Nancy Cunard:
Brave Poet, Indomitable Rebel

Nancy Cunard:

Brave Poet, Indomitable Rebel

1896-1965

edited by hugh ford

Chilton Book Company
Philadelphia   New York   London

To All Nancy's Friends,
who made this book possible;
     and
To Thérèse, Solita, John and Walter,
who helped from start to finish.

foreword

The writings collected in this volume to document the life of Nancy Cunard require a brief description. To begin, this book is neither a biography nor an autobiography, though it contains the materials of both. Miss Cunard's opposition to even the gentlest suggestions that she compose her memoirs, or entrust them with biographers, could be formidable, and few dared to bring the subject up a second time. Yet, and some may regard this as evidence of her paradoxical side, she herself chronicled whole events of her life which can only be viewed now as possessing a significance beyond any importance they might have claimed at the time they happened. The most incisive rendering of a single episode appears in "Black Man and White Ladyship," a rather scurrilous, exceedingly frank description of the calumnies that led to the permanent separation of Miss Cunard and her mother, Lady Emerald. But more illuminating, partly because they are quieter in manner and concerned with happenings that occurred over a great many years, are Miss Cunard's two books on George Moore and Norman Douglas, *G.M.* and *Grand Man,* which, although rightly described as "memories" of the two authors and not in any strict sense biographies, nevertheless contain nearly as much information about Miss Cunard as about the principals themselves. Reading them we rapidly grow accustomed to her presence, so often sustained by a flair for dramatic announcements. On one occasion, for example, she demands of Douglas: "Now how and where did we next meet?" Presumably unable to remember, she informs us of her own whereabouts: "On return to France I went immediately to another session of the League of Nations." Elsewhere we come upon this pronouncement: "And now I was possessed of a new idea which went down on paper on April 1, 1931, the making of an Anthology on the Negro race"; and, later, this one: "The war began in Spain and I went there as a journalist, arriving on August 11 in Barcelona . . . Spain took hold of me entirely."

The happy fact is that Nancy did turn memorialist often enough and long enough to set down some quintessential events of her life.

Scattered throughout her books (besides those already mentioned, the massive miscellany *Negro*, the booklet *Authors Take Sides, Poems for France*, and the informal history *These Were the Hours* provide either additional information or amplification of data), these personal passages comprise a fascinating and valuable documentation, and, incidentally, betray conspicuous and welcome lapses in her opposition to autobiographical writing. The selections from her works reprinted here, then, will give her a voice, a voice often droll and witty, always articulate and honest, as well as a responsible and crucial role in the creation of her own portrait.

Despite Miss Cunard's somewhat ironic tendency toward self-revelation in her own work, it is nevertheless true that any writing done, or even planned, about her usually evoked strong and even hostile reactions, for which no easy explanation exists. But as Leonard Woolf observed and as Nancy herself must have discovered, she was vulnerable, and not just because she was ingenuous or sometimes incapable of distinguishing friends from enemies. Rather, it lay in insisting upon baring herself—totally, unprotected, usually alone—to all the world, regardless of risks and dangers. Naturally people noticed her. The temerity with which she fluttered the causes she embraced always produced instant attention, followed by notoriety and, inevitably, attack, the most infamous being the offensive launched against her in 1932 by several tabloids in New York and London that contended that perverse, hardly scholarly, motives explained her visits to Harlem. However bravely she stood up to harassment and ridicule—and she was often very brave indeed—however unperturbed the surface remained, there was not enough carapace to prevent hurt. Thirty years after, wounds made in 1932 had not completely closed. Of course in time she came to loathe and, one might add, to fear the maliciousness of which she knew the press capable, and as she grew older her antagonism to anything written about her stiffened. Journalists and scholars who drew her fire were sometimes forced to make apologies and occasionally paid her substantial libel fees. Especially infuriating in more recent years were remarks she found about herself in chronicles of the twenties and thirties, nearly all of which were written by friends. I once looked at her small collection of these books and discovered the margins filled with testy notes to the authors who, I gathered from Nancy's jottings, had either set down misinformation about her or else had thoughtlessly perpetuated some annoying gossip. To my suggestions that they had probably been faithful to their own observations, she remained adamant; no, they had simply blundered or written nonsense. "Look!" she concluded. "See what happens when people write about you."

What would she say about the contents of this book? Would the poetry reprinted here from her early volumes annoy her? It is true that Nancy seldom mentioned the many poems she wrote before she was thirty-five, though she did occasionally enjoy hearing them read. Would she object to the selections from Aldous Huxley's *Point Counter Point*, Michael Arlen's *The Green Hat*, or Robert Nichols' *Sonnets to Aurelia*—that is, to witnessing the literary metamorphosis of herself once more? A little perhaps. She often said that Arlen, or "The Baron," as she called him, who cast her as Iris March in his novel, "had made a lot of money with *The Green Hat*—and for such nonsense, too—but no need to begrudge him that." As for *Sonnets to Aurelia*, which Nichols dedicated to her, that book was an inexcusable display of "poetic license." Of what Huxley had tried to divulge about her through the character Lucy Tantamount, I never heard her utter a word.

Nancy sat—rather fitfully, one suspects—for many portraits which, when grouped as they are here, manage to evince her bold yet resplendent beauty and intimate that her mystique could tantalize and evade the artist's métier. Would she enjoy seeing herself again in Alvaro Guevara's baroque, Edwardian portrait; in Adrian Allinson's painting, "The Café Royal," herself seated at a table in the foreground; in Oskar Kokoschka's brooding, haggard full-length study; in Constantin Brancusi's sylphlike, lambent bronze; in Wyndham Lewis's cubist drawing; in Eugene McCown's elongated, surrealistic pose; and in John Banting's sedate yet subtly mercurial portrait; or, in the photographic studies by Man Ray, Cecil Beaton and Islay Lyons? In all likelihood, yes, but some she had never liked and had, conveniently, almost forgotten they existed.

Her journalism, however, would be another story. Nancy labored prodigiously on newspaper assignments. Rereading her articles on life in Harlem (*Negro*, 1934), her impassioned accounts of the exodus of refugees from Spain (*Manchester Guardian*, 1939), the description of Paris just after liberation (*Horizon*, 1945), and, more scholarly than journalistic, her account of the operations of her Hours Press (*The Book Collector*, 1964) could only give delight, for each records what she came to regard near the end of her life as a supremely precious moment of living, a time when energy and devotion and intelligence had been tested and had somehow miraculously triumphed.

Would an equivalent joy come from discovering what her friends have written about her? It is difficult to believe that their recollections could cause any serious displeasure, and whatever slight twinge they might produce would surely pass when she recognized (as she would) the honesty that directed them. For that one quality she passionately admired, demanded of all her acquaintances, and kept unfailingly alive in herself. Such remembrances then as these, set down by friends whose opposition to gossip matched Nancy's, would please, amuse and perhaps only occasionally ruffle her; she would accept them as affectionate and respectful attempts to memorialize her, and, above all, she would be relieved to find them only faintly eulogistic and touched to discover them laced with love.

Of Nancy's legions of friends only relatively few are living (even from among this gathering of memoir writers several have died since the volume's inception), and many who are alive will, I fear, forever remain unknown—all the anonymous hotel clerks, train porters, barmen, refugees and menial workers she befriended wherever she traveled and lived. Unsurprisingly, her friends were always a remarkably colorful collection of people, as diverse as her own enthusiasms, if not as ardent—the sort of brilliant mélange represented by the contributors to this symposium, among whom are novelists, poets, artists, publishers, journalists, a cinema critic, an art dealer, a bibliophile, an interior decorator, a sculptor, an actress, and a small band of admiring academicians who alternately roused Nancy's ire and approbation. They live scattered throughout the countries she knew intimately: France, England, Italy, Germany, Morocco, Chile, the United States. Some are older and others considerably younger than she was when she died in 1965, at sixty-nine; a few shared her company for more than forty years, others under five. But for Nancy age was unimportant and irrelevant, and consequently it never encumbered her relationships with people.

Here then are the documents that comprise Miss Cunard's portrait: what she wrote of herself, what friends and acquaintances said of her; what novelists and poets extracted from her character for their books, and what artists managed to synthesize for her portraits. All these are arranged according to the chronology of her life, regardless of the dates of their composition, so that the narrative unfolds orderly and without interruption. The only looseness in the chronology occurs when a memoir writer has surveyed a rather large part of Miss Cunard's life instead of a specific period.

The division of Nancy's life into six parts was made for reasons other than convenience and organization. As the contents of each part will reveal, her interests at a given time could be almost obsessive—certainly totally engrossing—and thus the most clearly defined pattern discernible in her life consists of these periods of intense activity.

It will be noted that this memorial book is dedicated to those friends of Nancy whose interest and support made it possible. Without exception they responded kindly and generously to my requests for remembrances and memorabilia. They wrote gladly and always without gratuity. Occasionally one may notice slight contradictions in their writings. These I have allowed to stand, first, because they in no way invalidate the "truth" of what they say, and second, because it seemed to me that these very contradictions might enable the reader to glimpse for himself the often contrary effects Miss Cunard had upon people. However, whenever I was certain a factual error occurred, I made corrections.

For convenience, I have provided biographical data for each contributor in the section called *Notes on Contributors*.

Hugh Ford

Trenton, New Jersey

acknowledgments

The editor wishes to thank the following for permission to reprint material in this work:

Mr. Harold Acton and Methuen and Company, Ltd. for excerpt from *Memoirs of an Aesthete*, copyright 1948, by Harold Acton, by permission of Methuen and Company, Ltd.

The Book Collector for excerpt from "The Hours Press," by Nancy Cunard, by permission of *The Book Collector*.

Chatto and Windus, Ltd. for poems from *Aurelia and Other Poems*, copyright 1920, by Robert Nichols, by permission of Chatto and Windus, Ltd.

Curtis Brown, Ltd. for excerpt from *The Green Hat*, copyright 1924, by Michael Arlen, by permission of Curtis Brown, Ltd.

Miss Janet Flanner and The New Yorker Magazine, Inc. for excerpt from "Letter from Paris," copyright 1956, by Janet Flanner, by permission of The New Yorker Magazine, Inc.

Sir Rupert Hart-Davis and Rupert Hart-Davis, Ltd. for excerpts from *GM, Memories of George Moore*, copyright 1956, by Nancy Cunard, by permission of Rupert Hart-Davis, Ltd.

New Directions Publishing Corp. for excerpts from *The Autobiography of William Carlos Williams*, copyright 1951, by William Carlos Williams, by permission of New Directions Publishing Corp.

Mr. Roger Senhouse and Secker and Warburg for excerpts from *Grand Man, Memories of Norman Douglas*, copyright 1954, by Nancy Cunard, by permission of Secker and Warburg.

The Viking Press, Inc., Publishers for excerpt from *Paris Was Our Mistress*, copyright 1947, by Samuel Putnam, by permission of The Viking Press, Inc., Publishers.

The following acknowledgments are due for the illustrations:

To Mr. John Banting for his portrait of Nancy Cunard and the photograph he took of her in Barcelona in 1937;

To Mr. Cecil Beaton for his photographic portrait of Nancy Cunard taken in 1930;

To Bircham and Company, London, England, for the portrait of Mr. George Moore by Mrs. S. C. Harrison;

To Mr. Luis Enrique Délano for the photograph of Nancy Cunard and others taken in Madrid, 1936;

To Mr. Marcel Duchamp for permission to reproduce, and to Mr. Duane Michals for the photograph of, the sculpture of Nancy Cunard by Constantin Brancusi;

To Mr. Ian Greenlees of The British Institute of Florence, Florence, Italy, for Wyndham Lewis's sketch of Nancy Cunard;

To Mr. Oskar Kokoschka and Dr. jur. Bernhard Sprengel for the portrait of Nancy Cunard painted by Mr. Kokoschka in 1924;

To Mr. R. Alistair McAlpine for "The Café Royal" by Adrian Allinson;

To Mr. Henry Moore for his photograph of the "Ring Stone";

To Mr. Clyde Robinson for the photograph of Nancy Cunard taken in Majorca, 1959.

In addition to all the friends of Nancy Cunard whose reminiscences appear in the following pages and to whom I shall always be deeply grateful, I should like to extend sincere thanks to Solita Solano, Miriam Benkovitz, John Banting, Walter Lowenfels and Walter Strachan for suggestions, guidance and, above all, for their encouragement and support; to Joyce Brodowski, whose assistance has once more been generous and invaluable; to John F. Marion for his interest and belief in this project; and, finally, to Thérèse Ford for the numerous tasks that only she could do so well.

Hugh Ford

Trenton, March 1968

contents

III *Migrations: New York, Moscow, Geneva*
1930–1935

VI Turning Back: Mallorca, Toulouse, Lamothe-Fénelon, Cap Ferrat
1946–1965

list of illustrations

(Picture insert is between pages 170–171.)

prologue by langston hughes

Nancy: A Piñata in Memoriam
If one could break it in her honor

Nancy Cunard was kind and good and catholic and cosmopolitan and sophisticated and simple all at the same time and a poet of no mean abilities and an appreciator of the rare and the off-beat from jazz to ivory bracelets and witch doctors to Cocteau but she did not like truffles at Maxim's or chitterlings in Harlem. She did not like bigots or brilliant bores or academicians who wore their honors, or scholars who wore their doctorates, like dog tags. But she had an infinite capacity to love peasants and children and great but simple causes across the board and a grace in giving that was itself gratitude and she had a body like sculpture in the thinnest of wire and a face made of a million mosaics in a gauze-web of cubes lighter than air and a piñata of a heart in the center of a mobile at fiesta time with bits of her soul swirling in the breeze in honor of life and love and Good Morning to you, *Bon Jour, Muy Buenos, Muy Buenos! Muy Buenos!*

I

Growing Up: Nevill Holt and London

1896–1919

introductory by arthur waley
Three Nancy Cunards

I knew, but only very slightly, three Nancy Cunards. The first was a raw, Scotch-looking girl of about sixteen whom I met at Munich. She was dowdily dressed, simple, straightforward and quite unconscious of herself and her alert governess. George Moore had seen and praised a poem she had written. That was what she was going to be—a poetess.

Long, long afterwards someone who said she was Nancy Cunard rang me up towards midnight and said she was with some friends at the Eiffel Tower restaurant. Would I join them? I had already gone to bed and it was some little while before I arrived. I was led up to a lady bedizened in every possible way, with snaky bangles, gold anklets, startling rings. She was very drunk and had no recollection of having phoned to me.

The third Nancy I met at tea-parties once or twice, after the Second War. Eager, charming, very subduedly dressed, bristling with pamphlets, with protests one must sign, poems by Africans one must read.

I never saw her again.

nancy cunard

Childhood and Beyond

The passages printed below are taken from *G.M., MEMORIES OF GEORGE MOORE* (London: Rupert Hart-Davis, 1956), an evocative portrait of the Irish writer, Miss Cunard's "first friend," who until his death in 1933 kept a watchful, if sometimes troubled, eye on her literary and personal life.

I suppose I was about four years old when I first remember G.M., and I suppose I may, in some sort, even call him "my first friend." He came so often to Holt, generally on lengthy visits, and appeared then to be so much of the place, talking to me always in a manner beyond my years and taking so much interest in all that concerned me, that he is the central figure of childhood, and it is thus I think now of George Moore who was always known as G.M. to his friends. If I knew him first when I was four, he must have seen me first in a nurse's arms. He used to say that I was a romantic child. Be that as it may, I shall perhaps be guilty of romancing here and now—if only once in all—about the first time I remember G.M. talking to me. It may well have been the first time of all; I cannot affirm it was, being then still very small.

My desire to learn to read was acute and there was an early reverence in me for those who wrote books. Easy words, "dog" and "cat" words and much else, had been mastered, but the longer phrases and abstract terms still gave me so much trouble that I feared I should never read properly. A book in my hands, accompanied with a little pretence, was my evening pleasure for an hour in the nursery, or even in a roomful of guests, as in the Hall at Holt, where, on that occasion, curled up near a great fire of logs resting on ashes hardened to stone by the passing years, I "read."

It may well have been the first time G.M. spoke to me when, to my dismay, he approached, saying:

"Nancy, you have a book. Can you really enjoy it at your age? Let me see. Oh! *The Violet Fairy Book!* So you have got beyond *Reading without Tears!*"

In the next three paragraphs Miss Cunard wrote the only description of her father, Sir Bache, I have been able to find and perhaps the fairest and most penetrating portrait of her mother, Lady Maud Cunard.

G.M. had met my mother in 1894, before her marriage, and his description of that first meeting with her, then about nineteen, was vouchsafed me considerably later and was a memory precious to him. One can see why: her looks and charm, for a start. Her tastes were musical, literary, artistic, she loved and promoted good conversation by her own sporadic outbursts of airy, fantastic wit, and developed a remarkable gift for entertaining on a large scale. Later on all of this went *con brio furioso* but the times at Holt evoke words like "spacious, comfortable and leisurely."

The gardens developed throughout the years and the swards grew smoother, while straggling bushes were cut, bullocks' blood administered in bucketfuls to yews of hesitant growth, and topiary much practised by my father. Chopin's Third Ballade and Beethoven Sonatas were played with skill and feeling by my mother, who would be reading the classics and contemporary French literature half through the night. It was in the tower room above the porch that my father spent most of his time, hammering silver, carving coconuts elaborately to mount them into cups, and making other things with his able hands. Thoroughly conservative in his ideas, he was manually an ingenious, gifted man in all his manipulations of wood and iron. The silver leaves on the dinner table were the result of months in "Sir Bache's Tower." The silver fox, life-size, on a stand in the oak-panelled Breakfast Room, was a parting gift from the five hundred members of his Hunt.

Somehow I felt—and was—entirely detached from both, admiring and critical of them by my own standards, those of a solitary child wondering much in silence how life was going to be. It seems fantastic now to think of the scale of our existence then, with its numerous servants, gardeners, horses and motor-cars, now that all this has floated away forever and time wears such a different dress.

The house-parties in the early days at Holt consisted of somewhat diverse people, smart and worldly, good riders to hounds and race-goers, men of wit and women of fashion, politicians and diplomats, whereas the men guests, at least, became more intellectual as the Augusts and autumns proceeded and the host was away shooting and fishing lengthily in Scotland.

My picture of Holt is one of constant arrivals and departures during half the year, of elaborate long teas on the lawn with tennis and croquet going on, of great winter logs blazing all day in the Hall and Morning Room, with people playing bridge there for hours on end.

Beautiful and exciting ladies move about in smart tailor-mades; they arrived in sables or long fox stoles, a bunch of Parma violets pinned into the fur on the shoulder. Summer-long, in shot silk and striped taffeta they stroll laughing and chatting across the lawns. All these toilettes with their ruchings and flounces, the veils with big, smart spots on them, the feather boas (a *lie de vin* one especially) made me long to grow up and wear such things as well.

Flowers were everywhere, including hothouse blooms and sometimes orchids brought by somebody from London or his own conservatory, and a glory of azaleas filled the great Chinese bronze incense-burner in the Hall (now in the British Museum). It was in the Morning Room they sat most, in that long, low, harmonious place with a stone floor and many oriental rugs strewn across it, that grew yearly more luxurious because of an increasing number of Italian damasks, cushions, and brocades. Every ray of sun seemed concentrated in the four window-seats decked with old Chinese bowls of potpourri. The two oak writing-tables, one at each end, were elaborately appointed with everything to hand for the distinguished calligraphy of those times. Art-books and new novels lay about in profusion; here a great box of "candy," there a box full of aromatic Russian cigarettes.

When not discouraged from doing so, I loved "showing people the house," but it was mainly in the garden I found myself alone with G.M., after trying to drag him up King John's Tower into the wonderful attics beyond. Sometimes I succeeded and sometimes he knew how to be firm. Often he strolled about full of his thoughts underlying a vacant eye, and many a time were they interrupted by my chatterings. They would be about the cedar trees, or the tramps that came by on the road under the terrace generally at sunset, a bottle and a red wipe sticking out of their pockets—generally dirty, slouchy men with stubbly chins and anger in their eyes. Those tramps excited me and I told G.M. I wanted to run away and be a vagabond. Or I would tempt him to the great rubbish heap near the orchard, all strewn with fragments of lovely porcelain cups. On the way there might come a flash of colour: Mrs. Empson's cat. To G.M.'s delight, it was a tortoiseshell, for tortoiseshell cats were getting more and more rare, he bade everyone observe. Should we go and see if the jiggles were working in the rose garden? The jiggles—what could they be? What one of the gardeners called the leaden gargoyles recently put up to spout over the lily-pads. Or should we get out of the sun in the cloresters? And what might *they* be? The same man's name for the Cloisters where we often had tea under the plaster plaque of *my great-grand uncle, Robert Emmet, the Irish patriot*. Would he do this, would he do that, would he perhaps climb into my cedar and sit with me in the crook of the main branch and have a taste of my little store of beechnuts in a stone bottle? . . .

His questions rang with mine and were as numerous, there being so much of "why?" in nature, he said, before you get as far as wondering about people. As for the skylarks, ah, that is another mystery. The time will come, Nancy, when Shelley's poem will be a great joy to you.

By now one might have thought he would have mastered my dog's name, "that nice fellow Buster," a gay Scottish terrier with a withered leg who sometimes went for walks with him alone.

Buster and G.M. are bound to each other in one flurried childhood moment that still makes me hot to think of, although it also seems to me a normal reflex in someone carried away by indignation.

At tea that day in the Cloisters, G.M. was showing off to a waltz thumped out on the piano. He had been expounding on "what a dab" he used to be at *le double Boston* and there was some discussion about the correct way to reverse, which, dancing alone, he was illustrating. But now Buster got in his way and he kicked Buster very hard, the howls were excruciating. It must have been like a stone from a sling that I hurled myself at G.M. and gave him a furious slap in the face. Everything stopped in consternation, and never out of a man's mouth opened by stupor came a larger, rounder "OH!"

"Nancy has slapped me! Oh! It is that horrid dog's fault—Boxer, Brewster, whatever the beastly dog is called!"

They were very angry with me indeed, far more so, once the shock over, than was G.M. On the whole he understood. Of course he should not have kicked the poor dog; but then, Bouncer should not have got in his way.

Confined to the schoolroom for two days in disgrace, I could see G.M. from the window blandly wandering about, looking at the rooks and whistling motifs from *The Ring* which he did often with great proficiency.

There were no admonitions from him about the slap; the incident was forgotten (though not by me) and it must have been soon after that he made a stand in my defence during another explosion in the household.

Creating a furore, Elinor Glyn's *Three Weeks* had just come out and there cannot have been many well-appointed houses without the novel, aptly bound in purple, containing the green-eyed lady with red hair who spent so much time on a *tiger-skin*.

So much talk was there of Mrs. Glyn's "audacity" that I felt I too must read about Paul and his temptress. My week with *Three Weeks* in bed in the clandestine hours of dawn was a very great enjoyment. So that was an adventuress—beautiful, perfidious, dashing, and exactly what I wanted to know about! She blazed awhile across the repressions of my childhood. It also chanced that *Three Weeks* was the very first novel I read.

One of G.M.'s frequent remarks to me was "You are so secretive," and it would be untrue to say that he, or anyone else, was a confidant, and yet. . . .

On this visit he had been put in the Knight's Room where he worked all morning. Had he been in his usual Long Room the incident might never have occurred, as one generally did not pass that way to another part of the house. His door was open, and going by on some errand during the short break in Lessons, I was called in. What impelled me suddenly to tell him my secret I cannot think. We would often talk about books, although never yet about books such as this:

"So you have been reading *Three Weeks!* And what do you think of it?" he asked with real interest.

I told him it had thrilled me, but that *Too Weak,* although very unkind, had made me wonder if there were not, well, some exaggerated things in it, for of course, put that way, the story did seem absurd. We must have talked for twenty minutes, while I asked myself how severely punished I should be if the matter were discovered.

Discovered it was and on the spot; the governess happening to pass by stopped unseen, took in the conversation and the result exploded that afternoon: Nancy has been reading *Three Weeks!*

Astonishment and annoyance soon passed into uproar because G.M. came out firmly on my side, and as I stood there crimson with defiance, saying "Why not? Why not?" there was an increasing vehemence in all his words:

"What is the ha-arm in that, will you kindly tell me? Why should she not read *Three Weeks?* It may not be good literature, but what possible ha-arm can come to her from reading it? I strongly advise you not to thwart her curiosity, which is a natural thing, for you will only drive it underground. What possible ha-arm can there be? She is not a silly girl. . . ."

"But she's not yet twelve years old!" was the indignant reply.

Above all, he was in a pother lest I should think he had given me away. Oh my Lord! he adjured me, surely I would not go and imagine that? Indeed no, I assured him; besides, the ugly eavesdropping had come out meanwhile. This was one of the times when he was an ally against authority; it greatly endeared him to me, and of course we were in disgrace together for days.

Many were the walks that G.M. took with the governess and myself. Often on such occasions, at an age when I ran much and fast, I would leave them on the road breasting a stiff wind, G.M. holding on to his bowler, and be off with the dogs in the fields, catching them up in the midst of their talk on French literature, a discussion, maybe, of Barres's *Les Deracines,* or concerning the philosophy in *Thus Spake Zarathustra. Maitresse-femme* as she was, highly educated and a great reader, how out of place was Miss Scarth with so juvenile a child. She should never have been a governess (although Vita Sackville-West enjoyed her), least of all to me, who had every reason to hate her and her detestable temper, her punishments and outrageous discipline, while admiring her intellect in what, later, I would call "a purely objective way." It seemed to me that G.M. noticed this disproportion in ages and natures, even if he did keep silent about it, merely dropping a hint or two, while saying that she was a remarkable woman.

The usual morning walk would be along the road to Drayton as far as the top of a steep hill, a mile and a quarter from Holt. Here the land falls away on one side in a great, rolling expanse, a gigantic flank tufted with gorsebushes. On the left of the road were ditches that attracted me; in one of them a hollow thickly overhung, somehow became "my house." I would run ahead to be there two minutes or so before, catching me up, Miss Scarth called me to follow. But a house must have contents, and these I thought of as "works of art": some oddly curved root, a stick stripped of its bark, the wood gleaming with polishing, a few of those fierce sea-green flints stacked by the road, a beautiful shard of pottery, a small blue, empty medicine-bottle picked up unseen.

Somehow this harmless fancy had to be kept dark, so many things being forbidden that I developed a sense of what would become so. Yet one day—that will certainly have been when we were alone—I showed it to G.M. Now why, said he, could I want such a "house"? I told him that I liked to make or invent things of my own, ready, should he mock me, with the explanation that one could shelter here from the wind. No sneerer at fancies was he—the flints attracted him too—and murmuring that I was a funny child of nine (or was it ten years old now?) he ambled on.

It was in the spring of 1911 that G.M. left Dublin to live in London once more, the house-parties at Holt were coming to an end and I now saw much less of him, being busy with day-classes and soon sent abroad to Munich and Paris for further studies.

On our last walks at Holt he would talk to me about French painting and English poetry. I had shown him a few of my own poems and was reading some of his books, comparing his writing with that of other contemporaries and finding nothing else like it. As for his preoccupation with style—one could see his signature on every page.

But I could not follow him at all when it came to "objective verse." A baffling word, in this context, is "objective," until suddenly one has understood.

"Shelley's *Hymn of Pan* is objective, what a beautiful poem it is, Nancy. And *Kubla Khan,* and Poe's exquisite lines *To Helen.* Perhaps the finest poetry is objective, in French as well."

And he would quote from memory the delicious *Sonnet en Quatorze Mots,* breathing it out in a hush of admiration:

Fort
Belle
Elle
Dort;
Sort
Frêle,
Quelle
Mort.
Rose
Close,
La
Brise
L'a
Prise.

Objective verse being already much in his mind, thirteen years and maybe longer before his anthology *Pure Poetry* was published, he urged me to help him in finding "objective" poems throughout the whole of English literature that might be made into a volume, while I remained unable to grasp the difference between objective and subjective poetry.

Part of a letter has survived:

Hôtel St. James et d'Albany, Paris,
May 1912

I suppose you are too young to write 'pure poetry,' poetry about things, but remember that that is the only poetry that lasts. You remember our unmade anthology. The Hymn to Pan, Shakespeare's songs, etc., Gautier's sonnet to the tulip:

'Moi je suis la tulipe,
une fleur de Hollande'
One truth I have gathered and it is, that the artist should avoid sentiment as he would the plague—sentiment passes away like the

clouds. There is not a tear in Shakespeare; and what is most strange is that this age, into which sentiment hardly enters at all, will only read sentimental books and look at sentimental pictures. It is difficult to define sentiment. Perhaps you will understand why I am writing this to you better if I say that 'ideas' are the bane of modern literature.

"Not a tear . . ." Has the unsentimentality of Shakespeare ever been put that way before?

[That ubiquitousness which so characterized Miss Cunard for most of her life was already in evidence in 1912 and 1913, years spent getting an education abroad and discovering, as the following passages explain, the secrets of ancient streets.]

It was then, on his return—I had seen very little of him in the past two or three years, having been abroad and grown up meanwhile—that I said to myself: "Here is G.M. and shall I feel that I must begin to know him all over again?"

Naturally we talked of Holt, which seemed already far away in time and had now passed into other hands. He, for one, would never see it again and took a melancholy pleasure in recalling some of its aspects, here a room and there a field and a walk; no one would ever love it again as well as we. And up came a curious memory:

"Nancy, you were a funny child. Do you remember what you said to me in the churchyard at Holt? You bade me come to it with you and we sat on one of the beautiful old gravestones, you and I. Then you said to me: 'I often come here alone. And I often wonder where we go after we are dead.' You were about five years old then. Don't you remember, Nancy?" But I did not remember.

Many were the questions at this time that he asked me about myself. Had I really been as discontented in Paris in that *pension de jeunes filles* as he thought I looked when he came over in the spring of 1913? Indeed yes; I was bored to death for the first three months. Having worked hard in Munich at music and German the autumn before, I had tasted of adult life, had been taken away from it and put in a place where I could go ahead at nothing, the lessons being almost infantile if one knew French. I felt out of tune with it all, despite the three charming sisters who ran the pension. Things changed with the literary classes of Professeur Bellessort; it was the Russians and Scandinavians, that term, and they were of great interest to me. Music saved me; I was going later to three concerts a week, the Opera as well, with Marie Ozanne, the sister I was able to detach from the rest, on those occasions. Wonderful was the further discovery of César Franck, already played at Holt; most particularly of César Franck.

G.M. was delighted to talk of Turgenev and reminded me of his insistence years ago that I should read *Torrents of Spring* and *A Sportsman's Sketches,* two of the finest books ever written. And then returning to the subject before him, he questioned me about the possibility of my having been through a *crise de mysticisme,* for many, said he, at the age of sixteen or seventeen go through that, no matter what they become later. Had this happened to me?

No—certain old churches in Paris were a delight and I lingered long in them, but not more lengthily were my eyes lifted among the vaultings than they were used around me in the old streets near the Rue Mouffetard—the Place de la Contrescarpe, Rue de l'Epee de Bois, Rue du Pot de Fer, Place d'Italie—while talking German with Frau Schmutzler once a week; she was worn out by our enormous walks. My *mysticisme* was in those streets.

I remember nothing very definite about G.M. during that London season of 1914, my first *and* last, I swore to myself, as one ball succeeded another until there were three or four a week and the faces of the revolving guardsmen seemed as silly as their vapid conversation among the hydrangeas at supper. He came to lunch sometimes at my mother's in Cavendish Square; I have no particular memories of it and was often away. He was there several times while *Ezra Pound,* at tea, would be stressing the need of helping James Joyce; no doubt he applauded my mother's eventual success in obtaining for Joyce a sum of money known as "The King's Bounty." In a letter of 1916 G.M. says he is sure that Joyce's talent is deserving of recognition. Yeats too came there in 1916, but I was in the country at the time a performance was given in the house of his play *The Hawk's Well,* and saw him only once: "hard and mystical at the same time," I thought. G.M.'s quip about Yeats looking like a large, rolled-up umbrella left behind by some picnic party, made long ago in the Irish days, suggested a different side of the aloof, austere figure.

nancy cunard

Poems from Wheels

Miss Cunard's first poems, seven of them, appeared in Edith Sitwell's anthology *Wheels: An Anthology of Verse,* published in 1916. Reprinted below are "Wheels," the title poem, "The Carnivals of Peace," and "From the Train."

WHEELS

I sometimes think that all our thoughts are wheels
Rolling forever through the painted world,
Moved by the cunning of a thousand clowns
Dressed paper-wise, with blatant rounded masks,
That take their multi-coloured caravans
From place to place, and act and leap and sing,
Catching the spinning hoops when cymbals clash.
And one is dressed as Fate, and one as Death,
The rest that represent Love, Joy and Sin,
Join hands in solemn stage-learnt ecstasy,
While Folly beats a drum with golden pegs,
And mocks that shrouded Jester called Despair.
The dwarves and other curious satellites,
Voluptuous-mouthed, with slyly-pointed steps,
Strut in the circus while the people stare.
And some have sober faces white with chalk,
Of sleeping hearts, with ponderance and noise
Like weary armies on a solemn march.
Now in the scented gardens of the night,
Where we are scattered like a pack of cards,
Our words are turned to spokes that thoughts may roll
And form a jangling chain around the world,
(Itself a fabulous wheel controlled by Time

Over the slow incline of centuries.)
So dreams and prayers and feelings born of sleep
As well as all the sun-gilt pageantry
Made out of summer breezes and hot noons,
Are in the great revolving of the spheres
Under the trampling of their chariot wheels.

THE CARNIVALS OF PEACE

Had I a clearer brain, imagination,
A flowing pen and better ending rhymes,
A firmer heart devoid of hesitation,
Unbiassed happiness these barren times
With pleasure in this discontented life,
Forgetfulness of sorrow and of pain,
Triumphant victory on fear and strife,
Daring to look behind and look again
A-head for all the slowly coming days,
See nothing but the Carnivals of Peace,
Forget the dreams of death and other ways
Men have imagined for their own decrease. . . .
I'd write a song to conquer all our tears,
Lasting for ever through the folding years.

FROM THE TRAIN

Smoke-stacks, coal-stacks, hay-stacks, slack,
Colourless, scentless, pointless, dull;
Railways, highways, roadways, black,
Grantham, Birmingham, Leeds and Hull.

Steamers, passengers, convoys, trains,
Merchandise travelling over the sea;
Smut-filled streets and factory lanes,
What can these ever mean to me?

robert nichols...

Sonnets to Aurelia

Sonnets to Aurelia (1920), addressed and dedicated to Miss Cunard, probably preserves at least the emotions of Robert Nichols, though it may contain only a particle of the "truth" of their relationship. Many years later Miss Cunard wrote briefly about both the poet and his book of sonnets.

"I would not call Nichols an exhibitionist although, in those days, he came precious near it; I would recount the awful need he had of dramatising himself. Indeed, I would say, there are his *Sonnets to Aurelia,* dedicated to me, of which he sent me the entire manuscript, loose sheets, first drafts, errata, final versions, all bound together in sumptuous crimson with a golden N set above a wreath of bay-leaves round his name. These sonnets tell of every kind of lurid occasion that never arose at all between us—poetic licence if ever there was."

SONNET II

Seeing your eyes I know where sorrow is,
So steadfastly they contradict your youth,
So ag'd a blue tincts their drugged irises,
So blank are the pupils fixed on deadly truth.
Who gave you these most terrible of eyes,
That never, never, never know to weep,
That have become my life's unpitying spies,
Nor sleep themselves nor suffer me to sleep?

Fell Fortune you such gifts of sorrow made
The torment, which she deals you, to express,
Thus an afraid world to make more afraid
By utterance of all possible haplessness,
So, in her end, to silence such as I
Who to Her power your being would deny.

SONNET XIV

Your sunflower hair falling about your head
Is pale as from blonde orichalcum spun;
Your eyes are blue as your small mouth is red,
Pursed up as if pronouncing the word "one."
Your fingers, with their fiery stone, are slim;
Shallow your breast and swift your tenting side,
And your cool-costumed suppleness of limb
Gives you an air of ease and delicate pride.

The slenderness, purity, and magnificence
Of the magnolia's alabaster flower
Are yours, and from you floats an effluence
Of a like cloistered and voluptuous power:
Thus limn I you, knowing, alas, too well
That outward heaven hides an inward hell.

SONNET XV

Now that the summer of our love is past,
And no green shoots of all the tender grain
Which on each other's heart we reckless cast,
Spring up, but new weeds upon old weeds gain,
How must we mourn or in more bitter mood
Each lay to each the onus of this fate,
That what once seemed the promise of all good
Should now in proven ill be terminate.

Oh, of our myriad kisses did outsum
The celestial jewels of an August night,
Think! and, when minded to be rash, be dumb,
Lest, looking on past bliss and present spite,
We curse the hour each first of each was seen,
And wish what then was had now never been!

SONNET XVI

But piteous things we are—when I am gone,
Dissolved in the detritus of the pits,
And you, poor drivelling disregarded crone,
Bide blinking at memory between drowsy fits,
Within the mouldering ballroom of your brain,
That once was filled fantastically bright
With dancers eddying to a frantic strain,
What ghosts will haunt the last hours of the light?

Among the mothlike shadows you will mark
Two that most irk you, that with gesture human
Yet play our passion heedless of the dark:
A desperate man and a distracted woman,
And you mayhap will vaguely puzzle, "Who
Is she? and he? why do they what they do?"

iris tree

"We Shall Not Forget" for Nancy Cunard

The delicate dance of her walk through London streets, November perhaps, high heels, high fur collar hugged to her small face which wore an inward smile and the pearly flush of a rose shell. Charlotte Street, Percy Street, to the Eiffel Tower restaurant, or some other fugitive haunt unknown to our parents.

Lady Cunard had changed her name from Maud, considered common, to Emerald, a jewel in which she sparkled, surrounded by her brilliant collection of guests. Naturally she dreamed for Nancy such partners as would lead her through further vistas of yellow velvet rooms and green velvet lawns. My mother dreamed that her two younger daughters were still children, and my father that we would land safely on the stage with him and Shakespeare, in the wake of my eldest sister, Viola. I was then seventeen, Nancy eighteen. I studied at the Slade, and Nancy was just back from the finishing Pension of Mlle. Ozanne in Paris.

We had first met at classes when small, and she invited me and my sister, Felicity, to a tea party. I remember disliking a pale little girl who had, perhaps, usurped one of the interesting toys. When I confided this to Nancy, she rebuked me sharply: "If you don't like my friends you ought not to come here." A snub which shamed me then, but now seems significant of so many loyal defences and offensives that influenced her life and caused the breach with her mother, which lasted until death. Nancy had always referred to her mother obliquely as "Her Ladyship," already suggesting the opposed standards later climaxed in her blistering pamphlet *Black Man—White Ladyship*.

This persistent antagonism may have concealed an overt appreciation of that unique personality which partly formed her own, and whose inspired irrelevances Nancy took such pleasure in mimicking. At our last meeting I noticed the same oddities of speech and manner, with their instant penetration and airy dismissal of a subject. What began as mock mimicry had been converted through the years into second nature. But at the period of which I write we were bandits, escaping environment by tunneling deceptions to emerge in forbidden artifice, chalk-white face powder, scarlet lip rouge, cigarette smoke, among roisterers of our own choosing: Augustus John and his gypsy models at the Cafe Royal; Horace Cole, genius of practical jokes; Osbert Sitwell, happy fantasist, who later brought our poems to "Wheels Anthology." Studio attics with the then young wise owls of the Bloomsbury clique; stray Tommies who proffered rides on motor bikes; and the "coterie" crowned by Diana Manners, which included the most brilliant and exuberant spirits united at the various Inns and outings; Cavendish Hotel, Cheshire Cheese, pubs in Limehouse, river barges, cab shelters and a secret studio which Nancy and I shared for secret meetings with the favourites, or poems by ourselves. Those were the early days of First World War, when desires were heightened to a brief fulfillment before sacrifice and the last prodigalities were showered upon our beautiful intemperate young men. Intemperate not merely to assuage, but to augment their thirst for exploration through all the realms of being, released as they were on the wave of a new epoch.

For them it was an epoch of romantic discovery which had outgrown the strictures and sentimentalities of Victorian-Edwardian England, yet kept its manners and classical scholarship; articulate, satyrical, poetical. Transition and danger were in the air. We responded like chameleons to every changing colour, turning from Meredith to Proust to Dostoievsky, slightly tinged by the *Yellow Book,* an occasional Absinthe left by Baudelaire and Wilde, flushed by Liberalism, sombered by nihilistic pessimism, challenged by Shaw, inspired by young Rupert Brooke, T. S. Eliot, Yeats, D. H. Lawrence; jolted by Wyndham Lewis's *Blast* into cubism and the Modern French Masters, "Significant Form," Epstein's sculptures, Stravinsky's music (booed and cheered); the first Russian ballets and American jazz; nightlong dancing, dawnlong walks; exultant, longing, laughing loves unspotted by respectable sin.

All this, in a quick year or so, was not the battered old hat with new trim sometimes worn today, when almost everyone can paint, write, think, cohabit without censorship and with so many models to copy—but the green emergence of trends we now accept and which then (pejorative yet attractive) belonged only to the few. While seeking for identity, most of us feel less vulnerable in disguise.

Nancy and I loved dressing up for the Chelsea Arts balls, given at Albert Hall, designing our own costumes, influenced by Beardsley and Bakst. This was before the Teenage revolution when girls of our age were subjected to a sudden "coming out" from caterpillar to butterfly, long hair up, short frocks down, as debutantes for court and courtship. This flattering but difficult change suggested further transformations, a thousand masks through which to face cold eyes—or warm, perhaps?

Actually, the dressing up itself was the best part, because excitement and desire made the scintillating dusk before us seem like the entrance to a new world peopled for joy. Tomorrow would be conjured from tonight, and put on the half envisaged form of some companion-lover who would lead us beyond the boundaries of order and sleep with no foreseeable return to yesterday. Dinners arranged for the ball were belated by the chaos in each mirror, strewn with discarded images, taxis throbbing at the door, midsummer rain, on the way to champagne at other mirrors of Apaches, Bacchantes, dying swans, and though by now too self-engrossed and fluttered to focus upon anything beyond the haze of our own reflections. I still see Nancy, crowned with feathers, streaming with ribbons and simmering expectancies.

At the ball itself we were lost—or I was—Nancy usually found a temporary companion-lover, but mine put on dissolute or merely comic faces that swirled away in a circling dazzle of moths. Mothlike, we fell from lamp to dark, the dazed darkness greening to dawn in Hyde Park. On one occasion we were arrested for swimming in the Serpentine, and emerged in dripping feathers and velvets to receive a summons, returning scared to our solemn doors and stealthy, clockticking stairways. After this, though latch keys were confiscated and curfew imposed, we somehow tricked the watch.

Most of all we enjoyed the parties given by George Gordon Moore, galloping American millionaire, who flung his fortune into every hot pursuit, friends and their follies, horses and their games, until they left him, bankrupt but unbowed, still cantering—I hope—across the slightly tamed Wild West, with a yell to the last coyotes.

His parties coursed on from dinner, supper to breakfast, bursting from white to red camellias, rocketing with champagne and the new sound of Negro Jazz and Hawaiian bands. Though a great friend and admirer of Nancy, it was for Diana Manners that the parties were given. She invited the guests, and when she left, lights and music dissolved. Diana was not a pale beauty, but dazzlingly white and fair. Her presence always brought—beings—to such feasts something of myth and legendary revival, glory Greece, grandeur Rome, plus the clowning, gongleure escapading of Villon. After one of these revels we came home on a horse-drawn hay-cart—how; from where? The dance tunes singing through our limbs as we mounted into country sunlight.

Nancy sometimes sang, in a surprisingly deep contralto, refrains of those popular songs—songs that are so precise in their recall, not of past fashions, but of the mood when they first became familiar, whether drear, joyful, or desolate: *Oh, You Beautiful Doll!* This joyful desolation echoes still, but the immediacy of her living voice, which I used to imitate so often, is stifled on dead paper. She spoke in highpiping notes, punctuated by odd stresses and pouncing exclamations of jubilance or rejection: "Ohh!" "Ahh!" The obstinate, staccato "No!" An inward mirth simmered through sentences which revealed by hint or sudden swoop some peculiar detail which for her was key to an obvious situation. She was both delicate and shocking. Not exactly witty, but perceptive and always surprising—no dull dinginess obscured the quality of crystal, neatly crisp, gracefully turbulent, arrogantly disruptive, brave.

Unlike me, she was devoutly studious; read, spoke, wrote many languages fluently, and published poems in English, French, Spanish. These poems and critical essays reflect another side of her nature, pensive, purposeful, gleaning as she spent herself. Physically magnetic, she attracted many men, though to us, some of her chosen favourites seemed lacking in further distinction. Her eye was never for the obvious, and it may have lighted upon attributes to which we were blind, or provided those enchantments that often were abruptly disenchanted. Too proud for vanity or its regrets, she confessed in a sonnet:

All were there,
This life's alarmers, sowing their future harvests,
Rife weeds of conflict—
                    all but one
That I name never, Jealousy.

The country . . . I remember a weekend with her father, Sir Bache Cunard, at Haycock, Wansford, in a hunting landscape of brown fields and hedges. As a child she rode to hounds, but had long discarded habit and tweed for brighter plumage; an exotic bird in the eyes of Sir Bache, who probably wished her more like the ducks and partridges that, as hobby, he carved out of silver and polished coconuts. Having turned his back on past failures in a world of which she reminded him, there remained a wistful fondness, but no vital contact between them. George Moore, the Irish writer, was Nancy's imaginary, if not actual, father, and she revelled in repeating his phrases of astonished wit and the spiraling gestures that wafted them away.

My mother had rented a large-roomed house called Glottenham Manor, in Kent. Nancy came there often, and together we walked through rusty autumn woods or across hop fields, to the village station, when her young admirers arrived on farewell leave, before departing to the now bloody fields of battle. Together we had braved the panic of first bombings over London, and watched their fires redden on sky and river, ourselves burnt out by the terrible gaieties of last encounters, now made unreal by the realities of war—all the metal and struggle, trains, ships, mourning, noise of unknown distances from which we were excluded as figures of illusion—a theme that left its shadow on us both in different ways. By ourselves then, we tasted the guilt of our immunity, reproachful pain accusing those it spares. And the grave evenings at aftermath in Glottenham seeped through us with their chill of loneliness and death. . . .

I have emphasized the earlier period of our intimacy partly because later there were so many gaps caused by travel in different abroads. After the war we were neighbours in Paris; Nancy having rented a ground floor flat; I an attic, on the Île St. Louis. It was during her association with Louis Aragon—I was too absorbed by personal dramas for more than a fairground jostle with the carousel of friends that whirled around them: André Breton, Blaise Cendrars, René Crevel, Tristan Tzara, Marc Allegret, Ernest Hemingway, Janet Flanner, Cocteau crowing on the "Boeuf sur le Toit," and the permanent parade of genius and their molls from Café Dome to Café Rotonde.

Though we still exchanged poems and journeys together in Provence, through the various courts of love, Nancy now gave herself to the wider problems surrounding friends and lovers, igniting her torches from theirs, yet following her own. One much disputed loyalty to an American Negro (*Black Man—White Ladyship*) fired her to battle for recognition of his people, compiling and publishing her "Negro Anthology." Another friendship drew her to Spain during the Civil War, in which she participated actively on the side of freedom and composed a series of Spanish poems. Because of these and further deviations from the United status quo, she was refused permission to re-enter America, where she had hoped to join her closest companion, whose absence in Europe left her solitary at heart.

I know little about these later phases owing to our own separation of over twenty years.

Whatever the motives of her mysterious quests, they were not prompted by ambition, snobbery, material comfort or mere wantonness, but kept their urgent direction of desire and, surely, its fulfillment? For her each new experience was response to the odd accumulated with collectors' zeal. I see in her an abstract of this rarified collection that crystallized in glittering pyramid, all rubble swept away, all dust—which never was her element.

Over so long a lapse our old friendship awaited tenuously for renewal, which both must have realized could only be of memory, frosted beyond hope for the same things that had bound us—

Loneliness—death . . . ?

It was with shock that we met by accident eight years ago, one frigid, sunlit day in a street of Rome. She wore her high fur collar and walked with the same defiant spring; the same heavy African bracelets at her fine wrists, the very bright, light blue eyes glinting from dark shadow paint; bright side curls at her cheeks; "Beavers" she called them. I wore my customary flamboyant rags, drooping fringes, dog at heel. But these external defiances of time made its tricks more harrowing, working their change from within by imperceptible stages, as each defeated struggle etched, scratched, indented our faces, invading the design, yet sparing the pretensions. Our styles were fixed unalterably, and, fluent within their habit, the tempers became feverish, made restless by the confines each had fostered.

Feverishly taking up a lost refrain, we seemed like performers from the city, who sing for provincial orchestras, supplying one another with applause lest either be discomforted.

I wish we had grimaced at these contortion mirrors which, after the first, startled ripples subsided, composed themselves in clearer images— enjoyment even—for now we seemed like migrating birds alighting together on a lake of passage, feeding and gliding. . . . While lunching at a Tratoria, we attempted to sketch the maps of our lives during separation and reanimate the living forms that had filled them.

Brave and brisk as ever, she had grown very fragile, coughing a lot, smoking continuously with the familiar deft-fingered, airy gestures, the fluting voice and simmering laughter. She spoke of plans for a new book, and described the house she had bought in a remote French village—yet I gathered that her days there were lonely, somehow malevolent, bereft of surrounding sympathy or love.

I wonder—did we search for the affection, the whole exultant answer to affirm us: "Look, we have come through?"

Nancy was very proud. She had an arrogant disdain for any weakness, any crawling or interference in her freedom. Instead she reared up like a mettlesome horse to stamp them down, impatiently tossing aside the persuasions and forces of time, which beset the body, if not the mind. Condemned at last to face these desolations, hers was the spirit that would balk, but never bow.

So, as we left the wine-warmed restaurant for winter dusk, jostled by staring Italians and halted by traffic lights, the threat pursued us of those small calamities which repeat, absurdly, in a last phase the bold dramas of the first.

We had arranged to meet again on New Year's midnight, when bottles hurled from windows crackle the Roman streets and a smell of powder from exploded rockets fills the air.

I missed the appointment. . . .

Two years later, I found at Positano, a seachanged, blue glass bottle-top on which the initial "N" was inscribed. I sent it her as jewel with a poem. The following poem she wrote to me long ago, about "Glotten-ham," returns her to that Autumn spring in her dress of applegreen:

IRIS OF MEMORIES

Do you remember in those summer days
When we were young how often we'd devise
Together of the future? No surprise
Or turn of fate should part us, and our ways
Ran each by each; we picked the future's woof
Adventure searching, till these Sussex hours
Should bring us new adventure, while the flowers
About us waved in harvest plumes. Aloof
The house stood dark in green and gold of hay,
The house that we would leave fresh in the morn
To run the country on some quest forlorn,
Greeting the hop-pickers upon our way.
And there were wandering journeys to the sea
In dusty trains; there thrilling on the sands
Your scarlet dress grew vivid, and your hands
Evoked with witty gesture, palms of glee,
Things we had laughed at lovingly—for then,
Ah even then we loved our memories—
Till later under pale quiescent skies
We travelled homeward tired of towns and men,
Telling our dreams more slowly. So the moon
Crept up the stony hill between the hops,
(Full fields of ghosts become, where shadow stops
Across our stride;) and all the stars of June
Breathed up the poignance of unbounded roses.
We heard the rustle in the sombre trees
Heavy with bats and owlish noise; the breeze
Brought on its flutter sound of gate that closes
Far in a meadow. Sometimes you would tell
Stories to chill one in this midnight hour,
Until your fancy trembled at the power
The story held to frighten you as well.
The air grew full of dawn and we would yet

Talk of our morrows and our yesterdays;
Outside the birds grew tremulous with praise
In the hot sunrise. We shall not forget
The slumbering hours of hayfields where the river
Between its hedges near the passing train,
Faltered unseen and voiceless, then again
Flowed out with dipping birds and fish a-quiver;
For here we wandered silent, read strange things,
And had, how often, many a verse essayed,
Truant unfinished poem—as they played
Their shadowy game in the mind's fairy-rings,
Unseizably they mocked at our endeavour.
Then were there later days, with autumn rain
Damp in the haunted house, and so again
You would become a legendary inventor;
Weaving dark plays by firelight till sunset,
And thunder passing hence great moths came out
Sealing the redescended calm no doubt. . . .
Iris of memories we shall not forget.

david garnett
Nancy Cunard

It was in the early summer before the war started in August, 1914, that I first saw Nancy Cunard. I was with Francis Birrell talking I think to "Saki," or to Geoffrey Fry in the Cafe Royal when a party came in with one or two of Sir Herbert Beerbohm Tree's daughters and stopped to greet my companions. With them was a young girl—Nancy —who made a great impression on me. She was very slim with a skin as white as bleached almonds, the bluest eyes one has ever seen and very fair hair. She was marvellous. The world she inhabited was that of the rich and smart and the gulf between us seemed then unbridge-able. But the fact that she should appear in the Cafe Royal at all, even without her mother's knowledge, might have made me see that it was not.

Some months later I saw her again with a young officer in uniform and was told that she was married and that he was in the Guards.

I don't think I saw her again until after the war, unless peering down from the gallery at the people in the stalls or in the boxes I saw her at the Russian Ballet with her mother. After the war I got to know her, meeting her usually at the Eiffel Tower in Percy Street kept by an old Austrian—Stulich—who was popularly supposed to have been ruined by cashing cheques for "the Bright Young People" of the twenties. Once for some reason I was alone with her in her room at the Eiffel Tower, but I was too shy to tell her how much she attracted me. I knew that she liked me, but there was never time to get to know each other well.

I met her with Henry—I have forgotten his surname—a Negro, whom she said was a brilliant musician, and I went back with them to a basement in Greek Street or Frith Street where they were living. But Henry did not talk and I thought that he was ill suited to the almost dangerously thin woman with a skin whiter than the ivory bracelets that encrusted her arms both below and above the elbow. They must have been very heavy and Nancy was reported to have used them as weapons when in a rage. While Henry said nothing, Nancy talked in that shrill voice that I thought was Shelley's, but with a personal accent that was hers alone. She was always certain that what she saw was the truth and there was no room for doubt. This vision drove her. Though she was an intellectual, she was of a kind uncommon in England—for she was an extremist, following her belief *jusqu'au bout:* into messes that might be thought unsavoury.

Not long afterwards my friendship with George Moore brought us together. The book I was writing when I got to know Moore was the story of an English sailor who married a Dahomey Negress and my treatment of it pleased Nancy, because she was involved with Henry. I spent several hours with both of them. Henry, serious silent and very dark brown and glass in hand, and Nancy and I talking. She always assumed that I agreed with everything she said. On the whole I did agree—but with the shameful reservation that there were usually two sides to every question. That was inadmissible. Her devastating statements were punctuated with a high laugh and the rattle of a dozen ivory bracelets on her thin arms.

A few years later, I suppose, and Nancy was hunting for me everywhere. George Moore was very ill after an operation for prostate gland and I was the only one of her friends that loved him. I visited Moore in his nursing home in Langham Place on the afternoon that Tipperary Tim won the Grand National but I did not mention Nancy to him because I knew that her public quarrel with her mother must have upset him. And I was shy of talking about her because he and Nancy were so extraordinarily alike in features and colouring that it seemed probable to me that she was his daughter. But G.M.'s illness brought Nancy and me closer together than we had been before and it led her to talk about Sir Bache Cunard whom she had loved as much as she loved Moore. She told me that he had lived for long stretches at the Haycock Inn, Wansford, and that she used to go there and stay with him as a little girl. When Nancy spoke of Sir Bache, or of G.M. or later on of Norman Douglas, she was transformed. Love and reminiscent pleasure muted that shrill passionate voice and I perceived she was capable of a delightful humour. In all this I was able to share, for I loved G.M. and since she was sure of that, we could tell each other anecdotes of how ridiculous he was. She could have great humour —for instance her story of meeting Tommy Earp on the channel boat when they were each travelling alone to Paris. Tommy said in his squeaky voice: "Not very good at making love, Nancy, but I'll try."

But how I wish I had been ten years older or Nancy ten years younger, because then perhaps I might have been an old man whom she could love, as she loved Norman, and she could have been "my hill and stream companion."

I went to a party in her rooms in the Eiffel Tower at which Ezra

Pound and Alistair Crowley and other horrors were present. And once I met her with Aragon.

We met once or twice during the Spanish Civil War and I made my Anti-fascist affirmation in the memorandum she circulated to writers and published.

During the war years I heard nothing of her, except from her cousin Victor Cunard who was a colleague of mine in the Political Warfare Executive. Then after the war, Rosemary Hinchingbrooke (now Peto) brought her over to lunch at my house in Huntingdonshire. She was the same as ever: emaciated and beautiful and the long eyes like glimpses of the sea, and the voice like seagulls.

She wrote to me when she was ill and I went over from Menton where I was visiting Clive Bell who was there during one of the stages of his last illness.

She was in pain. It was almost unbearable seeing her wasted to nothing. But when she spoke about pain and about the poem she was writing about it, she spoke impersonally. And then we talked about Clive and the humour, which was often absent, came back. Suddenly we were very close and I tore myself away, not because it was unbearable, but because she was exhausted.

sir rupert hart-davis

The Girl at the Writing-Table

I first remember Nancy in 1918, when I was eleven and she was twenty-two. She and my mother, who was thirty-one, had taken a house together for the summer holidays. It was just outside the village of Kingston Bagpuize in Oxfordshire, and to my nine-year-old sister and me, who had known no settled home since 1914, when my father enlisted and our London house was given up, it seemed the Earthly Paradise. It was a largish, rambling, rectory-type house, approached up a long drive and surrounded with gardens, lawns and orchards. (I have never been back and probably it is, or was, much smaller than I remember.)

We came to it first in a dogcart from Wantage station—my mother, my sister, myself, and Nancy's French maid, Palmyre. My mother, ever ready to make the best of a bad bargain, saw that we were a trifle subdued by the uncompromisingly flat fields, and said to Palmyre: *"N'est-ce pas que c'est beau?"* To which Palmyre replied: *"C'est un peu lugubre,"* and was soundly rated for her lack of aesthetic perception.

And when we arrived, there was Nancy, much the same as she was to remain for more than forty years—elegant, bone-thin, with the same high squeaky voice, perhaps rather fewer bangles on her arms than she later carried, smoking, drinking, very "Bohemian" in her habits. She ate, as always, very little, preferring salads made with dandelions and other wild plants to the orthodox lettuce. Her unsuitable and short-lived marriage was already over, though she was still everywhere known as Mrs. Fairbairn.

My sister and I spent the long daylight hours playing outside, while inside the house there seemed to be a perpetual party. The guests were variegated—young officers, wounded and whole, artists and writers, Augustus John in the uniform of a War Artist, "Chile" Guevara the poet, St. John Hutchinson the lawyer, that mysterious character The Icelander (said, I believe rightly, to be imperfectly house-trained), Henry Mond (later the second Lord Melchett), the courtly and magnificent Lord Ribblesdale, the Sitwell brothers, over from some camp or barracks, and a forgotten crowd of others. Drink (I suppose some form of fairly potent cup) was dispensed from huge glass jugs, and there always seemed to be plenty.

Once my father came home on leave from France, suspected that some guest was my mother's lover and threatened a fist-fight. Nancy, my mother, my sister and I locked ourselves in a bathroom till the din had subsided.

Between the wild parties there were quiet days, without visitors, when Nancy would spend all day in the drawing-room writing. "Sh!," we were told: "Nancy's writing a poem," and at intervals one of us would tiptoe in with a cup of tea, put it quietly down on the writing-table, where Nancy, smoking continuously, sat locked in battle with her Muse (her first book of poems, *Outlaws,* was published by Elkin Mathews in 1921) and tiptoe out again. Those days gave me an impressive and romantic view of the poet's calling that I have never quite lost.

Nancy's great love at this time was a charming and handsome young man called Peter Broughton-Adderley. He won my heart by spending hours giving me cricket-lessons on the lawn. He was killed shortly afterwards, in the last months of the war, and perhaps if he had lived and married Nancy, her life might have been happier and less tumultuous.

After Bagpuize Nancy recurred in my life, but less frequently after my mother's death in January, 1927, and always in a different and an unexpected place. I never visited the Hours Press, but was an original subscriber, and only wish I still had a full set of its productions, particularly Louis Aragon's translation of *The Hunting of the Snark,* which ends: *"Car le Snark était un Boojum, voyez-vous."*

I remember her gay flat in the Île St. Louis, thickly hung with outrageous pictures and African carvings; a chance meeting by the roadside in central France, where Nancy and Aragon were eating a huge dandelion salad with their omelette and bottle of wine; her last home in the Dordogne—a converted farm-building surrounded with wringing-wet knee-high grass, and in its living-room Manet's *Étude pour Le Linge* (inherited, through her mother, from George Moore) shining like a jewel in a granary.

I never saw Henry Crowder, and was mercifully unexposed to Nancy's long vindictive feud with her mother ("Her Ladyship," as she always referred to her), which embittered so much of her life.

When I became a publisher, Nancy appeared as author, and I treasure the memory of the interview at which she showed Jonathan Cape an enormous dummy of her anthology *Negro*. He spent some time painstakingly explaining how the book's bulk could be reduced and its format improved. "But you don't understand, Mr. Cape," she squeaked at him: "this *is* the format." And indeed it was, for she had already had the whole book set up in that unwieldy form. (It was eventually published by Lawrence & Wishart, very few copies were sold, and the rest blitzed, so today it is rare and costly.)

I spent five years of the second war in the army, seeing nothing of Nancy, but directly I set up my own firm in 1947 she reappeared. I was too late to get her book on Norman Douglas (1954), too late even to persuade her to change its title from *Grand Man,* and when I did succeed in bringing out her book on George Moore (*G.M.,* 1956) I had a job to dissuade her from calling it *Whiles July* (she had a great gift for bad titles). When I edited and published George Moore's surviving letters to her mother (1957) she was all helpfulness and light.

Her last years were shadowy: no more lovers, too much liquor, chips all over her shoulder, periods of virtual insanity, but when I heard of her final collapse and death in Paris I forgot all that, and remembered only the friend of my childhood, the girl at the writing-table. "Sh! Nancy's writing a poem."

II

Independence: Paris

1920–1929

introductory by hilaire hiler

Nancy Cunard

I found that Nancy had a very advanced formulation of equity, ethics, and morals. It was as exceptional as it was different from the ideas usually held in connection with "proper" behavior and—in my opinion —of a much higher order. It was free from hypocrisy!

Once, when I needed friends very badly indeed I found that Nancy was the most steadfast, generous, and unselfish friend that I had. I'm not ashamed to say that her conduct was touching to the point of tears. If such qualities were not unique they were certainly most unhappily rare.

introductory by len lye

NC

Nancy, I didn't know. I only saw the prow of a gondolier nosing the Nile. I only saw a white praying mantis beguine benignly clunking ivory bracelets praying her wheel clinking ice in her drinks

She was my idea (as an Aussy aboe) of Paris from London and any night was right to hear Mantis prayer on arms of bone poised on the Glass stem, a fresh water not an ocean prow sailed by

The 'beguine' was the Paris dance to Cuban bands in Paris while I sat on a 'monkey' barge in the Thames and did swims and a *Colour Box* to the Cuban cuts

But first I had aboed my way to London working the stokehold of the twenty-two thousand ton White Star Liner "Euripides" for nine hell hot weeks of sweating slavery

Nancy shook her ivory loose from that Cunard stuff with the help of African boy friends and I knew how it mainly was with my Calypso girl friends

Uniquely Nancy made a vague polarity all around my retrospect of those welling concentrics flung out from white & black, ivory & glass, skin and bones

She was OK by me out of the corner of both eyes

As for the Hours Press it was part of the here we are ourselves

Like others who by time were fashioned into celebrities of the 1920's Miss Cunard in later years always stubbornly insisted that the "Jazz Age" (or whatever epithet was used to lend that decade a special aura) hardly added up to what it was often proclaimed to be. She showed her impatience with attempts at period-labeling in *Grand Man,* scorning the fashion "to exclaim about 'the wonderful 'twenties,'" and wondering, "Why this apocryphal swarming over times that seemed, then, in no wise extraordinary? Can it be in contrast with the peculiarities of today?" And there was more than impatience in what she remarked to Walter Lowenfels: "To hell with those days! They weren't so super-magnificent after all!"

These railings and taunts about the 'twenties (Miss Cunard, incidentally, spent most of the decade in France and nearly always in or near Paris) can perhaps be partly attributed to the value she eventually attached to the activities that filled her life after 1930: the assembling and publishing of a voluminous anthology, Negro; newspaper reporting at the League of Nations; writing and traveling in Spain during the civil war and, in 1939, going to the assistance of Spanish refugees; and even performing clerical work for the Free French in London during the Second World War. If the 1930's saw an almost frenetic involvement in social and political affairs, the previous decade contained all the beginnings of that involvement along with a full measure of the flamboyant and serious.

A glimpse at the itinerary of those years says as much about Miss Cunard's vagabondage (not to mention her stamina) as it does about her amusing and amazing coterie of friends. Typical was 1922. February, Sanary with Curtis Moffet and Iris Tree; March, Monte Carlo (a reporter for Sketch wrote: "Nancy Cunard looked charming in black, with a wonderful coral red hat . . ." (she) "is almost more like Lady Cunard than Lady Cunard herself."); April, Fontainebleau; summer, first at Eddington, England with Diana Cooper, Iris Tree, Aldous Huxley, Prince Farid, then at Deauville on the yacht Elettra with Marconi; September, visits to Hendaye, Fuenterrabia, Figueira, Guadelupe; October, Venice with Eugene McCown, Robert McAlmon, Osbert and Sachie Sitwell, Wyndham Lewis; December, Toulon. A whirligig of places, parties and faces!

What made the period so extraordinary, however, was Miss Cunard's ability to develop her own art and to inspire it in others, painters as well as writers, despite the full round of parties and travels. Always essentially a poet, she wrote continuously, dwelling often on the atmospheric and mysterious. A first collection of poetry, Outlaws, appeared in 1921, a second and larger volume, Sublunary, came in 1923, and a third, Parallax, in 1925. No doubt her most ambitious project began in 1928 when she founded what quickly came to be one of the few artistically and financially successful private presses of the time. Named the Hours Press, because, as she once remarked, it was "suggestive of work," it succeeded as a satisfying hobby and prosperous business for its owner and as an unusually remunerative outlet for its twenty-five writers.

Hugh Ford

nancy cunard

Glimpses of the Twenties

[Miss Cunard occupied numerous apartments while living in Paris, including one used by Modigliani at the time of his death. The apartment described below, however, was located on Île St. Louis.]

In my apartment there were then two Chiricos, two Tanguys and a large Picabia gouache of a man with four pairs of eyes, a body spotted all over with vermilion dots and one arm sheathed in black. (I think G.M. did not notice it.) There were other contemporary paintings and drawings, including several MacCowns, but not in the direct line of vision. There was also a comfortable settee in plum-coloured velvet.

[Although much has been written about the parties Miss Cunard attended, such as the Bal Beaumont, where she appeared dressed in a "slim, elegant pyjama-suit . . . worn with a very shiny, light topper and a mask," she could herself be a capable and spirited hostess.]

And it was Christmas Eve or Christmas night that I set him [G.M.] at the top of a long, narrow table of twelve at the dinner I gave for him in the room upstairs at the Rotonde. A dinner of twelve—how easy a thing to encompass in Montparnasse in those days. I hoped he would not mind, nor did he mind in the least, that everyone else except Brancusi was rather young.

But who were the diners? I cannot recall them exactly. G.M. sat flanked by two gorgeous young women. I think Marie Beerbohm, that wand of grace and punning wit, a niece of Max Beerbohm's, must have been there, and Dolly Wilde, handsome beauty and brilliant talker, niece of Oscar Wilde. Tzara and his fellow countryman whom I had met with him, the Rumanian sculptor Brancusi (a fine bearded-old-shepherd of a face and to my mind one of the great sculptors of all time) were certainly there, as were three young Americans, Eugene MacCown, the painter, Walter Shaw, then studying photography with Man Ray, and Jo Milward who wrote articles on art for American magazines, Iris Tree, the poet and daughter of Sir Herbert Tree, and Jan Sliwinski, the Polish singer and founder of *Le Sacre du Printemps* music-shop? Pierre de Massot, the French writer and his lovely Scottish wife, Robie? They were surely asked. Mary Reynolds, a beautiful American, friend of Marcel Duchamp and of so many artists? Nina Hamnett who lived then in Montparnasse? Maybe some of them came in after dinner.

Unforgotten is the vision of G.M. between those two young women, the singer and *diseuse* Yvonne Georges, with her Eton crop and immense, expressive eyes, and Clotilde Vail, whose long golden hair could be flung to the ground with a single shake to free it from the one pin or comb that held it up. Both had dressed themselves to perfection for him. They knew his eye for feminine flesh; well did they know the period that pleased him, and both of them were artists in taste. One looked like a Manet in black and white with something vaguely pink that nestled or floated; the other, in blue and green with a touch of yellow was a Renoir come to life. Thus, respectively, were Yvonne and Clotilde.

[Early in 1923 Miss Cunard first met Norman Douglas, who quickly became as attached to her as she to him. In the following pages she described the infuriatingly secretive talk with which Osbert and Sachie Sitwell sought to disconcert the already slightly nervous young woman as she waited for Douglas to appear. The passages below are from *Grand Man, Memories of Norman Douglas* (London: Secker & Warburg, 1954).]

It was nearly six years after *South Wind* came out in 1917 that we first met—with the Sitwells in Florence in February 1923. They had talked of you a good deal without saying anything very precise, and now, to my delight, they said we should meet. The aureole of legend around you was high in colour and, above all, mysterious. I would find it difficult, and even impossible, to say just what I was supposed to be prepared for! "You'll see! You'll see!" came from them delightedly, and not a word more.

In one of those preposterous *trattorie*, the name of which I forget, *Osbert, Sacheverell, myself*, and I think, William Walton, were dining. As the meal reached its worst stage, when the choice has to be made between pink *or* green *zuppa inglese*, Osbert and Sachie became more and more agitated. They seemed almost in a dither, for you were to join us—if you kept your word.

Again I ventured: would they not tell me just a little—say, at least, what you looked like, or if you were alarming, which at great speed evoked something like this:

"I'm-sure-I-don't-know-what-she's-going-to-think-when-she-*does*-meet-him, Sachie ... hmh, ... I suppose he is coming, what do you think?"

"Well, he *said* he'd come, Osbert."

"I'm-sure-I-don't-know-how-it-will-all-go . . . Oh, delightful . . . very, very witty . . . hmh . . . You're sure to find him that, but . . ."

"It's getting late, Osbert. It's past ten now and he said he'd come at ten sharp."

"Oh dear, what a bore. I must say I *do* hope he is coming, Sachie. Do you really think he will?"

"Well, he *said* he would, you know."

This went on for some time and I got slightly nervous.

"Will you please tell me if Douglas is difficult to talk to?"

"Oh no, not at all, I shouldn't say that, although of course . . . Well, you'll soon see. I suppose he *is* coming, Sachie, what do you think?"

(Was the famous author and personality going to appear in the light of some "cher maitre"?)

"What *is* so mysterious about him, Osbert, Sachie? *Is* there something so particularly strange? Why won't you tell me anything?"

"Oh dear . . . What would you say, Sachie?"

"Oh, I really couldn't, Osbert. . . ."

"Well, you'll soon see!", they plumped in chorus.

I could have screamed, I remember, at that moment. One had to shout anyway in that maddening place against the hubbub made by the garrulous diners in all the confusion of orders roared from one room to another, and the noise of the waiters colliding against our table, set, seemingly, between kitchen and lavatory. Of all the ghastly places to meet anyone in . . .

Nothing was to be got out of them, save, finally:

"I should be *careful* if I were you—hmh, hmh!"

I see now what they were doing! This was what Americans call "a great, big, build-up." And they were having such fun with me! That mysterious reputation of yours was too good not to be utilised, expressed to the last drop. Well, blessed be they as the divine instruments who—little knowing—brought you then and there into the perspective of my life!

Of course it was startling to be told at that moment:

"I should be *careful* if I were you. . . ." .

What could that possibly mean? A sudden, covert pill in my wine? A giddy moonlit drive round the town under the rug in an old cab?

"Oh come now—*do* say something about him!"

"Well . . . er . . . hmh, hmh . . . there's that little box of his. . . ."

"*What?*"

"I suppose-he-may-come-yet," said Osbert, hmh-hmhmming madly and hurrying away from my question.

Suddenly you were there beside us, having entered unseen, and you had a perfectly normal, if dignified and courteous presence: tallish, broad-shouldered, well-set, a man of fifty or so, I thought*—with a fine head, very clear-cut features, sharp tip to long nose, piercing blue-grey eyes of aquatic flint under thick, curving eyebrows, a rather florid or high complexion, an admirably neat outline of head and perfectly-trimmed, close-cut, partly grey hair—dressed in a mackintosh over a thick, well-tailored tweed suit—very forthright and straightforward in manner, as was at once apparent. Not in the least formidable! Beautiful bearing and beautiful breeding—*beaucoup de branche,* in fact.

You came and sat down beside me and after a moment pulled out an exquisite little *tabatiere* and offered me some snuff. At this, Osbert's and Sachie's eyes gave a leap—"There now, see?"—as I took some for the first time in my life, you telling me how it should be done, the right spot on the hand. I had a good sniff; it was strange and delicious. As I continued not to sneeze, I wondered if this would seem a sign of anything in particular to you, Apparently not!

We had a good, long look at one another. I remember *that* moment extraordinarily well.

"What do you find to do here?", you presently asked me.

"I've been in Florence two weeks now, and oh the rain! This year, however, it seems to come regularly every alternate day and I've been going by that. So, the fine days I do excursions, and picture galleries and churches in Florence the wet ones. It has worked out beautifully, so far."

"Pictures . . . ," you repeated, "excursions—where?"

"San Gimignano, for one. What a wonderful place in itself! And, of course, the Benozzo Gozzolis there, those frescoes. . . ."

"Benozzo Gozzolis!" The name of this painter set you off. *"What on earth for?"*

"Because I love his painting—that's all."

(I asked myself if you were playing at being a bit of a Philistine. Did I seem somewhat puzzling to you?)

". . . And Piero della Francesca, and Signorelli. These are my three favourite painters."

This was too much!

"What next?" you exclaimed, and offered me some more snuff.

(*Were* you playing at being a bit of a Philistine? A tweeded Scot, pooh-poohing at art? I was nonplussed now.)

"Isn't all that rather *Cinquecento,* my dear?" you asked suddenly.

It must have been an expression well-known to Osbert and Sachie,

* Actually 53 the preceding December—and I nearly 27.

judging from the laugh that went up, which added to my bewilderment, although it made me laugh as much as them. What could it mean, used thus?

That was the way we met. A curious first conversation—if it can be called such.

The next occasion we met was in Bologna in the autumn of 1924—a brief but gay moment. Would you not come to Venice—I asked—where I was spending a fortnight? This evoked a rapid "Not on your life!", for Venice was never sympathetic to you. It must be Florence or nothing. We split the difference, however, at Bologna. There is a slight mistake in Orioli's *Adventures of a Bookseller,* for he has chronicled that merry evening with a wrong date. And he has it that I was staying with you, and that this meeting occurred two or three years later on. He was after the 1479 Brecia *Aesop,* an extremely rare book—and *that,* it seems, is what brought us all to Bologna.

It may have seemed rather an odd trio that arrived by car, hot, dusty and in great need of refreshment which you joined us immediately in finding: Tristan Tzara, the Rumanian poet and founder of the *Dada* movement, Eugene MacCown and myself. Although Tzara knew very little of things English, you and he got on splendidly and this was probably the first occasion I listened to your remarkably good French. Could there but have been more time, time for *Dada* to be expounded . . . I mean, lightly touched on! To be sure, it was no longer in full flame as when it broke over all intellectual Europe immediately after the end of the war, having been birthed in Zurich in 1916. Tzara himself was now somewhat beyond it. I should have liked to hear you on the score of *Dada* philosophy, for there were many things in its attack on academic pomps that would have appealed to you. As we tucked into the *scampi* and all the other culinary riches, I thought what an agreeable subject this might be for one of Max Beerbohm's ineffable caricatures, this meeting of contrasts. For although Orioli shows that he had never heard of Tzara and *Dada,* the fact remained that Tzara was about the most universally known of cosmopolitan avant-garde intellectuals. Something like this, perhaps, as a caption to the drawing:

"Prandial first encounter between author of famous novel 'incorporating all known and several invented sins—South Wind' and founder of greatest modern iconoclastic movement—Dada."

Just as you were a storm-centre of legend, so Tzara was a sort of mystery-man of ethical and artistic revolution, pictured sometimes as a thunderous *ex-cathedra* giant, ominous, black-bearded, more full of blast than had ever been the hottest Futurist. How far from the truth! Neat, precise and sometimes very silent, Tzara sat gazing at you, taking in your personality. Who knows where we dined, but I remember yet the spread of dishes and wines and my pleasure at meeting Orioli—dear Pino—for the first time. There was an Italian child with you both, little Silvio, whose mother had asked you to take to an aunt nearby, and never had I seen a better-mannered small boy. He had ideas about me, though, according to Pino's book—he thought I would look like an asparagus with my clothes off; I seemed to him that long and slim.

Aragon and I were in Florence for a few days in October 1926, not long before the thirteenth unsuccessful attempt on Mussolini's life. The evolution of Fascism was visible—even in Venice where, somehow, it always seemed less noticeable. However, this month students there roared angrily along the streets and I came in for a share of this, for my rust-coloured mackintosh turned bloodred when it rained; it rained every day, and so . . . Earlier journeys in Italy had left certain memories—an excited man racing at me through a Roman street at night, having spied small red trimmings on my dark blue jacket; that old Neapolitan cabman who had whipped up his horse and left me stranded, recognising, quite correctly, certain sounds as the advance of a group of Blackshirts. What did *you* feel about this hysteria? Would you ever talk about Fascism? No! Simply not to be drawn! This was indeed disappointing to many of us who would have liked a good, long assessment from you, or even some stray remarks! *Not to be drawn*. As if there were some mute "Catch me!" at any suggestion of the subject.

Like Tzara, Aragon was much impressed by you. What beautiful French, and what a tremendous personality! Neither had ever met such a particular brand of old wine before—of sheer, elemental sun-warmth. And such an easy, spontaneous manner! Surely England nowadays. . . .

One evening you asked me about Venice. Now, what had that been like? I was longing to tell you, yet somewhat uncertain as to how much sympathy would be evoked by such things as "crises in the emotions," such matters as a rule enjoying short shrift with you! In all, it seemed to me what I thought you might call "a regular bumper crop."

Well, why not tell Norman everything—I thought—this once? *Nearly* everything . . . It had been the hell of a time in many ways—gay and mad, fantastic and ominous, and horribly dramatic too, for there was nearly a sharp physical tragedy. How would you react to the outpouring of so full a cornucopia?

I described all the people I thought would interest you—the joy of some, the bane of others; the petty intrigues and funny scandals; balls, fancy-dress galas and festivities—the whole hectic spin of Venice in August and September during the twenties, all the more exotic on account of its cosmopolitanism. I told you how much I liked the calmer hours when I would row with my philosophical gondolier, Angelo Trevisan, and how I loved pushing my oar in rhythm with his in a *sandalo;* of how much I learned from him about the difficult times of such Venetians as have to make enough money out of seasonal business and summer flummery to live on for the rest of the year. I told you of Augustina, an endearing, love-crossed maid, who fell on her knees embracing mine, begging me, weeping, to take her out of her unhappiness in Italy, where, she said, she would find no work after I had gone . . . And of Asterio Clerici, that dizzy, good-looking waiter, the story of whom is absolutely unprintable. Although it began in a would-be amorous manner, I felt sure it was hinged to the fear of unemployment and his dislike of the Fascist regime. He too had wanted me to take him out of Italy. Here you interrupted:

"Ha! Asterio Clerici—what do you expect with a name like that?"

"What a cryptic remark, Norman! Would that name account for such extraordinarily daring behaviour in public?"

"Lots of things that would seem extraordinary elsewhere are quite common in Italy. Young people often get excited and lose their heads. It's the *excitement* they like. And not only young people . . . Go on, go on. Tell me everything!"

Well, it had all been spectacular for several weeks—that blazing Lido strewn with society stars in glittering jewels and make-up—that brilliance of Grand Canal Barge-Parties—those spontaneous dawn-revels after dancing in some of the rather sinister new night-bars. A time came when everyone thought everyone else "crazy"—although Eddie Knoblock, despite my doubts, told me he thought *I* was the only sane person in Venice—an agreeable compliment from a most intelligent man! I told you how a great friend of mine had nearly committed suicide; it was only avoided at the last moment and all of that had been ghastly. And then, with the rains, had come the withdrawal of the great tide of people. And one night—well, this was something entirely new to me:

My cousin Edward Cunard and I had gone to sup and dance in the Hotel Luna and here we met some people so different to all I had ever known that they seemed as strange to me as being from another planet. They were Afro-Americans, coloured musicians, and they played in that "out of this world" manner which, in ordinary English, would have to be translated, I suppose, by "ineffable." Such Jazz and such

Swing and such improvisations! And all new to me in style! Well, so ravishing was it all that when they stepped from the band-stand at the end of their last number we rose to our feet with one accord and asked them to sit down and have a drink with us. The charm, beauty and elegance of these people—I told you—their art, their manners, the way they talked with us—these "Eddie South's Alabamians," as they were commercially called! *Enchanting* people, all four, whom we went to hear again and again and often talked with—Eddie, "the dark angel of the violin," Mike the guitarist, Henry at the piano and Romie at the drums . . . Bless them all. . . .

Now here is some curious English, Norman. Might it be Shakespearian? Listen well. You know in how rare a manner certain Americans express themselves. It seems that American Coloured talk has a parallel richness and is often stranger yet! One of these "Alabamians" is known as Banjo Mike—from Chicago. As attractive as a panther and rather like one—young, with a light brown skin, rippling blue-black hair. He has innate courtesy, beautiful clothes, and is practically illiterate, playing excellently by ear. . . . There he was one day in the street and I said, "How are you, Mike?" To which he replied with his charming smile: "Spunk's pretty high this morning!" Might that be old English—when "spunk" was "courage"?

And then, Henry—another man of great good looks, who is partly Red Indian. Henry tells me: "Mike is an angle-man." Do you see what *that* means? Would it be something in the nature of playing off one person against another?

But you had no ideas as to the possible origin or meaning of these two gems.

"Go on, go on—*tell me everything!*"

Well, at the end I gave a little fancy-dress dance, which had some picturesque touches, silhouetted against the windows open on to the Zattere. Here, at one moment, was an old nobleman, dressed like a Mandarin, down on his knees, most impudently beseeching the favours, then and there, of . . . And that figure of fantasy, rather like a Velasquez dwarf, who despite all his charm and wealth (or because of them) had had scandals all over Europe, who now ran hither and yon in consternation at having mislaid his little jewelled box and, oh dear, it contained cocaine! And right in the middle of the party, my gondolier, who—as he pointed out—was not a young man nor even of the dashing kind, taking me aside to confide his amazement at being so amiably solicited: "I could have understood had it been my nephew . . . but, *me?*" No harm, indeed, no harm—he laughed kind-heartedly—but Lord, how odd was the behaviour of some foreigners in Venice . . . At six or so in the morning the last to leave were three of the "Alabamians," and delectable was this view of them from above, going away in that bright Venetian sunlight with certain golden and other raven-haired friends of European blood . . . A new element had come into my life, suddenly. It was certainly too soon to pronounce oneself concerning its importance—one should never try to prise open the bud of the future. No! I was not going into *that* with you. And so, this was about all—except that, being very short of sleep and somewhat upwrought, I felt I was suffering from "extreme nervous exhaustion."

There was a considerable silence, and then you grunted, actually grunted one short remark:

"It all sounds like a regular good job-lot to me."

[One of the Alabamians, Henry Crowder, left the orchestra and became a factotum at the Hours Press, which Nancy had started at Réanville, Normandy, in the spring of 1928.]

Late autumn lay grimly over Normandy on my return, and the cold and gloom of dripping, and next of freezing country would have been unendurable but for the printing-work that went on day after day in grim tête-à-tête—with the talk running something like this: "Il faut aligner sur 25!" "Non! C'est un 'justif' de 30 qu'il faut; trois cicéros de douze par ici, quatre blancs par là"—and more technical jargon of this kind.

My printing was learned in French, and it pleased me to think of you having the same sort of conversations with your printers in Italian, but there would be smiles all round, *there,* I reflected, whereas here. . . .

After three months it became insufferable, and I persuaded Henry to leave Eddie South's "Alabamians" in Paris, if only for a time, and come and work for the HOURS PRESS. We had become very good friends after I left you in Florence and I was intensely interested—amazed too—at what I learned from him about the life of the American Negro. As you saw later, Henry became a great turning-point in my own. My feeling for things African had begun years ago with sculpture, and something of these anonymous old statues had now, it seemed, materialised in the personality of a man partly of that race. My sympathy with the Afro-American had, obviously, begun with music. At present something of both was in the house and part of it.

The adaptability of the American Negro! Henry, always a thoughtful, serious-minded man (although on occasion in rhapsodically rollicking mood) was sick to death of night hours, of all the drinks sent to him at his piano, of the fatigue attendant on the adulation of Montmartre and those interminable "crapgames" at dawn he and the other coloured musicians would be playing in the "Flea-Pit," too weary to go home and sleep. I got him away from all of that and we hired a piano for Réanville. Now he and Monsieur Lévy and I pulled the Press together on printing-day. Henry also did billing and circulars and parcels, laughing at the strange hierarchy of English titles as they have to be written for the post. And he drove the car too; he was indispensable. Thus Henry became part of THE HOURS.

raymond mortimer
Nancy Cunard

Everybody old, it is to be hoped, can look back to one person who was incomparably bewitching; and I have never met anyone to equal Nancy Cunard, when first I met her forty-two years ago. We had crossed to Paris on the previous day in the same boat, trains and (we discovered) reading the same book of poems, Roy Campbell's *Flaming Terrapin*. She had a ground-floor apartment looking south over the Seine in a fine old house at the corner of the rue Le Regrattier on the Île Saint-Louis. She would laughingly apply an early Eliot line to one of its rooms, painted dark red—"an atmosphere of Juliet's tomb." In those years there was nothing else lugubrious in her life.

What first struck one was her *regard* (there is no English word meaning not only the eyes—hers were an Arctic blue—but the way in which they confront the visible world). Next came the mixture of delicacy and steel in her build, hips, legs and ankles all of the slenderest, arms and wrists weighted with massive ivory bracelets from Africa that they seemed too fragile to support. Her walk also enchanted, the head held high with its short fair hair, and one foot placed exactly in front of the other, not with mannequin languor, but spontaneously, briskly, boldly, skimming the pavement. Never in her life, I believe, was she frightened of anything.

In those blissful days her ruling passion was for poetry, not politics. She was fascinated by the new surrealist movement, and was a close friend of Louis Aragon (the most gifted French writer, I think, of his generation) and René Crevel, who charmed everyone he liked until a desperate suicide cut short his so promising career. Her verse, however, was influenced by Eliot, not Aragon or Eluard. I introduced her to Virginia Woolf, who with her husband was running the Hogarth Press, and they published her book, *Parallax*. At this time she was still on friendly terms with her mother. I remember delightful evenings *à quatre* with Maud (she had not yet become Emerald), Sir Thomas Beecham and Nancy. Though the daughter never returned her mother's adoration, they had lots in common, entire courage, independence of mind and delight in the arts. Lady Cunard was the more bookish of the two, and would often read most of the night. A recent writer staggered me by suggesting that she took her views about books from a secretary who told her what reviewers had said.

Nancy's close friends when first we met included Iris Tree, like herself a gifted poet and a delicious character, Janet Flanner, always the most stimulating of talkers, and Marjory Craigie, brimming with humour and the glass of fashion. Nancy also took trouble with her appearance. Even later, when she spent any little money she had to spare upon helping friends in need, she chose with a sure eye whatever she wore. In all other ways she had never any use for conventionality. Like so many western sympathisers with Communism, she was a natural rebel and anarchist, who would have been the first to defy the party line if she had lived in Russia.

Though I saw little of her in her later years, we never had the slightest quarrel, (I knew that all argument with her would be futile); and we were always overjoyed when we did meet. The last time was at a mental hospital in a vast, preposterously ornate Victorian mansion. Roger Senhouse, always seraphically kind to her, motored me down from London; and going through long passages with pathetic figures muttering to themselves or groping for imaginary objects on the floor (cigarette-ends, violets, emeralds?), we found her at last, mercifully in a room of her own, and took her out to see Eton chapel. Apart from a few protests, quite calm, about fancied persecution, she was the old buoyant, responsive Nancy, delighting in details of the medieval frescoes and modern stained glass.

I think of her as a born enjoyer, whose idealism made her self-destructive. She pursued her own path, with no regard for her happiness, and untameable by experience. Four lines from her *Parallax* recur to my memory, though Nancy never went unpraised:

And Beauty walked alone here,
Unpraised, unhindered,
Defiant, of single mind,
And took no rest, and has no epitaph.

Poems from Outlaws

(*Outlaws,* Miss Cunard's first book of poetry, appeared in 1921.)

THE KNAVE OF SPADES

You are the Knave of Spades; I swear you are
No other personage, no other card
In any pack has that satanic eye.
You are the soul of highway robbery,
And you have nimbly mocked at all those toys,
Pistols and crossbones, horses, masks and skulls;
For you have been too swift in every chase
And now you hover round forgotten gibbets,
Staring, and laugh. Again you are a wild
Great stamping Tartar full of ecstasy;
Your speech is suave, yet like a scimitar
Cleaves the white air with blazing irony.
I love you, Longhi's darkest lurking shadow,
Appearing suddenly, as quickly gone
Back to your eighteenth-century lagoons;
I am not sure *you* weren't that famous snake
That is accused of having tempted Eve
With apple-talk; (you knew how well to lie).
I hope that I shall never live to see
In your dark face the sign of any pain
Or any creeping sorrow that spoils pride;
(The pride of devils that may never suffer).
I think you have been king of your desires,
First granting them, then turning them to dust;
Weirwolf, enchanter, sometimes Harlequin,
A bitter Harlequin of curious moods

When midnight trembles and the West meets East . . .
God knows what more, but I prefer just now
To think of you as that same Knave of Spades,
A fiendish rebel with no heart; and yet
You are my love, the witchcraft of my faith.

EVENINGS

Now when you hear the musing of a bell
Let loose in summer evenings, mark the poise
Of summer clouds, the mutability
Of pallid twilights from a tower's crest—
When you have loved the last long sentiment
Slipped on-to earth from sunset, seen the stars
Come pale and faltering, the blaze of flowers
Grow dim and grey, and all the stuff of night
Rise up around you almost menacing—
When you have lost the guide of colour, seen
The daylight like a workman trudging home
Oblivious of your thoughts and leaving you
Silent beside the brim of seas grown still,
Placid and strange. When you have lingered there,
And shuddered at the magic of a moon
That will not sleep, but needs your vigilance
And seizes on the musings of your soul
Till you are made fanatical and wild,
Torn with old conflicts and the internal fire
Of passion and love, excessive grief of tears
And all the revolutions found in life—
What then? your body shall be crucified,
Your spirit tortured, and perhaps found good
Enough a tribute for some ultimate art.

VOYAGES NORTH

The strange effects of afternoons!
Hours interminable, melting like honey-drops
In an assemblage of friends . . .

Or jagged, stretching hard unpleasant fingers
As we go by, hurrying through the crowds—
People agape at shops, Regent Street congested
With the intolerable army of winter road-workers
Picking; then in the Cafe Royal
Belated drunkards toying with a balloon
Bought from a pedler—streets and stations
Serried together like cheap print, swinging trains
With conversational travellers arguing on the Opera—
Newspapers, agitation of the mind and fingers,
The first breath of country dispelling undue meditation
With the reposeful promise of village firesides;
Greetings at meeting—But if I were free
I would go on, see all the northern continents
Stretch out before me under winter sunsets;
Look into the psychology
Of Iceland, and plumb the imaginations
Of travellers outlandish, talking and drinking
With stern strange companies of merchants;
I should learn
More than one could remember, walk through the days
Enjoying the remoteness, and laughing in foreign places;
I should cure my heart of longing and impatience
And all the penalties of thought-out pleasure,
Those aftermaths of degradation
That come when silly feasts are done.
I should be wise and prodigal, spending these new delights
With the conviction of a millionaire
Made human by imagination—they should be
The important steps that lead to happiness
And independence of the mind; then should I say
Final farewell to streets of memories,
Forget the analytical introspection
And the subjective drowsiness of mind,
Stamping into the dust all staleness of things outgrown,
Stand on a northern hill-top shouting at the sun!

THE WREATH

Love has destroyed my life, and all too long
Have I been enemy with life, too late

Unlocked the secrets of existence! there
Found but the ashes of a fallen city
Stamped underfoot, the temple of desires
Run through with fire and perished with defeat.
I would not speak the word of Disillusion
But have long felt the seal of melancholy
Stamped on my sombre autumn resignation.
My loves have been voracious, many-coloured,
Fantastic, sober, all-encompassing,
Have flown like summer swallows at the sun
And dipped into a wintry world of water:
Returned with laughing eyes or blenching face
From each horizon, from the Ever-New:
Passed through Adventure's net, struck at the stars
Flung by excitement recklessly so high:
Delved into precipices warily
And picked the jewel there from dragon-jaws:
Questioned the sphinx of Personality
Reading the puzzling riddles of the sand,
Bringing back prizes, bringing home defeat;
Sometimes to answers ancient questions turned,
Or driven on, flown like unbalanced moths
Round the perpetual candle of a sage,
Dropping to dust on Science's midnight.
They have gone forth like innocent crusaders
To win the ideals of mediaevalism;
They have set sail on roving western waters,
Searched for Eternity in worlds untame,
Fought for their lives against the rush of Time
And known the despairs of death, and war's dismay—
Of these my cunning crown is made, of these
Imperious leaves the sombre final wreath!

ANSWER TO A REPROOF

Let my impatience guide you now, I feel
You have not known that glorious discontent
That leads me on: the wandering after dreams
And the long chasing in the labyrinth
Of fancy, and the reckless flight of moods—
You *shall* not prison, shall not grammarise

My swift imagination, nor tie down
My laughing words, my serious words, old thoughts
I may have led you on with, baffling you
Into a pompous state of great confusion.
You have not seen the changing active birds
Nor heard the mocking voices of my thoughts;
Pedant-philosopher, I challenge you
Sometimes with jests, more often with real things,
And you have failed me, you have suffered too
And struggled, wondering. The difference lies
In the old bulk of centuries, the way
You have been fashioned this or that; and I
Belong to neither, I the perfect stranger,
Outcast and outlaw from the rules of life,
True to one law alone, a personal logic
That will not blend with anything, nor bow
Down to the general rules; inflexible,
And knowing it from old experience;
So much for argument—*My* trouble is,
It seems, that I have loved a star and tried
To touch it in its progress: tear it down
And own it, claimed a "master's privilege"
Over some matter that was element
And not an object that would fit the palm
Of a possessor, master-mind itself
And active-ardent of its liberty.

We work apart, alone; conflicting tides
Brim-filled with angers, violences, strife,
Each championing his own idealism,
Romanticism and sceptic bitterness . . .
The last I leave you, for this present mood
(The name of which you have expounded so)
Has turned against you, bared insulting teeth
And snarled away its rage into the smile
Of old remembrance: "You were ever so,"
Exacting and difficult; in fact the star
That will not, cannot change for all the price
Of love or understanding—mark you *now*
I have concluded we are justified
Each in his scheming; is this not a world
Proportioned large enough for enemies
Of our calibre? Shall we always meet

In endless conflict? I have realised
That I shall burn in my own hell alone
And solitarily escape from death;
That you will wander guideless too, and dream
(Sometimes) of what I *mean,* the things unsaid,
Vacant discussions that have troubled you
And left me desperate as a day of rain.

Then we shall meet at cross-roads in wild hours
Agreeing over fundamental fates,
Calamities of a more general kind
Than our own geniuses have kindled up.
But at the fabulous Judgment-day, the End,
We shall be separate still, and you will find
That Destiny has posted you once more
Back in the sky—and I shall be on earth.

william carlos williams
Nancy Cunard

[Staying at a pension in Villefranche in March, 1924, William Carlos Williams and his wife discovered they were living only a short distance from Nancy Cunard, who one day came to look them over.]

One day we entertained Nancy Cunard, surely one of the major phenomena of that world, and her cousin Victor. They came to look us over, Victor to sniff at the municipal gas tank beyond the mimosa to the rear of the pension, Nancy to invite us for a walk to Sospel back of Menton and to talk, of writing, of anything that was in her mind; and if there was anything that was not in that courteous, cultured and fearless mind, I have yet to discover it. Nancy was to me as constant as the heavens in her complete and passionate inconstancy. Out of passion, to defeat its domination, that tall, blond spike of a woman whose mind never, that I knew, was clouded by drink, kept herself burned to the bone. What else have the martyrs done?
    . . . Nancy had come down out of admiration and friendship for all of us and to look the situation over. She also was very fond of Floss (Mrs. Williams) and later protected her on more than one wild occasion. A tall wraith of a woman looking as though any wind might blow her away but without restraints.

[After several months on the Riviera, during which time the American couple was often entertained by Nancy, they moved on to Paris, where the poet, again in Nancy's company, found in her and in Iris Tree some elusive qualities hard to define.]

Who are these two young and arresting women, or any of them all, with whom we have been thrown during our brief stay in Paris? I speak especially of Nancy Cunard and Iris Tree, though we saw less of Iris than Nancy. Surely they were riding above the storm in the Paris that we were witnessing. Nancy Cunard, straight as any stick, emaciated, holding her head erect, not particularly animated, her blue eyes completely untroubled, inviolable in her virginity of pure act. I never saw her drunk; I can imagine that she was never quite sober.

If the Irish in her, through her American mother, made her daring, it was the German in Iris Tree that made her still, almost dull. She, stockier than her fellow Englishwomen, had she been mounted on a proper charger in mail, her thick blond hair brushing her shoulders, would have made an ideal picture of Sir Galahad.

There were the others but these two seemed to stand out for me—perhaps because they were absolutely remote from any desire I might have had toward them. They possessed Paris, as much of Paris as they wanted, but I couldn't make them out. I'm sure I didn't look at them as women. They were a momentary phase of a thing as fixed and permanent to me as the stones on which we walked. If I went to Paris again, I'd expect to find them just as they were at that time, young, detached from reality, without passion. They, young as they were, had had bitter early experiences without emotional response. There was nothing left in either of them. They were completely empty, and yet they were young, appealing and unassailable. No one could touch them to harm them in any way or be deeply moved by them. They were as quiet in their moods and as profligate in their actions (it was said) as figures cut from chalk, or so I addressed their images in my mind. For a strange reason, I felt a strong affection for them.

There was nothing I wanted to do about it; and I was happy to know that if there had been a possibility of raising a love from such stuff, it would be quite impossible to describe it.

It was a feeling such as one has in going about the corridors of a gallery of sculpture. The stupid believe that it is amusing to think of Galatea coming to life, but they haven't the slightest idea how far she would have to travel to regain breath. And if she should regain it, what a terrifying thing it would be: the past being something which we cannot even in our imagination resurrect. That's how I felt about those two English society girls, gross as I knew them to be. By their profligacy they were asserting a veritable chastity of mind which no one could disturb. The trouble of mind of a Clotilde, of a Mina, to me had come to some sort of resolution, but in Nancy especially, after some sort of purgation, it had reached a final end.

leonard woolf

Nancy Cunard

I do not remember exactly when or how it was that I first met Nancy Cunard; it must, I think, have been round about 1920. It was in 1925 that we printed and published in The Hogarth Press her poem *Parallax.* I never saw a great deal of her or for long at a time, but that made no difference to one's relationship with her. She seemed to drift in and out, in and out of one's room and one's life, but she was always the same Nancy, unlike anyone else in the world. When she was young, she was enchanting, and, though she lost, like all living things from daffodils and puppies to *les jeunes filles en fleurs,* the ravishing freshness of youth, she never lost that strange quality of enchantment. I had from the moment I saw her a great affection for her and she had, I think, an affection for me. One's affection was tinged with apprehension, or anxiety, for she had an air of vulnerability, deep down of sadness. Not that she was in the least sad on the surface of life; she was essentially gay, but often I felt behind or beneath the gaiety this vulnerability. I remember her vividly on two fortuitous occasions. One afternoon she drifted into our flat in Tavistock Square carrying in her arms a large fox made of silver. It had been presented to her father by the members of a Hunt of which, I suppose, he had been Master. She had just fetched it from the bank, and, according to her, it was the only thing which her father had left to her. She was amused by and laughed at her absurd silver fox, yet one felt that life had hurt her somewhat. The second occasion was some time later when again she drifted into our room, this time with John Strachey who later became a Cabinet Minister. They had spent the summer afternoon on the river and had lunch on Eel Pie Island. They described very amusingly the company on the island and the antics of a monkey which was kept in a cage there. The contrast between the two of them was fascinating. John was very much a Strachey, an intellectual through and through and, though not spiritually armour-plated, protected against life by an ultimate toughness. There was no toughness in Nancy and I can see her now sitting on the sofa, gay but vulnerable, unarmoured, with her mind not entirely upon Eel Pie Island, the monkey, and John, Virginia, and Leonard.

For Nancy was essentially one of those rare people whom Tolstoy called "sillies." He thought that they are the best people in the world. They have a simplicity, a purity, a nakedness of soul. They have no façade, no carapace to conceal or protect their inner being from people and the world and life. That is why they have that vulnerability which I felt in Nancy.

michael arlen

The Green Hat

[Among her many literary friends was Michael Arlen, whose novel *The Green Hat,* published in 1925, achieved considerable popularity, and in which Miss Cunard appeared as Iris March. The following excerpt comes early in the novel.]

I am trying, you can see, to realise her, to add her together; and, of course, failing. She showed you first one side of her and then another, and each side seemed to have no relation with any other, each side might have belonged to a different woman; indeed, since then I have found that each side did belong to a different woman. I have met a hundred pieces of Iris, quite vividly met them, since last I saw her. And sometimes I have thought of her—foolishly, of course, but shall a man be wise about a woman?—as some one who had by a mistake of the higher authorities strayed into our world from a land unknown to us, a land where lived a race of men and women who, the perfection of our imperfections, were awaiting their inheritance of this world of ours when we, with that marvellous indirectness of purpose which is called being human, shall have finally annihilated each other in our endless squabbles about honour, morality, nationality.

We have all of us a crude desire to "place" our fellows in this or that category or class. . . . You had a conviction, a rather despairing one, that she didn't fit in anywhere, to any class, nay, to any nationality. She wasn't that ghastly thing called "Bohemian," she wasn't any of the ghastly things called "society," "country," upper, middle, and lower class. She was, you can see, some invention, ghastly or not, of her own. But she was so quiet about it, she didn't intrude it on you, she was just herself, and that was a very quiet self. You felt she had outlawed herself from somewhere, but where was that somewhere? You felt she was tremendously indifferent as to whether she was outlawed or not. In her eyes you saw the landscape of England, spacious and brave; but you felt unreasonably certain that she was as devoid of patriotism as Mary Stuart. She gave you a sense of the conventions; but she gave you—unaware always, impersonal always, and those cool, sensible eyes!—a much deeper sense that she was somehow outside the comic, squalid, sometimes, almost fine laws by which we judge as to what is and what is not conventional. That was why, I am trying to show, I felt so profoundly incapable with her. It was not as though one was non-existent; it was as though, with her, one existed only in the most limited sense. And, I suppose, she affected me particularly in that way simply because I am a man of my time. For that is a limitation a man can't get beyond—to be of his time, completely. He may be successful, a man like that—indeed, should he not blow his brains out if he is not?—but he who is of this time may never rise above himself: he is the galley-slave working incessantly at the oars of his life, which reflects the lives of the multitude of his fellows. Yes, I am of my time. And so I had with this woman that profound sense of incapability, of defeat, which any limited man must feel with a woman whose limitations he cannot know. She was—in that phrase of Mr. Conrad's which can mean so little or so much—she was of all time. She was, when the first woman crawled out of the mud of the primeval world. She would be, when the last woman walks towards the unmentionable end.

Talking with her in that room was like talking with her as we walked on a windy heath: she threw out things, you caught all you could of them, you missed what you liked, and you threw something back. Now and then something would turn up in a voice which was suddenly strong and clear, and every time her voice was strong and clear you were so surprised that you did not hear so well as when she spoke inaudibly. She had none of the organised, agonised grimaces of the young lady of fashion. But one knew she was not a young lady of fashion, for she hadn't a sulky mouth.

Hers was that random, uninformed, but severely discriminating taste which maddens you: you try unsuccessfully to think that there is nothing at the back of it, nothing but a misty criterion of enjoyment. She used some words as though she had never heard any one else using them. "Nice," for instance, she used in a calmly immense sense. The word seemed turned topsy-turvy, and to turn everything else topsy-turvy. She did not like abbreviations, even lunch for luncheon. "What," she asked, "is the hurry?" I could not tell her. She thought that perhaps English was not the language for abbreviations and diminutives. She deferred to my judgment about that, and I said what I said. One just didn't discuss Barrie: there he was. "You can't laugh me out of him," she smiled, "by calling him whimsical." She had once enjoyed a book by Mr. Compton Mackenzie, a garden catalogue called *Guy and Pauline*. There was Hergesheimer. She put up a gallant, insincere defence for the Imagistes, but it turned out that she had never read any, and wasn't at all sure what they were. "They're short for poetry," I said coldly, "like nightie for nightingale." But perhaps the book she most profoundly liked was *The Passionate Friends,* with perhaps the last part of *Tono-Bungay.* "And, of course," she said, *"The Good Soldier,"* Mr. Ford Maddox [Ford] Hueffer's amazing romance. From a table she picked up Joyce's *Ulysses,* looked at it vaguely, dropped it absently on the floor amongst the others.

Poems from Sublunary

Sublunary, a considerably larger collection of poetry than *Outlaws,* was published in 1923.

HORNS IN THE VALLEY

This June the nights lay heavy until dawn;
Then did my heart devise in solitude
Of old romances—came an evocation
Across the valley mists at sound of horns
Deep in the forest springing. So again
When the last chord had died, Isolda rose
With pulsing signal of imperious arms
Uplifted in long tremolo of passion.
I saw the grasses bend before her lover,
Precipitate wraith that hurried to her calling;
And the lost echoes of their ardent voices
Grew in my sense with fading of the horns,
Sighing an ultimate song of death and love.
Then in the harbour of the risen moon
The dew lay solitary; no shadows there
Guarded these pale-faced lovers through the night,
And the lone tower was empty of its watcher.
But in that moment were they joined at trysting,
Come to the cadence of this midnight music,
And now are gone on silence desolate.

[Several poems in *Sublunary* brought forth comments from George Moore, among them "Horns in the Valley," which provoked the following remarks.]

. . . Your mind is opening, Nancy, and it is perhaps wrong for me to try to force it open with criticism. All the same I have to ask you if you are satisfied with the opening of "Horns in the Valley." To make plain my meaning I will attempt a rough translation:

This June the nights lay heavy and I sat
Night after night in solitude devising
Romance, until one night there came the sound
Of horns across the mist-brimmed valley—horns,
And mingling echoes calling from height to height,
From glen to glen—till in my heart awoke
Remembrance of the moment when Isolda
Quenches the torch, the signal for her lover;
And then the rapturous cries, too swift for song,
Cry upon cry and mutter upon mutter—
Until insistent love lead them at last
To the delayed fruition of their love.

It seems to me, Nancy, that we have now had enough of the Opera, and that the next verses should tell your belief that the evocative horns are not real horns inasmuch as the love-adventure of Tristan and Isolda is not in a single brief moment in time, but an immortal moment carried on through eternity which in certain moods is audible to us. I have no hesitation in recommending a remoulding of this poem to you, for it is the least good of the three you sent.

"Then in the harbour of the risen moon." I am sure this is not adequate expression. Do you mean the pool of light in which the moon floats? As a recompense for all this criticism I proclaim my allegiance to "Beaucaire."

(Letter from George Moore.
January 21, 1922.)

BY THE DORDOGNE

Leaving Cahors I go through feathery fields
Of ancient mustards golden to the sun,
They sway as if in mockery, where one
Grey steeple rises angrily and shields
A humble village with its shade severe.
To-day the Dordogne valley, green and flush
With myriad flowers, slumbers in the hush

Of noon; spring's coffers have been emptied here.
I pause at sunset on the giant plains,
Where sheaf of pigeons on the wind up-blown
Wheels with fierce feathers through the hurrying
                                                                skies
That stream above the earth; the evening rains
Hot light on these far furrows that are sown
With growing harvests, green before the eyes.

TOULONNAISE

She was a rebel governess
Who came from Toulon in the south,
Red cherries tumbling on her hat,
Loud laughter breaking at her mouth.

Came to the Midlands there to teach
A girl of seven sullen-hearted—
Her voice was full of life's adventure,
Her eye too gay, so she departed.

And I, the child of seven, wonder
In what far province of the south
After these years may rediscover
The cherries defiant of her mouth.

Lips that would snap with scorn then soften,
Chasing the scolding from her brow . . .
Thus I remember—comes the thought
We should not know each other now.

A VIS-À-VIS

I shall never forget the ancient courtesan
Of Bandol by the sea, a little town
Lost in that Mediterranean saison morte,
With its hostelry that treats small fry en pension.
Her florid face blinks at an early dinner,
Poor solitary meal she knows so well

Without pretence of book or conversation,
Drawing her scarf about her. Very still,
The venerable false cat, she sums one up,
And does not savour the varied memories
Of those that filled her life; the moonstones
                              gleam
In a golden setting upon each heavy arm,
Spoils of the past—If she would only tell,
Speak out the meagre mockeries of her mind!
Disapprobation peers from her eyes, and there
Is an acid smile as well, if smile be needed
Even now to dismiss inopportunities.
I think we angered her, as from the room
Between our voices shrilled, mosquito-like,
She moved in panoply of ancient taffetas.
But we forgot, flushing with local wines
Aided with metaphysical words, perhaps,
Forgot for an hour this siren of last century—
And then I saw her, sitting a little while
Before that tideless sea, alone, alone,
Spider at brood, now lulled in an intense
Malicious contemplation of the moon.

THESE ROCKED THE CRADLE

I think when I was born
(Under what unknown stars that keep my secret still)
The legendary fates attended me:
Dark whisperings went by
In the corridors whence I sprang,
They clung unseen
Malignantly to the new frail thing—
Chill fates, withering winds already desolating
The paths to be traversed.
Near to the grasp, out of reach, stood the fickle
                              sword
Of crooked courage, backbiting and self-defiant—
A mist of uncertainty
Was my fond nurse, to rock me on her boundless
                              breast;
And the outlaw,

The lurid wanderer of highroads that all children
                                        love,
He too was there—Could I have seen
I would have recognised this friend of nowadays
And said:
Clasp me, Adventure!
Seizing the vagabond
By a more kindly mood in that first hour.
All were there,
This life's alarmers, sowing their future harvests,
Rife weeds of conflict—
        all but one
That I name never, Jealousy.

TO THE EIFFEL TOWER RESTAURANT

Espéranto . . .
The seal on your letter sets me thinking
Of other days and places,
And now I have the past to kneel before my present;
Those old nights of drinking,
Furtive adventures, solitary thinking
At the corner table, sheltered from the faces,
Inopportune invasion of the street.
I feel
Sharp tugs at my memory's sleeve:
The sound of the clock going wrong,
The fleet
Procession of your waiters with their platters—
Drinks held long
In one hand, while the other unwinds a discussion.
I do not grieve,
I never grieve
For things gone by,
But all the matter
Of ten years in a childhood's land
That grudges colour to one (save on your tables
Of opulent fruits, trimmed foods, voluminous flowers
That lie most comfortably there waiting our appetite).
I say, all the matter
Of that decade

Comes back to me with your letter.
I feel the mist
Of the room that mocks the fog in the street;
The voices of those of us returned from distant
                                        journeys,
They could ring in my ears
From your evocation;
And since from choice
I have abandoned
Those groups that pondered through the night's
                                        perspective
Restlessly, talking of foreign towns,
I take this sustenance
From your hand only.
Think how all of France
Divides us now, and the Italian sky
That closes down abruptly on its sunset of six o'clock,
Without lamps in this cold October.
Is England sober,
Clad in its sullen winter moods already,
Or sitting expansively
At the tables in warmed intoxication?
And do you still contemplate
The varying destiny
Of the clients that always must return
To the Tower's beacon, to the Tower's cheer?
Small fry and gros bonnets.

I think the Tower shall go up to heaven
One night in a flame of fire, about eleven.
I always saw our carnal-spiritual home
Blazing upon the sky symbolically . . .
If ever we go to heaven in a troop
The Tower must be our ladder,
Vertically
Climbing the ether with its swaying group.
God will delight to greet this embassy
Wherein is found no lack
Of wits and glamour, strong wines, new foods, fine looks,
    strange-sounding languages of diverse men—
Stulik shall lead the pack
Until its great disintegration, when
God sets us deftly in a new Zodiac.

nancy cunard

The Hours Press

[The following account of the Hours Press appeared in *The Book Collector* (Winter, 1964).]

The Hours Press
Retrospect-Catalogue-Commentary
By Nancy Cunard

The Hours Press, La Chapelle-Réanville, Eure, Normandy was started by me in the spring of 1928, soon after acquisition of Le Puits Carré, a small, old, peasant house. I knew nothing of printing.

Some people are always asking the *why* of anything. All I can reply to "Why printing?" is that I had long wanted to learn typesetting by hand and the working of a hand-press, to produce mainly contemporary poetry. Ignorance, sometimes a deterrent, can also be surprisingly encouraging in that difficulty is not perceptible. Publishing was yet more completely unknown to me, while the handling of type and its results on paper were fascinating.

Various publishing friends shook their heads. One, John Rodker (founder of The Casanova Society, London)—was positively bewildered. Leonard and Virginia Woolf of the Hogarth Press (she had hand-set my long poem, *Parallax,* herself, published by them in 1925) wrote: "Your hands will always be covered with ink." Once I had begun, I noticed, laughing, how that was no deterrent, nor even true; plain petrol washes off all that good-smelling printer's ink as well as it cleans type. Those who find this "mucky," preferring to grapple with the niceties of lay-out, the problems of financial outlay, the dreadful ways of book-keeping—let them stop setting and printing at once!

Lucky was I when William Bird (greatly esteemed American newspaperman, alas, recently dead) who had founded and himself worked his Three Mountains Press in Paris on the Île St Louis, said he wanted to sell it—for a remarkably small sum, as I realised later. No man could have been kinder in finding me that *rara avis,* a printer who could still manage a hand-press while being a modern worker as well.

Bird not only procured him to come to me in the country, but came there himself to supervise the setting-up of this extremely handsome, over-a-hundred-years-old Belgian "Mathieu." The massive dark green iron lamp on top suggested it was of pure Empire date. A ramshackle little outhouse was quickly put in order, and into this the press and all accessories fitted ideally, set up by the two technicians Bird had brought with him.

What to call my venture? The name, The Hours Press, came of itself, and was not only pleasing to me but suggestive of *work*.

Of definite programme then I had none. Except that George Moore (my first friend since childhood, on account of his life-long devotion to my mother) wrote he would "like to start off your press with a good bang." He was going to send me something of his, which he soon did.

Louis Aragon (co-founder, with André Breton and Paul Eluard, of Surrealism) was then very often at Réanville. The only exception in all my work, which was in English, was his translation into French of Lewis Carroll's *The Hunting of the Snark*.

My own idea of printing solely unpublished contemporary poetry receded when Norman Douglas, Arthur Symons, Richard Aldington all offered me works of theirs—although, in those first days already, I did achieve *one* of the unknown—a poem by the Chilean painter, Alvaro Guevara. It enchanted me to set—all on my own—his *St. George at Silene*. Guevara, who had studied at the Slade, was already much esteemed as a painter.

Conditions at Réanville, from the start, were anything but easy. Constant interruptions of electric light, constant need of extras of diverse kinds for the press, not to mention dreadful arguments in writing with binders, were ever with us. Mercifully, the difficulty of different languages never arose, for there was none on my side, and my printer, Monsieur Maurice Lévy, was remarkably meticulous with the horrible spelling of English, of which he knew not a word.

After many a 16-hour day (mine, for it went on late into the night, especially at circularising times) it seemed worth while to move the press to Paris in the winter of 1929–30, where Georges Sadoul (now the celebrated historian of the Cinema) and another then Surrealist friend, André Thirion, immediately found just the right-sized, right-priced little shop, 15 rue Guenégaud, on the left bank, near the Seine.

Here began what I think of as my "second series of books" in which there was much more modern poetry, but far less typesetting for me. "Clerking," such as book-keeping and far too much business correspondence, and also talking to people, took all day long.

Meanwhile, reviews of the books were good, some of them very laudatory. The English booksellers were extremely prompt in their payments, long credit being impossible as my capital was too slender. As far as I could make out, I had almost doubled it in just under the first year—by sheer hard work, good authors, and good luck.

Had I but had a proper partner, who would have looked after the *business* of publishing as distinct from the choice of works to be done, and their design . . . that is, someone who could have handled the publicity, ledger-keeping side of it all, The Hours Press might have lasted somewhat longer. All that really interested me (apart from not losing money, this being a commercial, not at all an "amateur matter") was the hand-setting, choice of paper and of bindings.

So, the end of The Hours Press in 1931, once decided on, was rapid. I sold the Minerva pedal-press to the rising French publisher, Guy Lévis-Mano; the Mathieu was removed to Normandy, rue Guenégaud given up. The "after-end," so to speak, after the Second World War had passed over the very few remains, mostly ravaged, in Normandy, seemed to say: "None of this ever belonged to you." So much had happened in between. I was to learn, through the only two good friends in that evil village, Réanville, that "all was gone." German troops, expressly sent to my unoccupied house by the village mayor, had burned everything: furniture, irreplaceable African sculpture, many valuable books. Norman peasants had stolen the rest. All was gone— save what this dear couple, the Goasgüens, who ran the inn, had saved during the Occupation at the risk of their lives. Nor door, nor window left in Le Puits Carré; its well thoroughly fouled; what had been the bathroom floor covered with a "mattress of books" a foot deep, thoroughly stamped on for years.

A great friend of mine, Morris Gilbert of *The New York Times,* made one leap there, uniformed, in his jeep, two hours after the departure of the Germans. The Goasgüens took him at once to my house where, aghast at the sight, he picked up at random one volume emergent a-top of that "mattress": the signed, red leather edition of Douglas's *One Day.* Later, on leave in London, he brought it to me and Douglas with the words *"My* loot," while both of us lovingly inscribed it for him.

I continue to love beautiful print, such as my 16-point Caslon Old Face (to me the ideal size for verse) and my favourite paper, the Canson et Vidalon.

From Spring 1928 to Spring 1931 sounds a short time to set up a printing-publishing venture; but the not so very considerable knowledge I had gained the while served me very well indeed. Without it I should have been incapable of making my enormous anthology, *Negro* (designing of covers included), with the whole outlay of its doubled-sized 855 pages, the placing of some 550 illustrations, the proof-reading. Published in London by Wishart, 16 February 1934, in an edition of 1000 copies, it is now worth, I am told, over $60 in the US (some £20 in England) when (now rarely) a second-hand copy is procurable. And certainly The Hours Press books—most of them, all long since out of print—have greatly appreciated in value.

I think I have three things to thank for the (relative) success of the press: ignorance of the usual commercial procedure (overheads and wastefulness, etc.), good authors, and hard work at a propitious moment in the history of the private press movement.

harold acton

Nancy Cunard: Romantic Rebel

Another unconscious creator of myths was Nancy Cunard, who had inspired half the poets and novelists of the 'twenties. They saw her as the Gioconda of the Age, but never as her electro-magnetic self.

She was slim to the point of evanescence, and her voice evanesced in conversation to revive, surprisingly sharp and pointed, in a disarming query. Her small head so gracefully poised might have been carved in crystal with green jade for eyes, and this crystalline quality made some people think she was cold to the core. But she felt passionately about injustice: she was a romantic rebel, "to whom the miseries of the world are misery, and will not let them rest." She would not let them rest, and she would let nobody rest within her orbit, so long as there was a wrong to be righted by human means.

Gradually I watched the transformation of what the Press might describe as "a popular society girl" into a militant propagandist for miscellaneous prickly causes, fighting in improbable surroundings, for the Scottsboro Negroes, the Spanish republicans, refugees and down-and-outs of sorts, hardening her will to overcome exhaustion, courting physical discomfort, indifferent to calumny, smiling at risks. Her austerity was voluptuous. In the middle ages she would have become a mystic.

One of her quieter activities was the management of the Hours Press, in the narrow rue Guenégaud, where limited editions of contemporary poetry and prose, signed by the authors and numbered, were produced for thirty shillings or so.

On the back of a printed card which fell out of an unfinished book—how strange the fate of cards which are not torn up!—I find these pencilled words which evoke Nancy's shop: "Goodbye then—(6:15) this has been a ghastly day but now 'all set' (fair, set fair) after hysterical shop-stuff." And indeed the shop had an hysterical atmosphere; the printing press seemed to work in paroxysms, and everything else seemed ready to lose control. In that sloping street like one of Meryon's darkest etchings, fetishes from Easter Island and the Congo held rendezvous among freshly printed poems. "What are we doing here?"

they asked. "Let's run away. . . ." They refused to stay put. They disturbed conversation with their antics and distracted one's thoughts. Each contained a separate universe. One expected them to march out of the door and up the street, shouting slogans in a truculent procession. On the whole I think they were kindly disposed to my poems. "Wait a while," I could hear one saying, a rascal from the Gold Coast in a permanent state of excitement, "I rather like this about Harold Acton in his bath."

After the still birth of my "Five Saints and an Appendix," I despaired of my poems reaching more than a few friends, and Nancy's proposal to print an edition of one hundred and fifty seemed the happiest solution. It was a trifle optimistic, for I had not so many friends among the living. I gave her some poems which I entitled *This Chaos.*

The jagged blue on white collar-bone of a hare cover-design by Elliott Seabrooke, the whole production, belonged to 1930.

One of the poems, entitled "Soap," had appeared previously in *The London Mercury,* where it attracted the editor of *Progress* (published by Lever Brothers Limited in the interests of the Company and its Shareholders, Customers and Staff) who wrote for permission to reproduce "a poem which has, as you may imagine, a specific interest for us as soapmakers. We read it with admiration and relish. . . ." This led to an invitation to visit Port Sunlight, and I might have become the laureate of the soap industry but for my rendezvous with the last Medici, who seldom washed.

While *This Chaos* was printing, Nancy wrote a series of vivid letters from Creysse par Martel, Uzerche and villages in her favourite Dordogne, in which she spoke of "resting" after three crossings of the Pyrenees. But Nancy could never rest, whether she stayed "in a pair of peasant rooms, eating at an inn which was always ringing with succulent *patois*"—the *patois* would appeal to her more than the finest *pâté*—or sat under a tree "with the hottest possible sun switching round it like wooden horses, but with the Dordogne rushing below over the abandoned wash-boards." She was usually involved in a multifarious correspondence over some projected publication such as her *Negro* anthology, and jotting down poems and diatribes in between. She pursued several goals simultaneously with teams which were seldom worthy of her support.

The clock did not exist for her; in town she dashed in and out of taxis clutching an attaché-case crammed with letters, manifestos, estimates, circulars and her latest African bangle, and she was always several hours late for any appointment. A snack now and then, but seldom a regular meal; she looked famished and quenched her hunger with harsh white wine and gusty talk. Having dug through many layers of society to find only a crumbling foundation, she welcomed the primitive for a change, forgetting that simplicity can be even more deceptive.

While staying with Nancy at Chapelle-Réanville near Paris, I thought that her existence was symbolized by two pictures on my bedroom wall: one, by Picabia, a portrait of a chalk-white man with scarlet spots and six eyes, superimposed on either side of his head; the other, an early Victorian portrait of her grandmother. The furniture, a mixture of solid English and African, had counterparts among her friends.

Norman Douglas was a counterpart of her mahogany sideboard. Norman was fond of Nancy in his bluff way, and we all forgathered in Paris at what might have been called The Hours Press Hotel, in the rue Saint-Benoît. But Norman was also fond of regular meals; after running the whole gamut of Florentine *trattorie* he wished to sample as many gastronomical specialities as Paris could provide in a limited time, and he refused to be kept waiting. Himself punctual to the dot, he looked forward to his next meal with a ravenous appetite: "I'm in the mood for *kebab* to-day; I've heard of a first-class Turkish place, the most deleeshus coffee you ever tasted. Come on!"

"But what about Nancy?"

"We'll knock at her door on the way."

We would knock in due course, to find Nancy's room as crowded as if a party were going on, dense with cigarette smoke, books scattered over the bed. "Nothing doing. This is no place for us. Let's hop it," Norman would say. He disapproved of Nancy's hangers-on and grew more and more avuncular in their company. He enjoyed, however, making them sneeze: "A soupçon of snuff, my dear? Try it. It ought to clear your head." If this failed, he would offer a *Toscano* cigar, a real stinker, hoping it might act as an emetic. "In Burma the cheroots are rolled by young women between the breasts and thighs—deleeshus! That accounts, of course, for their fragrance."

Nancy was making arrangements to show a Surrealist film in London, which involved more confabulations in cafés than Norman was prepared to put up with. Rather grumpy, he was dragged along to visit André Breton. After one horrified look at the Dali dominating Breton's room—an intricately demoniac picture of William Tell in his underwear with a bright phallus protruding, and such details as the carcass of a donkey on a piano with a horse galloping over it—Uncle Norman said sharply: "I can't stay here. That picture will spoil my dinner. See you later, I must get some fresh air at once." Nobody could detain him. He had come to Paris to enjoy Nancy's company, but there were limits.

solita solano

Nancy Cunard: Brave Poet, Indomitable Rebel

In a Montparnasse café, on a rainy autumn evening in 1923, I first met Nancy Cunard. The rendezvous had been made for us by a young American painter, a protégé, whose talent soon gave out, who thought that Nancy and Janet Flanner and I would be sure to "get along." Nancy arrived late, but only one hour, which was quite early for her to be late.

How could I have said, but I did, "You are late," to that golden head set with sapphires.

"But of course, darling," she said kindly.

We "got along" indeed. The three became a fixed triangle, we survived all the spring quarrels and the sea changes of forty-two years of modern female fidelity, in a friendship which ended only in Nancy's appalling death three days after her birthday in March, 1965. Through a fantastic sequence of events, each typical of Nancy's progress through life, it happened that she spent her last birthday with me and another great friend, Elizabeth Clark, not moving from her blue armchair, refusing food, writing, writing, writing dementedly on her last long poem.

No one of us three knew that she was dying.

As the years passed by—the years of the Hours Press, the years of her immense history of the Negro race, the years of the Spanish civil war—it became more and more clear that to be in the presence of Nancy was more like coming to grips with a force of nature than being out for an evening of gossip and dancing after a hard day's work. The weather was seldom calm and storm followed storm at various degrees of violence. Her Ladyship's Vionnet and Poiret gowns, sent from London to Nancy twice a year and shared by us all, were now replaced by Nancy's own inventive taste and she took to wearing Spanish *guiches* beside her ears. Her collection of African ivory bracelets covered both thin arms from wrist to shoulder and were formidable weapons for proving arguments after midnight.

Much of Nancy's endearing gaiety was gone with the Twenties and though motives remained the same, provocations multiplied—mostly by privileged associations that only she was able to follow. It was impossible for her to work quietly for the rights of man; Nancy functioned best in a state of fury in which, in order to defend, she attacked every windmill in a landscape of windmills.

All the activities of her earliest causes—the right of a brilliant-minded child to study in her own way (three governesses whacked her on the knuckles), the injustices of governments toward the individual, the discrimination against races, servants overworked and underpaid—all such activities were set into devastating motion by a word, a look, a memory. Then with her special battlecry, "Up and at 'em!" off she galloped to break still another lance. Sleep? Warmth? Food? No! Somewhere someone was suffering. . . .

The greatest efforts and disillusions of her life were in the catastrophe of Spain. Refusing to accept the inevitable, she worked on and waited thirty years for her side to recruit its lost forces and try again with its left-over heroes. She learned—and as impeccably as she knew French, German, Italian—Spanish and Catalan and used them in a thousand letters and poems for imploring and insulting and for collecting quantities of pesetas for the prisoners' needs. In her emotional frustration and starvation, it was even said that she took angry lessons in dynamiting while waiting for the great day, during the time she was based at Toulouse. That would be in keeping with her proclamation: "I am not a Communist—I am an anarchist!"

The other cause for which she worked for twenty years was not a lost one. In a poem one could ask: Does the earth's halo hold enough gratitude for the fact that Nancy lived to see black become less black and white turn less white through shame.

The glands that spread anger are but two and so bafflingly small for causing so much havoc; these mere gobbets were the cause of Nancy leaving her home, her class and her country; because of them, she never had time to profit by the experiences of love, of guilt or remorse. By nature she was generous, loving and true-blue, but her vast anger at injustice embraced the universe like Valery Larbaud's grief, and there was no place left in her for the working of any other emotional pattern. Her life's purpose was to use her universal anger for the moral evolution of mankind. It was her mania, her madness. It was the key that had turned her on from infancy to the hours when she sat writing her last illegible words.

kay boyle
Nancy Cunard

I remember the first time I saw Nancy Cunard, and the last time, and all the times in between, as clearly as if we had met and laughed out loud together just half an hour ago. The quick humor, the laughter, were a part of the grave and considered gesture of putting one's life on the line for the things in which one believed. I learned that much from her right away; for Nancy never ceased putting her life and her heart and her livelihood on the line in the best way there is to do it, as if she were suddenly breathing fresh air.

The first time I saw her was in the late 'twenties in Paris, when all of us danced on a summer night in a square where an accordion and a violin and an old piano were being played. It could have been Bastille Day, for there were lighted lanterns hanging from the branches of the trees, and I can still see the startling, artificial green of the leaves, veneered with light, above the dancers' heads. Nobody marveled at the sight of a piano set out in the public street, because that was the 'twenties, and anything was possible: Robert McAlmon, for instance, leaping in entrechats higher and more spectacular than Nijinsky's as he yiped aloud his cowboy yipe; and Kiki of Montparnasse sitting on the piano whenever the dancing came to a stop, her tough, hoarse voice speaking into the temporary silence of Paris the words about love and longing and passion and abandonment. Even Nancy Cunard was possible then, a tall, small-boned woman with ivory bracelets from wrist to shoulder on her slim arms, bracelets girded on like ivory armor from shoulder to delicate wrist. Her eyes, blue and clear as sapphires, would have been a cause for wonder anywhere except in the ambiance of that decade in which we danced.

That was the first time, and because of the partners and the gaiety and recklessness around us, there was no time to talk. But from that moment, through her poetry, her letters, and her expanding legend, she became a far-reaching, constant light to steer a course by when injustices, prejudices, wars, or merely the petty outrages of daily life, cast one adrift. In spite of the seemingly perilous delicacy of her flesh and spirit, she was steadfastly there, steadfastly articulate, present where one was oneself hesitant to go, where the fighting was bitter enough to shatter a lesser woman's courage and heart.

The last time I saw her was in Paris in 1953, when we sat over a long lunch on the terrace of the "Closerie des Lilas" in the sun. We talked that day about the madness that then possessed my country, a madness in which my husband and I were embroiled: the dementia of McCarthyism. The next day we would be returning to America, and Nancy said: "We shall be listening for your words." For now, by some inexplicable twist of fate, it was we who had danced so wildly in the 'twenties, wearing green hats or horizon blue cloaks, in the theatrical armor of the earrings and bracelets that we wore, who had become the spokesmen for sanity at a moment when normal men and women had seemingly gone insane. Nancy's eyes were just as intensely blue in her economically designed face that day, but the armor of bracelets was gone forever. The ivory bracelets, some intricately and handsomely carved, some plain as horn, had been taken from her ransacked house in La Chapelle-Réanville (either by the French or by the Germans), during the Occupation. In the years immediately after the War, Nancy had searched for them through the museums of Europe, and I, living in Germany then, had helped ineffectually in the search. She had even made enquiries in South America, as if finding that armor of our youth would signal the restitution of many usurped things.

These were the first and the last times that we saw each other. The times in between are our real history, the chapters of it varying with the countries we met in, and the events that were taking place. It was a relationship that, from the first moment, never faltered. Its impetus and its heart grew stronger in the anguished period of the Spanish civil war, and grew deeper in our walks through the fields and across the snows of the French Alps. Whatever we talked of as we wandered the back streets of Montmartre or Neuilly together was confirmed in the letters we exchanged, and in the long poem I wrote for her in 1937, a poem dealing with the trial of the Scottsboro boys, entitled "A Communication to Nancy Cunard." During the war, when the Nazis advanced across Europe, it was not necessary that we see each other to speak in a like tongue of the things we knew were true.

Only after the fall of France, in the spring of 1940, did we lose contact with each other. Nancy was God knows where, and my husband and I were involved in the difficult problem of getting our family out of France, and, by way of Spain and Portugal, back to America. And then in the summer of 1941, a few days after our arrival in New York, I saw her photograph in a newspaper one morning, and in the brief story below I read that she was on board a ship then temporarily docked in Brooklyn. Nancy Cunard, the newspaper said, was not permitted by the Department of Justice to set foot on American soil, but was interned on the ship until it would sail again on the following day. That afternoon we went by subway to Brooklyn, and we found the dock, and found the ship, and even found someone in authority who turned his head the other way while Nancy came down the illicit gangplank, laughing softly at the sight of us there. We sat on packing-boxes and crates on the covered wharf in the summer heat, drinking beer from cans, which we, just fresh from Europe, had never done before. Other friends came throughout that afternoon, some journeying from Harlem, bringing more beer with them, and in time, as the gathering grew, a policeman or two joined us, and sat talking with us, and listened, as we listened, to Nancy speaking with English gravity and Irish wit of the things that stir in all men's hearts, and speaking with such simplicity that one was pleased to be alive. We could have kidnapped her that day, we could have fled with her in a taxi; but everyone, even the authorities, whoever they were, knew that Nancy had not the slightest interest in betrayal. Even Churchill's government knew it.

So our next meeting took place in London, in the winter of 1945, at a time when the V-2s were hitting every twenty seconds, each one of them wiping out eight city blocks when it fell. Nancy was in the uniform of her country, and my husband and I were in the uniform of ours, and we were proud, the three of us, of the fight to which we were committed. "How in the world did we get on the side of authority?" Nancy asked; "by what miracle? Are we really—you and Joseph and I—going to win in the end?"

The last letter I had from her was sent from the south of France, from Beaulieu, on February 2, 1965. With that letter came a reprint of her catalogue and commentary on her printing house, "The Hours Press," in which she stated with characteristic modesty: "I think I have three things to thank for the (relative) success of the press: ignorance of the usual commercial procedure (overheads and wastefulness, etc.), good authors, and hard work at a propitious moment in the history of the private press movement." The most important factor she did not mention: the uniquely luminous spirit of a woman who respected the vision and cherished the vocabulary of other women and men.

nancy cunard

Visits from James Joyce

[Shortly before the Hours Press closed, James Joyce came to Miss Cunard seeking her assistance on behalf of his friend, an Irish singer named Sullivan, who in Joyce's opinion had to be heard by Sir Thomas Beecham.]

Soon he came to the point: Sullivan, a very great Irish singer. Now, Sullivan was not getting the recognition he deserved and this must be set right at once. Well, Lady Cunard, my mother, was a very great friend of the orchestra leader, Sir Thomas Beecham, who should be made to realize that Sullivan must be engaged forthwith. Had Beecham ever heard of him? I could not say. Why was Beecham not interested? Well, what he, Joyce, wanted me to do was to use all my influence with Lady Cunard so that Beecham should hear, and engage, Sullivan. I presume Joyce thought this quite simple. What he probably did not know was that my relations with her were not of the friendliest; at any rate, I had no "influence" with her whatsoever—as I now tried to make clear. Joyce would have none of that and brushed it aside. I assured him that I would, of course, tell her that he had come to see me about the matter; more than that I could not possibly do. I thought he seemed annoyed and did not believe me. Sullivan *must* be engaged. And when I reminded him that he knew Lady Cunard himself and that she would be likely to listen to him, that too was brushed aside, and, somehow, I did not feel like recalling to him that she had been very instrumental, indeed, in 1917 or so, in obtaining public recognition for his great talent as a writer, recognition that could not have been more official, and on a financial plane, too. Joyce went on: Lady Cunard was in Paris now, Thomas Beecham as well, or soon coming, Sullivan was in Paris, and so they must be brought together. I must have said that this was more than I could do, but that he could accomplish it, if only he would get in touch with Lady Cunard; or why not directly with Sir Thomas? I fancy Joyce liked none of this. Obviously his mind had been made up: I, and I alone, must be the approach. "How displeasing it is to be put in a false position—maybe he has taken offence," I thought, as I sprang off the bed to try and guide him discreetly to the door after the half-hour's conversation. It was horrifying to see him grope, miraculous to see his adroit descent of the stairs, the tall, cathedral-spire of a man. As for Lady Cunard, would she even listen? She did not listen much.

And then, two weeks later or so Joyce suddenly reappeared at 15 rue Guenegard, near the Seine, where I ran my Hours Press. It was towards evening and several of us were there, although I cannot remember just who. I know we ran forward to greet him: would he not take a drink with us in our local bistro, perhaps even have dinner? I had talked to my mother, I told him; she had seemed to understand and had said she would tell Beecham, but there was nothing definite to go on, and, really, he himself should get in touch with her. Meanwhile, would he not sit and have a little drink with us? No, he would not. The point was Sullivan, who *must* be engaged for grand opera. Could I not realize the urgency of this? If I had tried already, I should try now much harder. And then he dropped a hint that, if things went well on the score of Sullivan, a little piece of writing might perhaps come to me for publication at the Hours Press. (The honour was materially cancelled out by my knowledge that the Press would soon be closing down.) In the end, a few days later, Sullivan did sing and was heard by Beecham. But what happened? I have a vague memory of some kind of complicated fiasco occurring that evening, and myself not even on the outer edge of it. How peculiar is this episode. I suppose it throws one of a million lights on Joyce, on the sincerity of his friendship for the singer, on his brooking no denial, while his tenacity was certainly revealed to me. That Joyce's manner with friends was very different to his formal way with me during these two unexpected apparitions, was easy to believe. How much I should have liked to observe the moment at which he became more human. At dinner, for instance, he "mellowed" a great deal, it was said. Who used that word? Robert McAlmon, who would talk and talk about the "Big Four:" Joyce, Pound, Eliot and Wyndham Lewis, in the early twenties—soon after the time I just knew Ezra and T. S. Eliot and Lewis rather well, all three. It is on record that Joyce "mellowed" over good wine and conversation. I saw him icy. How unfortunate that what brought us together at all was that erroneously conceived "use your influence with your mother."

Poems (Two) 1925

[Poems (Two) 1925, a limited edition of 150 copies, was hand printed in 1930 at John Rodker's Aquila Press, in London, and contained "Simultaneous," dated 1924, and "In Provins," dated 1925.]

SIMULTANEOUS

At one time
The bottle hyacinths under Orvieto—
At one time
A letter a letter and a letter—
At one time, sleepless,
Through rain the nightingale sang from the
                                    river island—

At one time, Montparnasse,
And all night's gloss
Splendour of shadow on shadow
With the exact flower
Of the liqueur in its glass.
        Time runs,
                but thought (or what?) comes
Seated between these damaged table-tops,
Sense of what zones, what simultaneous-time sense?

                . . . Then in Ravenna
The dust is turned to dew
By moonlight, and the exact
Splayed ox-feet sleep that dragged the sugar-beet
To dry maremmas
        Past Sant' Spollinare,
                Fuori Mura.

83 • *Independence*

In Calais Roads

The foam-quilt sags and swells,
Exact are the land's beacons to the sea—
Twin arms crossed, thrown across sleep and
                          a night-wind.
Time falls from unseen bells
On Calais Quays (that were sometime
                          a heart's keys.)
   Red bryony
Steeps in loose night-air,
Swelling—October crumples the hedge—
Or the wind's in the ash, opening the seed-pods.
        (The revolution in the weeds—
          Rain somewhere. Rain suggests
          Their dissolution to the seeds.)

                Midnight,
While some protract their trades
Forcing the line—sleep takes them,
But the baker
Cools at the sill, yeast auburn flour.

                Midnight
And trains perambulate (*o noctis equi*);
Faust is in hell that would have stopped the
                          horses of night
In their gallops, that would have galloped atop
                          of them
But was outpaced, overthrown for too exact
                          questioning.

          And in Albi
Les orguilleux sus des roues continuellement
                (hell's fading fresco),

And in Torcello
The mud-fogs now, and on all unknown
Ripe watery wastes
The rich dead silence.

Silence—or a nightwind on a lawn
Turning the pages, one by one,
                of a forgotten book.

IN PROVINS

So he ran out knocking down the brigadier—
Mince alors! said the officers to each other
In the hotel at the end of their Sunday meal,
                    fumant la pipe.

          And rain ran in new ditches
Beating on sooty walls, where the ramparts are
                              falling
In Provins, ville-haute—with the gale up the
                    winter's watery veins
In clipped crooked fields—wind in the nerves
                    of winter
     (the black branches)—in the streets'
                         draughty funnels.

Next morning the lieutenants cantered out in
                    clear sunlight
Past the Jardin Public, a place of shallow waters
                    rising.
What is left of old carvings . . . seamed fragments
                    in an odour of violets,
And from a café crept the unexplained scent
                         of frezias.
Sun descends on the streams, travelling down
                    the green water.
Against écarlate de Gand and bleu de Nicole they
          matched their *ners,* noir de Provins,
Famous cloth, fast-dyed in the Durteint, hard
                         river-water.

And Abelard
In these level meadows for two years was teaching.
And Thibaut leaned
From the high-town over a murmuring valley,
Thibaut, lord and love-singer, who ordered the
                    walls and a monastery.
Word and gesture all one now, dispersed by the
                    unrecording wind,
Other footsteps now, patterning the soundless
                         mould.

Dome on the sunset,
          blue dome on high hill-distance

Where the ramparts are falling—only a Caesar's
                              tower
Catches the wind still and the rain's minute
                              deteriorations.
The moon collects on puddle-water—
Lilac and prune-flush, suffusions then shadows of
                              nightfall,
Wing-rustle in quickset . . . and suddenly that
                                        hunting-music,
Delaying chords of horns, suspended chords
After silence.

All day I have had memories coming back at me
       with their gesture of meetings and partings,
And the sense of some moment in this place
          that is a memory to be.

By the roadside, what's past . . .
          then the *now* with its hotel bedroom
Where one traveller replaces another—
          (one traveller the abstraction of all—)
Time's seasons or shadows put forward,
                    remembered in the wallpaper—
Sad spring still frigid, summer with flies,
                    then the harvests beyond the octroi,
And the long sheet of winter wrinkled and knotted
                              with branches . . .
After the soldiers . . . shuffle and stamp in the
          clotted sawdust . . . the commercial gentry:
'Splendeurs et Misères'? mais mon vieux tu n'es
          pas de ton temps!

janet flanner

Nancy Cunard

On March 17th, six days after her sixty-ninth birthday, Nancy Cunard died here suddenly in the Hôpital Cochin. Both in Paris and earlier in London, she was one of the most astonishing personalities of her generation. During the First World War, she, Lady Diana Manners, and Iris Tree formed an inseparable trio of beauties—a kind of Mayfair troika of friendship, elegance, intelligence, and daring as leaders of the new generation of debutantes, who in evening clothes watched the Zeppelins from the roofs of the great town mansions and voted Labour in the opening peace. She passed her childhood at Nevill Holt, a vast, plain Georgian castle that covers considerably more ground space than the New York Public Library. At the tea hour in the great drawing rooms, where as a little girl she was occasionally permitted an appearance, she obtained remarkable, enduring visions of certain final remnants of Edwardian society, for her mother, the California-born Lady Maud Cunard, was a famous hostess with a compelling wit. Her father, Sir Bache Cunard, of the shipping family, was quieter and took up silversmithing and ironwork as a hobby. He made by hand a number of pony-size horseshoes, which he affixed to the castle's back-garden gate in such a way as to spell "Come into the garden, Maude," which infuriated Her Ladyship—one of Nancy Cunard's favorite family stories. She was a remarkably vivid and noted conversationalist and raconteuse; her vocabulary in both French and English was vast, precise as a dictionary when it suited the subject, and punctuated by racy slang—and, above all, by her own laughter—when she was telling something funny. Her laughter was like a descending octave; those who knew her well could recognize it anywhere and thus know that she was unexpectedly on the scene—in Venice, Vienna, Madrid, Florence, or Harlem, for she was a driven traveller, locomoting restlessly on her indomitable energy, slender though she was. She was famous, too, for what is called in French son regard—for her intense manner of looking at you, of seeing you and seizing you with her large jade-green eyes, always heavily outlined, top and bottom, with black makeup below her thick, ash-colored hair. From her childhood, which was lonely, she was an interminable reader and a book lover. She became a kind of general Egeria to the postwar London literary generation, knew everybody, was known by everybody. Aldous Huxley used her as the main female character, Marjorie Carling, in *Point Counter Point,* and she was Iris March of Michael Arlen's *The Green Hat.* She was a contributing member of London's *Blast* group for new writing and art forms, and its Wyndham Lewis drew some excellent Cubist portraits of her.

In the early twenties, she began living in Paris, in an Île-Saint-Louis flat. There she became connected with the just-beginning Surrealist group and with one of its founders, Louis Aragon. Now that she was freed of her English background (or so she hoped), her personal radical convictions and tastes soon took their decisive shape. Associated through Aragon with Communism, she herself was probably only a poetic anarchist, and certainly was against any government you could mention, being impassioned for her own liberty, for everybody's liberties. In 1934, her ardor for the cause of equality for Negroes, which dominated the rest of her life, resulted (after four years' documentation, museum studies, and travels in North and South America) in a gigantic, eight-hundred-and-fifty-five-page anthology called *Negro,* of which the *New Statesman* said, "No review can do justice to such a volume." It was the first book of such scope—of such unlimited immediate hopes for the Negroes—and it had an unusual list of distinguished contributors. It contained translations by Samuel Beckett, articles by her friends Ezra Pound, Harold Acton, and Norman Douglas, by Raymond Michelet, René Crevel, William Plomer, George Antheil, Alfred Kreymborg, Langston Hughes, Countee Cullen, and so on and on, with dozens of photographs of African tribal artwork. From then on, she was speeded up by history itself—by the Spanish war, which she attended on the side of the Loyalists, and then by the Second World War, in which her country house in Normandy (she was in London, working for the Free French) was occupied by the Nazis. They threw her fine collection of rare modern books, some of which she had published, and her Negro sculpture and masks into the well, along with a sheep's carcass. After the war, she concentrated on publishing, and on her Hours Press, in Normandy, about which she recently wrote a book, to be brought out soon by the Southern Illinois University Press and in London. Over its pre- and postwar years, the Hours published short works—original or reprints, often in de-luxe format—by George Moore, Norman Douglas, Richard Aldington, and Robert Graves and Laura Riding. In 1930, there appeared the first one-volume edition of Pound's *A Draft of XXX Cantos*—a major undertaking—and also *Whoroscope,* by Samuel Beckett, his first separately published work. She had never heard of him until he won her Hours' prize of ten pounds for a poem on *Time,* his being free verse on Descartes. In the middle fifties, London publishers brought out two memoirs she had written—a word portrait of Norman Douglas called *Grand Man* and *G.M.: Memories of George Moore,* a great friend of Lady Cunard's whom Nancy Cunard had known since childhood. This last was a first-class veracious study—a penetrating atmospheric picture of Moore as a fin-de-siècle Edwardian Irishman. Years earlier, in the twenties, this correspondent, on a visit to London, had been taken by Nancy Cunard to have tea with him in his house in Ebury Street, with its Monets and Manets on the staircase wall and G.M. in his study upstairs, already deep in his bread and butter and first cup of tea. At once, as Nancy drank hers, she asked him why, since he had accepted French Impressionist painting when it was new in Paris, did he refuse the new art of the École de Paris? First he answered that he had been young in Paris then, and no man could be young twice about new art; then he added, with distaste, "I have seen a canvas by your Cézanne—a portrait of a peasant by a peasant." Laughing but persistent, for she always enjoyed the struggle of discussion, she asked him whether he had read James Joyce's novel of genius, *Ulysses.* He had read it, G.M. said, "But it is not a novel. There is not a tree in it."

Over the last two years, she had been writing an endless poem against war called *Visions Experienced by the Bards of the Middle Ages.* In 1925, when she was twenty-nine, her friends Virginia and Leonard Woolf themselves set the type at the Hogarth Press for a long poem of hers because they so admired and relished it. It was called "Parallax," has been out of print ever since, and is so nearly forgotten that it is like a new poem today. Its subject is apparently a young male poet. This is the third stanza:

Come music,
In a clear vernal month
Outside the window sighing in a lane,
With trysts by appletrees—
Moths drift in the room,
Measure with running feet the book he reads.
The month is golden to all ripening seeds;
Long dawns, suspended twilight by a sea
Of slow transition, halting at full ebb;

Midnight aurora, daytime, all in one key—
The whispering hour before a storm, the treacherous hour
Breaking—
So wake, wind's fever, branches delirious
Against a riven sky.
All houses are too small now,
A thought outgrows a brain—
Open the doors, the skeleton must pass
Into the night.

Stanza eight continues:

Think now how friends grow old—
Their diverse brains, hearts, faces, modify;
Each candle wasting at both ends, the sly
Disguise of its treacherous flame. . . .
Am I the same?
Or a vagrant, of other breed, gone further, lost—
I am most surely at the beginning yet.
If so, contemporaries, what have you done?

walter lowenfels
Nancy Cunard

"I see Lillian yet," Nancy Cunard wrote me in 1959. "It was a party in your studio, and her flowing, glowing, tumbling, splendid hair burst above her as you danced together wildly. I see you one night somewhere in Montparnasse with Dan (one of my Afro-American musicians), and I see your book, *Finale of Seem,* on the table. And I remember Dan saying to me how very much he liked it; the subtleties in so many of these poems were to his mind; I thought at the time: "a musician understands"—it was through his *sensuality*.

"To hell with those days! They weren't so super-magnificent after all!"

The days were 1929, and I see Nancy, too—tall, very thin, a childlike blonde face, African bracelets on her arms, a petition for the Scottsboro Boys in her hands.

I have only realized during the past few years that among all of us in the avant-garde in Paris, Nancy was by far the most advanced. She was doing something about the central issue of our time, the Negro people.

Yet, I don't ever recall a discussion with Nancy on the "issue." She was the most personal person I ever knew. She didn't talk about issues; she did things. She had close Negro friends; she wore African ornaments; she also collected and showed friends African sculpture. In 1934 the great anthology, *Negro,* Nancy edited was published.

I have a copy at my side as I write and I have never seen anything like it. It is an enormous book, measuring ten by twelve inches, containing 855 pages. And what pages! Other books present one or another aspect of Negro life—political, economic, artistic. Nancy's book presents the total account of a people in all manifestations and in many continents. Music, poems, art, sculpture in Africa, the Americas, the Caribbean—she shows the Negro fighting oppression with his total creativity.

The book is a historic and creative document. Without it, Nancy cannot be understood as she was in the early 'thirties when she was working on it.

One day at lunch in Paris Nancy told Norman Douglas and me that she was going to Africa with a Negro. Later Douglas told me the British Foreign Office had exerted every pressure to dissuade her, informed her they could not be responsible for her safety, and refused to give her traveling papers.

The trip to Africa with a Negro companion was one of her ways of opposing "colonial oppression." In quotes, because she would not have used that phrase, and only now—I realize what Nancy knew, and proved she knew in what she was actually doing.

We knew, of course, that Nancy had rejected her upper-class British background to be a poet and to live among poets and artists in France. There was a revolting story going the rounds at that time about Lady Astor saying to Lady Cunard in a loud voice at a London social function: "Well, Maud, what's new with Nancy now? Is it dope? Or gin? Or Niggers?"

Suddenly I cannot tell you about Nancy, living. She is dead, in Paris, at 69. A letter just in from Langston Hughes: "I don't know anyone to send condolences to—except ourselves—she was a wonderful woman. . . ."

I wrote him, "Yes, we must console each other. Nancy had many lives, but always a special one with poets. That began when she was in her twenties and part of the avant-garde movement in London, post-World War I. Then later in Paris, with Aragon, Breton and other French and American poets. And this went on to her last days, when she sent me an intricate sonnet in five languages, written to the Internationals of the Spanish civil war.

"Few of us get to be as alive as Nancy was to so many things. Her death is like dousing an incandescence. I feel part of our lives has been dumped into the abyssal plain in the middle Atlantic, never to be recovered.

"We lost touch in the early 'thirties when I left France. After I was arrested, 1953, she wrote me (and also to the judge sitting on my case), and we had been close friends again, by mail, ever since. A few years ago she sent me her memoirs, *These Were the Hours*. She was having difficulty getting the book published—it was organized around the books she published at her Hours Press. I suggested that she revise it, with the help of a mutual friend, Hugh Ford. This she did and the book will be published by the Southern Illinois University Press."

Perhaps the best portrait of Nancy is contained in her own letters that reveal her never-ending search for an integrity she was always finding and never exhausting and her swiftly changing moods, as in the following letter, from which I have already quoted:

Dearest Lo,

My thoughts are so often with you—I was so upset and continue to be about the stroke that came to Lillian. When can we have seen each other last, you, Lillian and I? I suppose it must have been all-too-pretty-soon after we first saw each other (in terms of now-years!) say in 1931? "To pastures new" (I went—said you). All the Afro-American years . . . the Spanish years . . . the War years . . . the "Return" years . . . Dear me: must one now count in decades? That is all too often what comes into my mind. Meanwhile you and Lillian went back to America, "some time then" (though when?), and then you did much journalism—how rightly— And then it was our Norman who circuitously yet smartly put us in touch again . . . By the way: about Norman who was born under the sign of Saggitarius as we remember:

In this house NOW are "Les Sagittaires" and they are absolutely terrific: wood beetles eating their way, all day and all night into old beams and new, the floors, the wooden partitions, etc. If this sounds important, I'm sure it's not; yet important enough to warrant a chemical "intervention". Maybe Kenneth MacPherson would say this is one of Norman's last shafts . . . and true it is that—from the enormous catalogue of "de-pesting" chemists list—I would MUCH rather it were a sagittarean than a mere tick-tick-tick.

What's the time now do you suppose? Twenty to ten p.m. How I wish we three were here together, to eat some French beefsteak and swallow, fully, some of the thoroughly potent Corbières red wine. The mouse (1, 2?) in the kitchen will be my sole companion this still-soft early October night. My thoughts with you as I bend over the solitary stove.

To return to CONTINUITY: This is possibly ONE of the reasons why I liked so well your "Finale of Seem". (We had that in one of your letters: why did I like it so well?) I think you're a wonderful poet, dear Lo! Saying this raises (to me, at least) the whole question of "What is beautiful poetry?" I, *personally,* would say something like this:

The surprise (sometimes shock, even) of one image progressing, slowly or swiftly, into the next: the "startlement". It is indeed hard to analyse, and that, certainly, is no kind of analysis. I think a definition of beautiful poems would probably have to be done in (almost) three arts: Poetry, Music, Painting. (Some would add: Sculpture. I don't have that personally). The sparer, the finer, in the way of language (again, to my mind, and, very much so, to yours,

I'd say). All of this is a muddle, and to say what one feels to the end there should be a thorough ANALYSIS—a thing one has wondered about all life, or much of it—of WHY A POEM IS FINE. Norman got a good definition into words: "That of the inevitable ring". But that is too slight, too restricted to what he, personally, liked. Epitaphs and epigrams—"dee-li-shoos", of course, but where was Norman when it came to passion? Norman the understander, the splendid analyst, the critic, the maker—but not THE POET. Mysterious certainly, is poetry. Far more mysterious (to me, always "to me") than the wildest painting. Music is "secret"—but how much closer to poetry. In all the centuries, the birth, development and use of words, seems to me far more ODD than the communications between the other two of the three ARTS: Writing, Painting, Music. "Glacier-ages ago"—can one not imagine the warm urge of dancing—music? And the ("tomorrow-is-another-day" of someone sitting down—all sad, belike—to limn a . . . panner—remembering last night's frensy? That, at least, is how I would like to think of it, of some of it.) But words! Languages! Trip-ups everywhere!

Have you ever done just what you thought would be best, and (even) nicest to do? I, never! Or maybe one has, very briefly. I can think of a very few completely "finite" moments in it all. There was a day (and the date was Aug. 31, 1936, at exact sundown) in a desert in Aragon—and I alone (of course) sitting on the sand, gazing (after "funeral meats" with a young, dark, strong, peasant woman whose little dead daughter I had photographed in a coffin two days before), gazing at immensity. It had been a day that got out of hand, somehow. And the "somehow" was because of her gratitude that there had been someone there, even with the smallest camera, to take a picture of her child. She had plied three of us (one Spaniard, one German and self) with the saltiest ham in the mountains of the world; she had—in fact—made all three of us somewhat drunk, saying: "The time for weeping is now over; partake: I am grateful to you". (What country else do you think this could be in?) And then, I, who thought I would take "a thundering long walk", realized (in all my thoughtlessness) that—"even I"—would do better than set off the unknown, unknowable 15 or so kilometers. Ashamed of myself was I, for I was on a sort of consignment of time at that early date. "Prudence" prevailed, and, shaking off the two companions I walked straight in front of me and found the desert. (Dali has painted deserts, but certainly not that part!) It was nothing like North Africa (as I saw later, with Norman), but infinitely finer. I sat myself down on the earthy-sand, utterly at peace. And then came a man asking why it was empty? To which he replied "Empty? But of course! Because some think one way, and others another way. Such is the story of this land". Maybe you see which land exactly it was. To me it was infinity, and after death, and "realization of all one's desires", and any other simile or image or comparison you can think of. It was total and complete. And so, naturally, for how many reasons, I went back to that country—but NEVER AGAIN found just that.

How it remains, or comes back, does it not? I suppose a composer would put this into music. It wouldn't be I who would understand his meaning—yet we might be talking of the same land. How far, that desert, from the Hemingwayesque vision . . . Bah! And yet I like Hem very much. (Now WHY did he, with all his success etc., not go into "things" more?!)

None of this will seem mysterious to you. I am sure we are in complete agreement!—on the arts, and modes, and—people.

But a mouse in the kitchen for this evening's company. My thoughts are with you, with my fingers on this machine, dearest Lo.

"MONSIEUR, Vous me pardonnerez tout le decousu de cette lettre"! We must not be too hard on the French because of their incredibly archaic way of expressing themselves—some of them.

Dearest Lo! I am drinking ONE last pre-prandial rum to the health of yourselves. So much love to you both.

Nancy

oskar kokoschka

A Letter to the Editor

Many thanks for your kind letter in which you tell me that you wish to reproduce my picture of poor Nancy Cunard. Of course you have my permission and, again as a matter of course, free of charge. I would only like to receive from you a copy of the book.

I hope it will contain some of her more recent poems which I had no opportunity of knowing. We were such good friends. I am very, very sorry to learn of the passing of this exceptionally fascinating personality.

With kindest regards.

Yours,
Oskar Kokoschka

mary hutchinson
Nancy: An Impression

If my husband St. John (called by Nancy "Hutchie") were still alive, he would tell many a story about Nancy, for he saw much more of her than I did. He was very fond of her and saw her in many different places, often in London at the Eiffel Tower restaurant with Iris Tree and Marjorie Craigie, her two best women friends in her early years; sometimes in the English country at Bagpuise, sometimes in Venice; or taking long walks with her, carrying a picnic, in the hills behind the Côte d'Azur.

Sometimes she came to our house on the river in Hammersmith, and to our cottage on the Chichester estuary, where after a sudden scribbled indecipherable note in pencil she would arrive.

I can see her now appearing at a party in Hammersmith handing me a present, a ladle made of horn; and again near Dieppe, where we were in the same place as George Moore, emerging out of the dark Forêt D'Argnes into the sunlight, opening a bright parasol; and in Paris where she lived for a time in a ground floor flat on the beautiful Île St. Louis surrounded by a regal suite of Boulle furniture. How one wishes that while she lived in France she could have gone on with her Hours Press and developed her interest in publishing work by gifted and unusual writers (she was one of the very first to recognize Samuel Beckett). She could have dropped anchor in such a harbour. As it was she seemed to be always on the move—buffeted by storms— agitated—dissatisfied—unsatisfied—always attended by a different companion. What was she seeking? A victory? Or stability somewhere?

In consequence she has probably been called fickle, but she was unforgetting, and loyal to her friends. The times she spent with George Moore and Norman Douglas, my husband and those whom this book records, were probably her most serene.

It is true that whenever I saw Nancy I was struck by her appearance. In some early letters I described her as she seemed to me then and as I still think of her. In 1919—"Miss Nancy Cunard is wonderful, made of alabaster and gold and scarlet, with a face like Donatello's

Saint George; a lady who would fit into the early court of Louis XIV or Boccaccio's world. . . .

"She arrived yesterday in a scarlet hat and with a trunk full of clothes. . . . In conversation she has the bird habit. She hops rapidly over everything and daren't be silent. I was amused by our relationship. We had long talks in our nightgowns. I felt devoted to her but millions of years old." We were about the same age!

In 1924—"I met Nancy. She kept up perfectly her façade, behind which one seems to see a shadow moving—an independent, romantic and melancholy shadow which one can never approach. The façade was exquisite, made of gold leaf, lacquer, verdigris and ivory."

Her way of talking was like her staccato way of walking and like the changing companions and places. "Where," one would ask, "is Nancy? In Spain? In Mexico?"

Her character I am sure must be described as deeply disturbed and violent, subject to fierce angers, fierce indignations, fierce enthusiasms. Fiercely she battled for the revolutionary, the oppressed, the insulted and injured, identifying herself with them perhaps.

In her bright uniform she paced the earth carrying their banners.

At her tragic end she seems to me to have been in a battle again— of protest and despair—from which she attained at last rest for her "perturbed spirit."

III

Migrations: New York, Moscow, Geneva

1930–1935

introductory by samuel putnam
Nancy Cunard

While some were endeavoring to forget, live down, their past, there was at least one member of the Anglo-American Left Bank colony who paid the penalty for being some decades ahead of her time. Few persons have been more misunderstood than N.C. She has set forth her own case in an article which she wrote for the final (no. 5) issue of *The New Review*. Entitled "Black Man and White Ladyship," the article in question was a violent attack upon Miss C's mother, Lady C., and upon British upper-class society in general (with a sideswipe at George Moore) for its color prejudices. For Miss Cunard was defiant enough of conventions to have a black man for a friend. This created a scandal in London, a scandal which later was echoed by the columnists and sensational press of New York; but anyone who will read her statement will not fail to perceive that it was more than a personal matter with her, that she was fighting for a principle. She was making in real life, and in the callous 20s, the same challenge Lillian Smith's *Strange Fruit* was to make in later years.

N.C. was essentially an honest rebel against her class and what she took to be its narrow outlook; she had made a thorough study of Negro art, culture, and anthropology. A visit to her Paris studio, a talk with her there or at the Café Flore, and one went away convinced of her sincerity.

nancy cunard

New Directions

[The "new element" that had come into her life, the history and culture and, above all, the problems of the Negro people, profoundly shaped Miss Cunard's activities for the next few years. It brought on a hasty closing of the Hours Press, as the compiling of the anthology, *Negro,* demanded more time and as she felt increasingly drawn to participate in Negro struggles. It also ended whatever ties remained with her mother, as she announced in a pamphlet called "Black Man and White Ladyship." In the first paragraph below Miss Cunard traced her interest in Africa to a very young age.]

About six years old, my thoughts began to be drawn towards Africa, and particularly towards the Sahara. Surely I was being taught as much about El Dorado and the North Pole? But there it was: the Desert. The sand, the dunes, the huge spaces, mirages, heat and parchedness—I seemed able to visualise all of this. Of such were filled several dreams, culminating in the great nightmare in which I wandered, repeatedly, the whole of one agonising night, escaping through a series of tents somewhere in the Sahara. Later came extraordinary dreams about black Africa—"The Dark Continent"—with Africans dancing and drumming around me, and I one of them, though still white, knowing, mysteriously enough, how to dance in their own manner. Everything was full of movement in these dreams; it was that which enabled me to escape in the end, going further, even further! And all of it was a mixture of apprehension that sometimes turned into joy, and even rapture.

"Black Man and White Ladyship"

An anniversary is coming and that is why this is printed now, and the reason for its having been written will, I imagine, be clear to those who read it.

By anniversary I am not, indeed, referring to Christmas, but to the calendric moment of last year when the Colour Question first presented me personally with its CLASH or SHOCK aspect.

I have a Negro friend, a very close friend (and a great many other Negro friends in France, England and America). Nothing extraordinary in that. I have also a mother—whom we will at once call: Her Ladyship. We are extremely different but I had remained on fairly good (fairly distant) terms with her for a number of years. The english channel and a good deal of determination on my part made this possible. I sedulously avoid her social circle both in France and in England. My Negro friend has been in London with me five or six times. So far so good. But, a few days before our going to London last year, what follows had just taken place, and I was unaware of it until our arrival. At a large lunch party in Her Ladyship's house things are set rocking by one of those bombs that throughout her "career" Margot Asquith, Lady Oxford, has been wont to hurl. No-one could fail to wish he had been at that lunch to see the effect of Lady Oxford's entry: "Hello, Maud, what is it now—drink, drugs or niggers?" (A variant is that by some remark Her Ladyship had annoyed the other Ladyship, who thus triumphantly retaliated.) The house is a seemly one in Grosvenor Square and what takes place in it is far from "drink, drugs or niggers." There is confusion. A dreadful confusion between Her Ladyship and myself! For I am known to have a great Negro friend—the drink and the drugs do not apply. Half of social London is immediately telephoned to: "Is it *true* my daughter knows a Negro?" etc., etc.

It appears that Sir Thomas Beecham, in the light of "the family friend," was then moved sufficiently to pen me a letter, in the best Trollope style, in which he pointed out that, as the only one qualified to advise, it would, at that juncture, be a grave mistake to come to England with a gentleman of american-african extraction whose career, he believed, it was my desire to advance, as, while friendships between races were viewed with tolerance on the continent, by some, it was . . . in other words it was a very different pair of shoes in England especially as viewed by the Popular Press! This letter (which was sent to the wrong address and not received till a month later on my return to Paris) was announced by a telegram "strongly advising" me not to come to London until I got it adding that the subject was unmentionable by wire! I was packing my trunk and laid the telegram on top—time will show. . . . We took the four o'clock train.

What happened in London?

Some detectives called, the police looked in, the telephone rang incessantly at our hotel. The *patron* (so he said) received a *mysterious message* that he himself would be imprisoned "undt de other vil be kilt." Madame wept: "Not even a *black* man, why he's only *brown*." Her Ladyship did not go so far as to step round herself. The Popular Press was unmoved. This lasted about a month and I used to get news of it daily, enough to fill a dossier on the hysteria caused by a difference of pigmentation.

The question that interested a good many people for two and a quarter years (does Her Ladyship know or not?) was thus brilliantly settled.

But, your Ladyship, you cannot kill or deport a person from England for being a Negro and mixing with white people. You may take a ticket to the cracker southern states of U.S.A. and assist at some of the choicer lynchings which are often announced in advance. You may add your purified-of-that-horrible-american-twang voice to the yankee outbursts: America for white folks—segregation for the 12 million blacks we can't put up with—or do without . . .

No, with you it is the other old trouble—class.

Negroes, besides being black (that is, from jet to as white as yourself but not so pink), have not yet "penetrated into London Society's consciousness." You exclaim: they are not "received!" (You would be surprised to know just how much they are "received.") They are not found in the Royal Red Book. Some big hostess gives a lead and the trick is done!

For as yet only the hefty shadow of the Negro falls across the white assembly of High Society and spreads itself, it would seem, quite particularly and agonisingly over you.

And what has happened since this little dust-up of December last, 1930? We have not met, I trust we shall never meet again. You have cut off, first a quarter (on plea of your high income tax) then half of my allowance. You have stated that I am out of your will. Excellent— for at last we have a little truth between us. The black man is a well-known factor in the changing of testaments (at least in America), and parents, as we all know, are not to be held responsible for the existence of children.

Concerning this last I have often heard Her Ladyship say that it is the children who owe their parents nothing. But I am grateful to her for the little crop of trivialia that has flowered this year:

Mr. George Moore—(at one time her best friend and thence my first friend) whose opinion I was interested to have on the whole matter, which I obtained by the silence that followed my frank letter to him— was said to have decided not to leave me his two Manets as he intended, but has subsequently contradicted this. . . .

Her Ladyship's hysteria has produced the following remarks:

that—no hotel would accommodate my black friend.

that—he was put out of England (exquisitely untrue, for we came, stayed and left together after a month).

that—she would not feel *chic* in Paris any longer as she had heard that all the chic Parisians nowadays consorted with Negroes.

that—I now wrote for the Negro Press. (One poem and one article have appeared in the *Crisis,* New-York.)

that—where would I be in a few years' time.

that—she does not mind the Negroes now artistically or in an *abstract* sense but . . . oh, that terrible colour! (I invite Her Ladyship to send in writing a short definition of a Negro in the *abstract sense*.)

that—she knew *nothing at all of the whole thing* till Mr. Moore read her my letter. Now, to be exact: my letter to Mr. Moore was written Jan. 24 whereas Her Ladyship severely put through it several friends of mine in the preceding December, and had her bank signify to me on Jan. 21, 1931, that owing to the exigencies of her Income Tax . . . I suspect Her Ladyship of having conveniently forgotten that what seems indeed to have struck her as a bomb exploded before many witnesses in her own house. (This is very interesting and I don't doubt the psychologists have many such cases on their books—the washing of hands, let us add, by the main party.)

I am told that Her Ladyship was invited to a night-club, saw some coloured singers, turned faint and left . . . yet at least one paid coloured entertainer has been to her house.

I am told that she believes all the servants in a London house gave notice because a coloured gentleman came to dinner.

AND I AM TOLD

that Sir Thomas Beecham says I ought to be tarred and feathered!

It is now necessary to see Her Ladyship in her own fort, to perceive her a little more visually.

In the Sunday Express of Nov. 22, 1931, can be read in detail of how Her Ladyship spends a fortune on clothes she never wears. "I have not the faintest idea of how much I spend on clothes every year—it may run into thousands. I have never bothered to think about it. But that is because I do not have to bother about money." (Which tallies interestingly with her bank's statement concerning the exigencies of her Income Tax—see previously.) . . . "I want to tell you candidly why it is that so-called 'Society' women spend so much on their clothes. It is not that the cost of each garment is so very large; it is simply that we won't be bothered."

The Market may be going on at any time, and generally is. Others play it but Her Ladyship plays it best. Rich Mrs. XYZ will be "taken out" if she guesses or takes the hint that she is to do her duty by . . . (the object varies). No sign of the hint ever being administered! But the participants are well-trained, each is looking for what the other can supply, and each felicitously finds. Many results have been come by in this excellent manner. Snobbery opens purses, starvation fails.

Her Ladyship's own snobbery is quite simple. If a thing *is done* she will, with a few negligible exceptions, do it too. And the last person she has talked to is generally right, providing he is *someone*. The British Museum seems to guarantee that African art is art? some dealers, too, are taking it up, so the thick old Congo ivories that she thinks are slave bangles are perhaps not so hideous after all though still very *strange;* one little diamond would be better . . . though of course that is different.

Her Ladyship likes to give—and to control. It is unbearable for her not to be able to give someone something. But suppose they don't want it—what does this *mean?* Her reaction to being given something herself generally produces the phrase that people shouldn't do such things! Yet the house is full of noble gifts.

Another time it is Communism. "You don't mean to say those people you talk of are communists? they couldn't be, no-one as intelligent, as intellectual as they are . . . You can't *know* people like that," etc. . . . And away with the troubling thought. Her Ladyship is the most conscientious of ostriches and when she comes up again she hopes the *on*pleasant thing has disappeared. Perhaps it doesn't really exist. She is also a great cross-questioner and all her ingenuous ingenuity is seen at work on the picking of brains. As those she puts through it are generally less quick in defence than she is in attack, and as she has a fantastic imagination she generally arrives at some result. Look out! as in the farce, evidence will be taken down, altered and used against you. It will make quite a farce in itself. She is a great worker for she is never content to leave things as they are. In digging away she may turn up some startling facts. She is shocked. She is suspicious. All is not as it should be. She does not recognise . . . there may be no precedent—why it may even be scandalous . . . it *is* scandalous! it is unheard of!! WHAT is to be done? Why, talk about it! What do people say? A mountain is thrown up by this irreducible mole. There—of course it is *monstrous!* It cannot be true . . . and, though it is she who has informed the world, she is astounded presently when it all gets out of hand and falls back on her in anything but gentle rain.

Her Ladyship is american and this is all part of that great american joke: *l'inconscience*. Here she is, ex-cathedra at the lunch table, here she is telling some specimen A1 illiterate of the greatness of the last great book, here—wistfully puzzled by some little matter everyone knows, here—praising rightly, praising wrongly, making and missing the point all in one breath. Generous to the rich, trying always to do the right thing (serve only the best champagne, the food is always perfect). One day the footmen have frayed trousers. The butler has taken a leaf from Her Ladyship's book and explains that *no good enough* ready-made trousers are procurable in London, and that the tailor being dear, and slow . . . he falters. There is a scene. The interior economy is impeccable.

Are intellectuals generally the least biassed in race questions? Here are two reactionaries:—

A little conversation with Mr. George Moore in Ebury St.

Self: Yes, people certainly feel very differently about race. I cannot understand colour prejudice. Do you think you have it?

G.M.:   No, I don't think so.

Self: Have you ever known any people of colour?

G.M.:   No.

Self: What, not even an Indian?

G.M.:   No—though my books are translated into Chinese.

Self: Not even an Indian . . . such as might have happened had you met, shall we say, an Indian student. Don't you think you'd like to talk to an intelligent Indian or Negro?

G.M.:   (*calmly*) No. I do not think so. I do not think I should get on with a black man or a brown man. (*then warmly, opening the stops*) I think the best I could do is a yel-low man!

Thus Mr. Moore—after a whole long life of "free" thought, "free" writing, anti-bigotry of all kinds, with, his engrossment in human nature, after the *injustice* of the Boer war, as he says himself, had driven him out of England. . . . There is no consistency; there *is* race or colour prejudice.

Sir Thomas Beecham's remark about the Negro making his own music left me puzzled, and I don't doubt, puzzled for ever. Her Ladyship was evincing a very querulous astonishment at the Negro (in general) having any achievements (in particular). I was informing her that, for one, everybody knows the Negroes have a particular genius for music. At which Sir Thomas condescendingly remarked "They make their own music too." The tone of this pronouncement was so superior that I remained too dumb to ask whether at that moment he meant tribal or jazz. And Her Ladyship, far from being quieted, became as uneasy as an animal scenting a danger on the wind.

This is all what's aptly enough called *"Old* stuff." What's actual since some twenty years is a direct African influence in sculpture and painting. None but fools separate Africa from the living Negro. But the american press is constantly confusing their civic nationality with their blood nationality; (the 12 million blacks are the loyalest, best *americans;* a Negro in the States has written a good book, therefore he is a good *american* writer; the same of the coloured musician, the coloured artist, etc.).

"In Africa," you say, "the Negro is a savage, he has produced nothing, he has no history." It is certainly true he has not got himself mixed up with machinery and science to fly the Atlantic, turn out engines, run up skyscrapers and contrive holocausts. There are no tribal Presses emitting the day's lies and millions of useless volumes. There remain no written records; the wars, the kingdoms and the changes have sufficed unto themselves. It is not one country but many; well over 400 separate languages and their dialects are known to exist. Who tells you you are the better off for being "civilised" when you live in the shadow of the next war or revolution in constant terror of being ruined or killed? Things in Africa are on a different scale—but the European empire-builders have seen, are seeing to this hand over fist. And what, against this triumph of organised villainy had the black man to show? His own example of Homo Sapiens on better terms with life than are the conquering whites. Anthropology gives him priority in human descent. He had his life, highly organised, his logic, his customs, his laws rigidly adhered to. He made music and unparalleled rhythm and some of the finest sculpture in the world. Nature gave him the best body amongst all the races. Yet he is a "miserable savage" because there are no written records, no super-cities, no machines—but to prove the lack of these an insuperable loss, a sign of racial inferiority, you must attack the root of all things and see where—if anywhere—lies truth. There are many truths. How come, white man, is the rest of the world to be re-formed in your dreary and decadent image?

A Journey to Africa

[The difficulties of persuading Norman Douglas to accompany her on a trip to Africa in 1931 are humorously recounted in the following passages. In 1938 Miss Cunard did visit Tunisia with Douglas.]

At last a time had come when it seemed I might close the Press, take on no fresh work and go away for a little. I was beginning to think about Africa. Would Henry also not like to see the land of some of his ancestors? Enthusiastically received by him, the idea was beginning to swing like a pendulum—positive—negative—all affirmative of an evening when many of us, French, English, American and Coloured poets, writers, artists or musicians—would be together in some café (your nice friend Walter Lowenfels, the American poet whom I had published, was often one). Everything then seemed possible! The negative swing came in the morning when it did all appear rather difficult. What of the cost, the time, the general span of such a journey?

Well, there you were now in Paris telling me you didn't know what you wanted to do next, that you felt like travel. There you were, getting on magnificently with Henry, who, like so many other friends of mine in different spheres, was fascinated by you. Africa! Not yet in my conscious mind was the plan to make that big book about Africans and other Negroes which later became my *Negro Anthology*. Yet the subject was there in bud—thanks to what I had absorbed from Henry's vivid and descriptive accounts of Afro-America—all of it latent, incubating quietly and soon about to stir. There was also African sculpture, which, as you knew, I liked immensely and had learned a little about. Could I not learn a good deal in Africa of the Africans themselves, they in their endless diversity? And again, what of their music? As a pianist and composer, Henry could do good work in that field. . . .

What about you—would *you* like to go with us?

"Now Norman, you keep on telling me you don't know what to do next—which is surprising. How about Africa? Shall the three of us go?

"Anything you say, my dear. I'll go anywhere."

That is how it began.

I took you at your word. In a way, it seemed rather a curious trio, you, Henry and I. And, in another way, what could be more natural?

"Where shall we go? The Gold Coast sounds wonderful. Or Nigeria? Yes, Nigeria, Benin City for one. I would love to see whatever is left of that. The finest things of all come from . . ."

"Anywhere you say *except* Nigeria. Because it's British, and there will be the Colour Bar, and it will be damned awkward on account of Henry being coloured."

You looked rather glum, adding quickly:

"The more races, *and* peoples, *and* ages, *and* sexes there are together the better *I* like it. But that's not the way the British official mind works! We should have trouble—maybe serious trouble—if we went to Nigeria with an American black man!"

"Oh how disgraceful! The imbecility of it! All the more reason, indeed, for going. I feel sure there is nothing *illegal* in this. . . ."

(Whenever I hear the word "official" I think of legality.)

You remained silent.

"Now, come, Norman, why shouldn't two British citizens be travelling with an American citizen of Colour? We should even be on a sort of 'mission,' collecting data and music—at least, Henry and I would be, and you would doubtless find all sorts of wonderful inspirations. What has 'the official mind' to do here? It can't be against the law!"

"*You can get around laws—but you can't get around customs!*"

"Well—all right. What about Dahomey—French?"

"Anywhere you say, my dear. Just let me know when you think of starting and I'll go with you."

We got no further that day. Nor, maybe, for several days. Meanwhile, what did Henry think? *Did* you want to go or not? Henry laughed a good deal, then in all the serenity of his great smile replied "Opinion reserved."

My perplexity! This, paramountly, was the right time. I thought I had enough money for Henry's fare and mine; I could arrange to leave the Press; I did want to go to Africa, and so did Henry.

It was you who came back to the subject:

"Well, Nancy—what about our trip? When are we going to think about where we are going, eh? And how we're going to get there, and *when?*"

"Let's have another drink over this, Norman. Let me see . . . Dahomey perhaps? That would be by a French Line."

"Not on your life!"

"Good heavens, why not? No Colour Bar on French boats!"

"That's not what I mean at all. A French boat! Catch me! They're not safe, most of them, ha! If there's a heavy sea they're liable to sink *at once*—and the life-boats, all except *one,* are perfectly useless. Only the crew know *which one* doesn't leak! Then, when there's an ugly rush of passengers for the life-boats, the crew make a rush for the good one and keep the passengers out of it with their revolvers. . . ."

(That should have told me!)

"Well then, an English boat. We could . . ."

"Not on your life! The passengers will go to the captain in a body and complain about the presence of a black man with us. *I* like Henry —and so do you, ha! But the ordinary run of British passengers, and what's more, of British *colonial* passengers *and officials,* don't understand these things. They might like Henry when they got to know him—I daresay they would—I don't see how they could help it—but they won't give themselves the time to get to know him and they'll go in a body to the captain. Damned awkward, my dear. You'll see! I know them!"

(Both of these sallies at terrific speed.)

"Well then . . . a German boat?"

"I've nothing against a German boat. Now, you make all the arrangements and tell me just *when* you want to start—and where you want to go—because I don't suppose *you've* made up your mind yet . . ."

This sort of thing went on a few days more, intermittently.

"Norman, I have begun to investigate boats and their destinations. If it has to be a German boat, the place they go to seems to be—mainly—Portuguese West Africa—somewhere down that way. What do you say?"

"That will do very well."

It now seemed almost a point of honour to proceed with the plan, although I had considerable doubts, and each time I talked to Henry he shook his head and his laughter increased. I noticed that you and he never referred to it in my presence! And we went on meeting for meals and seeing a good many different people in Montparnasse and at St. Germain des Prés; and I continued working in my Press—and in bed.

Why on earth could we not decide? Should it all be quietly dropped?

"Norman—*Yes or No?*"

"I've already told you, I'm perfectly ready to start—tomorrow, if you like. But you must make all the arrangements."

After two or three more days of this, I thought "It must be dropped." Then again you came back at me:

"Well, when do we leave—and where do we go? I'd like to get away."

"Right! Now, tomorrow morning, Norman dear, you come with me to the Woermann Line and we will see about boats, prices, sailings, everything, *together*."

You came with me and studied those promising folders. Where was it these fine luxury liners went? To *Waalfisch Bay*—a port in South West Africa. Right. And the prices of cabins and passage? Right. And the date of the next sailing? Right.

But *not* right at all, for me, the land of which Waalfisch Bay (also called Walvis on some maps) seems to be the main port. Why, this is almost South Africa! Not even Angola, Portuguese West Africa, but the enormous territory where the Germans practically exterminated the Herreros in 1904—a civilisation of hides, cattle and leatherwork! Not an ounce of old carved ivory, not an inch of work in bronze or in wood—and where much, if I am not mistaken, is a series of great deserts, including even maybe the famous Kalahari? However, there it was. We now had the facts in hand—price-boat-date. *Your* move next! Once there one could go on elsewhere—possibly to the Congo? I was too tired to think. *You* would now have to decide. (And then, of course, we could begin all over again—only this time it would be much quicker.)

Henry had met you only rather recently, but it seems that he knew you much better than I (at least in this respect), for his laughter after being told of our expedition to the Woermann Line and the result it had produced: Waalfisch Bay (and all that was to be expected of the country) was monumental. When able to speak, he said: "Oh can't you see, Norman never had the *slightest* intention of going?"

That was the end of it all. For when you said a few days later:

"When do we start—have you done anything more about it?" I suggested that your role now in the whole matter was to make all the arrangements. At which some nebulous but remarkably valid objection arose on the spot, and, well . . . nothing happened at all. This was on a much more serious level than it may sound in retrospect—and a most peculiar kind of joke to be having with me, I told you. To which you replied:

"It's not a joke at all, my dear. I'm perfectly ready to start tomorrow!"

The mystery has remained to this day.

But really, Waalfisch Bay, with its *Alice in Wonderland* name, what better could have been found to cap such a Snark of a plan?

It was you who went to Africa not so very long after!

Would one call that the theft of an idea?

Nothing of the kind! It was to visit an old friend of yours—Eric—in Nairobi. And, in due course, four or five engaging pages came to me out of that journey—your contribution to my large Anthology, *Negro,* quite unique in the whole body of the book.

The Scottsboro Boys

[In 1933 Miss Cunard started a Scottsboro Defence organization and sent appeals for money which was forwarded to William Patterson, secretary of a similar organization in the United States, to be used to defray costs of defending the Scottsboro boys at a re-trial before the Supreme Court.]

The Scottsboro case was going on, that abomination of racial injustice, and I sent you (Douglas) the appeal I made that was more particularly addressed to authors. Would you sign the protest? Yes! As did immediately André Gide and many of the writers in Britain. The facts of the monstrous frame-up of these nine Negro lads arrested on a false charge of rape, repeatedly tried and condemned in a lynch atmosphere, were becoming well known. You would have liked one of my voluntary helpers in collecting funds for the legal defence: George Burke, some times unemployed and some times a pedlar—the way he threw his heart into everything that interested him, a cockney princeling rather than a down-and-out. George had very much of your *London Street Games* flavour.

Writings from NEGRO

[*Negro,* published by the British firm of Lawrence and Wishart in 1934, entirely at Miss Cunard's expense (around £1500), is indeed one of her most impressive projects. Numbering over 800 pages and containing 385 illustrations, it contains information on nearly every phase of Negro life, compiled by commentators as diverse as George Antheil, Harold Acton,

Earl Browder, William Carlos Williams, Ezra Pound and Mike Gold. Working almost alone as collector and editor, Miss Cunard made two trips to Harlem, in 1931 and 1932, and spent most of the next year in England readying the book for publication.]

And now I was possessed of a new idea which went down on paper on April 1, 1931, in the form of a circular: the making of an Anthology on the Negro race and its affiliations; there would be a good many people here and there, I knew already, who would collaborate. The vast subject so well known in the United States of America was little known in England, where one point of view was even "Why make such a book—aren't Negroes just like ourselves?" While I could see what was meant by this intellectual and scientific point of view, I could assure whoever it was who asked the question that if Negroes be like us their lives are mighty different!

I was for some weeks in Harlem, New York, capital of Afro-America—amused, annoyed, perplexed and interested by American ways—Negro as well as white, as I began collecting the personal and other data for my Negro anthology.

How regrettable it is that we (Douglas and N.C.) never went through those extraordinary anonymous letters that came to me the second time I was in Harlem . . . They were pre-eminently material for your inspection. The arduous anthological road held many surprises and this time there had been enormous publicity, blather and ballyhoo about me in the American press (*all* of it, not only Hearst's!). There were some outrageous lies, fantastic inventions and gross libels. Such things would have been properly dealt with in English courts, where the question would have been put: "What is all this *about?*"— the answer given: "A large book is being prepared on the Negro race, *and it is factual.*" Exactly that; not more. But in the United States the race-hysteria exploded, and surely its most ornate and rococo outbursts were embodied in this spate of frantic, unsigned and threatening letters! I was "sure going to be taken for a ride. . . ." Amusing enough, all of it—far more amusing yet at a distance, back in France, with half a ton of literary and sociological material for the book. And now on the Île Calypso in the Dordogne river I sat working on Afro-America, turning for light relief to all these frenzied menaces which outnumbered by far the other messages—friendly ones those, from people who did sign their names, commending my interest and praising the line taken towards people of colour.

[Miss Cunard's own contributions to *Negro* number six, five articles and a long poem entitled "Southern Sheriff." "Harlem Reviewed," the first printed below, and "The American Moron and the American of Sense—Letters on the Negro" show the lively quality of her reporting and the equally animated reactions it evoked.]

HARLEM REVIEWED

Is it possible to give any kind of visual idea of a place by description? I think not, least of all of Harlem. When I first saw it, at 7th Avenue, I thought of the Mile End Road—same long vista, same kind of little low houses with, at first sight, many indeterminate things out on the pavement in front of them, same amount of blowing dust, papers, litter. But no; the scale, to begin with, was different. It was only from one point that the resemblance came to one. Beginning at the north end of Central Park, edged in on one side by the rocky hill of Columbia University and on the other by the streets that go to the East River, widening out more and more north to that peculiarly sinister halt in the town, the curve of the Harlem River, where one walks about in the dead junk and the refuse-on-a-grand-scale left in the sudden waste lots that are typical of all parts of New York—this is the area of Harlem. Manhattan and 8th Avenues, 7th, Lenox, 5th and Madison Avenues, they all run up here from the zone of the skyscrapers, the gleaming white and blond towers of down-town that are just visible like a mirage down the Harlem perspective. These avenues, so grand in New York proper, are in Harlem very different. They are old, rattled, some of them, by the El on its iron heights, rattled, some of them, underneath, by the Sub in its thundering groove.

Why is it called Harlem, and why the so-called capital of the Negro world? The Dutch made it first, in the 17th century; it was "white" till as recently as 1900. And then, because it was old and they weren't rebuilding it, because it's a good way from the centre, it was more or less "left" to the coloured people. Before this they lived in different parts of New York; there was no Negro "capital." This capital now exists, with its ghetto-like slums around 5th, bourgeois streets, residential areas, a few aristocratic avenues or sections thereof, white-owned stores and cafeterias, small general shops, and the innumerable "skin-whitening" and "anti-kink" beauty parlors. There is one large modern hotel, the Dewey Square, where coloured people of course may stay; and another, far larger, the Teresa, a few paces from it, where certainly they *may not!* And this is in the centre of Harlem. Such race barriers are on all sides; it just depends on chance whether you meet them or no. Some Negro friend maybe will not go into a certain drugstore with you for an ice-cream soda at 108th (where Harlem is supposed to begin, but where it is still largely "white"); "might not get served in there" (and by a coloured server at that—the white boss's orders). Just across the Harlem River some white gentlemen flashing by in a car take it into their heads to bawl, "Can't you get yourself a white man?" —you are walking with a Negro, yet you walk down-town with the same and meet no such hysteria, or again, you do.

Some 350,000 Negroes and coloured are living in Harlem and Brooklyn (the second, and quite distinct, area in greater New York where they have congregated). American Negroes, West Indians, Africans, Latin Americans. The latter, Spanish-speaking, have made a centre round 112th Street and Lenox Avenue. Walk round there and you will hear—it is nearly all Spanish. The tempo of the gestures and gait, the atmosphere, are foreign. It is the Porto-Ricans, the Central Americans and the Cubans. Nationalisms exist, more or less fiercely, between them and the American Negro—as indeed does a jealous national spirit between American Negro and black Jamaican. The latter say they are the better at business, that the coloured Americans have no enterprise. (Are we to see here the mantle of the British as a nation of shop-keepers on West Indian shoulders?) The American Negro regards the Jamaican or British West Indian as "less civilised" than himself; jokes about his accent and deportment are constantly made on the Harlem stage. And so they are always at it, falling out about empty "superiorities" and "inferiorities," forgetting the white enemy.

If you are "shown" Harlem by day you will inevitably have pointed out to you the new Rockefeller apartments, a huge block towering above a rather sparse and visibly very indigent part of 7th Avenue. These were built by the millionaire of that name, supposedly to better the conditions of Negro workers by providing clean and comfortable lodging for them, but inhabited, however, by those who can afford to pay their rents. The Y.M.C.A. and the newly built Y.W.C.A.—more institutes for "uplift." The Harlem Public Library, with its good collection of books on Negro matters, and just a few pieces of African art, so few that the idea strikes one vexingly: why, in this capital of the Negro world, is there no centre, however small, of Africanology? The American Negroes—this is a generalisation with hardly any exceptions—are utterly uninterested in, callous to what Africa is, and to what it was. Many of them are fiercely "racial," as and when it applies to the States, but concerning their forefathers they have not even curiosity.

At night you will be taken to the Lafayette Theatre, the "cradle of new stars" that will go out on the road all over America and thence come to Europe. It is a sympathetic old hall, where, as they don't bother ever to print any programmes, one supposes that all the audience know all the players; it has that feeling too. Some of the best wit I heard here, and they can get away with a lot of stiff hot stuff. Ralph Cooper's orchestra was playing admirably that night they had "the street" in. This was to give a hearing to anyone who applied. They just went on the stage and did their stuff. And the audience was *merciless* to a whole lot of these new triers, who would have passed with honour anywhere out of America. The dancing of two or three of the street shoe-blacks, box on back, then set down and dancing round it, was so perfect that the crowd gave them a big hand. No-one who has not seen the actual dancing of Harlem in Harlem can have any idea of its superb quality. From year to year it gets richer, more complicated, more exact. And I don't mean the unique Snake-Hips and the marvellous Bo-Jangles, I mean the boys and girls out of the street who later become "chorats" and "chorines" (in the chorus), or who do those exquisite short numbers, as in music the Three Ink Spots (a new trio), adolescents of 16 or 17 perhaps, playing Duke Ellington's *Mood Indigo* so that the tears ran down one's face.

There was a new dance too, one of the sights of the world as done at the Savoy Ballroom, the Lindy-Hop. The fitting third to its predecessors, Charleston and Black Bottom. These were in the days of short skirts, but the Lindy is the more astounding as it is as violent (and as beautiful), with skirts sweeping the floor. Short minuet steps to begin, then suddenly fall back into an air-pocket, recover sideways, and proceed with all the variations of leaves on the wind. For the Lindy is Lindbergh, of course, created by them in honour of his first triumph. These Tuesday nights at the Savoy are very famous, as is the Harlem "Drag Ball" that happens only once a year. To this come the boys dressed as girls—some in magnificent and elaborate costumes made by themselves—and of course many whites from down-town. A word on the celebrated "rent-party" that the American press writes up with such lurid and false suggestions. This is no more nor less than an ordinary evening dance in someone's house. The "rent" part is its reason for being, for the guests give about 50 cents to come in, thereby helping pay the rent, and they buy liquor there which, as everywhere in dry America (and doubtless it will go on even if prohibition is entirely abolished), is made on the premises or by a friend. The music, as like as not, comes from a special kind of electric piano, a nickel a tune, all the best, the latest ones.

But it is the zest that the Negroes put in, and the enjoyment they get out of, things that causes one more envy in the ofay. Notice how many of the whites are unreal in America; they are *dim*. But the

Negro is very real; he is *there*. And the ofays know it. That's why they come to Harlem—out of curiosity and jealousy and don't-know-why. This desire to get close to the other race has often nothing honest about it; for where the ofays flock, to night-clubs, for instance, such as Connie's Inn and the Cotton Club and Small's, expensive cabarets, to these two former the coloured clientele is no longer admitted. To the latter, only just, grudgingly. No, you can't go to Connie's Inn with your coloured friends. The place is *for whites*. "Niggers" to serve, and "coons" to play—and later the same ofay will slip into what he calls "a coloured dive," and there it'll be "Evening, Mr. Brown," polite and cordial, because this will be a real coloured place and the ofay is not sure of himself there a-tall. . . .

This applies of course to the mass of whites who treat Harlem in the same way that English toffs used to talk about "going slumming." The class I'm thinking of is "the club-man." They want entertainment. Go to Harlem, it's sharper there. And it doesn't upset their conception of the Negro's social status. From all time the Negro has entertained the whites, but never been thought of by this type as possibly a social equal. There are, however, thousands of artists, writers, musicians, intellectuals, etc., who have good friends in the dark race, and a good knowledge of Harlem life, "the freedom of Harlem," so to speak.

"You must see a revival meeting," they said to me. "It's nothing like what it is in the South, but you shouldn't miss it."

Beforehand I thought I wouldn't be able to stand more than ten minutes of it—ten minutes in any church. . . . When we got into the Rev. Cullen's on 7th Avenue (the Rev. is the father of the poet Countee Cullen) a very large audience was waiting for the "Dancing Evangelist" (that is Becton's title because of his terrific physical activity). A group of "sisters" all in white spread itself fan-wise in the balcony. There was a concert stage with deacons and some of Becton's 12 disciples, and the 7 or 8 absolutely first-class musicians who compose the orchestra, of whom Lawrence Pierre, a fine organist and a disciple. Nothing like a church, an evening concert.

The music starts, a deep-toned Bach piece, then a short allocution, and then the long spirituals, the robust soloist that a massed chorus, the audience, answers back. They begin to beat time with their feet too. The "spirit" is coming with the volume of sound. At this point Becton enters quietly, stands silent on the stage, will not say a word. They must sing some more first, much more; they must be ripe ground. How do they reconcile Becton's exquisite smartness (pearl-grey suit, top hat, cane, ivory gloves, his youthful look and lovely figure), the whole sparkle about him, with the customary ponderousness of the other drab men of God? A sophisticated audience? No, for they appear to be mainly domestic workers, small shop workers, old and young, an evidently religious public, and one or two whites.

A new spiritual has begun; the singing gets intenser, foot-beating all around now, bodies swaying, and clapping of hands in unison. Now and again a voice, several voices, rise above the rest in a single phrase, the foot-beat becomes a stamp. A forest shoots up—black, brown, ivory, amber hands—spread, stiffened out fingers, gestures of *mea culpa* beating of breasts, gestures of stiff arms out, vibrating ecstasy. Far away in the audience a woman gets "seized," leaps up and down on the same spot belabouring her bosom. It comes here, there—who will be the next? At one moment I counted ten women in this same violent trance, not two with the same gestures, yet *all* in rhythm, half-time or double time. A few men too less spectacular. Then just behind me so that I see her well, a young girl. She leaps up and down after the first scream eyes revulsed, arms upstretched—she is no longer "there." After about a minute those next to her seize her and hold her down.

The apex of the singing has come, it is impossible to convey the scale of these immense sound-waves and rhythmical under-surges. One is transported completely. It has nothing to do with God, but with life—a collective life for which I know no name. The people are entirely out of themselves—and then, suddenly, the music stops, calm comes immediately.

In this prepared atmosphere Becton now strides about the stage, flaying the people for their sins, leading their ready attention to this or that point of his argument by some adroit word, a wise-crack maybe. He is a poet in speech and very graceful in all his movements. His dramatisation is generous—and how they respond . . . "yeah man . . . tell it, tell it." Sin, he threatens, is "cat-foot," a "double-dare devil." And the sinner? "A double-ankled rascal," thunders this "adagio dancer," as he called himself that night, breaking off sharp into another mood, an admonishment out of "that inexpressible something by which I raise my hand." There are whirlwind gestures when he turns round on himself, one great clap of the palms and a sort of characteristic half-whistle-half-hoot before some point which is going to be emphasized— and the eloquence pours out in richer and richer imagery. Becton is the personification of expressionism, a great dramatic actor. You remember Chaliapine's acting of Boris Godounov; these two are comparable.

Then, "when the millenniums are quaking it's time to clap our hands." It is the moment for the "consecrated dime," and the singing begins again, but the trances are over; other preachers may speak later. This ritual goes on from eight till after midnight, about four nights

a week, and sometimes both the faithful and the evangelist are so indefatigable that it goes on for 24 hours. These services, really superb
concerts, are the gorgeous manifestation of *the emotion* of a race—that
part of the Negro people that has been so trammelled with religion
that it is still steeped therein. A manifestation of this kind by white
people would have been utterly revolting. But with the Negro race it
is on another plane, it seems positively another thing, not connected
with Christ or bible, the pure outpouring of themselves, a nature-rite.
In other words, it is the fervour, intensity, the stupendous rhythm and
surge of singing that are so fine—the christianity is only accidental,
incidental to these. Not so for the assembly of course, for all of it is
deeply, tenaciously religious. I have given all this detail about the re-
vivalist meeting because it is so fantastic, and, *aesthetically* speaking,
so moving.

If treachery and lying are its main attributes so is snobbery flourish-
ing in certain parts of Harlem. "Strivers Row;" that is what 139th
Street has been called. An excellent covering-name for "those Astorperi-
ous Ethiopians," as one of their own wits put it. There are near-white
cliques, mulatto groups, dark-skinned sets who will not invite each
other to their houses; some would not let a white cross their thresholds.
The Negro "bluebloods" of Washington are famous for their social
exclusivity, there are some in Harlem too. I don't know if a foreign
white would get in there, possibly not. The snobbery around skin-
colour is terrifying. The light-skins and browns look down on the
black; by some, friendships with *ofays* are not tolerated, from an un-
derstandable but totally unsatisfactory reaction to the general national
attitude of white to coloured on the social equality basis. A number of
the younger writers are race-conscious in the wrong way, they make
of this a sort of forced, *self*-conscious thing, give the feeling that they
are looking for obstacles. All this, indeed, is Society with a vengeance!
A bourgeois ideology with no horizon, no philosophical link with life.
And out of all this, need it be said, such writers as Van Vechten and
Co. have made a revolting and cheap lithograph, so that Harlem, to a
large idle-minded public, has come to mean nothing more whatsoever
than a round of hooch-filled night-clubs after a round of "snow"
(cocaine) filled boudoirs. Van Vechten, the spirit of vulgarity, has de-
picted Harlem as a grimace. He would have written the same way
about Montparnasse or Limehouse and Soho. Do places exist, or is life
itself as described by Paul Morand (another profiteer in coloured
"stock")? Claude MacKay has done better. The studies in inter-colour
relationships (in *Ginger Town*) are honest. But his people, and himself, have also that wrong kind of race-consciousness; they ring themselves in, they are umbrageous. The "Negro Renaissance" (the literary

movement of about 1925, now said to be at a halt, and one wonders on whose authority this is said) produced many books and poems filled with this bitter-sweet of Harlem's glitter and heart-break.

This is not the Harlem one sees. You don't see the Harlem of the romancists; it is romantic in its own right. And it is *hard* and *strong;* its noise, heat, cold, cries and colours are so. And the nostalgia is violent too; the eternal radio seeping through everything day and night, indoors and out, becomes somehow the personification of restlessness, desire, brooding. And then the gorgeous roughness, the gargle of Louis Armstrong's voice breaks through. As everywhere, the real people are in the street. I mean those young men on the corner, and the people all sitting on the steps throughout the breathless, leaden summer. I mean the young men in Pelham Park; the sports groups (and one sees many in their bright sweaters), the strength of a race, its beauty.

For in Harlem one can make an appreciation of a race. Walk down 7th Avenue—the different types are uncountable. Every diversity of bone-structure, of head-shape, of skin colour; mixes between Orientals and pure Negroes, Jews and Negroes, Red Indians and Negroes (a particularly beautiful blend, with the high cheek-bones always, and sometimes straight black hair), mulattoes of all shades, yellow, "high yaller" girls, and Havana-coloured girls, and, exquisitely fine, the Spanish and Negro blends; the Negro bone, and the Negro fat too, are a joy to the eye. And though there are more and more light-coloured people, there is great satisfaction in seeing that the white American features are absorbed in the mulatto, and that the mulatto is not, as so often in England, a coloured man with a white man's features and often expression as well. The white American and the Negro are a good mix physically.

THE AMERICAN MORON AND THE AMERICAN
OF SENSE—LETTERS ON THE NEGRO

Here are examples of some of the wild letters received by me at the time I was in Harlem, New York, collecting part of the material for this book. The American press, led by Hearst's *yellow sheets,* had turned this simple enough fact into a veritable racket. Despite all the "liberal attitude of progressive whites" and the recent "New Negro" movement whereby Americans learnt with incredulous amazement that there is a distinct Negro literature, any interest manifested by a white person, even a foreigner to America (such as myself), is immediately transformed into a sex "scandal." The American press method (one of America's major scandals), led by the world-famous "yellow press" of Hearst, is to invent as vulgar and "sexy" a story as possible, to which any official denial merely adds another "special edition." The American public is intended to believe that no white person has ever stayed in Harlem before. But everyone knows that many thousands of whites actually live in Harlem, married to Negroes, or domiciled there.

No chance is ever missed by the American press, and the type of American that believes it (vastly preponderant), to stir up as much fury as possible against Negroes and their white friends. To do this the sex motive is always used. As in the South it is called the lie of the "rape" of white women by black men, so in the North it is always the so-called "scandal" of the inter-racial relations. The Hearst publications *invent* black lovers for white women. A reporter goes round to try and bribe the hotel people into saying that such and such a Negro is staying there—communicating rooms, etc. (This is the case in *my own* experience.) As of course there is not such a good "story" in scandalising about plain coloured X, some well-known coloured star or personality is always picked (one instance of this was the late Booker T. Washington himself, at the age of 60 or so). In that way the Hearst press hopes also to damage the star's professional reputation. If individuals persistently behaved in this manner amongst themselves, they would be locked up as criminals or insane; but what is to be done when this is one of the pillars of American society—the press? The equivalent to the jailing of individuals is of course the total suppression of the American press. An illuminating comment by Americans themselves on their newspapers is that journalists have got to write *something*—the papers have got to be filled every day, you know. . . .

It is necessary to explain to the English reader (I think?) that "caucasian" in the U.S. is used as a self-awarded title of white man's superiority. It has no more to do, geographically, with the Caucasus than "nordic" (same meaning) has to do with Scandinavia.

I should like to print all the raving, illiterate, anonymous letters—some are very funny indeed, mainly from sex-maniacs one might say—but what is to be done? They are obscene, so this portion of American culture cannot be made public.

Of course there are other letters as well—some 400 or 500—from Negroes and friendly whites, commending the stand I took and the making of this anthology. Of the anonymous threats, etc., some 30. Most of them came in a bunch, just after the press outcry, May 2, 1932. Examples:

"Miss Nancy Cunard, you are insane or downright degenerate. Why do you come to America to seek cheap publicity? you have not gained any favor but a whole lot of hatred. If I saw one of your publications I would be the first to suppress it. Furthermore I and a committee are appealing to the U.S. department of Labor to have you deported as a depraved miserable degenerated insane. Back to where you belong. If you dare to make any comparison you had better look out for your life wont be worth the price of your black hotel room. You for your nerve should be burned alive to a stake, you dirty lowdown betraying piece of mucus. (Here follows a sentence which might be considered obscene and which is not, therefore, printed.) K.K.K. 58 W 58." (I suppose this purports to come from the Ku Klux Klan, or possibly the writer only stole their "signature.")

"Dear Miss Cunard,—It is very gratifying indeed to know that in these trying days someone deserts the great make-believe world and devotes her time to a real problem dealing with humans. Your determination to do your OWN work in so noble a cause has inspired all of us who devote our lives to the service of others and we most sincerely congratulate you.

"Out here in the mountains of South California we operate a small boarding school for boys. Our place is very beautiful and the setting is most inspiring. We would be happy to have you avail yourself of our hospitality and to come out and visit us at any time. You will find this a wonderful place for rest, quiet and study.

"May success crown your every effort and may the example you have given the world be the means of creating interest in the conditions of the Negro in this country. Being a Virginian, the writer fully appreciates the status of the American Negro.

"Best wishes to you, cordially."

(This letter is from a California school, from the Headmaster.)

william plomer

In the Early Thirties

It was no secret that Nancy was not on good terms with her mother. I will leave it to others to enlarge upon this subject, but it has always seemed to me that they were in some ways much alike, and that each resented or perhaps envied characteristics in the other which were very much her own. Possibly the wilfully independent Lady Cunard, wishing to direct or control Nancy, resented most Nancy's wilful independence.

Nancy told me of an incident which did nothing to soften her asperity towards her mother. After one of their quarrels Lady Cunard sent her daughter a peace offering. A small parcel arrived by special messenger. Nancy disdainfully opened it in the presence of a friend, and it was seen to contain a bracelet of fine and beautifully matched emeralds.

I don't remember exactly when Maud Cunard gave it out that she wished to be called Emerald, but she was known to be fond of that stone. How irritating it can be when people choose to give presents of what they themselves like! Nancy was certainly irritated, and saying something like "If she thinks she can buy affection with *this,* she had better think again!" She flung the bracelet across the room, and it lay smouldering greenly on the floor. When her friend had gone and she had cooled down, she thought to herself, "Well, after all, an emerald bracelet is an emerald bracelet, and as it's very valuable, I'll sell it."

She bundled it back into its box and took it round to Cartier's, or some place of equal eminence, in Bond Street, and said, "I'm Miss Cunard. I expect you know that my mother is very fond of emeralds. She has given me this bracelet, and I would like you to value it for me." As they deferentially bowed her out, she said she would look in again the next morning. She did so, and they broke the news to her that the stones were one of the most remarkable imitations they had seen, and were worth every penny of some derisory sum.

I have written elsewhere of Nancy's physical appearance, but there are two details I will add. In 1931, when I was living in Canning Place, off Palace Gate, she came along one cold and frosty afternoon, and was offered tea. She said she would prefer gin. There was at hand a bottle of Schnapps—no, she wouldn't have anything with it, thank you —and while tea was being drunk by others, she was asked to help herself. She did so, several times emptying a fair-sized tumbler.

"Oh, and thank you for the gin," she said quietly as she was going away, perfectly sober. "It quite warmed me up."

And it quite warmed *me* up to see so fragile-looking a woman so gracefully fortified.

Some months later, when I was occupying the top floors of a house in Redcliffe Road, she visited me one evening with two Negro friends. When she left she missed her footing and fell down on the rather steep stairs. She looked so vulnerable that without stopping to consider whether she might be injured I picked her up in my arms like a child and carried her down to the waiting taxi. I remember how astonished I was to find how extremely light she was. I felt as if I was carrying a heron.

Light and slight also was my contribution to her notable miscellany, *Negro,* but I was pleased to have been asked to make it. Worldly people and spiteful gossips used to speak scornfully of her fondness for Negroes and made it unnecessarily clear that they thought her heart stronger than her head. What if it was? Is love, followed by a loathing of injustice towards the species of the loved one or ones, a bad thing, especially when it foreshadows, long before most pundits and politicians, the way the world is going? Superficial persons thought Nancy's Negrophilism merely fashionable, because in the twenties jazz bands, Negro spirituals, Paul Robeson, Josephine Baker, and African sculpture were all the go.

In a flat Nancy had in Percy Street in London, there was a large carved wooden figure from Africa of a male nude. The zestful emphasis laid by the sculptor upon its maleness rattled Nancy's charwoman, who thought it, in more senses than one, a bit too much. In the same room I noticed, hanging on the wall, three top-hats strung together—a black one, a grey one (formerly belonging to her father), and a gold one, of the kind used by jazz bands. There was a label attached to them, bearing these lines:

"Yo ho ho,
Up on a tree,
Nearer to God,
Further from thee,
Says Old Regime,
As then dost see."

Her refusal to conform to what she regarded as "old régime"—or "old hat" (a current expression for *vieux jeu*) was admittedly willful but not merely frivolous. Her Negrophilism was passionately serious, and its influence augmented other influences already at work. And ultimately of great political importance in the world.

raymond michelet

Nancy Cunard

1931—Nancy met la Hours Press en sommeil, et bientôt le magasin de la rue Guénégaud sera presque constamment fermé. Au début de l'année, Henry Crowder, le pianiste de jazz qui avait été son compagnon pendant ces dernières années, et dont elle avait édité un recueil de compositions, a regagné NEW YORK. Cette liaison prolongée avec un Noir Americain a, bien sûr, fait scandale en Angleterre, et provoque d'orageuses discussions entre Lady Cunard et sa fille. "On" fait la leçon à NANCY comme si elle était une petite fille mal élevée qui déshonore sa famille. La riposte ne se fait pas attendre: Nancy entre en rage et songe à écrire un pamphlet sur cette histoire.

Ce fut là sans doute son premier heurt, dramatique et décisif, avec la réalité, et avec la société dont elle est issue. A Paris, durant sa liaison avec Henry Crowder, elle n'avait pas eu à souffrir du préjugé racial; mais l'Angleterre, du moins la "société" anglaise réagit tout autrement.

A Cagnes-sur-Mer, ou elle a loué une maison en haut de la colline, derrière le Chateau des Grimaldi, elle écrit très vite un pamphlet qui sera imprimé sur place, et, sans être mis en vente, est envoyé à tous les amis, à tous les ex-amis qui l'ont lâchée, aux journaux qui se sont fait l'écho du scandale. Une photo de presse l'illustre et résume le thème: c'est celle de Lady Cunard, en robe de soirée, photographiée à une réception de gala aux côtés d'un prince hindou du plus beau noir. . . . Pourquoi donc ce qui ne fait pas scandale lorsqu'il s'agit d'un richissime hindou, même s'il est très noir de peau, devient-il intolérable s'il s'agit d'un musicien noir américain: Au fait: est-ce que le préjugé de couleur ne se double pas d'un préjugé de classe sociale?

La publication de ce pamphlet marque la rupture bientôt définitive de Nancy avec ses origines, et sera le début d'une nouvelle évolution qui la verra désormais, souvent avec véhémence, aux côtés de ceux que ne satisfait pas un ordre en apparence bien établi.

Son séjour à Cagnes se prolonge. Sont là: Georges Antheil, le musicien, le peintre Hilaire Hiler, Raoul Ubac, Georges Sadoul, et non loin, René Crevel que viennent visiter Paul Eluard et Georges Auric.

Peu à peu se forme en elle le projet d'une autre réplique plus consistante qu'un simple pamphlet de quelques pages: montrer, démontrer que le préjugé racial ne repose sur aucune justification, que les Noirs sont des gens aussi intéressants que les Blancs, qu'ils ont derrière eux une longue histoire sociale et culturelle, et que ceux qui les rejettent comme des sous-hommes ignorent tout de leur histoire passée, de leurs civilisations, de leurs luttes, de la lente reconquête de leur liberté. C'est ainsi que prit corps le livre auquel elle allait travailler pendant plus de deux ans: "NEGRO", énorme encyclopédie, "livre collectif" s'il en fut jamais, livre actuellement introuvable en dehors de quelques exemplaires dans des bibliothèques, et dont les derniers exemplaires, demeurés dans la maison française de Nancy, à la Chapelle-Réanville, près de Vernon, furent détruits pendant l'occupation allemande.

A l'origine, le plan de ce livre est encore vague. Nancy multiplie les lettres qu'elle expédie, un peu au hasard, aux amis, à tous ceux qui pourraient, pense-t-elle, lui apporter des documents ou une collaboration quelconque.

Le livre se fera ainsi, ballotté de résidence en résidence (car Nancy ne tient pas en place), au gré des réponses et des collaborations qui s'offriront. Pendant l'année 1931, on empile les dossiers, les correspondances.

A la fin du printemps 1931, Henry Crowder est revenu des USA. Nancy décide de repartir avec lui à New York et d'aller habiter à Harlem, dans le quartier noir, et de voir elle-même comment les choses se passeront. Elle descend dans un hotel noir. La réaction ne tarde pas: la presse flaire un scandale à exploiter, d'autant plus qu'il s'agit d'un grand nom de l'aristocratie anglaise! Bientôt les lettres anonymes et les menaces de mort se succèdent. Quelques semaines après, il ne reste rien d'autre à faire qu'à fuir et regagner l'Europe. Henry Crowder l'accompagne, et, avant son retour définitif aux USA, fait avec elle un long périple en Allemagne, une Allemagne encore républicaine: tour de tous les musées ethnographiques, particulièrement riches en documents sur les cultures africaines.

Automne 1931—Hiver 1931-32: deux longs séjours, TOULON d'abord (au Mourillon, à l'Hotel de la mer) puis à BRUXELLES (à Tervueren, aux portes du Musée du Congo). Le livre prend corps. Le plan se précise. Les correspondances se multiplient, souvent difficiles, car beaucoup comprennent mal qu'il s'agit de collaborations bénévoles, et non rétribuées! Certains des meilleurs amis s'excusent, ou s'en tirent par une pirouette et quelques phrases: tel Norman Douglas dont Nancy reproduira dans "Negro", telle quelle, la réponse farfelue . . .

Au printemps 1932, Nancy décide un second voyage en Amérique:

cette fois aux Antilles, Jamaique, Haiti. En fait elle prolonge son séjour surtout à la Jamaique. De retour en France, l'été 1932 s'écoule en Dordogne. Nous avions découvert le charme d'un de ces nombreux villages de la vallée: Carennac.

Nous logions dans l'ancien prieuré où Fénelon, dit-on, écrivit les aventures de Télémaque. 250 ans après, c'était un tout autre livre qui s'y faisait: Nancy écrit, traduit, adapte . . .

Je crois que c'est cette année là qu'elle se prit de passion pour ce pays incomparable. Nous vagabondions beaucoup: Saint Céré, Castelnau, Loubressac, Puybrun, Padirac, Souillac, Beynac, Domme, Gluges. . . . Plus tard, bien plus tard, elle devait y revenir puisqu'elle acheta une toute petite maison a Lamothe-Fénelon où elle vécut une partie de ses dernières années.

A l'automne 32, nous rentrons à Paris. Il faut finir "le livre" pendant l'hiver: on s'installe tant bien que mal dans sa maison de La Chapelle-Réanville, qu'elle avait en vain essayé de vendre. Elle n'avait pas trouvé d'acheteur pour cette grande maison. Entre temps elle avait transporté à Paris presque tous les meubles, qu'elle avait empilés dans la boutique de la rue Guénégaud désormais fermée. Il ne restait à Réanville que le strict minimum. Pendant 3 mois, nous y campâmes, travaillant un peu plus tard chaque nuit, si bien que, couchés au petit matin, nous recommencions la journée à la nuit tombante d'hiver. Au début de 1933, le livre est terminé et Nancy part à Londres pour s'occuper de l'impression.

Ceci est une vie de Nancy, mais ce n'est qu'une des vies de NANCY . . . car Nancy menait de front 3 ou 4 vies parallèles, qui parfois s'entrecoupaient, parfois se contrariaient, parfois restaient indépendantes. D'une heure à l'autre, elle pouvait totalement changer, devenir quelqu'un d'autre. C'est pourquoi sa personnalité pouvait être aussi fascinante, et aussi épuisante pour ceux de ses compagnons qui participaient vraiment à cette vie, qu'elle brûlait pas les deux bouts.

Car il ne s'agissait pas de sautes d'humeur. Nancy avait d'effroyables colères, souvent injustes dans leur excès, car elle poussait chaque sentiment à l'extrême, au risque de la faire basculer dans cette zone dangereuse où il explose et détruit tout autour de lui, mais au départ elles étaient toujours justifiées. Il s'agit d'autre chose. . . . Nancy fuyait en avant, sans jamais se reprendre, sans jamais se retourner, en brûlant tout derrière elle, les choses qu'elle avait aimées, les gens qu'elle aurait aimés. Comme elle le fit encore, dans un dernier sursaut, la veille de sa mort, alors qu'elle était presque inconsciente . . .

Que fuyait-elle? J'ai vécu plus de deux ans avec elle, et je ne le sais pas. Je le sentais, c'était parfois effroyable. Mais un garçon de 19 ans ne vit pas sur les mêmes rhythmes qu'une femme de 35 ans, même s'il est violemment amoureux, et celle qu'il croit connaître lui demeure impénétrable.

Mais j'essaierai pourtant de parler de cette fuite en avant.

Nancy jouait à la fois plusieurs personnages, personnages au sens de la "persona" des Latins.

Elle pouvait être ivre pendant des heures, sans cesser d'être lucide, au bord d'une certaine déraison, et pourtant toujours en équilibre.

Il lui arrivait de me dire qu'elle avait besoin d'un jour de solitude absolue. Elle en sortait non pas détendue, reposée, mais plus violente encore. D'ailleurs elle ne supportait pas une solitude prolongeé. Elle la craignait. Même la solitude à deux ne lui était tolérable que dans de rares moments d'équilibre parfait avec les choses, avec les paysages, avec les pierres où elle se trouvait vivre. Dans ces moments parfaits, elle était alors d'un romantisme que nul n'aurait soupçonné chez une femme apparemment aussi précise, aussi dure. Alors coulait un lyricisme éperdu qu'elle reniait quelques heures après, comme si elle regrettait de s'être livrée à nu. La solitude l'effrayait: lorsqu'un compagnon la quittait, il lui fallait tout de suite une autre chaleur humaine à côté d'elle. Il lui est arrivé de cueillir ainsi au passage le premier venu qui lui tombait sous la main, même s'il était parmi ses amis le moins indiqué pour vivre à ses côtés, quitte à le renvoyer—et de quelle façon, et avec quelle hauteur!—quelques jours après, voire même le lendemain.

Nancy menait sa "quête sexuelle" comme sa quête émotionnelle. Elle a eu de nombreux amants noirs, presque tous des musiciens, certains qu'elle a aimés passionnément, que pourtant elle a quittés, ou qui l'ont quittée, brûlés par cette flamme qu'elle nourrissait en elle . . .

Elle a eu des amants blancs à qui elle a donné le meilleur d'elle-même, et certains s'en souviennent encore qui sont encore vivants (j'écris ceci en 1966). On a écrit sur ces amours des poèmes qui sont parmi les plus beaux poèmes d'amour que des Français aient écrits. J'aimerais pouvoir les reproduire ici, mais c'est à ceux qui ont aimé Nancy et que Nancy a aimés qu'il appartient de les laisser relire.

Nancy pouvait pleurer d'émotion, à 35 ans, comme l'aurait fait une jeune femme surprise par un amour inattendu et soudainement surgi. Nancy pouvait être dure comme une femme indépendante habituée à se jouer des hommes. Elle pouvait être une amoureuse toute simple, toute passionnée, et le lendemain, incapable de choisir entre deux hommes qu'elle aimait, elle tentait de se construire une vie invraisemblable, où elle déjeunait avec l'un, passait l'après midi avec le second, dinait avec le premier, et passait la nuit avec l'autre: dans chaque situation elle allait jusqu'au bout, que ce fût simple, que ce fût compliqué, que ce fût logique ou absurde, que ce fût dangereux ou non.

Il lui fallait tirer de chaque instant tout ce qu'il pouvait donner.
Nancy flambait.

Car il ne s'agissait pas d'accumuler les sensations, ni de les collectionner. Rien de plus éloigné d'elle! S'il en avait été ainsi, elle aurait sombré dans le drogue. Or cela ne l'intéressait pas. C'est ce feu qu'elle portait en elle qu'il lui fallait sans arrêt attiser, activer, renouveler . . . surtout, qu'il ne vînt pas a s'éteindre!

J'ai vécu deux ans avec elle. Elle avait donc 35 et 36 ans. Jamais elle ne s'est abandonnée un jour à ces instants que chacun connaît dans sa vie, où on laisse les choses aller vers le vide, vers l'absence de tout. Nancy ne s'arrêtait jamais. Elle repartait en avant et il fallait la suivre, et jouer chacun de ses personnages. Qui ne la suivait pas cessait d'être de ses amis.

Que fuyait-elle, que cherchait-elle?

Elle avait peur de la mort. Ceci fait partie de ses rares confidences abandonnées. Elle se persuadait violemment que, morte, elle vivrait autrement. Je me souviens d'une longue discussion avec le jeune surréaliste Pierre UNIK qui, tranquillement athée, lui disait qu'il n'attendait rien de la mort. Elle le contredisait farouchement. C'est pourquoi l'animisme africain la passionnait.

Dans l'un des articles que j'ai écrit pour "Negro", je me suis efforcé de montrer que la notion de "mentalité primitive", inventée par Levy-Brühl, et en vogue ces années là (1930), n'était qu'une construction sans fondement. Je tâchais de montrer que l'esprit africain était capable des mêmes réalisations industrielles que les Européens, en dehors de toute influence directe de ceux-ci, donc était armé de la même logique, mais qu'en plus il était ouvert à d'autres choses, à d'autres perceptions que 20 siècles de rationalisme, latin nous avaient fait oublier. Et je citais quelques observations singulières dont les manifestations de télépathie n'étaient que les moindres, relevées, exprès, dans des relations de missionnaires peu enclins à la complaisance.

Or cela la fascinait. Elle me fit connaître un Ashanti que la police coloniale d'une "Gold Coast" qui n'était pas encore le Ghana, avait fait fuir en Europe. Il paraissait détenir des pouvoirs singuliers, mais seulement par moments, comme si ce n'était plus que les lambeaux d'un savoir bien plus vaste et qu'il ne dominait plus. Elle vit cet Africain souvent, pendant des années, comme s'il avait représenté pour elle je ne sais quel espoir, quelle protection contre le néant. Il lui arrivera d'ailleurs plus tard, dans les derniers jours de sa vie, de se croire africaine, et de penser que sa vraie vie n'était plus ici en Europe . . .

Voilà quelques unes des vies de Nancy.

Il y en eut d'autres: celles d'avant, celles des années 1925, 26, 27, au grand soleil surréaliste, celles d'après, au temps de la guerre d'Espagne, celles ou elle découvrait Beckett, et imprimait Aldington, Aragon, Ezra Pound. . . . Je laisse à ceux qui la connurent alors, le soin de la raconter et de la perpétuer.

MARS 1965—"FIN DE PARTIE"

J'emprunte ce titre à Beckett qu'elle fut la première à decouvrir et à éditer (en 1929 je crois).

Nancy vient d'avoir 69 ans. Quelque temps avant, elle a eu un accident: fracture col du fémur câssé. Depuis des mois elle vit à St Jean Cap Ferrat, presque immobilisée. Elle ne se soutient plus qu'avec l'alcool. Elle ne mange presque plus.

Est-ce qu'elle sent la mort venir? Un dernier sursaut la jette dans le train de Paris, alors qu'elle ne peut marcher seule et qu'il faut la porter. Elle veut revoir, je pense, quelques uns des gens qu'elle a aimé tout court. Elle arrive chez moi soudain, portée par un chauffeur de taxi. Elle délire doucement, tranquillement: elle mettra à la porte les deux médecins que l'on appelle le lendemain, successivement. Elle veut voir Beckett, Sadoul, Aragon. Georges Sadoul arrive dans la nuit: elle commence un long, un délirant monologue qui nous rappelle invinciblement, à Sadoul et à moi, les interminables ressassements des personnages de "fin de partie" à l'approche de la mort. Le lendemain elle disparait, après avoir brûlé "des tas de papiers" (dit-elle au téléphone). Sans doute s'évanouit-elle dans le taxi qui l'emmenait. Elle est transportée a l'hôpital, dans le coma semble-t-il. Elle meurt deux jours après. Quand on l'a hospitalisé, elle pesait 29 kgs. Elle a été incinérée au cimetière du Père Lachaise.

J'ai hésité à raconter cette mort dérisoire et affreuse. Pourtant il ne s'agit pas de mourir proprement ou pas proprement. Même cette affreuse "fin de partie" est un des personnages, un des rôles de Nancy. Et je trouve une grandeur tragique à cette folie qui emplit les derniers jours de Nancy et la mène tout droit à cette mort dérisoire.

eugene gordon

"The Green Hat" Comes to Chambers Street

If I had known what Nancy Cunard was doing that May afternoon of 1932, or better, where she was doing it, certainly I would have gone straight home. There, on the backside of Beacon Hill in my two-room-and-bath apartment overlooking Chambers Street—that rocky lane which slanted down toward Charles River between fishmarkets, push-carts, women, vegetable stands, children, overturned trashcans, dogs, kosher chicken markets, men, Chinese laundries, and radio repair shops, and where patterns of concord arose from the very discord of sounds, I would have reread Miss Cunard's letter asking for a "contribution" to her anthology.

Then, to satisfy myself whether I had written an unbiased account of the Negro's relation to the United States "radical movement"—whether what I had written was the contribution she expected—I would have studied it again. Its working title was "Blacks Turn Red."

Not knowing where Miss Cunard was doing what (though, if I believed New York reports in the Boston paper I worked for, she was chasing and being chased by lustful Negro men, wherever she was)—indeed, there being nothing at the moment to remind me of her—instead of going home I went to a theater which showed foreign films and newsreels. The time being May, 1932, I had been on the *Boston Post's* writing staff 13 years to the month, the first three months (1919) in the city room. If my 90 days as a reporter had been extended to 13 years I should likely have remained unknown to Nancy Cunard and she unknown to me, except as curiosity prompted me to read the scandal stories about her. Hiring me on May 1, the city editor assigned me to the Natural History Museum. When my series of brief stories ended, the editor said he was "lending" me to Charley Lincoln. The "loan" was a "gift."

The feature department, under Charles H. Lincoln, was completely autonomous. That benevolent autocrat required his staff to be at work not later than he and he came in at 10 A.M. My hours in the city room had been from 9 A.M. to 5 P.M. or later. Any who wished to leave the feature department desk earlier than 4:30 P.M. stated his reason to

Lincoln and left. Any wishing to remain after 4:30 could. No limit was set on one's time in the office. My contributions during that period to *Mercury, New Masses, Nation, Plain Talk, New Theater, Opportunity: Journal of Negro Life,* and *International Literature* were done in that isolated, silent old room with its encyclopedias, unabridged dictionaries, and innumerable books of reference, long after my daytime associates were asleep in Waltham, Brookline, or Cambridge. Nancy Cunard in London first knew about me from some of these writings.

On the afternoon in question I was late quitting the office, so late, I recall, that the newsreel was ending as I was pushing into my theater seat. The newscaster as I sat was pronouncing the words "Lady Nancy Cunard" and I just glimpsed her vanishing profile. I sat thinking, naturally, more of what I had missed than of what the feature film was about. The news sequence showing Nancy Cunard, when finally it reappeared, was brief: she allegedly was entering "a Harlem Negro hotel." She was in America "supposedly collecting material for an anthology." The leading female character in Michael Arlen's *The Green Hat,* which I owned, was Nancy Cunard, as was, said the newscaster, Lucy Tantamount in Aldous Huxley's *Point Counter Point,* which I didn't. Upon leaving the theater I went at once to the library, found Huxley's novel, and went directly home to read it. Making my own meals was one of my most pleasurable pastimes.

It probably was that passage in the novel where Lord Edward associates certain kinds of supper dishes with certain days of the week that set me thinking that today I'd have what he has on Tuesdays and Thursdays, these being "steak-with-chips" days. There was practically nothing in my icebox. I worked out a menu of steak, if I could find one at this late hour, a cucumber salad, hot biscuits, and . . . the phone rang. A woman asked, cautiously but pointedly: "Eugene Gordon?"

Having been reassured, she called: "Hullo, Eugene!"

I didn't know the voice. Before I could word a suitably polite apology, she said: "I'm Nancy Cunard. You promised . . ."

"Oh!" I hardly believed. "The shipping heiress of today's headlines?"

Her slow, husky laugh ended abruptly, punctuated by a pause. The pause was a period where an exclamation point would otherwise be. I imagined her expressing wry amusement and tolerant disapproval of her treatment by the press, and I believed, quite guiltily, that she had expected better of me.

She was saying: ". . . and you promised to get it to me, remember, but . . ."

My cutting in was a suggestion that a brief trip to Boston might be worthwhile, I suddenly catching myself, wondering whether *brief trip* was inferred to mean that if she came she could get quickly to hell out. True, I could imagine *Post* reporters and photographers among scandal birds from other papers scavenging after her around the entrance and up the staircase of 198 Chambers Street. "But, of course," I said, "it'd be foolish to expect you in Boston for something you can get by mail."

Her laughter was sheer mirth. "Forgive me, Eugene. Didn't you hear me? I am in Boston! I . . . we arrived today. I'm . . ." She was conversing with someone in the background, and, hearing my number and street mentioned, I realized, startled, that I could be rescued from between the horns of this dilemma only by the logic of impending events: whether or not I was "ready" for their visit. Who, I wondered, is with her? They were on their way.

She was talking to me again. "Lawrence Gellert is with me. Do you know each other?" They were taking a cab, she said, leaving me wondering, further, how long it would be before my bell rang.

"Goddammit!" And I pulled the window shades down and stuffed the tabloid into the oversized tin wastebasket and pushed it under my desk. I cleared a sizable spot on the desk and, damning "Blacks Turn Red," laid it in the clearing. I made sure that neither *The Green Hat* nor *Point Counter Point* was visible, not knowing—and I have never learned—what she thought of either.

I stood in the center and looked critically around the room at the glittering black floor. I threw myself into the red leather chair; bounced up. I paced. I peeked round the drawn window shade down into the night lighted street. The downstairs push-button trilled the bell in the kitchen. Standing on my landing atop the iron staircase, I looked down beyond Lawrence Gellert at this woman as the narrator of *The Green Hat* looked from his window upon Iris (March) Storm, visiting, for the first time, her brother Gerald March, stinkingly pickled in whiskey in his top floor flat "above a mean lane in a place called Shepherd's Market." Nancy Cunard was wearing a *green hat!* "I could not see her face for the shadow of the brim," says the narrator (nor could I), "for it was a piratical brim, such as might very possibly defy the burning suns of El Dorado."

If I endeavored to simulate the narrator's thought and feeling about Iris Storm, I don't recall—my effort was wholly involuntary and unconscious. For I was excitedly aware at every step they advanced upward that what we three were concerned with was life—not its reflection—brutal and ruthless, we being among the people trying to manipulate life's social forms to our advantage.

I was then aware, suddenly, that Miss Cunard and Gellert were not being followed into the building.

Feeling the need to consult Lawrence Gellert's recollection of that evening, I here stopped writing and after a few days' search I found him in his Greenwich Village home. How did I receive Nancy and him that evening? Did I serve refreshments? What did we talk about? I was stiff-necked and reserved, he told me, as I stood back in the room, away from the open door, waiting for them. I recall instead taking the hand of each, in turn, drawing them into the room, and shutting the door.

She was thin-faced, and her height was inches below tall. I remember most clearly the bold, direct probing of her impersonal green eyes: they quit staring into mine long enough to examine the rest of my face, and, the over-colored lips hinting tentatively at a smile, green eyes now sparkling, she was again probing me through my eyes. I realized later that we thus faced each other just a few seconds. They seemed then like minutes.

I reminded myself that this woman was *not* a fictional Iris March but an actual Nancy Cunard.

I directed her to my work chair at the desk and handed her the manuscript. Her left cheek inclined against the left palm, downcast eyes framed in a half circle of the tight fitting green hat's turned-up brim, she read with concentration and speed. She handed Larry each page as she finished it and he, reading less rapidly, arranged them. Presently, she looked up, smiling as to herself, saying, casually, "Very good"; then emphatically, "Very good!" She took the sheets, folded them, and put them into the handbag.

She rose from the desk and sat deeply into the cushioned red leather chair, relaxed, smiling as at something pleasantly remembered, tilting her face and changing its angle with that of its green frame.

She was disinclined to talk about the press harassment, but talked with intensity about going to the Negro worker's natural habitat. Incredibly, I listened, restraining an impassioned protest: let her begin considering the Negro's interest if she didn't consider her own. Her going into the Deep South as she had gone into Harlem, I wanted to say, would end tragically for Negroes and for her. I believed she was talking for its effect on me and that she had no intention of going South.

She said something about *Negro* (the anthology) as being a better title than *Color,* and, incongruously across the back of my mind flitted the half-formed idea that if the anthology, whatever she named it, was to be filled with stuff as hastily written and as carelessly read and accepted by its editor as mine had been, I'd have scant respect for it and less for its editor.

It would have been too easy at that moment to criticize her; and, more consciously than not, perhaps, I for that reason did not speak my opinion. I have ever since been glad that I did not.

No newspaper the next day mentioned her coming to Chambers Street. With the connivance of friends she had momentarily eluded the New York press. Wolfishly vicious in its competition for news susceptive to mischievous interpretation, the papers knew of her trip only as it ended. The New York *World Telegram* (May 21), a few days after she had left that city unrecognized by reporters, stated that Nancy Cunard had "returned from a weekend trip to Boston" and to the Grampion Hotel in Harlem. As a hoodwinked reporter remains unforgiven by his boss, the hoodwinker seldom escapes the reporter's retaliation: Miss Cunard, the *World Telegram* wrote, was "an extremely slim woman with generous use of makeup, wearing a black leather jacket, a dark dress, a tight-fitting green hat and two dozen of her collection of 402 ivory bracelets."

The *Boston Post,* having been scooped on its own beat, had staggered out of its shock by Sunday, though the best it could do was a fabricated innuendo-allegation of a police search for "one Ansel Collbrooke, colored," supposed to have "deserted his white wife and six children" at about the time Nancy Cunard was ending her "weekend." The *Post* hinted at "Collbrooke's" taking a trip with Miss Cunard to Jamaica, "said to be" his birthplace.

The Negro press' motive in pursuing the Boston fabrication was different from the daily press': the Baltimore *Afro-American,* the New York *Amsterdam News,* the Chicago *Defender* and the Philadelphia *Tribune,* lacking such facilities as enabled the monopoly press immediately to make known the (frequently dreamed-up) new or unusual, often reflected in their stories, rewritten from the enemy dailies, the whites' prejudice. The reason sometimes lay in a shortage of formally trained Negro journalists and sometimes in the "competitive system's" demands for "results" regardless of how obtained.

As in the July 16, 1932, Afro-American "Cunard-Collbrooke" story (rehashed from *Post* tidbits), results are sometimes crazy: the paper saw profit both in publicizing "Collbrooke" as possibly a criminal and in proving him to be a model of civic virtue. Its trouble lay in its ignorance of how to execute such a feat. Here is the *Afro's* two-faced performance:

Face One: Made up of gossip and innuendo.

"Miss Nancy Cunard made the front page again this week when she was discovered boarding the S.S. Orizba, Wednesday, July 6, with a man who registered (as) Anselmn A. Collbrooke, for Havana, Cuba.

"The Boston police would like to see Mr. Collbrooke about the stolen car of a Mrs. Meta P. Lewis. He apparently drove her Oldsmobile to New York and changed the license plates without her consent or knowledge."

Having detailed several nasty allegations, the *Afro-American* breaks off that section of the story and, in the same breath but in an accusative tone, performs with the following:

Face Two: Presumably its own.

"Mrs. Collbrooke has told inquirers that her husband has gone to Havana on business. The condition of the family has improved since Collbrooke, a man of education and a former Elk exalted ruler, secured employment with Miss Cunard. He has paid off the mortgage on his home and made arrangements to send his wife an adequate weekly sum while he is serving Miss Cunard.

"The fact of Collbrooke's employment and of his care for his family is suppressed by the white newspapers because of the desire to use him to humiliate the white Englishwoman."

The *Afro* was lucky that the second part of its name was *American* and not Englishman, or it may have shared the misfortune which overtook British Allied Newspapers, Ltd., when in the King's Bench Division of the High Court of Justice, on July 14, 1934, a settlement was announced of three actions which Miss Cunard claimed from it and from the proprietors of *The Empire News, The Sunday Chronicle,* and *The Daily Dispatch* damages for libels published in those papers.

Scurrilities of the type published by those English newspapers and their counterparts here compelled me to begin seeking the truth about this woman who, lied about or not, was more than commonly remarkable. Previously, I must say (and this despite our correspondence), I had been altogether indifferent to what she was doing or to what was being done to her. I now dug out "Black Man and White Ladyship," in its envelope since she dispatched it to me months previously. Reading it for the first time, I saw sharply the reason for her having been stigmatized as a shameless renegade years before her visit to Harlem.

There began to happen to me what might have happened before Nancy Cunard came to Chambers Street. I was determined later to defend her wherever I was when she was attacked. I determined, above all—when I had examined *Negro*—to honor her by using its accumulated riches in talks and in classes relating to that part of United States history which had been ripped out of its context and discarded.

Four-thirty seemed delayed beyond all sense on the afternoon *Negro* was delivered at the *Post*. Finally, at home, I tore the eight pound volume from its wrappings: NEGRO in bold red letters strolled from the upper left corner diagonally across the cloth bound cover. I had little appetite that evening for anything else, leaning over the book on my desk much as Nancy two years before sat reading "Blacks Turn Red," I learned from her starkly but eloquently written Foreword her answer to the first question I would have asked: Why did you begin this prodigious task? Because "It was necessary to make this book—and, I think, in this manner (an anthology of some 150 voices of both races)—for the recording of the struggles and achievements, the persecutions and the revolts against them, of the Negro peoples." But why was it necessary? Her answer emerged as I read in turn her contributions, beginning with the Foreword: "Harlem Reviewed"; "A Reactionary Negro Organization"; "The American Moron and the American of Sense"; Scottsboro and other Scottsboros"; "Southern Sheriff"; "Jamaica, the Negro Island"; "Colour Bar."

In "Harlem Reviewed" she saw that Negro "capital" totally, and afoot, its "ghetto-like slums" around Fifth Avenue; the "bourgeois street, residential areas, a few aristocratic avenues or section thereof . . ." The Negro population in Harlem, wrote Miss Cunard, "is always increasing but the houses do not expand"—nor do traditional ghetto walls—"hence overcrowding in all but the expensive middle-class lodgings."

My unexpressed criticism of Nancy Cunard's wish to go South is proved by her book to have been unjustified. She should begin thinking of the Negro's interests, I said to myself that night on Chambers Street. Her past and continuing proof of concern for the Negro people —always ahead of concern for herself—entitled her to first place among investigators who ought to go into the Deep South. But if she had gone she would have suffered perhaps a more horrible death than Mrs. Viola Liuzzo in Alabama 33 years later.

As I wished I had asked Nancy why she allowed "The Colored Girls of Passenack" (by William Carlos Williams) in the anthology, I wish I had found a way to tell her that I didn't fully agree with her criticism of the NAACP and W. E. B. DuBois. Though the NAACP leadership, both nationally and locally, was reactionary, individual members of the leadership getting their salaries from the men whom the rank-and-file (and the leadership, too) knew belonged to the oppressing class, there were both among leadership and rank-and-file those men and women who wanted to plunge ahead. W. E. B. DuBois was among such men, though he was not ready to plunge quite so fast and in the direction Miss Cunard in 1932 was pointing. He did, later, and was heroic in meeting the test of his convictions. Negro organizations in the United States in the very nature of their compositions cannot be totally reactionary. The NAACP today, of course, owing to its rank-and-filers, is certainly not reactionary.

I recall chiding Nancy in Moscow for saying in *Negro* that the Negro press was his worst enemy. I knew she had written it in passion, so tried not to be rough. But her voice was sharp when she demanded my reason for disagreeing. My explanation was this: when I say the Negro's press is his worst enemy I'm saying his lesser enemy is his oppressor. But his oppressor is the cause of the Negro newspapers' behaving as they do—even to imitating the enemy papers' methods. Well, is the slave worse than the master? She thought a while. She murmured what sounded like "Touché."

When I next saw Nancy (and for the last time) I had been in the Soviet Union about a year, having left the *Post* on May 1, 1935. I knew she was coming, on her way to Spain, but I didn't know precisely when she would arrive. So her showing up at the *Moscow Daily News,* where we from New York and our colleagues from London worked, hoping to learn Russian quickly, and where Soviet citizens worked in order to learn English, I was only one among a crowd that greeted her. She had come directly from France, where she seemed never to cease being grateful to the English (small e) Channel for keeping so much distance between her and Her Ladyship. Members of our staff from London all knew and liked her.

She and I sat in the dining room over glasses of tea, she asking again questions first put to me in her answer to my letter of thanks for my copy of *Negro.*

The time of year was somewhat later than May, the third anniversary of our first meeting. The only detail I remember of Nancy's dress is the green hat. (I had intended the next time to ask her opinions of Iris March Storm and Lucy Tantamount. Which did she prefer? Again, I remembered when too late.) It could have been her mood of detachment, a looking in an entirely new direction—the prolonged silence; an occasional hint of a shrug; green eyes, if like stones, veiled in mist. And when, sitting there, she asked again what had happened to Colebrooke, I could at least divert her for a moment with the news that some Negro papers, just before I left Boston, had allegedly turned up two other men with the same name, each spelling it Collbrooke. We agreed the papers, probably frightened at her successful suit against the London scandal sheets, were thinking about a possible "alibi."

lawrence gellert
Remembering Nancy Cunard

Dear Nancy,

I've just learned that a group of your friends from the whole world around are gathering together their recollections of you under one cover and I am hastening to join them. And I hope to be not too late for the rendezvous. While I would attend as a mourner with the rest, knowing you I'm sure that you would not want us to confine the occasion to one of sorrow and mourning your departure. Rather you would like us to give thanks to whatever Gods may be for the wonderful talents you were endowed with at birth, the long span allotted to you here on earth together with the means and opportunity for a most useful and rewarding lifetime, which you lived to its utmost capacity.

I remember you relating how you discovered injustice, or what seemed like injustice to a four-year-old child in that plush, sheltered English countryside home where you grew up with Iris Tree and Lady Diana Manners, as playmates. How one day the gardener when bringing the usual daily bouquet of fresh flowers for your child's room was questioned by you—whether he had a little daughter like yourself. And he said yes, and she was about the same age. And you wanted to know whether he brought her flowers every morning also. He shook his head. No, of course not. Why not, the little inquisitor wanted to know. The gardener explained that since the garden belonged to your father, if he took them for his daughter he could be arrested for stealing. And that seemed monstrous and stupid and a lot of other thoughts the four-year-old child could muster no words for as yet.

I remember when you came to America seeking out the people who were to contribute to the anthology *Negro,* which has since become a landmark in Negro culture, how the elevator operator at the Theresa Hotel in Harlem, where you had registered, was bribed to lie to newspaper men that you shared communicating rooms with the great Negro singer Paul Robeson, and how the yellow press blazoned and strewed the slander across the land in bold headlines—"Nancy Cunard and her black lover in Harlem." Reporters actually rented apartments across the street with a view of your window and took pictures with telescopic lenses of everyone that went in and out. I remember the daily stint of vile racist letters, and how you scolded me because in the sorting of them you caught me hiding the most scurrilous to save your feelings. You admonished me: "I'm used to it from home; we have suffered from it too in Merry England; the color bar they call it over there. The hatred with the English is a bit more subtle but just as vicious. I'll give you a pamphlet I wrote on an anniversary called 'Black Man and White Ladyship,' she's my mother. She has been persecuting me for my interest in the Negro race and she has had influence enough to keep me out of some countries, through the embassy officials and as likely as not by her characterization of me as a 'nigger lover,' which was leaked to the press here by the British Embassy at her urging and behest. Remember she was an American originally and came from Virginia and has never relinquished the southern attitude toward 'niggers.' "

I remember borrowing keys from a friend of mine for his Dutchess County farm, where we took you to escape further persecution. Up at that lovely place lilacs were just coming into bloom and you became even as a child again, with the long arm of hatred and persecution that reached beyond the sea after you forgotten. Your cooking, my dear, was horrid. But you were too busy to pay attention to details. You were busy writing, writing, writing, endlessly corresponding with half the world it seems. I still remember the beverage you brewed. You added coffee one day, water the next, coffee the next, and so on for weeks on end. But I didn't complain. Your work was all consuming and important.

I remember walking into a little country store with you and the proprietor was too busy to wait on us. His nose was pressed into a newspaper with a headline spread across the front sheet: "Nancy Cunard Disappears from Harlem." Fortunately, the country bumpkin didn't recognize you, and we fled for safety before he even looked up. How you laughed.

I remember how one day you shook yourself, explained it was time to get back to work, as though ten hours a day at the typewriter was mere play and vacation time, and so we locked up the farm and sped back to New York, to pick up various contributions for *Negro* that you had been corresponding about during the weeks on the farm, and to see a lawyer about a law suit against the press for slander, particularly the *Daily News*. But since you were advised it would be necessary to stick around for trial dates, you decided against it finally. And then we traveled on to contact and collect from more writers, both Negro and white, the poems, articles, pictures that were to be parts of the work. I remember we took the Fall River Line boat and stayed on deck all night watching the stars while you unfolded to me the dream you had about the book and the hope that it would contribute to that distant day of Negro liberation. We arrived in Boston. I remember Sterling Brown walking with us on Boston Common and writing a poem about the three of us at the cradle of American independence— an English lady, a Hungarian immigrant's son, and a descendent of slaves, the three of us strangely met with and with one and the same objective toward which we were pushing: the full equality of the black race. Other places and people we visited too, in Washington and Philadelphia, and everywhere Nancy you were gathering your material.

I remember when our funds became exhausted, and we tried to peddle (unsuccessfully) a Manet painting left you by George Moore, the special friend of your family, and when we could not sell the painting and the Scottsboro case needed money urgently you gave me a gold cigaret case which had been presented to you by the Prince of Wales, crest and all, and I took it to Ladine Young, wife of Walter Duranty, who advised me to take it to her husband for all the money I could shake out of him, and he would give it to her and she, in turn, would return it to us for auction so that there might be additional money for the Scottsboro Defense Committee. It turned out exactly as Ladine planned it.

I remember another time you came to America. It was during the second world war and you wired me. They would not let you off the ship at Gowanus Canal, Brooklyn, not even to let you replace a few necessary items you had run out of during your voyage and incarceration. And when I came to see you and accompanied you with the authorities that took you to Ellis Island for deportation because of "moral turpitude," a most dangerous alien, you discovered a Chinese there, also being held for deportation, he to Chiang Kai-shek's China where he faced the loss of his head. You enlisted my aid not in your own behalf, but rather you said I should see to it that the Chinese, who had written a radical book called *Hanging on Union Square,* was permitted to remain in this country. Through your influence and industry, even though in custody on the Island, forces were mobilized which eventually had Congress pass a special law to permit the Chinese (I forget his name) to stay here.

But I must not forget I'm not alone remembering. You touched other lives in your activities, in many other fields and they too are here to testify to your unstinted energy and devotion. So, for me, it remains merely to pledge that their work in which your anthology *Negro* stands as your monument, a legacy and landmark to the race, will go on with your inspiration. Farewell, dear Nancy . . . and salud.

georges sadoul

"The Fighting Lady"

S'il y eut jamais, dans ce siècle, une Lady, une grande dame dans le vrai sens du terme, par son intelligence, sa culture universelle, son courage, son désintéressement, ce fut Nancy Cunard.

Je la rencontrai pour la première fois à la fin de 1925 ou au début de 1926 à Paris, Place Blanche, au Café Cyrano qui est comme une dépendance du Moulin Rouge et où les surréalistes se donnaient alors rendez-vous deux fois par jour, à l'heure de l'apéritif. Il y avait là Louis Aragon, André Breton, Paul Eluard, Benjamin Péret, René Crevel, Max Ernst, Philippe Soupault, etc. L'allure de Nancy frappait et retenait. On voyait d'abord ses yeux très bleus, assez étranges, son visage fin et osseux, la crinière léonine de ses fins cheveux blonds, puis on s'étonnait de voir ses bras minces recouverts, des poignets aux épaules, par des bracelets africains en ivoire, dont elle avait la passion.

Je ne la vis alors que de loin, sans échanger avec elle plus de quelques paroles, et je n'eus pas l'occasion de fréquenter son bel appartement de l'Île Saint-Louis, au coin de la rue Le Regrattier et du Quai d'Orléans. Elle y vivait assez peu. Elle courait l'Europe. Ces années 1925–1927 elle séjourna certes à Londres, sa ville natale, mais elle visita aussi les Pays-Bas, l'Espagne, l'Italie, en compagnie de Louis Aragon. Dans tous ces pays elle visitait les musées, s'intéressait aux arts "classiques", aux "arts nègres" et se passionnait davantage encore pour le spectacle de la rue, pour la vie quotidienne, pour les gens.

En 1927, elle abandonna son appartement parisien pour Puits Carré, une maison de paysans achetée et aménagée par elle en Normandie à la Chapelle Réanville, non loin de Vernon, sur un plateau entre la Seine et l'Eure. A une extrémité de cette maison longue et basse la chambre à coucher, à l'autre un grand salon, avec les précieux meubles anciens hérités de son père, et une baie dont la glace encadrait un paysage paysan digne de Corot. Elle avait fait dégager, dans sa chambre, les jaunes pierres calcaires des murs. En bas d'un escalier menant au premier étage se trouvaient, singuliers balcons au ras du sol, deux meubles en fer à cheval, sur les barreaux horizontaux desquels étaient enfilés ses bracelets d'ivoire africains cinq ou six cents, un millier peut-être, certains larges comme des manchettes, d'autres plus étroits, sculptés de figures humaines et d'animaux sauvages. Près de sa chambre à coucher une salle à manger verte entourée de meubles bas où étaient posés des tableaux signés, Chirico, Georges Malkine, Picasso, Yves Tanguy, et pas mal d'idoles africaines.

Dans une dépendance près de l'entrée de Puits Carré, Nancy Cunard installa au printemps de 1928 une presse Mathieu fabriquée en Belgique au début de XIXe siècle, d'un pur style "Empire" et tout un stock de beaux caractères anciens "Caslon" et "Garamond". La première impression de cette presse me paraît avoir été au début de 1926 une très mince brochure en français de 8 pages sous couverture de bristol violet tirée à 25 exemplaires que Nancy Cunard n'a pas fait figurer dans son catalogue de la Hours Press sans doute parce qu'elle ne portait ni ce label, ni aucun achevé d'imprimer. *Voyageur par l'auteur de "Voyages"* contenait seulement quatre vers, plus tard reproduit dans *La Grande Gaité "L'auteur de Voyages"*, Louis Aragon avait avec Nancy Cunard composé ce petit texte, tiré ensuite par eux sur la presse à bras de Réanville. Après cette initiation à l'art de l'imprimerie, elle prit comme collaborateur un typographe professionnel Maurice Lévy. Avec son aide elle imprima à Réanville huit livres, dont *La Chasse au Snark* de Lewis Carroll traduit pour la première fois en français par Louis Aragon qui avait rédigé son texte, très remarquable, en trois jours, et qui tint à composer lui-même, avec le plus grand raffinement typographique, sa page de couverture et de titre.

Sauf cette exception française l'*Hours Press* s'était vouée à la publication de textes anglais, sur beau papier, à tirage très limité, comme le faisait à Londres l'Hogarth Press, de deux de ses amis, Leonard et Virginia Woolf qui avaient édité en 1925 son poème *Parallax*. Mais à cette époque de romantisme révolutionnaire, où la menace d'un coup d'état fasciste n'était pas imaginaire en France, Nancy Cunard pensait aussi qu'un jour sa Press de Réanville pourrait servir à des publications illégales antifascistes. Elle était prête à se mettre à la disposition d'organisations clandestines. Cette déclaration d'intention me surprit, venant d'une dame anglaise si noble et si riche. J'en attribuais le mérite au seul Aragon. J'avais tort. La suite de la vie de Nancy me le prouva.

Il me faut bien parler de leur rupture puisque franchissant le "mur de la vie privée", leur vie commune et leur séparation a fourni leur matière à quelques uns des plus beaux poèmes de *Roman Inachevé*. Je retrouvai Aragon à Paris en septembre 1928, désemparé, désespéré, hanté par l'idée du suicide, vagabondant d'hôtel meublé en hôtel meublé. Il vint alors habiter chez moi, 54 rue du Chateau, dans une petite maison du XIVe arrondissement de Paris, qui avait été celle de Jacques Prévert, Yves Tanguy et Marcel Duhamel. C'est là qu'il s'unit à Elsa Triolet et que commença, après un dramatique passage, la deuxième époque de sa vie.

Je devins alors l'intime d'Aragon et Nancy, de lui séparée. Elle vivait alors avec Henry Crowder, un athlétique pianiste noir américain rencontré à Venise, dont elle devait publier un recueil de chansons, *Henry-Music,* illustré en couverture d'un très beau photomontage de Man Ray; Crowder ayant sur ses épaules les bras de Nancy, entièrement recouverts de ses bracelets africains. J'étais alors secrétaire de Gaston Gallimard et lecteur aux Editions de la NRF. Fin 1929 je perdis brusquement cet emploi, et me trouvai dans une situation d'autant plus difficile que, poursuivi devant les tribunaux, pour avoir écrit une lettre d'injures à l'élève reçu premier à l'Ecole Militaire de Saint-Cyr, je m'imaginais poursuivi et traqué par la police, surtout quand j'eus été condamné à trois mois de prison avec sursis.

C'est alors que Nancy Cunard m'engagea pour travailler avec elle à l'Hours Press qui, abandonnant Réanville, vint s'établir à Paris, 15 rue Guénégaud, tout près de la Seine, rive gauche, en face de l'Hôtel des Monnaies, dans une petite librairie achetée au poète vénézuélien d'expression française Gattegne, auteur notamment d'*Orenoque.* Il y eut en devanture quelques livres et des objets nègres et dans la vaste arrière-boutique, la vieille presse, et une plus moderne "Minerve" à pédale. Nancy Cunard engagea comme typographe un ouvrier nommé Rigaud, nom qui la frappa beaucoup car elle avait beaucoup connu le dadaiste surréaliste Jacques Rigaud, qui venait de se suicider, et qui inspira à Drieu La Rochelle deux nouvelles célèbres: *La Valise Vide* et *Le Feu Follet.*

Je fus un bien mauvais collaborateur pour l'Hours Press, tout préoccupé que j'étais par "l'affaire de Saint-Cyr" et handicapé par ma quasi impossibilité de tenir une conversation en anglais, comme par une optique limitant mon horizon aux seuls surréalistes français. Je prêtais peu d'attention aux "amis de Nancy", à ces écrivains et artistes qui passaient très souvent rue Guénégaud. Sans doute fus-je très impressionné le jour où je serrais la main de James Joyce, ayant été dans mon adolescence fasciné par *Dubliners* et *Dedalus,* mais c'est avec trente ans de retard que j'ai compris avoir rencontré alors le dessinateur Len Lye, qui peu après renouvela de façon stupéfiante l'art de l'animation cinématographique par *Rainbow Dance* notamment; ou Samuel Beckett, qui écrivit une chanson pour Henry Crowder, et se trouva plus tard traduire—entre autres—un des mes articles en anglais. Sans parler de cet homme étrange et contradictoire, Ezra Pound, dont l'Hours Press publia pour la première fois en volume les fameux *Cantos.*

En septembre 1930, me croyant plus que jamais poursuivi par la police, je quittai Paris pour aller me réfugier à l'étranger, et passai la frontière d'une façon fort simple, mais que j'imaginais illégale, pour aller à Moscou retrouver Elsa Triolet et Louis Aragon. Revenu de là-bas malade, bouleversé par la mort de mon père et notre différent avec nos amis surréalistes, j'allais pour quelques mois m'établir et me rétablir en Suisse jusqu'au printemps de 1931 où Nancy me demanda d'aller la rejoindre à Cagnes, près de Nice, sur la Côte d'Azur.

Elle songeait à liquider l'Hours Press, elle avait rompu avec Henry Crowder, elle vivait alors avec mon ami Raymond Michelet, plus jeune qu'elle, avec qui elle commençait de préparer un ouvrage monumental *Negro*. Nous déjeunions habituellement tous les trois à la terrasse d'un petit restaurant, proche du château Grimaldi, d'où nous nous découvrions vers Vence, le superbe paysage des montagnes provençales. C'est là que nous avons appris et commenté les nouvelles venues d'Espagne; le roi renversé, les soulèvements populaires, les églises brûlées . . . A travers Nancy je fus quelque peu initié à la lutte menée par les noirs des U.S.A. pour l'égalité raciale, à l'action de la N.A.A.C.P., au combat mené par le Dr DuBois, à ce qu'on appelait *Black Belt* et *Dixie Line*. Tandis qu'elle vendait les équipements de l'Hours Press à Guy Lewis Mano, dont les éditions poétiques G.L.M. tinrent, durant les années 1930 un rôle éminent, je fus très désolé par la rupture avec les surréalistes, un long séjour en U.R.S.S., puis en Espagne avec ma première femme Nora. La crise économique était très grave alors en France, et les chômeurs nombreux. Nous vivions difficilement et je n'avais pu trouver que par intermittence des emplois temporaires quand, au printemps de 1935, Nancy nous offrit de nous héberger ma femme et moi pour quelques mois à Réanville, que je quittais seulement un jour par semaine pour aller à Paris faire quelques menus travaux de journalisme.

Nancy Cunard n'était plus elle-même dans une situation très aisée. Elle n'avait plus comme jadis de chauffeur, de cuisinière, de femme de chambre, de gardiens. Elle se préparait à vendre les meubles précieux hérités de son père. Elle avait en 1930 rompu de façon éclatante avec Lady Cunard, sa mère ayant été scandalisée de la voir vivre ouvertement, à Londres, avec le noir américain Henry Crowder. Il m'arrivait de me perdre dans la nuit en parcourant à pied les quelques 12 kilomètres nous séparant de la gare de Vernon, pour retrouver cette maison solitaire, assez étrange, d'autant plus que Nora, ma femme, y sombrait parfois dans un demi délire. Mais la gentillesse et la noblesse naturelle de Nancy Cunard y faisait régner un inimitable climat. Elle vivait alors seule à Réanville, s'étant séparée de Michelet après qu'ils aient terminé la rédaction de *Negro* qui avait été plus qu'une anthologie, une véritable encyclopédie de la question nègre, telle qu'elle se posait dans le monde entier au début des années 1930. D'autres sont plus qualifiés que moi pour dire l'importance capitale de ce recueil, auquel j'ai eu l'honneur de collaborer, avec plusieurs de mes amis français surréalistes ou non.

Vint alors la guerre d'Espagne, qui marqua en Europe le début de la deuxième guerre mondiale, l'affrontement des fascistes et des anti-fascistes. Nancy Cunard prit naturellement le parti des républicains, et fut à Madrid celle qui devait publier en 1950 un recueil de poèmes écrits par elle directement en français *Nous Gens d'Espagne,* se comptant désormais comme l'une d'entre eux, comme une parmi tous ceux qui, levés avant le jour, combattirent dès 1936 pour la liberté du monde. La "Lady" qui durant les années 1920 avait couru le monde était devenue à Harlem et à Madrid une "fighting lady".

Pour mieux définir ce qu'elle était devenue, dans le courant des années trente, et ce qu'elle resta jusqu'à sa mort, le mieux me parait être de reproduire son autobiographie, le portrait de l'artiste par elle-même qu'elle publia en 1947 dans l'édition française du recueil *Poèmes à la France.*

"Cunard Nancy—Que vois dire de moi-même? J'aime la paix, la campagne, l'Espagne républicaine et l'Italie antifasciste, les Noirs, leur culture africaine et afro-américaine, toute l'Amérique latine que je connais, la musique, la peinture, la poésie et le journalisme. J'ai toujours vécu en France depuis que j'en ai eu la possibilité, en 1920.

"Je hais: le fascisme parmi toutes les nationalités également. Et le snobisme et tout ce qui va avec. Deux oeuvres: *Negro,* grande anthologie sur les Noirs. *Authors Take Sides,* enquête adressée aux écrivains britanniques au sujet de la guerre d'Espagne et du Fascisme. Plusieurs volumes de poèmes."

Il n'y eut qu'une brève trève entre la fin de la guerre espagnole et le début de la "Drôle de guerre" en Europe. Ces six mois, Nancy Cunard les occupa surtout à des démarches pour essayer de faire libérer ses amis républicains espagnols internés par le gouvernement français dans des camps, sitôt après que la victoire de fascistes alliés à Hitler ait obligé à passer les cols des Pyrénées. Quand la guerre eut été déclarée à l'Allemagne fasciste les portes des camps ne s'ouvrirent pas pour autant, car la propagande officielle française accusa allors ceux qui, Espagnols ou Français, avaient combattu Hitler et ses alliés, d'être devenus les complices et les agents d'Hitler. Elle fut terrible pour beau-coup la grande nuit de la "Drôle de guerre" où les soldats français avaient reçu l'interdiction de tirer un seul coup de fusil sur les Hit-lériens, de l'autre côté du Rhin. J'ai retrouvé une lettre de Nancy, écrite au début de cette dure période, et qui décrit, à mots couverts, ce qu'était alors le climat français. Elle vivait alors à la Chapelle Réan-ville d'où elle continuait d'envoyer des articles à divers journaux anglais.

"Je suis ici depuis le premier août, date à laquelle j'ai ramené avec moi de Perpignan un ami espagnol que j'ai retrouvé par le plus grand des hasards dans un des camps. Et depuis un autre qui est le frère d'un des premiers d'ici, et que j'adore aussi. De temps en temps, je vais à Paris porter des articles à la Censure(!) quand je ne fais pas à la Censure d'Evreux (autres!!! Je trouve ces capitaines très gentils, quoiqu'ils coupent constam-ment des petites choses que j'ai prises dans la presse française.

. . . Je trouve Paris morose, pour ne pas dire plus. Je n'y vais que pour la Censure. TOUS nos amis partis, ou introuvables. Oui, Tristan (Tzara) que j'ai réussi à voir voici dix jours, en vitesse, m'a dit que Louis (Aragon) se trouve bien. J'en suis fort heureuse. A plusieurs reprises j'ai tâché de le voir après le 1er septembre, mais il devait déjà être parti. Je l'avais vu pour-tant (Louis) les derniers jours d'août. Quelles choses que toutes celles-là. Tzara m'a dit qu'il s'était fait inscrire comme volontaire.

. . . Je serais probablement allée en Angleterre, mais sans grand intérêt. Très contente de ne *PAS* être partie pour le Mexique (*avec les réfugiés espagnols* GS). Ce sont les Mexicains par leurs inconcevables lenteurs, mauvais vouloir et autres turpitudes qui m'en ont enlevé toute envie. Des trois des "miens" au Mexique je reçois de temps en temps des nouvelles; un s'est trouvé la possibilité de faire une maison d'éditions. Ce "mien" des miens a trouvé après des semaines de peines un emploi comme marchand de poissons! Non ce pays-là ce serait bien pour flâner, mais pour accomplir un travail sérieux pour moi veux-je dire . . . non, non, non.

"Le tout c'est de savoir ce que je peux faire de mieux pour la défense, pour y participer. Eussé-je été seule ici, quand tout commença que je n'y serais pas restée plus d'une heure. J'étais à Paris, le 1er Septembre cher-chant fièvreusement un emploi de presse, de reporter "au front" ou près du front. Ou je me serais engagée dans une chose militaire quelconque. Mais voilà. Les journalistes vont au front différemment que dans tel autre pays.

. . . De Perpignan, Maison des Intellectuels, aucune nouvelle depuis le début. Je me demande ce qui se passe avec ces 14 qui y restaient. L'argent a complètement tari, alors? Le Comité Britannique y fonctionne toujours. Pas vu Pablo Neruda. Ni vu les Alberti. (Le poète espagnol Rafael Alberti, et sa femme Marca Teresa Leon, après avoir quitté Madrid, peu avant la prise de la ville, dans un des derniers avions, habitèrent quelques mois chez moi, à Paris, puis partirent au début de la guerre pour l'Amérique latine.) Vicens (Ami espagnol de Garcia Lorca et de Bunuel, mort en exil vers 1957) m'a écrit qu'il ne savait ce qu'il ferait. Un des miens est 27 fois blessé et pour ce, réformé, ou le serait a vue. Insondable avenir. . . . Mais je voudràis, je devrais avoir un travail plus actif et plus utile. Quant au *Manchester Guardian,* ayant travaillé pour ce sacré journal, le meilleur qu'il y ait en Angleterre, pendant des mois, surtout au moment de l'exode catalan, et ayant reçu des masses de lettres, toutes pleines de compliments des lecteurs, et ayant réussi à faire imprimer par ce journal des appels, etc. Qui ont rapporté beaucoup d'argent, beaucoup bon en réponse simplement: "Rien, Nous ne pouvons, etc., etc."

. . . Je n'ai de nouvelle de presque personne. J'ai écrit, je m'aperçois, mon poème annuel, inspiré par la voix d'Hitler à la radio, et que je t'enverrai puisque tu lis l'anglais. Ah oui la Radio, nous en avons loué une et j'adore ça: toute la musique qui en sort avec tous ces bruits qui explosent, et les voix d'hommes d'état à 3 heures du matin. Régime d'hiver; feux de bois humide, fumées, poêles revêches, pluies, des fois peu de soleil, calme, plutôt peu d'alcools que beaucoup.

. . . Que de fois je pense à cette magnifique lettre de toi qui n'était vu dans le noir de la nuit avec ses chandelles dans le village de Creysse, où tu m'avais fait mon horoscope: "caractère violent, dépenses folles." Et tout ça s'incorporant dans la vie quotidienne avec Henry Crowder au piano qui nous avait apporté des boeufs, Henry composant ces musiques si modernes et si rares, entouré de villageois, des oies et des seaux d'eau qu'il nous fallait chercher tous les jours.

Tu parles c'est bien cette France-là que j'adore. C'est ce Front-là qu'il faut sauver. On le sauvera."

C'était le temps où l'on parlait de pendre son linge sur la Ligne Sieg-fried. Et les radios françaises diffusaient cette chanson plus optimiste encore. "Viens Hitler sur la Ligne Maginot. Nos petits gars ils t'attendent là-haut. Si jamais le temps te presse. Ils te botteront les fesses . . ."

Le front qu'il fallait sauver devint le front intérieur, après que la débâcle eut amené sur les Pyrénées—ou dans les Stalags—les petits gars de la ligne Maginot. Nancy Cunard avait quitté à temps, j'ai oublié comment, Réanville pour Londres. Bientôt parvinrent en Angleterre les poèmes de Résistance par ses amis Aragon, Eluard et d'autres qu'elles ne connaissaient pas ou dont elle ne put percer le pseudonyme. Nancy contribua à les faire connaitre et traduire, à les défendre aussi contre les attaques de certains français réfugiés à Londres. Elle publia en 1944 aux éditions de la *France Libre* un recueil de *Poems for France* dédié au pays alors occupé et à sa Résistance.

Ce fut quelques semaines seulement après la Libération que je la retrouvai, à la fin de l'été 1944 à Toulouse, où se trouvaient alors ses amis Tristan Tzara et Léon Moussinac. C'étaient surtout les Pyrénées qui l'avaient attirée dans le sud-ouest français. Elle croyait, comme nous tous alors, que le régime de France ne survivrait pas à celui d'Hitler. Elle voulait être la première à assister à la libération de l'Espagne qu'elle avait été l'une des dernières à quitter, lors de la défaite républicaine. Ce fut sans doute une des raisons pour lesquelles elle quitta Réanville. Sa petite propriété normande avait été occupée par les allemands, qui l'avaient mise au pillage malgré les efforts de vieux amis, les Goasguëns, propriétaires du bistro voisin. Le mobilier avait été brûlé, avec beaucoup de livres, et de précieuses sculptures africaines. Il ne restait plus grand chose de sa collection de bracelets en ivoire, ni de ses précieux tableaux. Le Puits Carré avait été comblé avec des détritus où se mêlaient quelques sculptures nègres et des bracelets. Ils avaient disparus avec des papiers personnels et certaines choses auxquelles Nancy tenait beaucoup, deux albums des gravures originales d'Hogarth, un album de coupures de presse tenu depuis son adolescence. Il n'y avait plus une fenêtre à la maison. Elle n'avait pas les moyens matériels de réédifier ce qu'avait été Puits Carré. Elle vendit sa petite propriété pour pouvoir acheter non loin de Souillac et de Creysse Presmartel, La Mothe Fénelon, une autre maison de paysans. Si les express de Toulouse passaient non loin de La Mothe ils ne s'y arrêtaient pas, et les communications n'étaient pas faciles avec ce pays perdu dans les splendides solitudes des Causses. Nancy venait de temps à autre à Paris, et descendait souvent chez nous. Mais nous ne sommes allés la voir qu'une seule fois, en 1958, en route vers les Pyrénées. Sa nouvelle maison était fort belle. Elle y avait recréé, en plus petit, ce qu'avait été Réanville. Au mur quelques tableaux sauvés du désastre. Le plus précieux, un Manet, ayant appartenu à George Moore et dont elle avait hérité de sa mère morte quelques années plus tôt, elle était obligée, par crainte d'un vol, de le garder enfermé dans un coffre à Souillac. Nous avons merveilleusement déjeuné chez l'aubergiste du pays en qui elle avait un ami très sûr. Nous ne l'avons pas quittée sans de grandes appréhensions. Elle avait largement dépassé la soixantaine et paraissait plus que son âge. Elle marchait avec beaucoup de peine. Et le chemin escarpé qui conduisait à sa petite maison était à peine carrossable. Elle n'avait pas d'auto, ni le téléphone; qu'un accident lui arrivât dans une maison bien difficile à atteindre, et à chauffer, ne risquait-elle pas de mourir seule, faute de soins? Ma femme voulut lui trouver quelqu'un qui s'occupât d'elle, ou la convaincre de vendre La Mothe pour acheter à Paris ou en banlieue un petit appartement où nous pourrions veiller sur elle. Nos efforts n'aboutirent pas. Notre inquiétude fut très grande quand nous avons appris qu'à la suite d'un scandale dans un pub londonien elle avait été internée dans un hôpital psychiatrique. Avec Aragon, qui lui conservait sa fidèle amitié, nous nous sommes demandés comment la tirer de là, n'ignorant pas que les lois coutumières anglaises sont bien sévères pour les "malades mentaux".

Il nous restait un espoir, son cousin Victor Cunard, qu'elle aimait et qui l'aimait bien. Elle avait passé plusieurs mois après la guerre dans son Palazzo de Venise qu'il habitait pendant la belle saison. Le Festival m'appelait professionnellement dans cette ville italienne. Je connaissais un peu le "cousin Victor" et j'avais l'adresse de son Palazzo. J'étais certain de le convaincre de tout faire pour tirer Nancy de ce mauvais pas.

Lorsque nous sommes arrivés ma femme et moi aux environs du Palazzo, nous avons demandé où il se trouvait exactement, à la première femme venue. Nous avons eu du flair. Elle faisait parfois des ménages pour le cousin Victor. Elle nous a désigné, à cent mètres de là, son Palazzo, et a aussitôt ajouté: "Vous venez sans doute pour l'enterrement, mais vous arrivez une heure en retard, le cortège est déjà parti". Deux jours plus tôt en effet, se trouvant à son balcon que la femme nous designa, Victor Cunard avait été pris d'un malaise, et avait presqu'aussitôt après rendu l'âme.

Cette mort subite nous bouleversa d'autant plus que nous avons alors désespéré de jamais revoir Nancy, faute d'une caution qui lui permit de quitter son hôpital. Elle en sortit pourtant, mais dans un bien mauvais état. Nous l'avons revue à Paris, puis à Saint Jean Cap Ferrat en 1964. Elle vivait alors chez des amis, dans une belle villa fleurie, ayant d'autant plus sagement renoncé à retourner à La Mothe Fénelon qu'elle avait eu, quelques mois plus tôt, un grave accident. Elle s'était appuyé sur un fauteuil qui avait basculé et une mauvaise chute lui avait vilainement brisé une jambe. Elle marchait avec beaucoup de peine, en s'appuyant aux meubles et sur les murs. Elle avait toujours été maigre. Elle était devenue squelettique. J'ai gardé en mémoire un "close-up" de ses deux mains où il n'y avait plus sur les os qu'une peau parcheminée. Et l'on ne voyait plus rien dans son visage que ses deux splendides yeux bleus. Elle se sentait très faible. Pour se remonter elle buvait un peu trop de rhum. Mais elle avait gardé tout son charme et sa resplendissante intelligence.

Au retour d'un long voyage en Inde et en Egypte au début de 1965, je trouvais dans une masse de courrier, une lettre de Nancy, datée du 12 février et où elle me demandait d'insister auprès d'un acheteur éventuel, pour que sa maison de La Mothe fut bientôt vendue. Elle ajoutait: "J'y laisserai *tout* hormis quelques livres, tous mes bracelets africains, tous mes albums et archives et quelques petits objets. Je viens de me casser le col du fémur, très gravement (accident avec le sol de la chambre ici). Opérée d'urgence à Nice, chirurgien merveilleux. Je passe sur tout le reste. J'écris tout le temps au lit évidemment. Masseuse tous les jours, pénible. Jambe droite à present incurvée. Passera peut-être un jour. Lequel? Mon livre sur l'Hours Press vient d'être accepté par l'Université du Southern Illinois. Première édition 10,000."

J'étais rentré du Caire dans les premiers jours de mars. Je voulus rencontrer l'acheteur éventuel de La Mothe, mais avant que j'ai pu le joindre au téléphone, ce fut Raymond Michelet qui m'appela le soir du 11 mars 1965 vers 8 heures. Nancy venait d'arriver chez lui dans un état terrible. Il avait besoin de notre aide. Nous avons aussitôt accouru, ma femme et moi, dans son petit appartment de banlieue. Un spectacle affreux nous attendait. Nancy Cunard avait perdu la raison et délirait. Elle était devenue plus maigre qu'un cadavre de Buchenwald. Elle ne pesait plus que 26 kilos. Avec son fémur brisé, elle ne pouvait plus se tenir debout. Etendue sur un divan, à demi-nue, elle parlait sans cesse. Comment était-elle arrivée chez Michelet? Deux heures auparavant, plus lucide elle lui avait expliqué qu'elle s'était brouillée avec ses amis du Cap Ferrat, qu'elle les avait brusquement quittés, elle s'était rendue à Nice, qu'on l'y avait arrêtée, conduite dans un commissariat de police, puis relâchée.

Comment avec sa jambe cassée avait-elle trouvé le moyen de prendre le train pour Paris? De se faire conduire alors à Orgeval chez des amies? D'y passer la nuit? D'arriver enfin chez Michelet? Une seule explication: sa formidable énergie avait su vaincre ses infirmités. Maintenant qu'elle était arrivée là, son esprit avait craqué, sa belle intelligence avait sombré, elle ne savait plus guère qu'injurier ses meilleurs amis présents et absents.

Elle avait pourtant retenu une chambre dans un petit hôtel du Quartier Latin, où elle descendait souvent et que fréquentaient beaucoup de ses vieux amis républicains espagnols. Nous avons tenu conseil, dans une chambre voisine, avec Michelet. Il ne pouvait l'héberger pour la nuit, moi non plus. Le mieux était de la loger à l'hôtel, car il était déjà près de minuit, et que nous ne pourrions avant le lendemain matin alerter des médecins et psychiatres.

Nous sommes partis, dans nos deux voitures pour le Quartier Latin. La chambre était bien retenue, au troisième nous dit le gardien de nuit qui connaissait un peu Nancy. L'hôtel n'avait pas d'ascenseur. Elle consentit à ce que Michelet et moi la soutenions jusqu'au bas de l'escalier, mais proclama son intention de le monter toute seule. Je restai près d'elle, mais elle m'interdit, sous la menace de coups, de lui donner la moindre aide, de la soutenir, de la toucher même. Et elle se mit à gravir, toute seule, l'escalier à reculons. Elle s'asseyait sur une marche, trouvait la force de se hisser sur une seconde, puis y demeurait le temps de reprendre ses forces et son souffle, dix longues minutes parfois. Cette lente ascension devait durer 90 minutes, deux heures peut-être, qui comptent parmi les plus longues de ma vie.

Je craignais que Nancy fut prise d'une crise violente, qu'on appelât la police, qu'on l'internat alors dans un asile dont nous n'aurions peut-être pu jamais la tirer. Fort heureusement son monologue n'avait plus le ton des invectives, mais d'une conversation presque mondaine. De temps à autre, des clients de l'hôtel montaient l'escalier, s'étonnaient de la voir assise sur les marches, avec sa toque et sa veste de léopard, ses bracelets d'ivoire. J'expliquai qu'elle était infirme et tenait à monter seule dans sa chambre. Ils passaient leur chemin. Parfois elle demandait aux passants par exemple s'ils connaissaient Pablo Neruda, et s'ils pensaient qu'il allait avoir le Prix Nobel.

Durant cette atroce et interminable "fin de partie", elle me parla surtout de Samuel Beckett, dont j'avais oublié qu'elle le connaissait. Etait-il à Paris? Pourrait-elle lui téléphoner? Viendrait-il la voir? Il avait beaucoup d'amitié pour elle. S'il avait reçu cette demande de rendez-vous, il se fut trouvé non en face de la Nancy Cunard qu'il avait connue, mais devant une de ses héroïnes qu'il montrait au théâtre, paralysées, enfouies dans le sable ou dans des urnes, revivant leur passe dans une série de phrases sans suite apparente. "Celle-là, avait dit Nancy parlant d'elle-même à la troisième personne, vient d'avoir aujourd'hui 69 ans, d'entrer dans sa 70ème année". Son jour anniversaire était depuis longtemps achevé, lorsque glissant assise sur le tapis du corridor, elle parvint enfin vers 2 heures du matin, le 12 mars, dans la petite chambre qu'elle avait louée. Elle refusa que je l'aide à monter sur son lit-divan. Nerveusement, à bout de forces, j'allais retrouver Michelet qui prit ma relève une demie-heure durant. Puis nous avons tenu conseil dans la rue déserte. Elle serait incapable de descendre l'escalier et de quitter sa chambre. Des ordres avaient été donnés pour qu'on lui apporta à manger qu'on ne lui donnat sous aucun prétexte de l'alcool. Elle n'avait pas un franc sur elle. Nous pourrions donc aviser, lui envoyer un médecin, lui éviter l'internement dans un asile psychiatrique, l'installer dans une clinique où elle serait bien soignée. Elle allait mieux d'ailleurs, elle était plus calme. Nous avions du temps devant nous. Elle pourrait passer quelques jours à l'hôtel, durant lesquels nous alerterions ses amis fidèles.

Je me laissais si bien tranquiliser, que je quittais Paris pour la banlieue, après avoir alerté un médecin, persuadé que Michelet, veillant attentivement sur elle, il n'y avait plus rien à craindre pour les jours à venir. Le repos lui ferait du bien. On pourrait alors la raisonner, la persuader dans deux ou trois jours, de sa propre volonté, d'entrer dans une clinique où elle se remettrait vite.

Mais dans la soirée plusieurs coups de téléphone me firent regretter, horriblement, mon départ. Dans la matinée elle avait reçu aimablement le médecin psychiatre. Il l'avait trouvée dans un tel état de délabrement physiologique qu'il n'avait pas voulu intervenir avant qu'on soignât son pitoyable corps. Elle avait aussitôt après son départ téléphoné à Michelet l'accusant violemment de lui avoir envoyé un "flic" camouflé en médecin et d'être lui-même un policier. Comme moi-même, et tous ses amis. Il accourut un peu plus tard à l'hôtel. Elle n'y était plus. Elle avait trouvé la force de descendre seule l'escalier et de prendre un taxi. Sitôt après son départ on s'aperçut qu'une épaisse fumée sortait de sa chambre. Avant de partir elle avait accumulé sur le tapis des papiers froissés et y avait mis le feu.

Où la retrouver? N'était-elle pas partie pour La Mothe, comme elle nous avais dit en avoir le projet? De retour à Paris nous avons réussi à nous procurer l'adresse de son ami l'aubergiste. Avec son incroyable énergie, elle avait peut-être trouvé la force de revenir dans sa maison solitaire. Nous allions appeler La Mothe Fénelon quand Michelet nous appela. Nancy était morte, le 15 mars 1965, à l'Hôpital Cochin. Comment y était-elle parvenue, nous ne l'avons jamais su, mais les infirmiers nous ont dit qu'elle s'était éteinte d'épuisement dans le calme le plus complet. Ce ne fut pas comme disent les gens "une belle mort", mais il y eut une terrifiante grandeur shakespearienne dans les derniers jours de cette prodigieuse "Fighting Lady", une femme d'exception, s'il en fut jamais.

louis aragon

"Nan"

I have tried and failed more than once to write a piece on Nancy. To reminisce about the old days and friends alive or dead is simply more than I can manage. And when I grope back to the Paris of the late twenties and early thirties I find so little that I might almost as well not have been there. But grand things still that make me glad I was, such as my meeting with Nancy and the long unchanging friendship it began. . . .

But with the passing time, the more I think of Nancy, the more I feel unable to write what I ought. I know how it will look, reading it. . . . I have too much to say and too much to conceal. And more: what I could write seems to me poor and weak, on account of what I feel. I pray you to understand that I cannot lie, and that all that I should write would sound to me like lies. It is just forty years ago I first met Nancy. It is why I answer you today. I hope your book will be, without me, what Nan could wish. . . .

wyn henderson

A Tribute to Nancy Cunard

I had not seen Nancy since the year 1932, when what I had fondly believed to be a warm and loving friendship was rudely disrupted by the lying malice of a mutual "friend." Yet the news of her death was a shock and the keen regret it occasioned revealed to me how many pleasant memories of her I had repressed.

We met while I was running the Aquila Press, which I had started in 1929 before the collapse of the American market had hastened its untimely demise. The occasion of our meeting was the projected publication of her *Poems (Two) 1925,* which we subsequently published in an edition of 150 signed copies set and printed by hand with an early abstract design by Eliott Seabrooke in bright scarlet on the white boards of the binding.

I can see her now with her delicate shapely head, rolling her pretty blue eyes with the mischievous expression of a naughty child she so often assumed, in this instance at the sight of the atrocious and horrifying paintings by Aleister Crowley with which he had temporarily plastered the walls of the press he had vain hopes of buying. Her keen visual sense was very properly outraged but not at the expense of her lively sense of humour.

She asked me if, when the Aquila looked like closing down, I would come and work with her at her Hours Press in Paris and when later she decided to go to America over the Scottsboro trial, I took over for her in her absence and with John Sibthorp, who had been our printer at the Aquila, produced the last five books the Hours Press published. But without the American market the writing was already on the wall, the hour of the little presses had already struck when the Penguin waddled in and the Eagle folded its wings.

The charming little Hours Press in the rue Guénégaud with its black and white tiled floor, its leopard skin divan and its handsome Boule desk that had belonged to her father, was a meeting place for writers round about five o'clock, the hour we officially closed and visitors to Paris from London and New York who were Nancy's friends often dropped in for talk and a drink about that time.

On one occasion I was standing up on a ladder hanging some printed sheets to dry on some lines ingeniously invented as a quick-drying technique by John when a woman walked in at the door. She was wearing a flat straw hat of the kind known as a "boater" with tweeds and flat-heeled shoes but was very striking looking. She asked for Nancy whose absence I explained as she stood below me looking up. She continued to stand there and suddenly exclaimed: "What a very fine pair of legs!" adding quite irrelevantly, "Why do you not publish an edition of Rochester, a splendid poet you English never really appreciated?" She turned to leave and I asked her name, to tell Nancy she had called, and when she replied la Duchesse de Clermont Tonnerre I realised, with great pleasure, that there standing before me was the original of Proust's Princesse de Guermantes. When on her return I told Nancy, she laughed and said, "I always told you I would like to cut off your legs just above the knee and have them stuffed as *objets d'arts* for each end of my mantlepiece."

When in gay mood we were setting out together for a party, she always called us "merrie wives" (we had both married and divorced Guards officers), but at other times she called me Dr. Johnson, whether on account of my bawdy humour or a tendency on my part to pontificate, I never knew.

Not the least attractive thing about her was her beautifully modulated voice that expressed so well a certain quality of dreamy charm that emanated from her in certain gentle moods. She was also a good hater and could be cruel and vixenish when angry, especially towards men. She was a great romantic and like most of them, her tenderness was roused towards ideas rather than individuals. How often the championing of great causes (in her case the Negro races; the Spanish Republicans) is an identification with the underdog, an outlet in abstractions for feeling or love that can neither be offered nor accepted in the case of individuals. Romantics are thus often both cruel and sentimental and, in the case of women, are often attracted by male homosexuals who make no demands. The Earth-Mother, All-Things-to-All-Men concept is nothing if not romantic and its adherents are quite wrongly classified as lustful wantons, *femmes fatales,* whereas, in fact, they are romantic, generous and technically frigid.

Besides her wit, Nancy had humour, a much rarer quality in women. On one occasion we were driving down to my cottage in Essex for the weekend, having with us Henry Crowder whose delightful *Henry-Music* Nancy had just published. My car was an old Austin seven with loose, dilapidated floor boards, and as Nancy looked down at them apprehensively she said, "I hope the floor won't fall through, I don't think I can run very fast in these high heels." She once described Marseilles from which she had just returned as "bunches of garlic-eaters clinging to clanging trams."

I often envied her her capacity for sustained effort, for concentration and sheer hard work. Printer John and I would sometimes work through the night, returning through the dark snow-covered streets with rats leaping out of the dustbins lining them, stopping at the workman's bistro opposite for a *vieux Marc* on the way to the hotel, the newly opened Crystal in the rue Saint Benoit, where we all lived. She told me she had often worked all night single-handed when a publication date was pressing. Staying with her at Puits Carrée in Chapelle Réanville, her country home at that time, I had often been impressed by her single-minded sense of purpose. Until the work in hand was completed no distractions were permitted. She was fundamentally an entirely serious, dedicated artist despite the heavy drinking she was prone to use as an escape.

A rare creature—unique perhaps—and despite the injustice she did me I shall remember her always with affection, and will always regard it as a privilege to have known her.

IV

At War; Spain

1936–1939

introductory by george seldes

Nancy Cunard

I knew Nancy Cunard only slightly; but enough to be impressed by her, to honor and admire her. We who talk and write about noncon-formity rarely have the courage to live the lives of nonconformists, but Nancy Cunard had the courage and paid the price society still de-mands. England and America are bad enough, but Nancy when I knew her was the dissenter, the rebel, the heretic in the Spain of today, which is still in the shadow of the 17th century.

I wish I had known her longer, and could make a contribution to her memorial.

nancy cunard
Spain

[With the publication of *Negro* behind her, Miss Cunard journeyed to Russia (she saw little of the country and remained only two months) and then returned to France at the outbreak of the Ethiopian war to become a journalist, first reporting for the Associated Negro Press at the League of Nations, and later, during the Spanish Civil War, for various British journals and the *Manchester Guardian*. It was while the war in Spain raged that the Hours Press equipment was unpacked and used to print six numbers of *Les Poetes du Monde Défendent le Peuple Espagnol,* which contained poems about the Spanish war by Pablo Neruda, Rafael Alberti, W. H. Auden and Tristan Tzara. In 1937 Miss Cunard polled British writers on their attitudes toward the Spanish conflict and published their comments in the booklet *Authors Take Sides.* Near the end of the war, she gave great assistance to Spanish refugees interned in southern France and personally obtained the release of the Spanish poet Cesar Arconada who, along with several others, lived in Miss Cunard's home in Réanville in 1939.]

Geneva! It was the first of several times I went there to the League of Nations, as a reporter, on this occasion, for the Associated Negro Press of the United States and a West African paper—to that Session which the Powers intended should give the quietus to Ethiopia and end the pleadings of Haile Selassie. Everything but reporting was out of the question for me during those strenuous days. . . . Of an evening, when the last words had been written and sent, with what disgust was one filled at the way "they" carried on—breaking their own clauses and covenants, with supra-human cynicism. Such was my baptism in matters of this kind.

Fifteen days or so after the end of this historical Session the war began in Spain and I went there as a journalist, arriving on August 11 in Barcelona. The whole next three months spent in towns, villages and going to the fronts were so engrossing that I could think of nothing else; and next I was in Tangier and French Morocco, where much was to be learned about the way Moors were impressed (mainly) into a war that was no concern of theirs.

The things of Spain took hold of me entirely and, back in France next spring it seemed of point to find out how writers in Britain felt about it all.

Would it not be good to send out a Questionnaire? I had soon composed one. The feeling was considerable among the writers in England, judging by the number of answers that poured in, and the way *Authors Take Sides*—as it was called when published that autumn—sold out immediately, some 3000 copies, I think.

We were in Narbonne at that moment, you (Douglas) sitting on the edge of my bed and I in it with a temperature of 103, an influenzal thunderbolt the very morning that John Banting was arriving from London with a camera to join me in a journey to Spain. You had come to see me off. You did not realise that a passport had now to be specially endorsed, which entailed "a valid reason," such as some kind of mission. The French made difficulties; the Spaniards honey-combed with spies in the Republican zone, were, naturally, prudent. Even the most accredited journalists often had considerable difficulty now and much, once in Spain, depended on being "listo"—personally resourceful in every sense. I had my ways and means, I told you, besides my credentials—but you seemed chagrined at not being able to buy a ticket and come with us. What would your stated "mission" have been?

"If you find me a child I will come to the frontier and take charge when you return."

And now John arrived and I sank back into my torpor.

What did you do with him all of that day? In great high spirits both of you came back—from Carcassonne. That is where you had been. But to Hell with its battlements and all that! In November night comes down far too early for sightseeing after lunch. As for *hastening* over lunch so as to climb up and down all those infernal crenelated walls—*what on earth for?* Besides, the wine in Carcassonne is very good! It had been an enjoyable session, I thought, judging from the mood of both—embellished with some fine drawings John had made of you. For my part, I was succeeding in sleeping and drugging myself out of the fever.

How would you have felt about all those drawn sabres and bayonets and angry French officials three or four days later at the frontier in Cerbère station? Unlike John, *you* would have realised it was touch and go. The French permit out of the country this time had to be a verbal one, promised by a difficult man who, I feared, *might* go back on his word at the last moment. And then? Then other means would have to be sought. But enter Spain we did.

And now came two absorbing months—first in the icy cold and

hunger of Barcelona, then in the slightly attenuated conditions of Valencia, and lastly in freezing, starving Madrid under the December shells. Everywhere, but here most of all, was that fortitude, that innate faith in its cause of the Spanish people.

But as to finding you a child—no. That was something I could not undertake, working all day as I was, unable to tackle the endless arrangements such a thing would have entailed. And there were many refugee-children in France already.

Back there in the new year of 1938, I don't seem to remember you in Paris for very long. Was it not in March that you and I and your eldest son, Archie, had that pleasant yet rather sad meal together in Vernon, my local town on the Seine? That small restaurant we ate in was bombed to oblivion just over two years later. We were, I remember, overshadowed by all that was going on; that month it was Austria. The picture of you and Archie remains in mind. Archie (whom of course I knew already), well-set like you, good-looking, of somewhat smaller feature and more rounded in face, golden-haired and blue-eyed, with a pleasant manner, and, at moments, something of *your* manner.

An awful premonition was gnawing the patronne of that little place and she told us repeatedly she felt something dreadful might be coming. "Ca va mal, ca va mal!" was already much to be heard. It was her own hotel she had in mind, those very days that Nazi boots were marching through the streets of Vienna. I think I have never read so many newspapers as at that time. The effect in English is a sledge-hammer; in French "un coup de massue," and I had both. One is worn out, suffocated, emptied of thought. All that remains is a furious sense of indignation. How much I would have preferred to be a regular press-correspondent, to have been right in the vortex at that time.

On return to France I went immediately to another session of the League of Nations, where the case this time was Spain; and then home after finding, in Paris, Narcisa—a Spanish refugee whose husband had disappeared in the massacres of Badajoz. She came to live with me at Réanville and helped me much with Spanish. What rich and complicated bacalao dishes she would cook, of which she made you a particularly fine one later on.

Suddenly you were there!—appearing unannounced in the middle of a lush, green June or July afternoon, with a tall, florid good-looking young American:

"Here we are again! And this is Hutch, my dear. He's only *just* come over from America, and he says he's *just* going back, too. I wish I could induce him to stay. . . ."

You had thought of bringing a good bottle of champagne with you from Etretat that day and we drank it slowly, sitting under my linden trees by the well. So this was Réanville, the house called "Puits Carre!" And what was *that* curious little building up there on the slope? The one-time Printing-Press, the HOURS—the tiny, converted stable where, years ago now, *One Day* had been carefully raised. Narcisa, despite her total lack of English, was much struck by you, telling me later that you were, obviously, "a great man." She could read that, she said, in your eyes most of all, although of course the whole manner of you indicated the fact.

Hutch and I went into the house for a moment so that I could show him The Hours Press books—was it not to him I gave my last available copy of *Pumice?* And there, sitting on the floor by the shelves, he looked at me hard and said:

"*Any* length of journey with Norman at the end of it! What a personality! As important to me as a scientist—I mean, his scientific writings are that—as a creative author. I had to meet him, just had to. And now I've got to get back to the States at once, so short is this vacation. But I'll be over again next summer to see him—if there's time."

What did that mean, "If there's time—if there's still time"?

What else but the possibility of war by then?

It seems to me we talked little of this under my lindens. You were in fine form, and . . . Dear me, yes! You certainly *would* come and spend a few days here soon.

"And then," said Narcisa, "Gervasito, my son, will see his first great writer from England."

For the moment she had lost him. No matter! Gervasito being a responsible boy of fourteen would soon send his address from whatever children's colony he was in. He would be the first Spanish child, you said, you would ever have met. By all means let him be here next month:

"*Leave it to me,* my dear. I shall know how to talk to him, despite the difficulty of the language."

No difficulty, however, existed; for Gervasito, lively, wide-awake and already as manly as could be, had, we discovered, learned excellent French.

And so, a few weeks later—August 8, I see, from a book of yours then autographed—the four of us would be sitting lengthily of an evening around those trees. I remember these few days as bucolic— the wine let down into the well to cool, everything done in a leisurely fashion and in perfect temperature, the rich Spanish dishes made by Narcisa, our walks and strolls, and—as late as midnight—Gervasito's strong young voice ringing out in the hot darkness, spiralling up and down Flamencos and new Republican songs, marching songs and those of the defence of Madrid. I think you were rather fascinated by him. In character he was very different from most Italian boys and he may have seemed slightly problematical? You got on famously together. And some time later told me you had an idea of going —of all places—to Goa! Did I think Narcisa would let you take Gervasito along? She was appalled at the thought. No, no, no! "El Douglas" was certainly a grand person, and a good one. But her son was all that was left her of the man she adored, of the country she had lost. . . .

Soon after our few days at Reanville I went to Spain again, to Barcelona only this time, where everything could be summed up now by that terrible word "hunger." It was, indeed, nigh-starvation—a fact that was getting to be understood, on account of the reiterated descriptions sent by journalists and various missions. With such hunger, how could anyone be surprised at people rushing into the smoking ruins even before the arrival of the rescue-squads? Those houses were reputed to be store-places! It might shock some to hear of emaciated citizens hunting about for a few dried beans in the shambles among the dead.

I returned from Spain to Paris on a rainy, cold day in October—ill from the sudden change back to proper food, without a penny (it was Saturday, too, and the Banks shut), and scantily clothed, having felt I must leave everything possible to bombed out people in Barcelona. Another touch of the friendliness that so often attends return lay in the fact that not one room was available in half a dozen hotels, the first of which expressed itself thus:

"Madame, all of your friends are here, where, I agree, you have lived lengthily. How could there be a room for you? There is Monsieur Douglas with two friends of his, and Monsieur Howard, and Monsieur Siepmann—all friends of yours, I repeat—and of course they are occupying the rooms, one of which, had things been otherwise, you might certainly have had yourself."

A hotel should be kept strictly to oneself, not generously indicated to others! And Paris seemed rather odd. How peculiar this absent-minded, worried look on the faces of those generally alert, change-counting people who were suddenly making slight arithmetical mistakes, saying *Ah, je n'ai pas ma tête aujourd'hui* . . . What was happening? I had seen no papers for forty-eight hours. Presently it became clear: the first day of "Munich week."

Soon enough I too felt I "had not my head today." Many people grew flustered, and some hysterical, as the aerial journeys of the states-men proceeded.

For me, that last winter of "Peace-in-our-Time" was spent entirely in writing articles and raising money for Spanish relief. My wish was to get back to Spain, and the *Manchester Guardian* agreed that I might go for them, paying my own expenses but duly accredited. Headed thus for the Cordoba front, events now came so fast that I had only reached Perpignan the day Barcelona fell. The refugees were starting to pour in over the frontier; the Prefecture carried out orders decided on long ago in such an eventuality. These were apparent to all in the attitude and deportment of the rancorous, fussy officials who made further difficulties in a difficult enough situation. Franco was very near the border now and so imminent was the end that Perpignan became, all in a day, the hub of the world "from the news-angle."

But who could be helped? Officialdom saw to that. So inimical was it to the refugees that many a case that could have been dealt with by warm-hearted French people individually and in groups was prevented from even being approached. Everything got worse from day to day.

For such, like that of the other two or three hundred journalists, was my day, every day of that cruel February:

Up at seven. On the road in a car by 8:30, or by train, to the fron-tiers at Le Perthus and Cerbère, and even to Bourg Madame in the snow. Over, on foot, several miles to the first Spanish village. Scenes of horror along the way. Questioning, noting, talking to hundreds of people in Spanish, memorising things to describe. Often no lunch, from lack of time. Back, come dark, to the unheated, freezing, dingy room in a horrible hotel where, by the worst light imaginable, ex-hausted and shivering, I would try to make consecutive sense in writ-ing out of the facts and impressions of the day. The three or four-page airmail despatch then had to go off to the *Manchester Guardian*. The first real meal and rest came generally about 10 p.m., when, between mouthfuls, one would be discussing events with some of the other journalists. An occasional alternative was afforded by those hour-long waits in the crowded Prefecture, preliminary to obstinate arguings and pleadings with angry officials and the grudging stamping of permits.

Maria Eyguisquiaguirre, that typical Basque name. . . . A tiny woman in black, a peasant, old before her time on account of the privations of war, her eyes raking the ground near the Port in Barce-lona just after an air-raid. Had I seen the fish-man, she asked me suddenly, as I passed? Well, no, there was nothing to eat, nothing, save what kind people had sent from France, a tin now and then. I had given her my address and her letter, a few weeks later, telling of the hunger, had been photostated; I had made it the start of a *food campaign,* which collected hundreds and hundreds of pounds in England, thanks to the publicity given by the *Manchester Guardian, News Chronicle* and *Daily Herald*. And now there were half a million refugees scattered all over France and in concentration camps there. I, busy with my own Spanish refugee friends at Réanville.

"Nancy Cunard." Painted by John Banting. *Collection of the artist.*

"Nancy Cunard." Photographed by Cecil Beaton, London, 1930. *Collection of Mr. Cecil Beaton, London*.

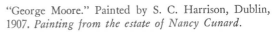

"George Moore." Painted by S. C. Harrison, Dublin, 1907. *Painting from the estate of Nancy Cunard*.

cy Cunard and Monsieur Levy at the old
press of The Hours Press, Réanville,
.

"Nancy Cunard." Painted by Eugene
McCown, Paris, 1923. *Collection of
Hugh Ford.*

"The Cafe Royal." Painted by Adrian Allinson, London, 1915. *Collection of Mr.
R. Alistair McAlpine, London.*

Above: Jeune Fille S *phistiquée.* "Sophisticat‹ Young Girl, N.C." by Co stantin Brancusi, Par 1925. *Collection of M‹ Teeny Duchamp.*
"We gladly give you t‹ permission to reproduce t‹ *Portrait of a Sophisticat‹ Lady,* a sculpture in wo‹ by Brancusi, which he to‹ us was a portrait of Nan Cunard, although she nev posed for it nor knew th she had been the inspi‹ tion of it (only much l‹ er). Our sculpture w‹ given by Brancusi to Tee‹ Duchamp around 1950 a‹ she had seen it in his stud since the 1920s."—Marc‹ Duchamp.
Photograph by Duane Michals.

Left: "Nancy Cunard Painted by Oskar Kokosc ka, Paris, 1924. *Collecti‹ of Dr. jur. Bernhard Spre gel, Hannover, West G‹ many.*

Right: "Nancy Cunar‹ Sketched by Wyndha‹ Lewis, Venice, 1922. *C‹ lection of the British In‹ tute, Florence, Italy.*

The Hours Press, 15 Rue Guenégaud, Paris, 1930.

Pablo Neruda, Nancy Cunard, Delia del Carril, and Luis Enriq
Délano in Madrid, 1936.

Left: Nancy Cunard in Barcelona, 1937. Photograph by John Banting. *Right:* Ring Stone given to Henry Moore by Nancy Cunard, 1964. Photograph by Henry Moore, 1967.

Nancy Cunard with Clyde Robinson, Majorca, 1959.

Nancy Cunard, Lamothe-Fénelon, Lot, France, 1963. *Collection of Hugh Ford.*

nan green

Nancy Cunard and Spain

Spain was our meeting point. Not the geographical entity Spain, and not the physical meeting point which, if I remember rightly, was a bar somewhere near Tottenham Court Road—in what year I cannot remember. It seems to me that I *became aware* of Nancy rather than becoming first acquainted with her, as one becomes aware of a particular instrument in an orchestra or a particular colour in a tapestry—and the tapestry was Spain: the Spain of 1936–1939. The Spain of the people who, at a certain moment in the long, confusing and crushing process of defeat undergone by democracy in the 'thirties at the hands of ascendant Fascism, decided that it was "better to die on our feet than live on our knees" and thereby aroused the hope and admiration of anti-fascists the world over.

We were both closely involved in that struggle; Nancy as a writer, a poet and a friend of those writers and poets whose genius flowered in the Spanish war "as if a rock had been struck and a spring had leapt out of it" (the words are those of John Lehmann, then editor of *New Writing*) and I as a member of one of the British medical units that went to help the beleaguered Spanish people. I recall her participation in the International Writers' Conference that was held in Madrid in the summer of 1937; I recall her contribution to a symposium of intellectual opinion that was issued at that time. She recalled, in a letter to me dated January 2, 1964, "collecting pence in Paris for the starving children of Spain in a large open sheet, probably on the first of May 1937 . . ." (she had come upon an old snapshot which awakened the memory). The love and admiration for the Spanish people which seized us at that time was the continuing basis of our friendship, which lasted to the end of her life.

During and after the Second World War, our correspondence was mostly about people—about Spaniards and the men of the International Brigades who, though defeated, would not accept defeat and fought on—in the concentration camps of southern France, later in the French Maquis, in North Africa and Italy, on the eastern and western fronts, the Spaniards confident (alas for their hopes!) that the defeat of Hitler and Mussolini would entrain the defeat of their ally Franco. I had become the secretary of the International Brigade Association which worked, during those difficult years, to protect the lives and safety of our fellow-combatants of other nationalities; winking them out, wherever possible, from prison or concentration camp, campaigning for the lives of those who fell into fascist hands, sending clothing, razorblades, money, letters, chocolate, food-parcels—whatever we could send to Spaniards and Internationals wherever we could hear of their whereabouts. I imagine few people know how many Nancy helped in her own way: now and then she would refer to it but one did not ask for details in those days. Much later, in a letter of March 1964, she spoke of having "suddenly been able to turn into an agent of Providence" to save a great friend of Picasso "from total disappearance in those French, February-1939, camps."

In 1952 I went to the Far East and our correspondence, for the next eight years, dwindled to Christmas cards. But almost immediately on my return Nancy sent me "the last of eight sonnets written *in* and on Spain in 1958—so obliquely on purpose because, at any moment, some plain clothes man may bear down on you to demand just what and why you are writing at all—it seemed natural to end the sequence with The Internationals," she explained.

SONNET IN FIVE LANGUAGES
THE INTERNATIONALS

Adesso è altra sosta, ma dove su Dante?
If the fire burn low, it is the same, I see;
Por mudo que vas tiras por adelante,
Et tout ce qui fut avant peut renâitre ici.
Noch gibt es einigen Moorsoldaten die
Are ready to spring to their appointed place,
E quantí altri, vicini e lontani . . .
Se no se dice, consabido és.
So mischt man Sprächen mit Hoffnung wohin man geht,
I treni misti vanno molto lontano;
May our suns and moons coincide in the rising spate,
Pero quien me dirá la fecha de este ano?
Courage persiste si le coeur conserve ses as . . .
Y cuando te toca el turno, ah! Cuanto cosecharás!

She added explanatory notes for each line:

(1) At this time comes another pause in history, but where is its Dante (to chronicle it)?

(2) If the fire burn low (the spirit perforce be dim, inarticulate) it is the same fire, I see.

(3) Muted art thou (Spain), but strivest ever forward

(4) And all that happened before might well come here again

(5) Some of the "Moor-Soldiers" still live. "Die Moorsoldaten" was the name given them by the inhabitants near the Nazi concentration camps in the nineteen-thirties, to the men they saw returning from the enforced, utterly senseless work with pick and shovel, digging dry ground, carting stones, making tracks, putting up yet more barbed wire etc. These men formed themselves into marching units, singing as they came and went in all that misery—songs of courage, of unending defiance. Alejo Carpentier, the Cuban musician, recorded one: "Die Moorsoldaten" and another, both in German; "Die Thaelmann Kolonne in den Strassen von Madrid" is its first line.

(6) They, and other Germans of the same feeling, would be ready to fight again (in case of need, against the Fascists)

(7) As would many another man, from far away and near;

(8) If such be not spoken of, yet it is well known

(9) Upsurge of tongues comes ever, mixed with hope, wherever one goes;

(10) 'I treni misti' in Italian means part-goods, part-passenger, and they go very far. . . .

(11) May our own (British) feelings coincide with all this (if it should come to pass),

(12) Though who can tell me the date of the year wherein such might be?

(13) Courage endures if the heart clings to its aces. . . .

(14) Ah (Spain) when thine own turn comest, much much shallst thou harvest!

In 1963 I began to collect material (and money) for an Exhibition on the Spanish war, to be entitled *Spain Fights for Freedom*. It was intended to be a very mobile and readily-portable exhibition; it turned out, unfortunately, to be rather cumbersome—partly because of the wealth of photographs, posters, documents and other relics with which we were inundated. The whole idea was exciting to Nancy, who sent money and began to bombard me with suggestions, names and addressess of people who might be enlisted in support of the project. She herself wrote to Picasso (who did not respond) and to Pablo Casals (who did, very kindly) and a spate of letters began to arrive, suggesting people to whom I should write for their interest.

A letter dated "Feb 11, or 12 or 13, 1964" begins: "You will excuse me (and also bless me) for my brevity. The light is failing—sometimes a very pleasant thing—and as, by accident, I have had to have my right leg cut open (to the bone or no?) to have two enormous cupfuls of 2- or 3-day old jelly extracted (with hardly any local anaesthetic) in Nice, some 10 days ago, I will have to get up enough courage in a minute to turn on the light. This preposterous (and deep) accident is the reason why I did not write sooner to thank you for your splendid letter about the Exhibition. I do so now, despite the infernal pain. . . ."

"The infernal pain" comes very often into her letters from then on. "While the Nice doctor was cutting his 8(?) inch slit in the leg, what should come back to me but the vision of the Spanish worker's forearm being lanced, without any anaesthetic at all, in the Escorial, improvised hospital, in Sept. or Oct. 1936. Looking for a 'dum-dum' bullet was the surgeon, explaining to me as he probed on, that such 'star-shaped' wounds were due to Dum-dum."

"Why have I not sent you the poem, the one at least specially to you?" she wrote on March 6. "PAIN, my dear Nan, plain pain. . . . I wrote you, not only in head but on paper (when I looked again it was practically unintelligible); all got too long, so I tore it up. I was telling you about the agony in my leg, of my pain, and pain and pain again—even of the doctor who obviously hates ALL artists (they all do) and most of all poets and writers—'those horrid pretentious people who think they can think.' What a war that can be: that between 'die reine scientifische Sache' and the creative whatsomedever—I for one hold that anyone should have a good mix of technical skill along with his-her own creativeness. . . . How can such a 'flesh-wound' hurt so? This is the first day it has not dragged on me like a ton's worth. To my amazement, walking, if slowly, is not more painful it seems than 'laying it up.' Now why? How can this possibly be?"

She found time, however, to write that a young friend ("a most creative, able and gifted young man") had been to see the Exhibition which had by now been shown in London. His letter, which she copied, read: "Just to tell you that I saw the Spain Exhibition in Hampstead and had a brief chat with Nan Green. I thought the exhibition impressive—photographs plus simple narrative, mounted on screens. It certainly hit one with Guernica and a lot besides and made one want to find out more and go to Spain and help start our generation enquiring about the Franco regime."

"So you see," commented Nancy, "with this one you have achieved

JUST what you wanted: not only historical fact in retrospect but the desire, among the young to know more, to assess for themselves, to judge what—to US—may seem, as you so rightly put it 'as far back as the Boer War.' I mean that our Spanish war is not that to us but that it can well appear so in the minds of the new generations."

In a postscript to the same letter she wrote: "My poem to you is well on the wing. It is getting pretty long—several pages—and is about (of all things) the Troubadours and Bards, with many a thought, many a consideration of our times and you know where. A curious come-together of continuity. . . . I will send it to you as soon as done. If only I were not so ill I would by now have walked into the mile-away Beaulieu, to ask the local printer how much he would charge to print up a few copies of the Sonnet to the Internationals, for a start. I have so many poems written on Spain that I wonder if they, in their differ-ent years, 'during and after' could not be done up into one volume . . . the poem to you is very strange. I cannot think how these two main thoughts came together, but there they are: welded."

Disparate Sequences from the long poem in the making:

"The Vision" Feb-March 1964

The subject, in a general way, is of what the bards and troubadours sang in those old Baronial Halls in pre-mediaeval times. But not only. It has to link up with "the country we have most in mind." As I can never write anything consecutively, I cannot yet say where this comes into the long-fat body of the Poem. As that goes on, I think it may come to book-length.

FOR NAN ESPECIALLY

No war is ever the same as the one before
For all its Flanders muds, its bombs and guns;
Time sees to that—and yet, unerring, runs
One same, fast thread of continuity.
"Grapple it to thy heart with hooks of steel"
Wrote Shakespeare, naming friendship. Not strange that here
These words return, to be loved and held most dear
By *us* who have one country most in mind,
Its steadfast pain in the blood, its nobility,
The force and vigour of its immortal kind.

Ay, grapple it well.

We, Irish, Scots and Welsh,
We, English of many shires and many sires,
Some of us know—how soon and, ah, how well—
What such-like friendship means, and so we went
To the dangerous, lovely land (some being new friends
Who's set their hearts, however, on taking a hand
(And how!) in its battles . . .

Well grappled to the heart still is
By us that far music in all its tragedy,
Its sombre purple and violet with yellow shot-through,
Its scarlet and black . . .
On such there's no turning back . . .

How well these things are known to me and you.

This, and her subsequent letters to me were signed "Nanción," a fancy which pleased and amused us both (canción—song).

"My leg is about cured," she wrote on May 14th. "The scar will be for ever—a fair slash. The emphysema is appalling and the lung specialist agreed that it is incurable, though, said he, it can be made less, providing. . . . Moreover, something most peculiar that I had best call vaguely rheumatism is well with me in perpetuo. What is all this? *Los años.* Food is mainly anathema. All I seem able to do is write THAT POEM. And that poem began with you, or rather it began— it did indeed—from the Exhibition. . . . So you see Spain will have done something to me again—after all the years. . . . I have the greatest difficulty in THINKING. With subconscious, unconscious? No difficulty at all. So what? To work, and work and work and work and work and work *over*. And my metres must be perfect, each—every one. I must be the one to be fully satisfied. But to construct, to THINK HOW—oh Lor! Yet it has to be done. Disciplina, Señora! Se acaba! POR FIN! I bid you farewell" (she wrote the last few lines in Spanish), "believing that with our love for a particular country you will excuse me for not begging your pardon."

This was the last intelligible letter I received from her.

A Poem on Spain

[Miss Cunard wrote many poems on the topic of the Spanish Civil War. "To Eat To-day" was printed in the *New Statesman and Nation* on October 1, 1938.]

TO EAT TO-DAY

They come without siren-song or any ushering
Over the usual street of man's middle day,
Come unbelievably—abstract—beyond human vision—
Codicils, dashes along the great Maniac speech.
"Helmeted Nuremberg, nothing," said the people of
                                        Barcelona,
The people of Spain—"Ya lo sabemos, we have suffered all."

Gangrene of German cross, you sirs in the ether,
Sons of Romulus, Wotan—is the mark worth the bomb?
What was in it? salt and a half-pint of olive,
Nothing else but the woman, she treasured it terribly,
Oil, for the day folks would come, refugees from Levante,
Maybe with greens . . . one round meal—but you killed her,
Killed four children outside, with the house, and the
        pregnant cat.
Heil, hand of Rome, you passed—and that is all.

I wonder—do you eat before you do these things,
Is it a cocktail or is it a *pousse-cafe?*
Are you sitting at mess now, saying "visibility medium . . .
We got the port, or near it, with half-a-dozen," I wonder—
Or highing it yet, on the home-run to Mallorca,
Cold at 5000 up, cursing a jammed release . . .
"Give it 'em, puta Madonna, here, over Arenys—

Per Bacco, it's nearly two—bloody sandwich it's made
          down there—
Aren't we going to eat to-day, teniente? *te-niente?*"
Driver in the clouds fuming, fumbler unstrapping death.
You passed; hate traffics on; then the shadows fall.

On the simple earth
Five mouths less to feed to-night in Barcelona.
On the simple earth
Men tramping and raving on an edge of fear.
Another country arming, another and another behind it—
Europe's nerve strung like catapult, the cataclysm roaring
          and swelling . . .
But in Spain no Perhaps, and To-morrow—in Spain, it is, Here.

john banting
Nancy Cunard

Most of Nancy's intimate friends are now either dead, too (and one has the chilly sensation of standing on a small rapidly eroding island), or they are forgetful or subjectively distorting. It must be recognized at once that her detractors have the subtly ulterior motive of throwing into disrepute her outlook on life and that of all others who hold a similar outlook. Thus the right-wing racists will say that of course she was "ineffably charming" but had a "fatal fondness for lost causes" and a "compulsive inclination towards self-destruction."

She needs no vindication against this perfidiousness, but it should be recognized for what it is worth—a typically underhand gesture of the variegated reactionaries—snide and slimy.

With the shock of the news of her death came a feeling of congratulation to her on her release from ten years of struggle against increasing ill health. Never one to "take it easy" or "relax and rest," the frustrations of illness were (for her) harder to bear than to most of those who love their pillows.

My earliest memories of her are about 1925 and associated with parties in London—parties at which serious conversations took place in the same room as the vigorous Charleston. She wore an icy emerald green velvet dress and was with Louis Aragon. At another party she appeared in a pale shell pink taffeta with a plunging back-line and both arms elbow-deep in beautiful African bracelets of ivory. When I danced with her I gently made the bracelets click and clank in accompaniment to the music of a small band. Years later she remembered both occasions but not me. Her eyes were large and lustrous and more startlingly turquoise blue than any I have ever seen—especially in artificial light. They gleamed from the almost Van Dongen eye shading surrounding them—a becoming fashion not to reach London from Paris for several years. But without this make-up the blue of her eyes was still intense. Her severely short straight nose and determined mouth belied her tender sympathy and her own special sense of humour. Her exquisitely small head was usually tightly turbaned, hiding a regular life fountain of light brown hair—near blonde but untinted and with a natural slight wave. (Years later she allowed coiffeurs to frizz it to my horror and I accused her of having it "fried" but of course she didn't give a damn.) Her beauty of movement and swift grace in walking were notable enough to cause plenty of trash to be put to paper—"a very gallant lady glided rapidly through the midnight news of old Mayfair" appeared in *The Green Hat*. She used to laugh about it: "Never mind. The baron made some money from it." (Michael Arlen's nickname.) We encountered him once in a side street in Cannes and exchanged a brief "hello." It was after a fairly "heavy" night in Haute Cagnes with George Antheil, Bob Brown and his wife. I was still unshaven and supporting with failure a heavy hangover, but Nancy always looked spruce under any conditions, for her physical vitality was as strong as her determination, which is saying quite a great deal.

I suppose that the dreary old (and, worse still, the young) Fuds and Duds would shake their empty heads and mechanically rattle out (like the jack pot prize from a "one armed bandit") the cliché: "She burnt herself out." And the worst of it is that this is one cheap way of describing her long hours through the night working at her hand press in France and later the gruelling shift work with the Free French in London.

Night was her time for work or for meeting friends in the "Boeuf sur le Toit." In Paris life went on much later than it does now and meeting her there with Norman Douglas or Samuel Beckett and André Breton, one might not imagine her Country Side at "Puits Carré, La Chapelle Réanville—9 kilometres outside Vernon and only an hour from Paris in the lush cornucopia of Normandy. She had found a large old barn built with that glowing honey coloured stone that abounds in most of France and converted it into a house with four or five bedrooms and a large sitting room. Naturally I loved every part of it, for each detail reflected her inventiveness—both visual and practical. Her wonder and delight in every detail of the countryside now reminds me of Colette's. The surprisingly short seasons for fantastic beetles was observed and insects and the changing pageantry of moths—a new species every evening—one with short white fur all over its head, wings and legs; another with folded wings like a splinter of silver, and one with a yellow body and transparent green wings. After twenty varieties we gave up counting. They came into the reading lamp and had to be saved from being smothered inside the sheets.

I did all the cooking on a woodstove which, carefully banked up with coke, stayed glowing for three days on end. She once confessed that she had always hated eating, but I am among those who with the aid of the fresh country produce of France, and country air succeeded in arousing quite a hearty appetite. The "square well" (so useful for cooling white wine) was shaded by two large lime trees ("lindens" or tieulliers not lime fruit) whose branches swept down nearly to the grass, forming a magnificent shady dining room (in June scented with the golden tasseled blooms). At night an electric lamp on a long flex from the house was hung amongst the branches. But in cold weather the warm kitchen with its Benin heads was our refuge. Nancy swept, polished and dusted with zest and conscientiousness. She was as fastidiously neat as any of the creatures of the woods she loved and with as much unforced natural ease. No fuss no bother. Everything was in place and shone there with its own personality respected.

Later the Nazis were billeted there by a French mayor of dubious sympathies and the square well was fouled and broken, doors torn off, African carvings looted (some ivory bracelets were found by village friends thrown fields away and returned to Nancy). Two paintings by Miro mutilated and books and papers strewn everywhere. A painting by Picabia was damaged, too. The place had to be sold, for Nancy had not the money to restore it. She accepted the loss stoically and in 1952 found a similar but far smaller barn at La Mothe Fenelon, a "coin perdu" in the Dordogne—a region she had always loved. Again the "ambiance" was of her own creating and once again everything came under the Spell of the Muse.

The walks were even more exploratory and one got lost more easily, which I suspect she rather enjoyed. (I did not.) The minutiae of wild life was richer than in Normandy and (as cook again) I found the produce even more varied and prodigious. One couldn't well go wrong with such materials at one's disposal. (The processing of comestibles is a sorry blow to English cooking.) Again we were busy at our separate tasks, Nancy dealing with correspondence sitting bolt upright in a bed neatly covered with letters and newspapers whilst I painted, wrote, cooked and drank with all four arms. (Such was her invigorating vivacity.) She gently (and privately) deplored my morning libations and when one day a wasp also indulging from the same glass in the Rhum Martinique gave me a sharp sting on the upper lip she said, "What a thing! Invite someone to a glass of La Mothe rum and a wasp welcomes him." So I had a grotesque "stiff upper lip" for a few days. It was again "Nancy of the laughing face" (a pop ballad of the 'fifties with a melody oddly full of Nancy). Again as at Réanville she would dart at some exquisite detail in the forests—moss, furred twig, bee, orchid, shade-bleached leaf or a Brancusi stone and profer it with feather-light hands for my appreciation and possible transmutation or delineation. "Nancy of the laughing face." (Even the words of it are not as banal as usual. Maybe the writer had someone in mind, and maybe these things do exist still, although it is hard to believe.)

But our long friendship was by no means one pastoral delight. To collect contributions and make personal research for the big anthology, *Negro,* Nancy asked me to accompany her to New York. I was very keen to do all in my power. We stayed in a hotel in Harlem and met many Negro writers and stage people, Eugene Gordon, Countee Cullen, Rose MacClendon and others I cannot remember. We went to two Baptist revival services which shook me with their incessant mass mesmerism. We met nearly all strata, I suppose, and it was a very great experience to me. After three days the press descended in full weight. Nancy gave an interview to about ten press men at once, expertly batting off the more stupid and destructive questions fired at her. I was half sick with horror but I need not have been, for she stood up to the barrage smilingly in her bright armour of belief and her quick wit. Later a "sob-sister" tried to tackle me and I had the satisfaction of turning the tables and cross-examining her on her own life and melting her into something quite human. The shower of abusive anonymous letters (one from the KKK) were revolting and threatening, but Nancy said that everyone whose name appeared in the press was subjected to this—especially women—in any country. She was disgusted enough but not alarmed as I was. She was head-lined in the gutter press for a week, then some other wonder took over her place. The Negro press read very differently of course.

There can be no doubt that Nancy has accomplished much towards the realization of the existence of racial injustice everywhere amongst people who would have remained in ignorance. Now the realization is universal. She was a pioneer—independent and allied to no organization. She has never been a member of the Communist party (any totalitarianism would be abhorrent to her) although she had Communist friends.

A few years later in October we went to Republican Spain illegally. Not being accredited journalists or members of any political party this was a difficult enterprise but she handled the entire matter as she had entered Spain once before. We found scanty accommodations in Barcelona, although everyone in the various organizations and elsewhere was as helpful and as friendly as possible. By an official car we went to beautiful Valencia, where we met Langston Hughes—a magnificent and a magnetising man—with his sense of humanity and wide understanding of life. I wish we had seen him more often. At last it was arranged to join a bus load going to Madrid. In the ten-hour journey across an empty countryside of red mountains there was one stop at a small village. At Madrid we stayed in the Hotel des Anges, already full of Red Cross people and foreign correspondents. It was now December and so cold that one had to add floor rugs on top of the bedding. Food was scanty. During occasional crashes from artillery, the housewives went in search of food. The capital seemed three quarters empty. One thought: "How brave these women are to stay amongst the bombs." Just a year later we had them from the same sources in London—only far worse—and the women queued for rations.

One day was memorable. Permission was received to visit the Prado. We agreed that we had never seen such big slow snowflakes that day. In the basements of the Prado experts had partly restored El Grecos taken from attics and churches in a black condition. Some 17th century armour was partly destroyed. The work was going on steadily with semi-famine, bombardment and icy weather outside. That afternoon we went to the partly ruined "Florida" hotel, where Hemingway was staying. He was just back from the trenches and resting on a bed. He made some remark about the stimulation of fighting which neither of us liked and commented upon our smoking a horrible mixture of herbs (all one could get) suggesting it might be "marijuana" and that we were too late to be put into a play he had just written about the "war tourists." We said we were glad to miss that honour. It was not a felicitous meeting. I thought that the (mental) "hair on the chest" seemed rather artificial and so did Nancy. Perhaps he was a good writer and made lots of money. Others can have him.

We returned to Valencia at dark winter dawn by means of an open truck, sitting on the floor. Gradually it became so filled that farmers were standing, their smocks blowing. Wine skins were passed round, songs were sung, and provisions exchanged. We reached Valencia in the middle of an air raid but were so tired that we could not move down from our top floor. Nancy was grazed from sitting on the truck floor and I ached all over. I collected all the war posters I could from the many organizations in order to show them in London. The only transport we could get from Barcelona was with a French truck driver carting oranges to France. He was a tall troglodite and it soon appeared that he was heavily "loaded" with drink. He could not find the right road and narrowly escaped several obstructing buildings. "When I find my road I hold it," he reassured us in a very slurred unreassuring speech. At last we shook free of Barcelona. But an hour later we stopped for him to sleep over the wheel. Revived he made a pass at Nancy, unnoticed by me at the time, was repulsed, and set off once more. Finally we reached the frontier, only to be sent back to Barcelona for another stamp on our passports. We were there just the allotted three months and lucky not to have been jailed. Nancy was much braver through the whole complicated and inspiring visit. We were both deeply impressed by the natural dignity and beauty of the Spanish people and by their warm and gracious hospitality. After that the last war and its thousand-told story passed. Let it pass. "C'est pour vomir."

Then in 1952 Nancy rented a flat in Anthony Thorne's house in "London's Little Venice." She became terribly ill and I marketed for her twice a week. Her face was swollen almost beyond recognition and she was out of breath. One preposterous but prosperous doctor (whom she had obeyed to the letter) told me that it was "all imagination" and that she drank too much. "I found her drinking wine at midday," he said. (She had been drinking very little for several years.) I suppose he was reluctant to admit his failure to diagnose, although I took care not to upset him by interfering. Later on asthma (chronic) set in—and anaemia.

She returned to France, and to Spain. There was a stormy scene with a pro-Franco English official and she was expelled. A confusion of discreditable reports followed. Arrests, drunkenness, illness and finally she was certified insane by one of her favorite cousins and her plump doctor. Rumours flew. She had bought a new dress (from the hook) and soaked it all night in the bath, i.e. she was crazy. (From old, I knew her clever adaption of ready-made dresses involving extracting the "make up" or glue in the fabric and clever needlework—changing buttons, etc., so this was quite a rational act to me.) She had "Persecution Mania." Anyone with her past activities would be a fool not to realize a possibility of persecution even in free England. In her speech there was far less of this than in that of the average English citizen. Finally after six months in a "bin" where a woman nearby screamed "Buggeress" at the nurses like a non-stop parrot and where there was no psychiatric treatment whatsoever, she was allowed out for weekends to stay with me in my flat. I wrote to her doctor again (very politely) informing him of this. In his reply he said "with so much liberty she *must* be mad not to leave." I was sickened and never told her of this, of course, since the medico (sic) was an old friend of hers. Maybe he did his best— At last she was free, spent six months with her old and good friend Louise Morgan at Battle and finally returned to France— her real country, for she spent most of her life there, grumble about it as she sometimes did.

The closing scenes of our deep friendship were terrible for me and perhaps for her, too. In April, 1962, I left Dover by sea in a thick mist and after a bad journey arrived at Lamothe. Nancy was quite unable to take her usual long walks but improved in health with the coming of spring until by July she was putting on weight in the right places and taking afternoon walks with some breathless rests. But at meal times she invariably reminisced about the last war. (World Bore II, I called it.) And from angles which surprised me she seemed almost to glorify "LaGloire" and to regard it as a genuine anti-Fascist war, so that we had some bad arguments about its aims and results. Never a personal note, of course, but upsetting enough. (I only hope not so upsetting for her. Anyway she always did enjoy a good old battle.)

It seemed to me that with her official reportage some of the "Establishment" had infected her outlook. She had not become a "Reactionary" or a jingoist but some of her outlook had undergone a change for the conventional, which I found unlike her with her courage and questioning revaluation of outworn and cancerous symbols. She seemed to accept them without agreeing with them. Her spirit was uncrushed and her zest in life undimmed in spite of frustrating illnesses. It is my everlasting regret that we were no longer "in accord" as we had been for nearly forty years. We exchanged letters, but things were never quite the same again.

"Niche 9016, Columbarium, Père Lachaise," is engraved in the minds of many—"in accord" or otherwise.

charles duff

Nancy Cunard: The Enigma of a Personality

I knew Nancy Cunard over a period of about thirty years—from the
early 1930s to the early 1960s—and during that time there were
stretches when we used to meet almost daily. One might think from
this that I ought to have known her really well. Yet now, when I try
to collect my thoughts about her, I cannot help wondering whether
I ever fully understood her, though I used to think that I did. For she
was a woman who was constantly showing new facets of her personality and nature, and there were times when she left me bewildered.
One had either to accept or reject the woman. As an example of this,
I can mention an occasion when she stated, without the slightest
qualms and with utter frankness, that she was anti-Semitic at heart
but could tolerate Jews. This statement, to my mind, did not fit anywhere into the jigsaw of her character, feelings and life as I saw them,
or tried to see them as a whole. She often sprang great surprises. Yet,
whatever she said or did, I could never think of her as anything but a
very good and worthwhile person whom one just had to respect. For
she was, above all else, a woman with a great heart, one which glowed
with kindness and good will, especially to those who, by some quirk
of luck—birth, race or circumstances—found themselves in an abased
position due to human injustice or plain misfortune. She could make
such people a part of her life for as long as she thought she could help
them, or help a cause which they represented. Long before I had met
her, she had taken up many causes. We know that, during her early
years in Paris after World War I, she helped many young writers who
were struggling for recognition. Some of them later became famous.
These acts of benevolence were never silly, or just the stereotype routine of a do-gooder. They were always purposeful. She became associated with the cause of coloured people, and in this field canalized a
great effort into the writing of her huge unique book *Negro*. In this,
one has to recognize that she did some excellent pioneering work in
the field of Negro culture, as well as in demonstrating that the Negro
was not, just because of the colour of his skin or for any other reason,
a kind of *Untermensch*, inferior to the white. In order to find grass

roots, she mixed freely among Negroes everywhere she went. She travelled widely, often roughly. This, for a woman who had been born in the upper crust of English society, caused her to be shunned by many of her old friends, dispossessed by her mother, and detested by innumerable others. It gave her lots of publicity of a malicious nature, and this in turn created a host of offensive myths and legends about her. I heard or read many of them. But one did not need to know her very long before realizing how absurd most of those stories were.

Her next great cause, that of the Spanish Republicans during the Spanish War, was perhaps her greatest, and certainly the most moving event in her life. From the first, and without hesitation, she was anti-Franco. Being Nancy, she put her whole heart into it. Possibly I know more about this phase of her life than of any other, or than most people. The very first thing she did was to allocate her house in France, and the whole of her income, to refugees from the Franco onslaught, and she did this with a snap of the fingers and at a time when she had practically no other visible resources. She said to me at the time: "It doesn't embarrass me in the least to do this, well knowing that it leaves me penniless," and with a smile she added, "I think I can make *some* kind of a living—a good enough one as I'm very ingenious at living on the smell of an oil-rag. You'll see!" And I did see. She got herself a job with the Free French at a derisory weekly wage and told me: "This is my purgatory, here and now. For, although I love France, I just detest most French people." There was no universal love of humanity about her: she was a precisionist and a selectivist in her loves and hates, and did not mind in the least whether she made mistakes. She said that, if the routine work she had to do for the Free French wasn't at times so difficult, it would have bored her. But they quickly found out that she was highly articulate *and* literate in both French and English. As a consequence, when there was some exceptionally difficult piece of translation to be done from English into French, it was given to her, and not to a French person who knew English well. Her French was perfect, the French of an educated French person who was also a sophisticate.

Her outspokenness and associations with Spanish refugees, and others who helped the Republican cause, caused her to be dubbed a Communist. Franco's supporters in most countries followed the example of *El Caudillo* in regarding *all* who were not with him as "Communists," and this notwithstanding the fact that in England and elsewhere many people of all political parties, as well as many Catholics, hated everything that Franco stood for. No doubt Nancy was in many ways, but not in all, a person who inclined to the political Left, but I never saw or heard from her any evidence that she was at any time a true red Communist. She knew nothing whatever about Marxism, and her whole nature revolted against *any* rigid way of thinking. She had not the mind for grasping or even trying to grasp any political ideology. Idealism suited her temperament better, and for it she courted a set of ideas and had a complex of emotions which on occasions seemed like a mystical faith. If she unabashedly approved the stand taken by the Spanish Communists, and innumerable others who were certainly not Communists, this was because she had firmly decided in her own mind that justice was on the side of whoever fought against Franco. Once she said to me: "Franco is a *small* man whose only creed is "Might is right." His Catholicism is a humbug, or otherwise he would not have himself photographed on his knees in prayer just for publicity purposes, would he? And what about all those Basque priests whom he allowed to be killed in his name?" If she was not an extremist in politics, she could at any moment be an extremist in words, for she never hesitated to express herself with the utmost frankness about *anything*. This often shocked the well self-controlled English, whom she regarded as the supreme hypocrites of this world. I finally decided that Nancy could not be regarded as a "political" person, notwithstanding all her associations or words. If anything, she was largely a conservative in feelings. When she was not this, she was essentially an individualist, perhaps even an eccentric to some people, including conservative friends and many others who forgave her for everything because of her palpable honesty and her frankness. Her ideas coincided with the party line of the Communists only when it coincided with her own humanitarian ideas. It always seemed to me to show ignorance of Communism to call her a Communist. For she never understood what Communism was or is. In her later years, she hardly ever mentioned the word. Systems of any kind were repugnant to her. For all that, she never resented the fact that many people continued to refer to her as a "red," and, when I asked her about this, she just shrugged her shoulders and said: "Let them call me anything they like! They don't matter."

She left the office of the Free French at the end of the war, and in a way characteristic of herself. One day, when we were having our frugal lunch together, she said to me: "I'm having a row with the French, thank God! I'm sick of them and their ways. Just think, a damned accountant has tried to swindle me out of a few shillings! How insulting! The man thinks I cannot add two and two! I intend to give him a lesson in more than arithmetic. I've put the matter in the hands of my lawyer and asked him to get me those few shillings *and* an apology." She won hands down, got the money and an apology from her chief, and then, having thanked him, handed him her resignation, saying that de Gaulle could have whatever else was due to her. She told me that she had saved up some money from her small pay and was going to give it to the Spanish Refugee fund.

I often speculated on *why* Nancy was just that sort of Nancy. There are some reasons for it that are not unconvincing, though she rarely mentioned any of them except one: her Irish ancestry. Did the causes of her general unorthodoxy and later way of life spring from a revolt against most things in the earlier way of life in which she had been brought up? Or was it against a parent or parents? She hardly ever spoke of her father, Sir Bache Cunard, but she did often mention her mother, Lady Cunard, that strange, interesting widow, who was rich and a well-known London hostess, famous for her hospitality. Her mother had had a work-a-day youth and gathered a fair fortune before acquiring what her husband left her. Lady Cunard did not ever mention those faraway days of her youth. She turned her back on them. She set her compass for English society, and arrived there, apparently with little difficulty: because, as well as having her wealth, she was lively, intelligent, witty and congenial. All went passably well until Nancy began to "mix with Negroes," of which her Ladyship strongly disapproved. They quarrelled in the 1930s, and, for two such strong-minded people, this meant the severance by mutual consent of the umbilical cord. Nancy's revolt had started long before that. The quarrel about Negroes was merely the culminating point. She had long abandoned all thought of becoming an accepted person in the upper crust of any society and, being herself, acknowledged no ties or restraints of any kind. This is a reasonable explanation of her revolt, but something more has to be added to it. Nancy had Irish blood in her veins from both parents. Her mother was entirely Irish by heredity. I long wondered why there was a rather familiar thread running through Nancy's personality and attitudes towards life. One day she told me of those Irish ancestors, and how one of them (on the female side) was closely related to Robert Emmett, the Irish rebel who had been hanged for leading an insurrection. She expressed such great pride in this that in a flash I (being Irish-Irish) thought to myself: "Surely this explains a good many things!" But still not everything. It may explain much of her romanticism, her idealism combined with a realism which ignored the windmills of life, and made her a combination of Don Quixote and Sancho Panza. Her regardlessness of consequences—once an ideal has been aimed at—is a quality which the Irish have shown again and again, not least in that Easter Rebellion of 1916. Yet, after all, these can only be speculations, for, apart from her kindness, even greatness of heart, her generosity towards bottom dogs, and all that, there still remain for me many mysteries in her personality. I shall not solve any of them, but I find them extremely interesting.

Many of our mutual friends at one time or another have agreed with me that Nancy's character, attitudes and personality could be at the same time transparently clear and still full of baffling contradictions. She could be highly intuitive and at the same time coldly rational. She was, of course, an intellectual, but with that went instincts of a cat: she was aware of a potential friend or enemy at a glance. She was both timid and fearless. She looked frail, but seemed to be able to stand up to fatigue and stresses better than many strong men. The list of these apparent contradictions could, I think, be extended almost indefinitely. But considered together, with the additional fact that, after she had deprived herself of a comfortable income and home, she willed herself to live on what, it seemed to me, would not nourish a sparrow —and this at a time when she worked hard all day and played half the night. The only answer I still find to the question of what made the woman tick is the not entirely satisfying one: her wonderful spirit.

Her book *Negro* and the poetry she wrote in French late in life gave me some clues for rationalization, or so I think. In *Negro* there is a vast panorama, much of which is made up of items and minutiae of often a seemingly disparate nature. Her later poetry in French is built up with flashes. Both of these methods, whether consciously or unconsciously applied, seem to be consistent with most of the other manifestations of her nature. Her minor and major activities always contributed to something bigger, perhaps to something which she did not necessarily grasp fully but felt strongly that it was there. Very slowly I came to realize that her personality, as reflected in her behaviour and speech, was made up of minute units which, rather like the glass particles in a kaleidoscope, formed the patterns of her life, and which, like those of the kaleidoscope, could change suddenly under the eyes of the onlooker, and form others quite different but basically consisting a reformation of the original units. Some kind of waves generated internally in her mind, or suggested from outside, produced these effects. How those waves came to be, or what exactly they were, is the nut of the enigma.

This brings us back to a conventional Square One in which lies the *born* personality, received from the genes, moulded by the environment of a gilded youth, and a moral revolt sharpened by the manifold and often disillusioning experiences of a life that moved well out of the ordinary.

Nancy is gone. The greater part of the enigma of her personality remains.

nancy cunard

Spanish Refugees

[Miss Cunard's most distinguished reporting was done for the *Manchester Guardian* in 1939. The articles that follow are only a few of many she wrote on the exodus of refugees from Spain.]

"THE EXODUS FROM SPAIN"

Vans, trucks, lorries, and buses continue to bring refugee women and children across the frontier at Le Perthus. The road is much better organised, and half of it is now free for cars to pass in and out of Spain. Pitiful little groups of refugees are still camping out, washing their clothes in the streams. At night there are small camp-fires all along the mountain. There are many babies in arms and infants at the breast.

The French soldiery is very much in evidence too; stacked rifles are by the roadside and squads of men being drilled. The control near the frontier is even more strict; while returning to Perpignan one is stopped four times by the Mobile Guards. On a Spanish bus one reads chalked in Catalan "No volem Italians!" ("We do not want the Italians!")

BREAD AGAIN

Everybody in the region of the frontier is going about with the same thing in his hands, or in a bag, or even on his back, and that is—bread. They are eating bread again, the white bread sent to them by France.

When I was sitting on a bench in Perpignan to-day an old peasant woman came up to ask me for a little money. These were her words: "I left Gerona with my husband the night before last. Eight 'planes followed us out of the town to the last bridge, machine-gunning us. We got to Figueras. If only you could see it—nothing but ruins, smashed to pieces. I made my husband get into a lorry there; he is ill, so I walked to La Junquera. We had 11,000 pesetas we had saved; we have worked all our lives. They gave us 28 francs for this at the frontier, and the bus from Le Boulou to Perpignan cost us 16."

This disastrous situation of the exchange is beyond words. Nearly all Spaniards arrive with various sums of money, but cannot, or can hardly, pay for a hotel room or a meal.

SAVING THE WORKS OF ART

It is fit to pay tribute to the leaders of a nation in its present agony who care in the way they do for the cultural heritage of their people. Perhaps one of the last official documents to bear the signature of Señor del Vayo in the old Castle of Figueras was that accepting that the Spanish paintings and works of art be taken to Geneva for safe keeping by the League of Nations. M. J. Jaujard, sub-director of French National Museums, was delegated on this mission to Dr. Negrín, as arranged directly after the fall of Barcelona with the other delegate for the International Committee for the Protection of Spanish Works of Art, Mr. MacClaren, of the National Gallery, London. At the moment of the signing of the document a violent bombing of Figueras took place, the electric current was cut off, and the signatures had to be apposed by the light of matches.

The report that some of the lorries transporting Spanish works of art were attacked by 'planes is confirmed in the local press here to-day. It adds that José-Maria Sert (famous Spanish painter whom I have known personally and whose work decorated the chapel of the Duke of Alba's palace of Liria, in Madrid) sent a telegram to the Duke of Alba in London asking that there should be no bombardments during the transport of the pictures and art treasures. These contain 400 or more paintings by Velasquez, El Greco, and Goya.

Yesterday, on Spanish territory between Le Perthus and La Junquera, I passed ten huge vans carrying these treasures; immense, solidly packed trailers attached to special motors and driven by French chauffeurs. The one I talked with was indignant over the conditions in which this work has to be carried out. "They attack even the works of art of a country," he said. "Can you imagine what it has been like getting away from Figueras during these air raids?"

MANY WOUNDED

Figures of wounded people coming in I have now been able to ascertain—at least, in part. Seven thousand—but this represents both soldiers and civilians—have been brought to France under the charge of Carmen Catalan Pastor. She was directing the transport of some of those wounded in the Figueras raids when I met her in Le Perthus, and told me that thanks are to be given to the French Minister of the Interior for arrangements made. At the Fort of Bellegarde, just above Le Perthus, there are now 2000 wounded soldiers. Another large hospital is at Le Boulou. In Perpignan, said Señora Pastor, are 3000. In La Junquera I saw many other disabled soldiers and wounded waiting to come into France.

Date: February 8, 1939

AN ARMY CROSSING THE FRONTIER

At Le Perthus, from nine o'clock this morning until 4:30, I have been watching soldiers pass between the two stone posts that are actually the frontier-line. They have come by in thousands and thousands, in groups, singly, and in numberless lorries. At the posts stand the French soldiers, who immediately search them for arms. The Spanish soldiers give up their arms in an orderly fashion. The piles of rifles, revolvers, cartridge belts, dirks, and even a knife or two grow throughout the day. Two machine-guns have been brought in; farther up, an armoured car.

But all this is only the beginning; we are told: "To-morrow the rearguard of the army, and afterwards—the army that has fought." On the mountains each side they come, so that the whole landscape seems to be moving. Soldiers on horseback, wounded men, women, children, a whole population, and cars and ambulances. Many of the ambulances are British and of the "Centrale Internationale Sanitaire," one of whose doctors tells me of the appalling lack of supplies, of staff, and of help.

In fact, there is enough of nothing save the now excellently distributed food rations which are made by France. There was a good supply of food at La Junquera, as the food parcels that had been intended for parts of Catalonia now taken by the enemy were being used there. All medical centres and staffs are over-powered, however; at Cerbère, for instance, a doctor told me, are 1500 wounded soldiers with hardly any sanitary necessities at all. Lack of sufficient transport for them is another difficulty. Dr. Audrey Russell, who is well known for her fine work in Spain for many months, said that she had just been able to get her last canteen into French Territory.

General Molesworth was another English worker at Le Perthus, where he was indefatigably trying to get the internationals together. "Only a handful have come through so far," the General told me. The vans of the Quakers pass. I see in front of me André Marty, the moving-force of the French in the international brigades; he has a bandage round his head and neck.

At noon a whistle blows, the frontier is declared shut. That will last for twenty minutes or so, that all those trudging up the hill may leave room for the next thousands to enter. A squad of forty "blues" in their French azure uniforms marches smartly down to relieve those at the frontier posts, over which fly in bright sunlight the flags of the tricolour.

A few shots ring out on the mountain; but the Mobile Guard who comments on them as I pass is saying: "That will be to empty the rifles; why should they want to fire at us?" It is so obvious that the Spaniards are glad to be in France. They have come with arms, which they give up, with cars and lorries and vans and trucks and petrol tanks and drinking-water tanks and what soon becomes a whole herd of horses grazing in a valley, and with small flocks of goats, and, here and there, a lamb on a string which seems to pull the old peasant who owns him up that terrible hill.

"Nada armas"—"No arms"—say most, although this morning's heap has grown by night, but maybe a chicken under the arm and certainly some food for the six-mile walk to the camp at Le Boulou. Meanwhile we can just hear the sound of bomb explosions down below, somewhere beyond La Junquera.

THE COMING DAYS

To-night and to-morrow and for how many days more the influx will continue. At Céret, driving back to Perpignan, there are other hundreds on the road who have crossed by mountain paths. It is dark, it is horribly damp and chill; some have lit small fires in the fields which will make some of the French population curse them and others say: "Humanity itself commands us to do all we can for such misery."

Spanish military friends are with me. They are saying: "Arenys is wiped off the map. For the Italian tanks to get in they had to clear whole mounds of bombed wreckage from the road."

Before many days are out "the others" will be at the frontier of France.

February 9, 1939

AT A REFUGEE CAMP

Some of the camps to which the Spanish refugees are going are not fit to receive human beings. The problem has been too vast to be dealt with as yet.

At the great central camp at Le Boulou are thousands of men, women, and children. On one side of the road is an enclosure with wire fencing. On the other the refugees who walked down from Le Perthus yesterday are lying, sitting, standing, doing nothing this cold end of a February afternoon. It is a horrible sight, and all of them, men, women and children, are in the utmost depression. This "camp" is a large, flat, bare area, the grass trodden down into a sort of grey compost. They sleep here, in the open. A few have rigged up some vague kind of shelter.

As for medical aid—just one case I saw will show the state of things. A woman lamented that she could do nothing for her child. She took off the little girl's bonnet and said: "These dreadful sores are the result of typhus." They come and stand around you and talk; they argue among themselves in front of you: "Are we worse off here to-day than we might be in Spain?" Then a woman cries out, "I shall never get into a train without knowing where it is going, for I have heard that they want to send us back to Franco." Other voices broke out: "Ninety-five per cent of us want to go to Mexico—anything rather than return to Spain as it will be under the Fascists." At the village town hall a girl I knew in Spain says she thinks the women she is one of in a long queue may get a permit to go to Perpignan some time soon. All the men, says a French guard, are going to Argelès; when? No one knows. In all of this families get separated; the men are taken from their families in some cases. Every phrase ends in "I don't know." As for the wounded—they are lying in the ditch among their crutches; a man limps by in obvious agony.

Somehow one becomes accustomed to such sights after ten days. But they become more real again when I try to set down just a fraction here and compare this mass-wretchedness with the "business-eye" of some Marseilles white-slave traffickers who have made their appearance. There are many pretty girls in the Spanish migration.

February 10, 1939

THE REFUGEES AT PERPIGNAN,
MISS CUNARD'S APPEAL

This is an appeal to all those who realise the magnitude of the tragedy of Catalonia, to all those compassionate and generous readers of the *Manchester Guardian* who may want to help alleviate the indescribable suffering of scores of thousands of refugees pouring in during the past week. To give you an idea of the number (the figures I have just verified at the Prefecture of Police here), 55,000 have come in and have been sent on from Perpignan to date. This does not include all those still in this region—10,000, 20,000? No one knows. And of those to come still less can be foretold.

I am writing this from the Centro Espagnol, the organisation that is the most deserving of help. As I sit in its big cafe about 200 people, women and children mostly, but old peasants talking their Spanish dialects too, are waiting for supper. Bales and bundles and clothes fill the end of the room. A daily average of 2000 hot meals is served here now. Perhaps as many as 3000 to 4000 people come through here in the course of the day. All of this is paid for by the regular subscriptions of the workers who founded this place in 1920. Not a penny of State aid do they receive. In February, 1937, they took in 120 Basque orphan children: these children are living here still and often have I seen them. The directors, Señor Bertran and M. Bonnet, are thoroughly responsible and devoted to their work. At present, as can be guessed, they are submerged by the task of caring for the refugees, most of whom arrive in a starving condition.

The Centro is entirely non-political and non-party. It has two other large halls upstairs, where I saw about 200 people, who had been escaping for as long as six or seven days, at last they were able to sleep without fear of bombs. All of the food parcels that filled the lorry I started in for Figueras, in Spain, on January 28, and which could not get through the beginning of that terrible exodus at Le Perthus frontier because the road was blocked, are now being utilised here— that is, those whose donors' consent has been obtained. The Centro is run with strict discipline and probity; that, I feel, I can vouch for, having been in close and constant contact with its organisers since September last. How intensely they need help! Even small sums will do much, for the English pound is worth 177 francs, and food is, of course, bought wholesale.

I have just investigated the report that La Junquera was bombed to-day, causing many wounded amongst the women and children being evacuated in lorries to Le Perthus. The facts are that Figueras had three heavy raids which killed 60 and wounded 200. Small bombs merely were used, to terrify the population. The road likewise was bombed and machine-gunned; so the wounded women and children, many of whom have been brought to the Hôpital Civil here (number so far unascertainable), were victims between Figueras and La Junquera. Such crimes as this are beyond comment.

delia del carril

Nancy Cunard

Nancy! I could indeed write a whole book on our everlasting friendship, nearly thirty years, to which distances and continents have made no difference.

Her profound love for humanity compelled her to participate body and soul in every drama that burst out in this, our sad world. She spent an unexhaustible heartful of energy in giving help. Help! the most exalted word in all languages. She also desperately needed a little dose for herself, but there were always others to think of.

The real image, the most faithful one, of her passionate, attractive good nature was given me by a simple and respectful Spanish woman who had migrated to France in that biblical exodus of half a million Spanish Republicans defeated by Franco, Hitler and Mussolini. She asked not to be forced to speak and give details, because she wasn't able to bear the high emotion that would be provoked in her. The one thing she could say was that in those terrible moments when the old folks and the children were suffering intensely and often dying of hunger, cold weather and desolation and when all doors and even windows there around were hermetically closed, only one person, a tall, slender, pale lady dressed all in white had come to them with a smile and a tender gesture, bringing milk and bread and sweets for the children. As I listened, first my heart and then my mind were connecting a dear name to that mythical apparition in the shape of an archangel fighting the beast for the sake of the innocent. Only one angel, and what if it was Nancy? And so it was.

I send you this with the inevitable tears that I cannot conceal.

V

*More Migrations
and Another War:*

*Santiago,
Ellis Island,
Havana,
London*

1940–1945

introductory by morris gilbert
Nancy Cunard

Nancy Cunard came by her rebelliousness by blood. She was a direct descendant of the greatest American who was also one of America's greatest rebels, Benjamin Franklin, through his daughter, who married a man called Bache. The name Bache was perpetuated in the Cunard family—probably in the important Staten Island branch—so that Nancy's father became Sir Bache Cunard. The name Bache he pronounced Beach; probably through that trait of misnaming names which is so endearing a characteristic of the English.

There was nothing rebellious about Nancy's father. His main distinctions were being a Master of Fox Hounds and a topiarist, two of the most conforming of all English activities. But there was other rebelliousness in the Cunard blood. Among Nancy's ancestors was a brother of Robert Emmett.

A third and, to me, vital rebel in Nancy's background was her mother, whom Nancy greatly resembled in basic character, however greatly they differed in their careers. Maud—later, Emerald—came surging into London society from distant, mysterious California, equipped with a fortune, great verve and great beauty, in the 1890s. This dashing woman was to go her own way, in her own sphere of defiance, until she died, a loyal partisan of the ill-fated King Edward VIII, later the Duke of Windsor, whom practically all but she, at that time, had fled.

Lady Cunard began and remained an original. This great hostess, presiding at the sumptuous estate of Nevill Holt, even entertained literary figures, a highly suspect impulse among titled Britons in those years. This was great for little Nancy who, at the age of about four, struck up a warm and enduring friendship with George Moore, then about forty.

This friendship was to be commemorated many years later in Nancy's best book, "G M," a memoir of the brilliant Irish novelist and connoisseur of art. Probably, G.M.'s influence had a big share in making her life what it was, although he deplored her left-wing traits as time wore on. She probably helped G.M., too. He spent a great deal of time at Nevill Holt. It is recorded by both her and Moore that on their walks in the country while she was still a child, he would send her scampering into the fields, to bring back and name the wild flowers she found. I have always suspected that Moore used these names in the works he was writing. . . . But she also pointed out and named the villages they could see on their rambles, and Moore recited these with affectionate appreciation, in a fine passage in one of his letters to Nancy's mother.

Those letters, by the way, are the beautiful expression of Moore's lifelong devotion to Lady Cunard. That devotion spilled over to engulf her daughter, too, and in Nancy's "coming out" years in London society, she was his weekly guest at lunch at his famous home in Ebury Street. An unprepossessing street, actually, and a quite modest, narrow row house, later somewhat unhinged in the blitzes.

At one such lunch, Nancy used to relate, she accosted Moore with an unexpected and rather astounding question. "G.M.," she said, "people around London are saying that I am really your daughter. Is that true?"

G.M., according to Nancy, had a trick of popping his eyes and blowing out his cheeks in moments of bewilderment. On this occasion, having done so, he made one of the most equivocal replies ever recorded. "My dear," Nancy quoted him, "I fear I cannot say." Then, in a burst of agitation, he demanded. "Nancy, you haven't mentioned this to your mother, have you?" Nancy reassured him.

Of Nancy's writing, Moore made a pregnant observation, which, I think, was to hold true during most of her career. Speaking of her verses in that early compilation, *Wheels,* in which her work was joined by verses of the Sitwells and others, he said, in effect, "Nancy has more genius than talent." This was to hold true, I believe, until the very end. Nancy wrote voluminously, both prose and verse. A year or two on the rim of a copy desk would have taught her the rigor she needed. She was always, perhaps, the gifted amateur until her memorial to George Moore, which had a really professional quality.

One is inclined to sympathize a little—not much—with editors confronted with Nancy's copy. So much of it so good—so much of it needing scrutiny and a blue pencil.

An anecdote in this regard brings up the second great influential figure in Nancy's life, Norman Douglas. Would that I, during the World War II years in London, had had the sense to record Douglas's comments on practically anything. As it is, only a few of them remain in my memory. One of them was apropos of Nancy's embittered comment about an editor of an art publication with whom she was having a tiff over some copy she had submitted. We were sitting in the pub we frequented in Curzon Street.

Norman sniffed. (That was his habit, before producing an aphorism.) "Every man," said he, "whose name ends in i-u-s is a - - - -." Just four vulgar letters.

Nancy, in those war years, was stupendous. She held down a tedious job in the French section of an American bureau, translating. She could have been at more important work, but what she was offered, she took, tedium and all.

At least, her work had the good effect of returning her to her beloved Paris, a few months after the landings. (She was later, it appears, to have gone against Paris, preferring her uncomfortable pied-à-terre in the Dordogne.)

But while in London, Nancy undertook to compile a book of poems about France at war. It was a good collection, with a number of illustrious names in it. But interviewing and entertaining the contributors—whom I, at one point, labeled the Meistersingers and the Minnesingers—required an enormous amount of time. My favorite was a short set of verses by Sylvia Townsend Warner (whom Nancy was to visit down in Dorsetshire). . . . Later, in Paris, Nancy translated the entire collection into French, and it was published.

This was no problem for Nancy, who was one of the few people I knew, probably not more than four, who spoke native English and were truly bilingual in French. A great many more presumed to be so.

That summer of the Normandy landings, I was to have the disturbing duty of reporting to her the wreckage of her beautiful country property at Réanville, on the edge of Normandy south of Vernon which is on the Seine.

At a briefing, one morning, General Wade Haislip, commanding the XV Corps, to which I was loosely attached, disclosed on his map that Réanville had been liberated. The Boche were still at Vernon, but I collected my jeep driver and sergeant and we started off by back roads.

I had never been to Réanville in its good days, but I had been made well acquainted by Nancy with two of her favorite people there or anywhere, Jean and Georgette Goasgüen—such a wonderfully antique Breton surname, as encrusted as the shell of one of those primitive Brittany oysters. They conducted the little local bistro, but on that great day, all there was to drink in the place was crème de menthe. The Boches had cleaned them out before departing.

I climbed out of the jeep, in my U.S. uniform with the curious patch which indicated to the well-informed that I was a civilian attached to the Army. I had no officer's marks of any kind, although my AGO card showed that I held the assimilated rank of lieutenant colonel. That was useful in hotel and air accommodation, since I followed after real lieutenant colonels and outranked real majors.

Jean and Georgette gave me warm greetings, and soon we proceeded to Nancy's place. I learned that Réanville's mayor was a wretched collaborationist, who had acquired several farms by driving out their owners, and was presently to force the Goasgüens from Réanville.

Nancy's showplace was a shambles. The mayor had, first, unlocked all doors so that the local peasantry had full entry to the house and dismantled or stole most of Nancy's beautiful house trimmings and houseware. The one property undisturbed was the fine Belgian press which William Bird had sold her in Paris and on which Nancy printed a number of exquisitely contrived writings by such friends of hers as Harold Acton and Norman.

One would have thought that Nancy had grown up a printer. Her typesetting and the format of the pages of her little editions were admirable. Her opinion was that she had inherited from her father a special gift for handicrafts, which she certainly possessed. None of her friends will forget the self-made clip-board which was always with her—crammed with her notes on any subject, all held together with a strong elastic band.

With the arrival of the Boches in Réanville, the mayor turned the house over to them, and their treatment of it was shameful. The floors were strewn with papers and worse, and books from Nancy's print shop littered the place, their texts torn out and otherwise defaced, ruined bindings tossed all over. I managed to retrieve about four practically intact copies of Douglas's *One Day,* and eventually got one or two to Norman, one to Nancy and kept one for myself. There were about eleven pistol bullet holes in an original Chirico, also on the floor, along with other destroyed paintings.

Nancy had great discernment in choosing the Goasgüens for friends. Jean, now getting along in years, had been shocked in World War I. He said he had been *concussioné,* and always shook a little. Georgette was considerably younger. She had been Jean's soubrette, when he had performed as a strong man in the *fêtes foraines,* the street fairs, lifting heavy weights. She had passed the hat for contributions, and now was a fine bistro keeper's wife.

Jean spoke an excellent French, without any of the crustations of Paris. One time I told him I had just come back from Geneva. He asked me if I had seen the *kursahl,* the casino, there. I said I had passed it, but it was closed. Jean drew himself up. *"O, Maurice,"* he said, *"tu sais, c'était le plus bel établissement de toute ma carrière d'artiste!"* Unforgettable words!

Forseeing that the mayor would be able soon to drive them out of Réanville, Jean looked forward to a life of moonshining calvados, applejack. He wanted to function in his native Brittany, on the coast, if possible, so that he could make deliveries by water. Here he was frustrated, and Georgette wrote Nancy, perhaps a year later, to recite their difficulties. They had, she said, traversed the whole of France, looking for an abode and work. Her piteous phrase was, *"Nous avons parcouru toute la France!"*

Eventually, they settled for a shop somewhere in Piccardy. I believe Nancy visited them there.

We hurried back to XV Corps camp, on the hill behind Mantes le Bel, that afternoon, and I sat down to write Nancy the wretched news of Réanville. . . . Later that year, I drove her down there a couple of times. She retrieved a few possessions, but viewed the whole calamity with typical fortitude. She never went back there to live.

nancy cunard

London at War

[Miss Cunard's trip to Chile, briefly mentioned below, was the beginning of a journey that lasted over a year and took her to Argentina, Jamaica, Mexico, Ellis Island, Cuba and finally back to England in August, 1941, where she remained until the end of the war. Most of the following account describes her numerous wartime activities in London and her return to France in February, 1945. The excerpts below are from *Grand Man*.]

Soon after this the nightmare began, the "Drole de Guerre Phoney War" period, with . . . myself in Normandy and in Paris, until, sick at heart and finding no sufficient field for my free-lancing, I decided to leave Europe and go with a Spanish refugee friend to Chile.

Maybe my going to Chile at the suggestion of Chilean and Spanish friends saved my life. Maybe I should have stayed in France, been interned, possibly shot, or taken the humiliating but necessary road to Bordeaux. . . . I reached England in August at the end of my interminable manoeuvres. . . .

We (Douglas) had one or two cosy evenings in Clifford's Inn, with a small pittance of whisky and ale wheedled out of good old Peele's, that so-often fog-enshrouded pub on the corner.

"Now tell me the real reason why you came back from Chile, or Mexico, or Trinidad or Cuba or wherever you were, gadding about all the time like a neurotic dragon-fly. Why did you want to come to England just now?"

"I've told you already, Norman dearest, that this is 'my' war too—in so far as it is (if only partly) against Fascism. That word seems out of favour here! Despite the great bombings, people do not seem to me to be very much aroused. But then, neither of us was here while they were taking place. Well, one is impressed by the fortitude of the English. . . . It took me about a year to get here from all those places in the New World and I was determined to get here. I could not have stayed there in the state of mind I was in after the collapse of France. Besides, if I can be of use. . . ."

"That's very patriotic of you, my dear."

"I am all for patriotism as I see it! To me it means fighting the common enemy in any way, in any country. I would like, preferably, to work in connection with France, within the scope of things here; and I have a very real admiration for England in its dire ordeal. Does that sound too literary to you? Well, while battling with all those negative officials and money-difficulties in the Americas, I did hope I might find some useful and interesting war work when I got here. Nothing so far! M.O.I., B.B.C., newspapers, translating. . . ."

There were sirens far away—thin scarves of sound waving about over some eastern stretch of Thames maybe, and they made us think that "useful work" could have been found, surely, for anybody in such a grand-scale war as this.

Ah that Preface of yours in *Alone!* You too had been through all this ridiculous search for a war-job in 1915 or 1916—you, the writer, editor, linguist, scientist. World War I seemed already over-staffed in England as far as *you* were concerned.

"Well, Norman . . . have you any ideas or feelings about the probable duration of this war?"

There was a pause:

"My dear, I have no hope for humanity, none whatever. There will always be people to make wars. The last one was going to be *the last one,* ha! Civilisation—pah! If it goes on like this, the use of many things will be forgotten, as happened in Italy after 1918.

The long snow and frost of all January and February transformed the world as seen from those high windows in Clifford's Inn, investing the towers and crenelations of the Law Courts with a strange nobility. We were, I remember, very comfortable in that little flat, and of course *that* is where *you* should have lived the whole time that had to be spent in London until the end of the war. No case of "wise after the event," this, but of "up went the rent." . . . What did we do the five or six days you stayed with me here? No cosseting, indeed, was needed and you were up and out early, making some kind of contact again with England; we would meet at Peele's for a snack-lunch, or in some other place in Fleet Street.

Well, what about London and its changes? You had not much to say; besides you had put a note or two for me on that paper! As for the black-out. . . .

Quite enough to evoke a quiet "Blimey" from anyone—as it did from you—the first two or three times. And it was also difficult to keep one's feet in proper control that particular week, as we discovered, linked to each other by arms of prudence as well as of affection, creeping in the dark over ice-covered snow, getting lost among the fantastic outlines of Carey Street and Fetter Lane and strange empty corners that had come into being through the Big Blitz. Where were we going between those un-London-like snowdrifts that night in the awesome solitude? To Otto and Louise Theis in Old Square. For on meeting you with me ("Theis, Theis?", you said, "the name of a river in Austria") they were anxious to see you again. Once there, a deliciously warm evening developed, with Otto—erudite man of good counsel—and Louise, her imagination a-shimmer like a jay's wing, her tomahawk swiftness! Peaceful indeed was this unpredictable little oasis where all else was excluded, the preciously saved brandy brought in on its tray, the hot, spicy sandwiches that seemed to come from another world. . . .

I urged you to stay with me as long as you liked, but the fever was on—that maddening search for "a place of one's own," for rooms, "for any kind of room" as it became later. It led you first to an unprepossessing hotel in Mayfair. The only good memory I have of that place which seemed to me such a harsh background for your return to England, is the occasion on which Dylan Thomas, standing one evening on its doorstep, was determined to go further, further—whatever obstacle lay in the way. He *must* meet you, he expounded to me again and again: "I will meet Norman Douglas, I will, I will! I must meet him—*now!*" An obstacle, however, there was: the heavy plate-glass doors were shut and locked at the preposterous hour of 9 p.m. We had left a fine cocktail party at John Lehmann's, prolonging it with some excellent confabulations at "The King's Arms" in Shepherd Market, and we had been talking of you. Now, as we passed your hotel, the urge came gloriously over Dylan. He was armed with a very stout stick and proposed to use it on the ungracious doors. (What can have been the matter with the academic idea of ringing the bell?) The stick waved frighteningly: "I *will* meet him, I will, I will!" Little as I knew Dylan, how much I admired his spirit. Finally he appeared to pay heed to my admonitions that you were always out at this hour. You would have liked him very much, I think, but not in a shower of broken glass and the accompanying hotel-comments.

Soon after I did find some work, in one of the Free French organisations in London. Who would have thought that a six-hour shift could be so exhausting? The rota seemed unmanageable here, the allotting of hours so unhappily made, that every one felt—and was—overworked. And then there were those six nights on end, too. We did not meet so very often now!

"Preposterous!" you hurled at me once. "What on earth do you do it for? You'd much better give it up!"

"Will that find me more congenial work in some other French department, or at the M.O.I. or B.B.C.?"

"But I thought you were doing a book at present?"

"I *am* doing a book—or rather, finishing that long pamphlet with George Padmore on colonial matters that I was at when this began. I can't just give that up, can I?"

You were the only person I saw all these times who soothed my exhausted nerves and took my mind off the horrible subjects we had to grapple with.

"And what on earth are they?", you asked.

It all came in through earphones—enemy-stuff from Paris, Berlin, Vichy, etc.—a good deal of it Jew-baiting. I was known as *Correctrice-Assimilée-à-Expediteur*—(a "Radio monitor," in language simpler than this delectable French appellation). My work was to correct all the script in French as transferred to paper by typists listening (in great weariness) to what came into their earphones. Pages and pages per day were processed thus with an accompaniment of aerial screech-ings on top of Vichy blasts. Twenty years of life in France all over the country and with all kinds of people had never presented me *once* with such types as those who ran this office, although my fellow-workers were all right. The typists, in fact, were often great fun, for they would have a good go (in their bewilderment) at enriching the melée with whimsies of their own—all phonetic errors, or nearly.

You too thought that a *centre de documentation* was delightful and were as mystified as myself as to what could be meant by *maintenir les oeux en amont*, whereas *un fait d'hiver parmi beaucoup d'eaux*— a wintry fact among many waters—seemed to us both pure poetry.

Well, what did you think? Forty people in all were employed in recording and transcribing enemy news and ballyhoo (much of it monitored by the B.B.C. in any case and thus available) and in pro-ducing exactly fifty-five copies of a daily, twenty-page, stencilled bul-letin which went to heads of Governments in exile and other impor-tant personages, whom we all felt could not have time or desire to read it.

There was much else to tell you in detail about the "political" at-mosphere in this place as we occasionally dined together before my night-shift, where I learned so much about fatigue . . . those endless hours when ears and eyes give out, the spine turns to rubber, and nerves alternate between strung catgut and damp, flapping sails: de-humanisation by exhaustion.

None of it brought a smile to your lips; I had been telling you about it in the hopes of a good tirade. You listened in complete silence, saying quietly at the end:

"And all of it perfectly useless!"

"How do I know for certain it *is* all perfectly useless? I feel some compunction. We 'girls' there all do! And I have got to have regular war work. The atmosphere of everything here. . . ."

"Perfectly useless. You'd much better give it up."

"What will I find to do instead?"

Square pegs in round holes appeared to be the answer.

After three months and more with the Free French, five other fellow-workers and I resigned the same week for reasons of health, but as I left the establishment the charming Monsieur F—, who had come sometimes to consult a file in our building, asked me if I would care to become his secretary. He assured me it would be "quite different to all this."

So I was soon again at work. And this time . . . I thought I should call myself "a filing clerk," bound to the ordinary eight-hour day, reading all the English papers, marking everything that seemed of interest to France, and then filing documents for the rest of the time. It was not exactly "creative," although my Monsieur F— enchanted me by his rather mysterious detachedness. Weeks and months passed thus—the landings in North Africa, the stupendous battle of Stalingrad; the turn of the tide at last, as was manifest to all. Yet it was a long, black winter. And *if I had kept even the briefest diary* it would have said things of us like this:

"Norman came to fetch me for dinner. Difficult and unnecessary to go far in the black-out. A certain gloom at the start. More lively later, but thrown out of everywhere by closing-hours. Norman certainly at work on that volume of extracts from most of his books—on the score of which, when lightly questioned, he will say nothing. Last night he told me as we clung tightly to each other in the pitch dark, walking between our respective rooms in Queen and Half Moon Street: '89 steps, my dear, between your place and mine. I count them every time we leave each other like this.' "

How I wished we could ever have managed to live under the same roof! But not once did there seem to be rooms available at the right moment. Back from my office in a not unpleasant trance of fatigue, I would eat my spam and boiled potatoes cooked on that dear little old gas-ring, drinking coffee, sitting on the floor by the gas-fire—sometimes "dreaming," now and then writing a poem. You would be well away long before then from our Shepherd Market haunts, dining with John Davenport or Desmond Ryan in Chelsea and Kensington, or with Viva and Willie King in that decorous house of theirs so full of good cheer, or with your publisher Roger Senhouse, or my cousin Victor Cunard, or how many of your other friends. We were pretty often together, too, of an evening—such as on that occasion with Neil Hogg and Professor Walter Starkie in the Carlton Grill, when you and the Professor looked as if to carry on with your jokes (classical subjects, mainly) and your ripostes long after any closing-time, war or no.

All those winter months merge for me, when not in my room or in the office, into one or two small, composite vignettes—a sort of conglomerate of the strange uniforms and foreign faces of Britain's loyal subjects from various parts of the world standing about in Pubs; or in cartoons of even "straighter" British, when, on my way home of an evening, I would come across the chap-in-the-cap and the man-in-the-mac, dallying sadly over their strength-depleted beer, mumbling away to each other: "things may be even worse when it's all over," and "at least we're not occupied here as they are in France."

At length the winter seemed to be edging towards spring. Should we go and look for it, I asked you one day, now no longer an office worker but doing a few articles for the M.O.I. and the proofs of *The White Man's Duty*.

"Go and look for what?"

"For spring, Norman! Why not at Epping? That forest, you know. . . ."

I took a number of snapshots of our "Looking for Spring day." We went in hopeful mood on top of a bus, for neither of us, I think, had been out of London for months and the thought of even a *soupçon* of some pale green buds was enticing. Alas! Like so much else, it was "not yet"—hardly more than a grey interlude between one darkness and the next, a mean, miserly day. And yet, London-wise, it was panoramic and distinctly evocative somewhere near the River Lea . . . And where the devil *was* Epping Forest?

So imperceptible when we got off that one wondered if it were visible only in summer. After a terrible pub-lunch we wandered on, looking for spring now in good earnest. Not a bud, not a spring! Merely a few moments in the icy wind, with a pale shaft of sunlight that made the snapshots just possible, and then back to London—by now "in the gloaming," "returned empty." . . .

"If I ask you again, Norman, how long you think the war is going on, you will say I am getting neurasthenic, but . . ."

"God alone knows—and He won't tell!"

"I must apologise for my awful gloom and dullness!"

"You can't give what you haven't got! Nobody can! We're in the grip, my dear, in the grip. . . ."

How we harped on the sombre chords that day—the old times in Italy and France and Tunisia. Should we ever get back? . . . how much more was to come? . . . and so on.

"*Lack-lustre,* dearest Norman, is what George Moore would have chosen, perhaps, after considerable thought, as a fitting adjective for a day such as this!"

"I suppose we ought to be thankful that we're at least still alive"—and muttering that old, national corrective of all Italians, *Pazienza!* you enfolded yourself in a silence well in keeping with the fog and murk we found enshrouding the streets of our national colossus.

A curious place in which to hear of the capture of Mussolini was that Yorkshire bus bringing me down from near the good grassy peak of Addleborough, the extraordinary news coming from the wireless of a wayside inn as we passed. By the time I reached London again there was a note from you:

> 2 Hereford Square, 27 July, 1943
>
> I have just found what I suppose is your copy of *La France Libre* at Ryan's house where I may have left it. Shall I bring it to you anywhere—a good excuse for a drink to the damnation of Mussolini. . . ."

As for *La France Libre,* although this was quite unknown to me at that time, they were to be the publishers, eleven months later, of a book of mine as yet unplanned! To this you contributed aid, giving me two telling little satirical poems by Neil Hogg for inclusion in that War Anthology, *Poems for France*—in connection with which it seemed to me I was writing all that autumn to every poet in England: "Have you a poem to send me connected with France since the war began?"

Autumn brought us closer to each other, for I had moved again and was now in Half Moon Street in a wonderful sort of "bed-sitter" and we resumed our pleasant rhythm of lunches in the pubs around here. One seemed to be having to think more and more about food, and of all the rarities, look what was produced by you:

> 2 Hereford Square, 19 Dec, 1943
>
> Dearest, I have three fresh eggs for you. So don't forget Tuesday, Queen's, 7:30.

We were often at the Queen's Restaurant, Sloane Square, including a dinner on your birthday this year, and for me it had memories that stretched far back. A night, for one, during the "old" war, with Augustus John, Sybil Hart Davis and Alvaro Guevara, when we dined so long and well that dear Augustus was dashing off exquisite sketches of everyone at the end of it on the tablecloth. Waiters in consternation were assured that piece of napery would be paid for and cut up on the spot, and I still have the little head thus drawn of me. Out of the question, alas, to be allowed to get into such an euphoric condition during *this* war, we sighed. If restaurants knew the importance they have in the moral as well as the physical life of people . . . Well, what then? Let us not get sentimental! It's bad enough when one is in bed at night with one's thoughts, you murmured. As for people's voices— sometimes they go on and on in one's head, continuing the conversation when one wants to sleep, and can't. To Hell with people!

All of that winter I worked on my Anthology of poems for France in the bed-sitter that could be made so warm, and small wonder, for £1.5s.—I worked it out—used to go into the electric meter every week. Often you came here after lunch and we brewed some of that delicious coffee. And once there was an enforced case of "where I dines I sleeps"—the last bus gone and the last Tube, with the nocturnal wails of "Taxi, Taxi" ringing in vain through the black-out all down Piccadilly.

Often *à deux* that winter, Christmas night is one of the times I think of frequently yet, in certain moods. There was a little party for you at which Morris (Gilbert) had supplied some munificent American whisky, and there you sat in my bed-sitter ensconced in all of its dilapidated late-Victorian comfort as five or six of us moved and conversed around you. Finally we were left alone. A distant Radio seemed to be drumming some complicated kind of rhythm and it merged with the languor in my mind, producing a sort of timelessness. . . .

"Come and sit by me on the sofa."

We sat for hours, I know, our arms linked, talking of the things we would do, later . . . later. . . . At present we were playing at being in the *Wagons-Lits*—the very sofa could be said to resemble one. We were crossing France towards Italy, and as romantic about it as could be! *And why not?*

Maybe this was one of the times you told me (the same sentiment was addressed to one or two others as well, on various occasions) that, when the time came, you would like to think of yourself as "putrefying gracefully in your arms, my dear. . . ." —a winning, if at first somewhat startling, remark! It makes me horribly nostalgic to think of that evening now. I cannot tell what kind of charm you had as a young man—nor yet at the age of forty. But, damn it, the charm you had then in 1943, at the age of seventy-five. . . .

The summer that followed was exciting—the Invasion swept on fiercely, with Doodle-Bug-Buzz-Bombs falling "like mad" all over London and around it. Alarming and ghastly as they were, I think of some nice moments with you, with you and Augustus John together in the lordly Pub or Lounge of the Pier Hotel at Battersea Bridge, where suddenly and mercifully the drink supply had generously expanded—to steady the clients' nerves.

"Some people swear we are in a regular track of the beastly things here—but at least one can have a proper drink, any number of drinks at present, ha!"

This "secret weapon number 1" appeared to worry you—and Augustus—less than it did many others, who could be heard saying it was "worse than the Big Blitz." Things were moving fast on the Continent and we were in good spirits the night Morris Gilbert and his cousin Morris Bishop (an erudite Professor of Romance Languages in an American University), and you and I sat under that long, rose-heliotrope sunset by the Thames, with crashes taking place two or three to the minute and some scholarly conversation proceeding the while between you and the Professor. And my Anthology *Poems for France* had come out exactly at the moment of the invasion; it was selling fast and you thought it a good production, considering the regulations for wartime books. Another long dinner together comes to mind—that rather dreamy occasion with Harold Acton in the very middle of the empty Ritz—of all places—safeish and silent, at least. Events were moving so fast that I feared a race had begun (in the eyes of the publisher, that is) between them and the work I was doing—the translation into English of Gabrielle Picabia's excellent, topical book on the Occupation of France; the publisher would tell the author that the book was "out of date." . . . And now the house I was in closed down, the French who ran it leave for France, and grieving that I could not go with them, I went to Oxford; at least I should enjoy your company some of the time there, while I hastened to finish my work.

Yet, I thought vaguely, you might get to France if only you would apply to go there *on a mission*—for such was, understandably, necessary; in your case it would be to write, to describe. As for my house at Réanville, now that a little news circulated between the two countries, every brief message that came from the two French friends there, the only two, said: "Nothing, nothing is left." It looked as if months more of suspense and anxiety were to follow—despite the fact that— yes!—the publisher (curses upon him) turned down the book I had long ago finished translating, telling the author that it *was* "out of date." One evening, now back in London, came the distant sound of heavy artillery: the hammering to pieces of Boulogne. Another evening, a gigantic bang which hung in the air interminably. And what might that be? The first of the V2s, somewhere in Chiswick.

Now, thanks to Aleister Crowley, I found myself living in Jermyn Street, in the house where the spiritualist-proprietress had actually named a room after him (for seances) and where, although she threatened me with her "I shall need your room soon," I managed to stay for months. In this light he was indeed my benefactor, for lodgings were impossible to find. How much *we* talked of him on one occasion! Did you think, for instance, that he really used those little phrases with which he *said* he began and ended *positively all* of his letters? Did he carry it as far as this:

"Messrs Buntleys Bank.
Dear Sirs,
Do what thou wilt shall be the whole of the Law.
Concerning the matter in hand . . ."

Ending with:

"Love is the Law; love under will.

Yours truly . . ."

A very fantastic figure, Crowley!

"*Nothing* in comparison to what he was," you assured me.

And all those scarlet and sable events, were they not connected only with people who flung themselves blindly into whatever mysteries he seemed to represent? You were inclined to agree, although even to me, what I had just said sounded a bit too easily "dismissive." Such a mixture of good and of horrible *taste* in that man. . . .

"He was hot stuff, and no mistake, my dear. They can stand a good deal in Italy, but in the end he was too much for them, and he had to go!"

Meanwhile I was an office-worker again, this time as a translator of English into French (with a good deal of military Americanese thrown in), striving to comply with the request to make it all sound as much like proper French journalism as possible. The eight-hour shifts at SHAEF in Kingsway were gruelling, left one no time for anything, but kept one from miserably brooding over that problematical return to France and what would be there to face one. Typing, and broadcasting at dictation-speed, all day or all night, I now knew the hurried step of the early morning worker, the muffled, dreary return of an evening, the sameness of "tomorrow and tomorrow and tomorrow."

And then Morris Gilbert came on leave and vividly described what he had seen in Normandy—the shambles of my Puits Carré, all due to the results of the animosity of the village mayor, for no fighting had ever occurred just around it. I see his gesture yet, holding out a battered copy of the red leather edition of *One Day,* in which you wrote a few words for him then and there while he told us: "A mattress of ravaged books, six deep, now covers the whole of the bathroom floor." He had found it emerging somewhere near the top. . . .

The criminal imbecility of wars—we had a lot to say about that some time later in Christmas week, on a background of tipsy soldiery in the Bodega back of the Café Royal.

"Could not all these international fights *really* be settled by some form of negotiation?", I asked you.

"Could? Of course they could! But they won't be. There'll be another war after this, and then another, *and* another—pah!"

(Ah—those "scratches on the rocks" of yours . . . that apt remark of Einstein's: "I don't know what weapons World War 3 will be fought with. But those used in World War 4 will be stone clubs.")

The turn of the year brought the great turn in events and now I was snowed under with the reports of the beginning of the agony of Berlin and other German cities, which no one in the office seemed anxious to translate. And my plea to go to France to do some press-articles was at length going successfully. I had often said to you in all the turmoil of news last August that I felt the end of the war would be in sight as soon as the liberation of France began. Now was the time to start my own private campaign; one, obviously, would have to be built up so as to get me back there! As I work at writing and as France is my home, what *could* be more legitimate than to do some writing on France for different English reviews? Starting with *The New Statesman,* it was chance unadulterated that took me to its office the very morning of the second—or Mediterranean—landings, in August—there that I heard the news, asking, at that very moment, if I might do some articles. But no; nothing doing at *The New Statesman.* And soon after this began my work at SHAEF.

What had been happening to the French national art-works during Occupation and devastation? Surely that was a matter, among others, of the greatest magnitude? In short, I thought of Dr. Borenius, editor of *The Burlington Magazine,* and an old friend, although not met for years. He came to see me at once, and there we sat, both of us wan and weary from office-work, in my rickety, bomb-shaken room in Jermyn Street—and naught to offer him but a cup of coffee. How grim and cold was all of this December; how symbolic—said he—of life nowadays. . . . Yes, yes, he would accredit me. . . . Alas, nothing would ever be the same again. We sat huddled over my small electric-heater. No, nothing— And in process of sad talk and nostalgic memories, he thought he discerned a palm-tree in the concave curve. . . . It was but a tiny breath of grease from my solitary, clandestine cooking, yet it caused him to sigh mightily for such far-away, inaccessible strands. Certainly, certainly, I should do articles for him—on art—in France. . . . Thanks also to Peter Watson and Cyril Connolly of *Horizon,* and to those of *Our Time,* there were now three accreditations and, after a mere three months of complete suspense, they were approved. Alas, it was I alone, and not the two of us, who took that strangely-muted train one dark night at Victoria on February 27. As it crept to the coast, during the all-night wait on board, the long rough passage and the still lengthier railway journey through French fields where so much had happened during the five and a half years (this was not even the main line to Paris any more), I wondered not only *when* and *where* but even *if* we should ever meet again. Of that return to France I spare you all my feelings but one: I could have wept that we were not doing this together.

Impossible to find words for the atmosphere in Paris, the "new ways," the emotion of it all! What had not died during the years of betrayal and defeat and passion and resurgence? Faltering and Lazarus-like, how bitter-bitter-sweet to me was that exultation of return.

[Eventually Miss Cunard did find words to describe the "atmosphere in Paris" in an article called "Letter from Paris" (*Horizon,* 1945), a part of which follows.]

LETTER FROM PARIS

March 1945

"Nous pensons que nous allons retrouver la liberté, quand retrouverons-nous l'égalité? Si seulement le pauvre pouvait manger, oui, manger. . . ." ("We think we shall find liberty again, but when equality? If only the poor could eat. . . .")

The letter with these symptomatic words from my village in Normandy came as I finished packing to return at last to France, after five years' absence, six months after the liberation.

It was a strange journey to Paris from Dieppe, not a beast in the fields, hardly a man or woman on the roads, scarcely a village en route. As the half-empty train crept, hastened, then stopped frequently and lengthily during its seven-hour run along these byways of railways, one noted many a bomb-crater along the line. *Le recueillement,* the communing with self, seemed to lie over the whole of the unpeopled landscape, a legacy of the misery of occupation; nothing here but silence and waiting.

At the sufficient but very "disciplined" meal they served us I talked to an eloquent French journalist whom I asked if *la misère* was very noticeable in Paris. "No," said he, "it hides there, the opposite of in the South, where *la misère* is almost on parade." At length, in the dark of night, illuminated at the station approaches by fine new powerful arc-lamps set high, we moved into Paris. With a surging tear I embraced the blue-bloused porter, a hefty man, who said with emotion that it had been *très dur* indeed the whole of these years. And so, Paris again, *at last;* Paris: twenty years of life, for twenty years my home.

I opened the window next morning on to a blaze of grey. Such the effect, from a high sixth floor, of all the roof-tones in the pure Paris sunlight that 26 February. One had forgotten these things. Forgotten, too, that one would hear facts from the very lips of people who had withstood and duped the Boches; how the "Myth of the Maréchal" never took in the great majority of the French, certainly not the working class, nor the *marchande de vins* on the corner (whose husband, killed in the last war, had fought at Verdun and "never thought much of Pétain anyway"); that vivid accounts of Allied bombings of Paris, "most terrifying but approved by us," would throb to the ear; that the concierge (mine is Mme. Stum, a tremendous *résistante* with a grand, resistant husband, both Bretons), might say, as she did say, that her son has just been killed as a *lieutenant des troupes de choc du Général Delattre*. . . .

I am glad that first day back in Paris is over. I know now what Lazarus felt after the tomb. It was terribly painful, and somehow I could not think this out, yet wanted to. Better far to have been flung back into some great street-day, a 1 May, a 14 *juillet*. I walked alone (and have never stopped walking since) down the whole of the Champs Elysées along the Grands Boulevards to the Bourse, glad to be alone, hoping I would meet no one I knew, hesitating on the threshold of what future. . . . Later on, Georges Sadoul, co-founder and present editor of *Les Etoiles,* a literary review started clandestinely, said to me: "Every one of us, Aragon included, felt like this on returning to Paris from exile or from the southern zone."

During the course of that walk, that re-establishing of contact with France, visual intake mercifully predominated. Three things immediately startle: those hats on the women, their fanciful high wooden-soled wedge shoes, and the extraordinary "man-taxis"—bicycle-drawn and motor-bicycle-drawn rickshaws, contraptions in plywood, wicker-work, metal, in anything that contains two people with the least weight of its own. Of the hats the Germans said to the French: "What would they have been like if you had WON the war?" (and it is easy to see how these great, often beautiful turbans came about it: it was indeed a "high-hatting" of the Boches, a sign of undashed spirit). Of the rickshaws people say: "Shocking. But at least strong men pull them and they make a great deal of money."

The Grands Boulevards are full, shops glitter, newspapers (alas, in a reduced form of only one page) are being sold; most of the cafés stay open till 8 or 9 at night, some shut a day or two per week. Salty, golden water called beer, quite acceptable cognac, and café national cost you six, ten, twenty times as much as the authentic things did formerly.

To force myself out of the extraordinary feeling of strangeness with which the return from exile troubled me during those first hours, I went to *Ce Soir,* one of the biggest dailies, installed with some eight other of the ex-clandestine resistance papers in the palatial offices of suppressed, pro-Vichy *Paris-Soir.* Within a few moments its scholarly, intellectual chief editor, Louis Parrot, was telling me of the immense number of new books, reviews, poems, plays and people that constitute the beginning of the "after the war" *efflorescence,* already well on the way. Yes, they are in advance here on what you might think would be the "normal" time-table. The war is not over, but activity in all things of the intellect and of the arts is already in its stride, because France is free of the Germans, because there is an *immense* desire and intention of renewing all the old links with the rest of the world as soon as may be, and because this is just characteristic of France's eternal, beautiful force of renewal.

Even to list new books and reviews and talk a little about the writers and other intellectuals would need a separate article, so here are merely some notes, rather at random:

Paul Valéry's *Bergson* is soon coming out. Aragon's new novel *Aurelieu* is extremely successful; likewise a new poem of his "La Diane Française"; Jean Paulhan is at the Nouvelle Review Française. Sartre and Camus have been constantly mentioned to me as the two outstanding new writers; *Les Mouches* of the former, *Mal Entendu* of the latter, are cited as THE books to read for a knowledge of what occupation was like. Vercor's *Marche à l'Etoile* (on the persecution of the Jews) ranks high. Marcel Arland's *Antarès,* with illustrations by Marie Laurençin, is announced. A very interesting work will be the book on Resistance-writers and poets by Louis Parrot. These, thanks mainly to Aragon's animating and organizing spirit, were grouped into the *Comité National des Ecrivains*—in both zones. *Les Lettres Françaises,* the big literary weekly, and *Les Etoiles* were its mouthpieces; both started clandestinely in the occupied and unoccupied regions. George Adam, editor of *Les Lettres Françaises,* has written a superb book, *L'Epée dans les Reins,* on the first of the Nazi years here; Claude Roy's *Les Yeux Ouverts dans Paris Insurgé* is brilliant reportage of the six great days that freed Paris.

Carrefour is another literary weekly. *Régards* has come out again. Praised as a vivid picture of occupation is a sort of diary by Jean Galtier-Boissière (who was editor of *Le Crapouillot*). There are indeed such literary riches, and the immediate present seems to overlap with such profusion on the immediate past, that it is impossible in a fortnight, doing widely different things and so many of them, to appraise, evaluate, analyse "trends"—least of all, predict. And there is still a sort of tendency to think of "two zones." Thus, Tzara, Jean Cassou, Moussinac and many others have made a capital of Toulouse. André Malraux and André Chamson are with the Armies. Eluard, whose productivity throughout, like that of Aragon under various pseudonyms, was immense, is in Paris. He has just written me: "I never want to leave France again." His public, which is pretty well everybody, adores him. Aragon and Eluard share about evenly, I should say, the gratitude of France, as poets, and as leaders.

On the left bank the literary cafés, the *Deux Magots* and the *Flore* are as full as ever. The latter, one hears, remained a perfect moral fortress against the Boches; the Germans hesitated to enter it. Today, it is a veritable centre of intellectual productivity; Sartre sits there writing lengthily when in Paris; there is almost a "School of the Café de Flore"—that of the most active of the numerous resistance groups. It is certainly an oasis in the desert of daily difficulties that have to be coped with: food, transport, lack of time to do things.

For—not a bus, not a taxi, the Metro like a Cup-Final crowd most of the time, the appalling cost of *everything*—gas without strength, electricity without heat, *ersatz* prevalent, ration-cards even for salt. Eighteen different slips of paper per month for various articles of food, but often these articles, meat and cookingfats particularly, are non-existent! Is anything on sale instead? NO, not until two weeks ago, when a tiny slice of American spam appeared instead of meat. Milk, chocolate and oranges are allowed only to children, and milk only to the youngest. The total lack of coffee (*Mélange National* is made of acorns, chicory and something else, but without coffee in it) save on the Black Market at anything like 1000 francs a lb., is a national disaster. Think of England without any tea whatever and you have the comparison, though lack of coffee is worse.

Yet the Parisian temper is good. It is patient, greatly troubled and denunciatory of all this beastliness in daily living, appreciative of the first needs of war, appreciative of the British and the Americans (definitely the great majority of French people are). *This is so in all classes.* I know two or three people who have returned to London from here saying "the French are furious, they think it's worse than under the Germans, and even preferred them." These people are either deliberately lying or saw only Fascists and fifth columnists—who of course continue to exist, and many a complaint have I heard that the "cleaning-up" process was not done quickly enough and is very far from thorough. The protagonists of "the French are furious" certainly never talked to the man in the street, nor to anyone else representative.

Despite all these difficulties of transport, of daily living, and the hesitation with which one meets friends in the bar or café, where a few drinks can run to several hundred francs, Paris IS Paris. Hardly damaged at all by bombs, save in some of its suburbs (badly so there), in the centre it is elegant, busy, rhythmical, alive with new plays and old, films, picture-shows, spring fashion displays.

The Germans have massacred, tortured, blackmailed, attacked psychologically and done much more, but they have emphatically NEVER dominated the spirit of the men, women and children of France. They have tried to make people as corrupt as themselves (and in some cases Vichy Fascists could give the Germans lessons in baseness and vice— a pretty small minority of people, these, however, out of the 40 million beings who live in France). Everywhere, in every class and region, the Germans were met with fortitude, with dignity and stupendous self-sacrifice, with the real *noblesse d'âme* of a fine and extremely resurgent people. All will be well here with the right handling, that is to say, if only things, things of daily life foremost, are done with as much honesty and vision as possible. Life can be rebuilt fast, I am sure. It will be part of the national honour that is in every ordinary normal man and woman to do this.

And in the time, first, of amelioration, then of well-being that one hopes is on the way, friendship and a deeper feeling than ever for England will be evident. *"On a besoin l'un de l'autre*—our countries need each other." THAT is what has been said to me more than anything else during the course of the first fourteen days back in France.

[Although Miss Cunard knew before returning to France that her home near Réanville had been damaged during the war, she was unprepared for the actual devastation that awaited her. *These Were the Hours* contains a longer and more detailed account of the destruction than that which follows. The following passage is from *Grand Man*.]

AGAIN RÉANVILLE

You and I had sat under those lindens at Réanville one year and two months before the catastrophe began and now I was faced with the shambles. Not a door, not a window remained. . . . Everything I had was here, and now almost all was gone. Jean and Georgette Goasgüen, those two of such true heart, to whom I owe all that does remain, had risked their very lives in saving what they could. And, as they began to collect and hand over all they had hidden, they told me shaking with indignation of the evil mayor—still mayor at that very moment. He, and none other, must be held responsible; he had left my house open to all after taking the keys from them, threatening to denounce them to the Germans if they went on protecting my belongings. French reservists . . . wandering waves of refugees and looters at different times . . . lastly the German soldiers billeted there, who had burned and destroyed every object except some books. The mayor (protector of other properties) had said it was "a very good house for them to be in"; at one moment, he had tried to sell it too, but was deterred by the broadcasts from England that such dealings would entail due punishment later. The spate of description raced on for days. . . .

Invisible blood and tears of ravaged books and pictures! Here a drawing by Wyndham Lewis under a tree. . . . There, among scattered pieces of type and shreds of African beading under the straw that all soldiers leave behind, were some fragments of coral, hammered to smithereens. What else among them but a leaf from that pastoral brooch you had given me once in Florence? The Germans had ceremoniously burned the whole set of last-century *Punch* on the grass, before stoning all my pieces of African sculpture that were still left and blazing them up in the kitchen stove. Stabbed papers, wounds and mutilations everywhere—the little printery with its heavy old beam sawn in two and the roof taken off—although the old Mathieu Press had defied them. On another out-building, the words *Achtung, Waffen!* The deep well fouled with excrement, a dead sheep, some books, smashed china and other fragments were in it yet. The German commander, gazing at my two abstract paintings by Tanguy and Malkine, had said he would hang me *if only* he could lay hands on me.

"*Tu sembles être une* pillouère *née*"—Georgette murmured, using the Breton word for *scavenger* as I raked through everything for days, coming across a few of your books, our Tunisian snapshots, the last copy of *One Day* (the unsigned edition this time) duly stamped, as was all else, with the hobnail mark of the beast.

I had not many thoughts for anything or anyone at this time, except that which occurred at frequent intervals.

luis enrique délano

Nancy Cunard in Chile
Recordando a Nancy

Estoy pensando qué podría agregar yo a lo mucho que se ha dicho y se ha escrito sobre Nancy Cunard, como no sea una impresión personal de ella, un recuerdo de los días en que la conocí, en el Madrid asediado de fines de 1936. Fue en la casa de Pablo Neruda, esa Casa de las Flores que aparece mencionada en un poema de *España en el corazón,* donde había tenido yo la suerte de conocer a cuanto poeta de Europa o de América llegaba a Madrid, desde Robert Desnos hasta Raúl González Tuñón, y también a los españoles de esos días, a García Lorca, a Alberti, a Miguel Hernández, a Cernuda, a Altolaguirre y tantos y tantos más. Pregunté quién era esa mujer de cuya piel, de una blancura azulada y translúcida, parecía estar ausente la sangre. Es imposible hallarse en presencia de un ser con ese aire tan absolutamente inédito de Nancy Cunard—su elevada estatura, su delgadez exagerada, los cabellos rubios y unas anchas pulseras de marfil que parecían crecer, ser más grandes en cada ocasión—sin interesarse por conocer algo suyo. No fue difícil saber cosas, pues la precedía la leyenda de su aristocracia desdeñada por ella misma; la de los salones literarios de Lady Cunard, su madre; la de sus relaciones con la poesía inglesa, con la bohemia luchadora de París, con el África oprimida; la de sus denuncias y sus grandes peleas con el colonialismo. No era difícil, repito, saber de quién se trataba, si los rasgos de Nancy andaban en muchos poemas y por lo menos en dos novelas famosas: *Contrapunto,* de su enamorado Huxley, y *El sombrero verde,* de Michael Arlen.

Como muchos otros poetas y escritores europeos, Nancy había llegado a España a ver por sí misma, con sus propios ojos—unos ojos suaves y de un desvanecido color celeste—el asalto del fascismo a la República, y al pueblo en armas, puesto de pie para rechazarlo con decisión. Anduvo por todas partes, se relacionó con todo el mundo, abrió ojos y oídos al rumor de la guerra desatada y más tarde desahogó todo su sentimiento en su lengua propia, la poesía. Pero hizo más que eso: para ayudar a la causa de la República Española se transformó en reportera, en periodista, en editora y hasta en tipógrafo. En París, con Neruda, se puso a parar con sus propias manos los tipos de las ediciones *Los poetas del mundo defienden al pueblo español,* que publicaron versos de García Lorca, Alberti, González Tuñón, Aragon, Neruda, Tzara, Guillén . . . También uno de la propia Nancy, *Para hacerse amar,* escrito en inglés y vertido al español por Vicente Aleixandre.

Hacia fines de 1939 o comienzos del 40, Nancy llegó a Santiago y la acogimos con calor chileno y una amistad que acostumbramos a otorgar de golpe, el primer día, al extranjero, y muchísimo más si es un artista, un poeta. Cuando pisó Santiago, sólo la conocíamos en persona Pablo Neruda y yo. Una semana después, Nancy era amiga de todos los poetas, de todos los escritores, de todos los pintores y, en fin, de cuantos por esos días nos agrupábamos en la Alianza de Intelectuales, con el ánimo puesto en las grandes batallas de esos días. La guerra de España habia terminado con el resultado conocido y los amigos españoles de Nancy estaban distribuyéndose, buscando el calor del mundo para pasar los días de un destierro que se creyó sería breve, pero que dura ya más de un cuarto de siglo. De los poetas y los artistas españoles que Nancy habia conocido en Madrid, algunos estaban en la Unión Soviética, otros en México y unos cuantos en Chile. No pocos languidecían en campos de concentración en Francia o comenzaban, como Miguel Hernández, a padecer una muerte diferida, de cárcel en cárcel, en la propia España ahogada por el fascismo.

Nancy vivió entre nosotros con extrema naturalidad, pues tenía un raro sentido de la adaptación. Hablaba el español y en poco tiempo era amiga de todo el mundo, se la veía en las reuniones de la Alianza de Intelectuales, en las tertulias literarias, en los bares donde solíamos reunirnos. Trabó amistad íntima con un escritor casi desconocido, a quien quiso ayudar, traduciendo al inglés un libro suyo. Era generosa, alegre y de una viveza y una penetración intelectuales muy notables.

En junio de 1940 viajamos en el mismo barco, entre Valparaíso y el puerto mexicano de Manzanillo: un barco japonés que se fue deteniendo en cada puerto, en cada caleta, y que tardó un mes en recorrer esa ruta. Allí conversé mucho con ella y aprendí a conocerla mejor, a valorar lo profundo de su espiritu de justicia, del fervor revolucionario con que había escandalizado a los salones literarios de Londres: ese ímpetu que la llevó a levantar el grito por los explotados negros de África y a atacar con extremada violancia, en sus actos, en sus escritos y en sus palabras, al fascismo, al clero y a la parte podrida de la tradición que desataron la guerra de España.

La última vez que la vi fue en la ciudad de México. Era sorprendente la soltura con que se desplazaba con sus ropas de inglesa, a todas luces chocantes con nuestro medio: sus faldas de *tweed,* su sombrero a cuadros, semejante al gorro de doble visera que los viejos dibujantes acostumbraban a poner en la cabeza de Sherlock Holmes, su enorme bolso de mano. Recuerdo que los mexicanos, no obstante su costumbre de ver tenidas inusitadas en las turistas de Estados Unidos, miraban a Nancy con una especie de complaciente extrañeza. Creo que desde allí partió a Europa y los años tremendos de la Segunda Guerra Mundial, que ya había comenzado, se la tragaron. Sé que ella debe haber estado luchando (otra cosa no se entendería en un espíritu como el suyo), pero ignoro dónde y lo que hacía. Después sólo tuve muy de tarde en tarde noticias lejanas de Nancy: que estaba enferma, que había sido detenida en Ellis Island, cuando quiso entrar a los Estados Unidos, y devuelta a Europa. Hasta que llegó la que debía ser la más dolorosa de todas: su muerte en Francia.

El recuerdo que guardo de Nancy Cunard es el de una mujer sincera a toda prueba, sin prejuicios hipócritas, una mujer que se entregaba a todo poniendo el corazón en sus causas, en sus luchas, en sus amores; una intelectual con comprensión plena, cabal, de su época y de todas aquellas grandes empresas por las que valía la pena pelear hasta la muerte.

Cartagena, junio de 1966

sylvia townsend warner
Nancy Cunard

A contribution to *Authors Take Sides* was my first link with Nancy Cunard. We had some correspondence about Spain, but we did not meet till the winter of 1942–43, when Morris Gilbert's work brought him on a visit to Dorset and she came with him. They, Valentine Ackland and I met for lunch at a hotel in Dorchester. Slender, long-legged, walking with a neat, slightly tripping gait, like a water-wag-tail's, she came in carrying with elegance a large onion. At that date every scrap of paper was needed for making Heads of Departments; it was ordinary for purchases to be unwrapped. But Nancy carried her onion with a difference. That same evening she and Morris dined with us. As they were leaving, she slid the heavy African ivory bracelets off her wrists and asked us to look after them. They would be safer in a Dorset village than in London. She looked sadly at her wrists when they were off. She would have felt much less denuded if she had stripped off her clothes.

Possibly the bracelets drew her back, for she came for several week-ends that winter. She prided herself on traveling light. Nothing was forgotten, nothing was crumpled, everything was fitted into the small-est possible compass: a tartan haversack, supplemented perhaps by a Dick Whittington spotted handkerchief. Settled in, she began to preen: a button was made fast, a lining re-stitched; the bracelets were fetched and devoutly polished; after that, she would polish her nails or do a little washing. On a desert island, in a jail cell, she would have kept herself spruce, well-kept, clean as a cat. Her temper was notorious, her life was wilful and erratic—and she was compellingly respect-worthy. Loyal, industrious, thorough, she had the qualities that make the sublimely good servant—a good servant in French, at that, for she was *courageuse:* an indomitable worker. She had another domestic merit: she was punctual. I have cooked many meals for Nancy and never known her late for one of them. Whatever she had been doing, however absorbing it had been, she would be ready—brushed and combed and creditable; and sitting upright and slightly formalised, she would converse agreeably, as a guest should. This frosting of social convention made her peculiarly entertaining, since it co-existed with a wide range of violent opinions and violent language. Even when she was drunk, it persisted, though *allargando* into solemnity and owlishness. "Nancy, you're tight." "Only a little, darling"—flawlessly enunciated. And when an explosion of feeling broke through this habitual *bel canto,* the effect was formidable.

Yes, she was formidable. But as it happened, I was not afraid of Nancy and we never fell out. Each of us sometimes found the other exasperating; but we saw eye to eye about Spain. It was that which cemented us. Her engagement with Spain, her implacable loyalty to what the democracies had allowed to become a lost cause, made her take a rather *de haut en bas* view of Britain's protracted series of Finest Hours. When she talked of life in London, it was muddle and officialdom she complained at, not danger and privation. Air-raids were no more than what we had asked for when we turned a deaf ear to *Arms for Spain* and a wall-eye on Guernica. The only air-raid I remember her referring to was one when incendiary bombs set fire to dumps of domestic fuel stored in Hyde Park. Among these was a dump of those singularly incombustible pellets called Boulet Bernod. "Actually burning," she said with enthusiasm. "What a strange sight!"

She had an eye to notice such details—it was part of the good servant side of her character, as was her power to nail a personality in a phrase. I asked her—she was then working for the Free French—what General de Gaulle was like. In a flash she replied: "Froid, sec et cassant."

This dash and dexterity in the spoken word flowered from the pains she took in writing. Her French translations of the *Poems for France* anthology were arrived at after countless expedients and discardings and considerations and consultings. I remember a postscript, the handwriting enlarged by triumph. "Darling! Got it at last, *de croupir longuement.*" This was poetry, and she was a poet. But she would be as self-exacting over something she was unconcerned by. Once, when she was staying with us, she brought down a commissioned translation of an article about French painters. It was quite unimportant, it was plain sailing, until a painter of marine subjects involved a technical term in rigging. Dictionaries were fetched, and failed. Sea-going authors were looked through, in case one of them came up with the term she needed. Telephone calls were made. The passage was really not of the slightest importance, but she must have spent over an hour on it. And reading through the final version, her face assumed the particular grimace of such moments: wary, censorious, bleak.

For though the application might be the same, the mood was totally different. Her concern with poetry was carnal and passionate: she pursued the word, the phrase, with the patience of a weasel, the concentration of a falcon: When a poem happened to cost her no trouble, she was as pleased as if she'd stolen it out of the church collection.

The other achievements were a matter of technical self-respect, to be classed with the packing and the polishing, the type-setting performed with un-inked fingers, the *serpette* slashing with authority among the brambles round her yellow house at Lamothe.

Early in 1944 she came to Dorset in search of a lodging where Norman Douglas would be warmed, well-fed, out of bombs' way and within reach of female attentions. I felt a heartless relief when this project fell through: it seemed to me that if anyone needed the female attentions, etc., it was Nancy. She was thin as a wraith and had a tormenting neuritis in her shoulder. This did not prevent her from walking with great speed and energy over the downs, nor from coming back with such loads of flints in her coat-pockets that silhouetted on a skyline her slender person gave the impression that panniers had been fastened on a cheetah. During the next hour or so, Nancy would be in the bathroom, working on the flints with a nailbrush. Then a towel would be spread over her bed and the flints laid out—to be admired, examined, graded: some for more polishing, others to be rejected. This capacity for magpie delighting was one of her prettiest charms. She used to collect beads (and sewed little bags exactly to contain them), shells, small nonsenses. When Valentine, at a rather later date, gave her nineteen mother-of-pearl "fish" counters, she recorded it in:

A NINETEEN OF PISCES

Nineteen little fishes
(Never been so clean)
Roach and dace
And tench and plaice
And dab and brill and bream.
Skate and hake
And flounder's mate
And spreckleback in stream.
Herring, grayling,
Whiting, spratling,
All together for an outing . . .
Cod and polk and carp and trout,
And that's *nineteen*—no odd man out—
All in a horn—not on a dish—
19's *my* number: I'm a Fish.

and signed it, with circumstantial exactitude: N. At 2 a.m. Dec. 11, 1953.

From the downs where Nancy collected flints we could see an unusual amount of traffic on the roads: camions and muffled vehicles of odd shapes. Everyone knew that something was going on and creditably few remarked on it. In March of 1944 a frontier was enforced along the South Coast. Non-residents must go outside it, residents must remain within. Once again, Nancy packed with her practised hand; and moved into Somerset. This disconcerted many plans, and she was in no condition to make out alone in a strange neighborhood. But when we met—and meet we did, for there was a conveniently situated little railway station on the borderline—her *bel canto* was unaffected. Shivering with cold, shrugging the pain in her shoulder, she walked up and down the platform beside me as though we were doing it for pleasure.

I remembered this when, many years later, I saw her good manners shining against a blacker adversity.

Pas de carence de vie ici, nenni—
Mais tant de paroles perdues pour dire "attendre."

So ends one of the poems in the group called *In Time of Waiting* which she wrote when she went back to Spain in 1959. They are poems of great force and anguish. Her patience cracked, her bodyguard of practical virtues deserted her, she behaved outrageously. On her return to England she was certified as insane and shut up.

The day we went to see her, the sun shone effusively on her place of detention. We were directed along a series of corridors to a door where we were to ring for admission. We rang, and heard a key turn in the lock; the door was locked after us, and we were directed to a more social corridor where we were put to wait at one of a row of little tables (flowers on it, of course) while an attendant went off with keys under her apron to tell Miss Cunard of our arrival. When she came towards us, she was so unchanged I could not believe it was she.

She was neither harshened nor subdued. She was pleased to see us exactly as she would have been if we had met outside. Her affection rang true. In that hygienic limbo she made us feel welcome, familiar and unconstrained. It was only when she began to talk of plans for when she was let out that I realized, with shock, that something had died in her; and thought, her objective has died in her. Whatever it was, she kept to herself. "It will have been funny," she had once written to me, from Port Vendres, where she was waiting, uncertain where to go next, "my life. How enormously much of it A-LONE."

anthony hobson

Nancy Cunard

I first met Nancy Cunard in 1941 or 1942 when she came with Norman Douglas to dinner in my father's house. I was eagerly looking forward to meeting her. Not only was she celebrated as a negrophile, then a rare and suspect cause, but she symbolised the Twenties for me, in my private mythology a lost Golden Age of happiness and licence. My recollection of the occasion has merged with later ones; I think she tried hard to make the evening successful, but Norman Douglas monopolised attention by his silences, hardly broken except towards the end when he said to her, "You remember going for a walk with me in the Tuileries Gardens one winter? You were wearing long green woollen stockings and a very short skirt. A crowd of small boys collected and you said, 'Look, Norman, they're following you.' 'No, Nancy,' I said, 'It's you they're following.'" Soon after they had to leave to make their way home through the blackout before the first air-raid of the night.

After that there were many lunches together, in the Savoy Grill or in small restaurants in Soho. Nancy's appearance, bizarrely evocative of the Twenties with her tall thin figure, waistless dress, bandeau and long string of beads, would make everyone look up as she came into the room. She herself was unconscious of the stir her entrance caused, having learned long before to ignore those she thought boringly conventional. As she crossed the room one saw her for a moment from outside, noticing the superficial eccentricity, only to be captivated immediately by her warmth of greeting, her distinction of poise and manner, her beautifully modulated voice and magnificent wide-set blue eyes. She always listened to one's doings with grave and courteous attention. Conversation was punctuated by the rhythmic clash of the rise and fall of her African ivory bracelets (illustrated on the cover of *Henry-Music*), worn seven or eight on each arm.

After the war we met only occasionally. In 1955 she wrote about a projected book on African ivory sculpture, unfortunately never completed although she collected two exercise-books of notes on examples in Germany, Switzerland and Holland. The sale of some of her books in 1961 started our correspondence again. This time it flourished, as by then I had become keenly interested in the Hours Press and her own poetry. Her letters (three in a single day, on one occasion) were very like her conversation, full of sudden exclamations: "How you would like my part of Lot—its roaring dialect!" "Don't miss the ANDES," she wrote before a journey to South America, and another letter improbably confided, like a character in a Firbank novel, "How I should have liked to be an actor—preferably of the male sex." Press-cuttings were often enclosed: "I don't know why I cut this piece out for you—beautiful writing, I think!" A description of Dali's *Apocalypse* was accompanied by her comments on "the bronze cover—what vulgarity, what splurginess without conviction, what a dreary colour it is!", and later, "it gives one the jim-jams."

Re-reading her letters one is conscious of a perpetual background of ill-health, bronchitis, congestion of the lungs, emphysema. They are mentioned but not dwelt on. A postscript in 1962, "I am *very ill,* and say it with rage!" is the nearest approach to a complaint. Normally her vigorous courage was in control, as in a letter written from hospital at Gourdon: "There are hours here which I actually enjoy: those at this terrible typewriter!"

In August 1964 my wife and I visited the cottage at Lamothe-Fénelon which Nancy had bought after the war. A neighbor was posted on the road from Gourdon to show us where to leave the car; from there a track wound past ruined walls to the house, a converted stone barn standing on a narrow terrace overgrown with rye grass. Nancy was waiting outside; she was erect as in the past, her eyes and voice unchanged, but her face had aged and her arms were painfully thin. After dinner we were shown round: kitchen, sitting-room and bedroom downstairs, Nancy's bedroom and *salle de travail* in the roof, filled with a mass of books, albums of press-cuttings, some African wooden sculpture, a few pictures and an abstract decoration by John Banting. We signed the visitors' book, almost the only signatures that year. Nancy's welcome was as warm as ever and she was quite unembittered by her relative loneliness (a French friend was spending the summer with her).

I had suggested to John Hayward that he should ask Nancy for an article on the Hours Press for *The Book Collector*. At first doubtful, she eventually became intrigued by the minutiae of bibliographical description. It was published in the December 1964 number and she was delighted with her offprints. "Despite morning shakes," she wrote on January 3rd, "I seize my pencil to thank you yet again for this lovely thing you have done for me." It was the last piece of her writing published in her lifetime. Three weeks later she suffered a severe fall in the South of France and broke her hip. The accident did not prevent her writing, but with the pain of the injury a new note of asperity entered her letters. An extraordinary twelve-page letter dated "Midnight 18-19 February" was like a violent spasm of life before the encroachment of fatal illness. A more serene postcard followed; then, entirely unexpected, the news of her death in Paris.

Nancy Cunard had two considerable achievements in book production, other than authorship, though both may now seem flawed masterpieces. *Negro* (1934), the anthology she edited and published, is an extraordinary document, if only for its mixture of names of the past (Pound, Douglas) with those of the future (Azikiwe, Kenyatta). Although possibly an enzyme in the fermentations of the Fifties and Sixties, it now reads more like an antiquarian record of past attitudes, and many of its protestations sound shrill to a generation who would be ashamed to deny (though not necessarily intellectually convinced of) the book's thesis—that the Negro is culturally and creatively the white man's equal.

"What was it moved you to enlist
In our sad cause your all of heart and soul?"

the West Indian poet Alfred Cruikshank once addressed her. This was a good question; a candid reply would have to take into account Nancy's dislike of "Her Ladyship" (*Black Man and White Ladyship*, a public attack on mother by daughter to which it would be hard to find a parallel). But what is now striking is less that the enquiry remained unanswered as the archaic sentiment of the question; no modern coloured author would talk about "our sad cause." *Negro* was the first serious and comprehensive documentation in support of the coloured races' claim to equal treatment; startling in its novelty in 1934, it has suffered the normal fate of *avant garde* works of being dated by events. But how much more vital it still is than most products of what Auden called the "low dishonest decade."

The Hours Press, which Nancy started and owned, published twenty-four books and pamphlets between 1928 and 1931. Though some of the poems seem to have been chosen as much for their attitudes of revolt as for merit (Aldington's *Hark the Herald* is hardly more than a belch at convention), the decision to print original works (exceptions were made for two old friends, Norman Douglas and George Moore), instead of the deckle-edged reprints of the classics favoured by most English private presses, gave the enterprise a genuine interest as well as its chief scoop, Samuel Beckett's first book *Whoroscope*, winner of a £10 prize offered by the Press for the best poem on "Time." (Seven years later she printed the first edition of Auden's *Spain,* beating Faber's to it by a month.) Nancy's talent for experimental design comes out in the wide and satisfying range of covers; the photo-montage of *Henry-Music* is the most successful, with Elliott Seabrooke's blue and white boards for *This Chaos* as runner-up. Brian Howard's *First Poems* and Bob Brown's *Words* have calligraphic patterns which anticipate the beautiful binding, blocked in red on black, of *Negro.* Nancy followed with pleasure the latter's rising price on the antiquarian market; with the Hours Press books it is a lasting memorial to her adventurous spirit.

ewart milne

On Nancy Cunard

I was over here in England for the war effort and working on the land when Nancy Cunard asked me to come and talk to her about the poems I'd sent her on the fall of France. It was in 1943, it must have been because her anthology *Poems for France* came out in London in 1944. Or it may have been earlier. Her room in a friend's flat was strewn as writers' rooms always are, papers with everything. She was tall and thin, vibrant with it, and when I'd spoken two words with her I felt lifted, because I knew that unlike so many politically active people, women above all, she really did know about poetry and really did love it. She was prepared to use poetry to further the cause of the Free French movement, but somehow I knew this did not mean she put the cause first and the poetry a long way behind. That was, and I imagine is, the British political fashion—and indeed it used to be the Irish fashion, too. But you didn't feel that with Nancy Cunard.

The second thing that struck me about her was her absolute fearlessness. I don't know whether it was she who had helped to smuggle Louis Aragon's poems out of France some time previously, but she did mention his poetry, and I gathered she knew him, and his wife, Elsa. Probably this was in connection with a piece of mine called "*July 14, 1942*" which she wanted to use in her *Poems for France* anthology.

When I say she was fearless in the expression of her views I mean she gave them forth as if no one could possibly have any other views. Her views mainly coincided then with the Communist Party line, I mean she had thrown herself into the anti-Fascist, anti-Generalissimo Franco fight long before, as well as having worked on the "anti-racialist front"—for the Negro Press of the United States—and was when I met her working devotedly for the "second front" against Hitler, and so on. She was the aristocratic rebel to her slender fingertips, and I fell immediately and completely under her spell. I told her I was not a member of any British political party, and not any longer a member of any Irish political party either. Nancy said she'd guessed that when she saw me because I looked a bit aloof, and we both laughed.

We met once again, and she showed me the French translation she'd made of my poem from *Listen Mangan,* "L'Histoire? Il ne reste que. . . ." which she wanted to include in the French edition of her anthology, *Poèmes à la France* (1947), but I don't want to give the impression that I was only interested because she was an editor. This was far from the truth. We liked each other, or let me say I'm sure I liked Nancy Cunard, and could have become devoted to her in no time, only no time was given, and she returned to France to carry on her work. She was a wonderful woman, a most brave person, and a poet herself who had the French rather than the British attitude to poets and poetry. Which is to say that she thought, felt, and held, that they were important; that being a poet conferred a standing and a dignity, and that poetry should be rightfully placed at the centre of social living, and not as was the case in Britain (and the rest of the world almost) on the margins.

We corresponded for a while, and she sent me two or three "Planes tanks guns" sort of poems of hers, obviously hating the planes, tanks, guns with all her splendid heart, but trying to accept and put up with them for the sake of getting rid of Hitler. This may seem like a big laugh today, but in 1943-44 we really did believe some of the propaganda, though I do not think Nancy Cunard would have felt the same about the Russians or the Soviet Union after Hungary. It would have been a case of "Tanks for the Memory" with her, too, I fancy, as it was for another woman friend of mine, who shook the Budapest dust off her feet at that time. For myself, all the perfumes of Arabia will not now sweeten the Russian hand.

But though we ceased to write I never felt I'd lost touch at all with Nancy Cunard, and the report of her death in 1965 was a great shock. I felt guilty, too. I felt she had been lonely in her last years in France. Not because it was France, she didn't want to live in England again, but just lonely. Her death happened only six months, or a bit more, after the death of my wife, Thelma Swinburne, and of a third friend, Mrs. May Keating, wife of John Keating the great Irish artist, a great friend of my wife's and of myself. All three women had been champions of human liberty, tolerance, and love in all things, and within nine months all were gone. Two of them had given me their friendship, and one had married me with her love. I feel I have one thing at any rate in common with Yeats, in that the women he loved had a greatness of their own, quite apart from him. I happen to think and believe that all three women I have mentioned here were great women, each of them after her fashion, and that somewhere all three fashions are indestructible.

VI

Turning Back:
Mallorca
Toulouse
Lamothe-Fénelon
Cap Ferrat

1946–1965

introductory by henri viers

Madame Nancy Cunard
Femme de Lettres à Lamothe-Fénelon

Bien avant de venir me fixer définitivement à Lamothe-Fénelon avec ma femme, enfant du pays, je venais chaque année en vacances dans cette petite commune. Le Parisien que je suis fut tout de suite séduit et émerveillé par ce lieu où flotte toujours le souvenir de Fénelon qui, comme chacun sait, fut le précepteur de Duc de Bourgogne puis archevêque de Cambrai et qui serait né, selon une tradition qui est restée vivace ici, le 6 août 1651 dans le château que sa famille possédait à Lamothe-Fénelon (Haute), qui portait à cette époque le nom de Lamothe-Massaut.

A cette tradition locale s'oppose une autre tradition, officielle celle-là, qui veut que Fénelon soit né au château de Fénelon à Sainte-Mondane (en Périgord). Ne soulevons pas de polémiques. . . .

Fénelon dans ses écrits a souvent comparé le ciel de notre beau Quercy, et celui de Périgord si voisin, à celui de la Grèce. Impregîné de ce sentiment, il avait d'ailleurs baptisé du nom de Calypse l'île qu'il voyait de son Doyenné de Carennac où il aurait écrit son "Télémaque."

Il est fort possible que Madame Nancy Cunard, grande voyageuse, ait été seduite, elle aussi, par cette ambiance et le charme de notre région qui l'auraient incité à venir se fixer pour la belle saison dans ce petit coin de France; quoiqu'il en fut, je ne tardai pas à faire connaissance avec elle.

Au premier abord, sa haute et mince silhouette, sa maigreur excessive, donnaient une impression indéfinissable qui s'effaçait bien vite dès qu'elle parlait car alors on était séduit par sa conversation.

Cette conversation était émaillée de quelques souvenirs des voyages qu'elle effectuait chaque année. Espagne, Portugal, Baléares, Grèce, Egypte lui étaient des lieux familiers. Après ces évocations, elle s'inquiétait aussitôt des travaux auxquels on pouvait se livrer.

Artiste-peintre, vieil amateur ayant, plus de quarante ans de métier, historien local ayant pris pour but d'écrire l'histoire des lieux qui entourent Lamothe-Fénelon, sans oublier celle de ce dernier, elle ne pouvait que s'intéresser à mes activités. Discutant sur l'âge d'une vieille tour ou d'un vieux moulin, sur quelques faits ou anecdotes locale de tradition ou d'histoire. Son jugement était toujours très juste et l'on tombait vite d'accord avec elle.

Nancy Cunard, femme de Lettres, avait acquis à Lamothe-Fénelon une petite maison paysanne qu'elle avait fait réparer et arranger très simplement et avec goût où elle aimait chaque année, au retour de la belle saison, à venir se reposer de ses voyages et où elle recevait souvent quelques unes de ses relations. Là, elle se livrait dans le calme à ses travaux de traduction en langue anglaise d'oeuvres de Grands Auteurs.

Lorsque le temps était beau, elle aimait s'installer pour travailler, sur une table rustique qu'elle avait fait placer sous un arbre, avec tous ses documents, et là, elle oeuvrait en fumant force cigarettes. . . .

A l'intérieur, elle avait embelli cette humble demeure avec de beaux tapis rapportés de ses voyages qu'elle avait tendus le long des murs, avec quelques tableaux, et aussi avec de beaux meubles anglais qu'elle avait réunis là. Elle aimait également décorer quelque étagère avec des vieux ceps de vigne tordus et de formes bizarres qu'elle ramassait au cours de ses promenades champêtres.

A l'extérieur, on trouvait des pierres ouvragées qu'elle avait recueillis dans quelque ruine, entre autres, une très curieuse pierre provenant d'un ancien manteau de cheminée d'une maison détruite. Cette pierre avait été retrouvée enfouie sous des gravats, et elle représentait, sculptée, une figure entourée de rayons, emblème du Roi Soleil, Louis XIV. Elle avait été très heureuse de l'acquérir et de la faire mettre en bonne place contre un mur de la maison. A quelques pas de cette dernière, on voyait encore des vestiges de petites bâtisses qui furent sans doute des dépendances de sa maison. Tout celà était bien enchanteur . . .

Pour rustique que soit son petit cottage, elle n'en avait pas moins fait installer un confort intérieur qui lui permettait de jouir pleinement de ce petit Eden.

Placée sur la pente d'une petite colline, sa propriété permettait d'avoir la vue d'un petit paysage reposant où se trouvaient quelques maisons dont certaines étaient les derniers vestiges des dépendances du château évoqué au début de ces lignes lequel, nous l'avons dit, appartenait autrefois à la famille de Salignac-de-Lamothe-Fénelon, château qui fut détruit à la Révolution et dont les pierres servirent à construire (ou à reconstruire) bon nombre d'habitations de Lamothe.

Maintenant la petite maison a été achetée par une dame qui est professeur d'Anglais à la Sorbonne à Paris; une antenne de Télévision domine le petit cottage qui, de ce fait a perdu une partie de son charme.

Madame Cunard a terminé son séjour sur la terre d'une façon bien tragique, nul ne la verra plus circuler, de sa démarche qui lui était propre, sur la route, venant à Lamothe-Basse faire quelqu'emplettes, mais par le prodige de la pensée il semble encore, lorsque l'on évoque son souvenir, la voir avancer de loin, dans les toilettes simples mais colorées qu'elle affectionnait, coiffée de son grand chapeau de soleil.

Toujours aimable, adorant les bêtes, une petite anecdote dépeindra sa sollicitude pour elles.

Lorsqu'elle avait àffaire à Gourdon ou à Souillac, elle ne manquait jamais, en prenant son billet de chemin de fer à la gare de Lamothe, de s'enquérir auprès de l'employé, des nouvelles du chien de ce dernier, et chaque fois elle laissait son obole "pour Fanor."

Madame Cunard, Lamothe ne vous oubliera pas. . . .

irene rathbone

Nancy Cunard

"I want a poem from you," she said.

"But, Miss Cunard, *I* am not a poet. You're mistaking me for someone else."

The occasion was a P.E.N. Club dinner at (I think) the Rembrandt Hotel, the period mid-1943. I had never met her before, though heard much about her, and now she had come threading between the tables, the dinner being over, and was standing, very tall, very slim, gracious and compelling, by mine.

"I mistake you for no one, I've *read* a poem of yours. Your only one? What do I care. You can't get out of writing another, and this time for me."

She sat and explained. She was in process of collecting, from every poet she knew or could get in touch with, contributions for a volume which was to be a tribute to France. We talked about it for a while. We parted. At that time I lived in the country, and during the days that followed I managed—lit at a distance by Nancy's zeal—to produce some verses. Not good ones, but apparently good enough. They were accepted.

The book came out in 1944. One read on the cover:

POEMS
for
FRANCE
Written by British Poets during the War
collected
by
NANCY CUNARD

And inside, on the page before the poems began:

"This volume is a manifestation of our faith in France, our appreciation and love of her people and culture, our admiration for the dynamic, organized force of her resistance, and an earnest [   ] of the conviction that our two countries must ever march together."

How she had worked! Among the mass of letters sent out, a proportion must have been answered unfavourably or not answered at all. So many poets were serving, so many abroad, so many if at home occupied to exhaustion with war jobs. But not only had Nancy obtained contributions to the number of seventy, but had herself composed a note on the life and work of each contributor—from the most famous to the least well-known. A labour of love is none the less a labour, and this book could easily have used up all her energies. Nancy referred to it as a sideline.

Her "real" task lay with one of the Free French organizations: Allié —SHAEF. Here, for long hours on end, by day or by night, she toiled at translating from French into English subject-matter that varied from the boring to the horrible: enemy stuff from Paris, Berlin, Vichy, and other places. She was known as Correctrice-Assimilée-à-Expediteur, or, more simply, as a Radio Monitor. About forty people, counting in typists, were employed at this ill-run office, where nobody knew beforehand what shift she might be assigned to, where the hours, especially the nocturnal ones, seemed intolerably extended, where eyes and ears gave out, and doubts arose as to whether anything at all that went on here was of the slightest use to the war effort.

When now and then I came up from the country and Nancy and I briefly met, she would declare her temper to be soured, her nerves ruined. By the air raids? Oh no, by the *job,* its too uncongenial nature, and by some of her fellow workers. The condition of nerves and temper might be as Nancy described; it was not to me noticeable. Fatigue was. And, as I knew, she was desperate to be in France again. The outbreak of war had caught her travelling in Chile, and *then* she was desperate to be in England—or became so as soon as the Continent by falling to the Germans had put itself out of reach. England was the country of her birth, after all, she admired its "stand" and must offer her services. She couldn't just footle on in safe America. More than twelve months, however, went by till she was able to secure a passage, and the crossing had had to be so deviously conducted, had been so beset by gales, icebergs and submarines, that she had found London by comparison cosy. Let it be blacked-out, let it be bombed. But let her never have to repeat a war-time transatlantic voyage. All right, but now France was her object. She had a house there, friends there, had lived there most of her adult life. How soon could her return be arranged? Surely, with Paris liberated, with the war moving to its end, with a solid stretch of service at her back, it should not be hard to get permission. . . .

By the time I next met her, she had got it. Having badgered authorities, pulled strings (she was a person who had them to pull), having endured what in her view were imbecile delays, she was off. I saw her off myself, so did her cousin Victor Cunard, at Victoria Station. It was a cold night in February, 1945. Nancy wore a pointed, furry, Russian-looking cap. Her face was small beneath it and her eyes shone. "How I envy you!" I said. "Follow me soon," smiled Nancy. I was in no position to do that—although I couldn't guess that I should have to stay cooped in this island, along with the bulk of my fellow-countrymen, for a full year *after* victory. At 10 P.M. the almost empty train heaved itself forward: a war-time train, grimy, unlighted, sluggish, unrepaired, its only glimmer Nancy's face at one of its broken windows.

Later we heard from her, or heard of her. Paris was still beautiful; hungry and fireless, but more beautiful than ever because of the absence of traffic in the streets. She walked those streets for days. Rejoiced to find certain friends alive, lamented the deaths of others. Collected facts. Wrote articles: some in French for *l'Europe,* some in English for *Horizon* and *Connoisseur.* We found them all, when they eventually and at different times came out, vivid, engaging, instructive.

At a point during her stay in Paris—or it may have been afterwards —she visited Réanville, the Norman village where she had lived on and off in the peace years. Only on and off, for she was a great traveller, but there she was *based*. Although she did not expect to find her house intact—a letter from Madame Goasgüen, wife of the innkeeper, had warned her of much damage—she was unprepared to see a shambles. Either that letter had been toned down out of mistaken kindness or else the good woman was no hand at description. Nancy stared, stupefied, at gaps in the roof, gaps where doors and windows had been, at charred remains of furniture, at piles of cinders, at trampled-on books that covered floors, were deep in filth and spoiled forever. The well in the garden she found choked and foul. All this depredation, she learnt, had been the work of German troops, *deliberately sent* to the unoccupied dwelling by the village mayor, a collaborator. Things irreplaceable had been destroyed: African sculptures, paintings, manuscripts. And things of lesser value, but of greater usefulness to troops, been stolen. Some portion, however, of what had once made a home was saved. The faithful Goasgüens, at risk of their lives, used to go out at nights on sporadic rescue operations. The saved stuff was in their granary. Nancy went to inspect it. The couple standing near were scarcely less downcast than she was herself. Nancy said they had housed these things long enough, that she would have them all removed as soon as possible and put in a Paris store. She clasped the woman and kissed her; kissed the man; thanked them both from her heart, and bestowed on them a sum of money that left them speechless.

Then began her hunt for a new home. She must strike roots again, but *not* in Normandy. For a time the search was fitful; visits to Spain, Florence, Venice broke into it. The shock she had received at Réanville seemed to have shaken the resolve to re-settle herself. Then the resolve hardened. She scoured the lands of Lot and Dordogne, and found at last, near a tiny village called Lamothe Fénelon, a house that suited her. It was scarcely more than a barn to begin with; she got the local builder to alter and add to it; in course of time took up residence, in course of time asked friends to stay. I was one of them.

How hot was that summer! How hot, peaceful, delectable, were other summers of the 1950's—at least those parts of them that I spent with Nancy. From the spare bedroom on the ground floor of her house, one stepped, wearing a dressing gown, straight into grass; then, at a long, rough, wooden table, sunlit at that hour, later tree-shadowed, one sat having coffee. The morning slid by. One tranquilly wrote or read. Nancy, in her room under the roof, typed letters. She had a vast correspondence, and the people she kept up with included rich and poor, black and white, French, English and Spanish poets, curators of museums, duchesses, old dressmakers, journalists. The rattle-bang of her machine continued till lunch time, when down she wafted. We had not seen each other since the evening before. Dressed by now, I helped to carry food from kitchen to garden. There was not a great deal of it; quite enough; and, as always, enough wine. Across the valley spread the wooded hills; on this side, half way up a hill, stood her house.

I used to comment on its perfect position, and Nancy agreed as to that. But one day, being in a despondent mood, she found fault with it as a dwelling.

"Primitive. Primitive and poorly equipped." Followed allusions to all the precious stuff destroyed in her former dwelling. Of course, what the dear Goasgüens had saved was here, she had had it transported from the Paris warehouse, had at last properly examined it, made the most of it, and eked it out with a few antiques bought at country sales and some horrid modern things—necessities—bought at shops. She had spent, she said, too much on the *structure* of this place to allow of her properly furnishing the interior.

Sitting with her over the remains of our meal, my back to the hills, my face to the red tiled house, I mentally saw its interior. The kitchen stove, ancient rather than "antique," interesting rather than adequate, was of fragile ironwork and had one hole at the top into which sticks were laboriously pushed and on which a pan took an hour to boil. The treads of the staircase were narrow to the point of peril. The four chairs in the sitting room light, pale and cheap. Yet, counteracting sparceness, there was a divan of sorts, Moroccan tapestries hung on the walls, and over the fireplace a painting by Manet. This, by far the most valuable of her possessions, Nancy had lately inherited from her mother. She had also lately inherited, but from quite a different source, those fat, grey volumes of a French 17th century dictionary that were ranged on a shelf by the stairs. She prized the dictionary, she prized at its worth the Manet, but there was one thing she seemed better pleased to own than either. Among the rescued stuff from Réanville had appeared her original set of The Hours Press books. That printing-publishing venture, at which Nancy had slaved from 1928 to 1931, personally hand setting the type, choosing the paper, getting young authors to send her their work and artists to design the covers, had been a glittering success; then by her own decision had ended. The press itself was sold, an example of each of its productions kept and treasured. What wonder she should have given them up for lost when, after the interminable war years, she had stared at her ruined house? But amazingly they were not lost; today they were here, in this house. The little cabinet she had had made for them contained the entire collection of two dozen—safe, dry, slim, distinguished, if damaged. It stood there on a side table, a witness to a period when she had lived at the most intense pitch of work and of joyfulness. Other books, "ordinary" ones, were strewn about the house, some she had sent for from London, some picked up in France. Few in number compared with those destroyed, they offered plenty of good reading matter for a guest.

"You have what's important," I affirmed. "Your interior is original, civilized, an emanation of yourself."

Nancy looked amused. "What's important! Ask the villagers *their* opinion. Where's my wireless, my TV set, my telephone? Where, outside, is a garage with a car?"

On a certain morning I heard, without asking for it, the opinion of at any rate one villager. Madame Achille, the builder's wife, who came daily to sweep floors and "éplucher les légumes," said to me, as she brought my café-au-lait to the garden, Nancy being still upstairs,

"She has no comforts, Madame Cunard, no modern conveniences. Elle est riche, pourtant." Baffled, deferential, stolid, the woman stood there.

I replied that Madame Cunard had rich relations but she herself was far from well off, therefore she went without certain things in order to spend on others. I refrained from adding that there were things she would go without *anyhow,* because she disliked them, and that a wireless was one of them. "What she cares about is foreign travel in winter, supporting at all times good causes, helping distressed friends, and buying, very occasionally, some small objét d'art."

I received a headshake. "Ce n'est pas normale, sa façon de vivre." There was added, as the woman moved away, "Mais nous l'aimons bien."

That I had realised. Nancy, the eccentric, the incomprehensible, who, when she journeyed about the country, went third class among peasants and baskets of live hens, whose clothes were of no known style yet somehow became her, who belonged to "le parti communiste" though springing from "la classe dirigeante," was taken a sort of pride in locally, taken perhaps advantage of, and treated at once as châtelaine and friend.

As to Communism, Nancy and I never discussed it. I doubt if she was interested in it—from the doctrinal point of view. Some man whose mind she admired, Louis Aragon or another, had years ago drawn her into the fold, and there she had unquestioningly remained. If one was "anti-Fascist," if one detested tyranny, if one burned to help the persecuted, surely the Party was the most hopeful set-up to adhere to. Quite simply Nancy saw it like that. She therefore failed to see that her own nature, that of aristocrat and rebel, would render her useless—worse, a menace—as a citizen of any Communist-governed country. Did she hope France would become one? Did she think that in such an event she, Nancy Cunard, would *last?* These queries were not put to her—nor often to myself. Over politics in the wider, the non-party sense, we were in perfect accord. Evils of the 1930's could still enrage us: notably the betrayal of Spain, where Nancy during the Civil War had been a reporter on the Republican side and in frequent danger of death, and to whose people she remained ardently attached. Yesterday's France under the Nazis was a constant theme with us. And at intervals we growled maledictions at today's America for re-arming and re-building Germany.

On those long walks we went about the country we would come on memorials to butchered maquisards: a plaque on the side of a house, a rough-hewn stone by a roadside or in a field. Once we hired a car. The place Nancy wanted me to see—she had been there herself before —we couldn't have reached on foot and returned from in the same day. It was a farm called Gabaudet. No village near it. A lost farm, lost in the distance, lost from life, burnt by the enemy. It had been a meeting place of the local maquisards, a few of whom escaped, but most were shot or hanged. We stood by the monument where their names were engraved and those words beneath their names, "Assassinés par les Boches, Juin 1944." We wandered between the blackened, broken walls of barns and stables. Silence round us. Acres of grassy tranquility.

"No, it's not possible," I said. Meaning I'd failed in mind to conjure up the flames, screams, horror of that hour.

At other times too I failed. The *settings* where these ghastly scenes had been acted out were of such smiling calm as to halt attention on their surface; deeper it was difficult to look.

The day of our expedition to St. Julien de Lampon, when we started early, carrying a picnic, was set fair. Up through the woods we climbed, on the opposite side of our valley, emerged at Les Tourrettes, a crumbling château, its courtyard given over to hens and brambles, and under a near-by lime tree ate our lunch. Below us lay another valley, a broad, open-to-the-sky piece of country: the valley of the Dordogne. Hills rose beyond it, the river itself was invisible from here.

We walked on, on and *downwards* now, along paths that skirted vineyards, cornfields, fields of lucerne, the hot clear sun in our faces, till, by the river at last, we struck a stretch of road and found ourselves in the main square of St. Julien de Lampon. Did we stop? No. Not the little town, but some point outside was our destination. Nancy marched me through. Then it confronted us: the tall stone tablet. There were between twenty and thirty names on it, women's names among them, and a few Polish names. All these young people had been "Victimes de la Barbarie allemande, Juin, 1944." The crime committed here at Lampon was on a larger scale than that at Gabaudet, on a smaller scale than that of other crimes up and down the country, but in character similar. The Occupants had got wind of a meeting of maquisards, stuffed as many as they could lay hands on into a barn, turned machine guns on to them, then burnt the barn—some of the bodies being still alive.

From Nancy fell a curse or two, unprintable. Slowly we turned from the monument.

Back in the town, we sat at a café drinking Evian water. It was after seven when we got to our feet and began making for home. Up by those fields again, up towards Les Tourrettes, we went, looking back now and then at a sinking sun in a stainless sky and to the stretched-out hills beyond the Dordogne. By the time we had dropped into our own, our narrow valley, had crossed our tiny stream, le Tournefeuille, and gained the high road, my legs were giving out. "Don't wait for me," I called to Nancy. She turned, smiled, encouraged me. There was only one more kilometre to Lamothe, she said. Thought I, "only" one more! Staggering, I followed her—and fell into the village inn.

What inn in England, I dazedly wondered, would welcome two women turning up without warning at nearly 10 o'clock at night?—

even though one of the two was an inhabitant and loved. But the kindly couple who ran *this* inn, Monsieur et Madame Bournioux, were charmed to see us and served us almost at once with soup, roast veal, red wine. Madame B. hung about our table, enquired where we had been, admired our energy, wanted details, and Nancy, vital as when we had set out in the morning, responded.

Rather less than a kilometre lay between the village and Nancy's house. The air had cooled and darkened, my legs were to a degree rested, and I was equal to the "short cut"—a steep, stony path between blackberry bushes—that Nancy as a rule preferred to the longer way round by the "lane." As she fitted her key to the door, I looked up at the stars.

"Would it be midnight?"

"Probably. Have a brandy."

"Dear Nancy, no. Bed for me. But what a wonderful, what a golden day!"

Other outings ended earlier. We covered much ground at that—and never got lost. Nancy was familiar with every path in the district. Small, seemingly endless paths led up to and away from hamlets, wound round mouldering manor houses, once the properties of "gentilhommes," now of peasants, and on which we dreamed of spending huge sums to bring them into repair. Fields shimmered in the heat; walnuts on a length of road cast shade. But we were seldom on a road. In my mind I invariably see her moving beside crops, beside pastures, through woods, moving with that tall grace of hers, that elasticity. While I, squat and square, often perspiring, always contented, plod at her back.

The garden was full of evening silence. We sat at supper. A bat blundered about. A silver quarter-moon confronted across the width of sky the rose of sunset.

"Read me some poetry, Irene."

Never in London used Nancy to pronounce my name that way. Here it was a habit with her. I liked it.

"Any special poem?" I asked.

"No. You read everything well."

Tonight I fetched from the house a poem of her own. *Parallax,* published in 1925 by the Hogarth Press, has here and there faint Meredithian echoes, but is a work of real originality. Each section is in a different metre, and rhyme is unused except, suddenly, in a single, splendid passage of a score of lines. It's long. I made no haste over it. The light just lasted till I had finished.

"Thank you," came Nancy's voice quietly. "You've made it sound— almost beautiful." Then, "But it's *young,* isn't it. I'd forgotten."

"Young and bitter and life-loving and crazy and joyous and sad. Young in the manner of the 1920's, and in yours."

Dusk had closed in. Nancy's listening face, propped on a hand, showed pale as the ivory bracelets that clasped her arm. It was a small face for a woman of her height, and the breadth of it beneath the forehead seemed taken up wholly by eyes. In a usual face, eyes don't extend to the outer edges. Hers did, and reminded one of the long eyes of ancient Egypt. Blue, between their thick black fringes, a deep speedwell blue, they not so much reflected what light was around at the moment as gave out light themselves. Even now, at dusk . . .

"Luminous," I murmured.

"You do say nice things about it."

Back came my thoughts. Nancy, naturally enough, had been unaware they had strayed from the poem.

"I'd like to see later ones . . . I have seen some . . . Do you ever *stop* writing poetry?"

"Only when I've a stout prose work on hand."

Her stoutest prose work, a stupendous achievement, an anthology called *Negro,* had come out in 1934, only three years after the closing down of The Hours Press. Which meant that in *less* than three years she had collected, sorted, and linked together with her own bits of text the varied mass of material forming the contents. Of normal proportions, and of far greater interest to the general reader, were the two prose works published in the early 1950's. These were: *Grand Man. Memories of Norman Douglas,* and *G.M. Memories of George Moore.* Each book enshrines a very different human being. To each Nancy had been devoted: to Douglas from young womanhood, to Moore, a friend of her mother's, from childhood. Discernment and wit, warmth and gratitude irradiate both portraits. Both, in turn, got a great spread of reviews.

"The reviews were good, yes," Nancy allowed, when I mentioned them. "But sales were not. Reviews ought to *sell* books. In my case they don't."

Dusk had become night; the moon was too young yet to have much effect on darkness. Our bits of talk were the only sounds in the soft, still air.

"You should write your own 'Memories,' Nancy. That book would sell."

"It seems so. More than one publisher has asked me for it."

"And since you're always hard up—chiefly through your own generous fault—wouldn't the money be welcome?"

"How welcome!" Then she shook her head. "No, not even for money. A book of that kind would bring in too many people. Numbers and numbers of them, men, women, friends of youth and of middle age, people who've let me down as well as loved me. Most might be pleased to read what I'd made of them. Some would be hurt. Others perhaps bring libel actions!" She said again, "No." She said, "The choice lies between writing the thing fully, in detail, no holds barred—specially where I myself am concerned—or not writing it at all. I choose *that*."

She stretched her arms: first sideways, then straight up. The African ivory bracelets on each slid from wrist towards elbow. Down came her arms again and stayed crossed on the table; her head sank on them. After a minute, seeing she didn't stir, I whispered good night, and went over the grass to my ground-floor room. It must have been half an hour later that I heard footsteps tip-tapping on those narrow, uncarpeted stairs and go along into the room above.

What I took to be, at the garden table, a drop into sleep may have been a drop into melancholy. Nancy did need more sleep than she permitted herself, for often she worked at night, and on occasions had a cat nap before we parted. But, aside from physical conditions, she was subject to rapid changes of mood. From being uplifted, she became despondent. From vivaciously good humoured, querulous, even stormy. The fair moods lasted far longer than the dark, which, in any case infrequent, occurred mostly at the day's end. Not when she and I were out walking, though she could be for a space subdued. Then suddenly something enchanted her: some simple thing, a leaf, a dragon-fly, a curious stone, the smell of hay. She was all sunlight.

But beneath these surface ups and downs, flowed, steadily, a stream of affection. So much affection flowed from her heart to her friends! They couldn't all have deserved it. Yet I never heard her *criticise* someone to whom she was attached, any more than I heard one good word from her about a person she disliked. She praised or she abused. She was warm and intolerant. And just as people in the wider world fell roughly into two categories, so did the inhabitants of Lamothe. Nancy spoke of some as "darlings," others as "salauds." Luckily, she said, there were fairly few salauds.

One afternoon, when we had been to the post office, we met on our road home a very old woman dressed in peasant-black and carrying a bundle of sticks.

"Why, it's Madame Marie-Paule," exclaimed Nancy.

The woman raised her eyes, the two cordially shook hands, and, after I had been introduced, fell into conversation. The poor creature, it seemed, was "très inquiète," she had had grave news of a married daughter in another part of the country; recovery was unlikely. I heard Nancy's sympathetic remarks, heard her offer to pay for the railway journey in case Madame Marie-Paule wished to go and see the daughter, heard gratitude and a refusal expressed, heard further exchanges, and then saw Nancy put her arms round the little bent body and hold it. It was an impulsive, swooping, sweet gesture; it brought comfort and tears.

"Vous êtes bonne, ma chère. Mais la vie est dure, ah, oui! Elle est triste, la vie . . ."

"What a pet," I said, when Nancy and I had resumed our way. "I'm sorry she's in trouble."

"And I wish I'd known she was. As a rule she's merry as a grig. Incidentally, she's the 'oldest inhabitant,' and her cottage almost the oldest in the village. I'll take you to see it sometime, but today . . ."

"Could I be allowed to contribute, if money's in question?"

"It isn't. She's poor, of course, but that journey would be beyond her anyhow. Her heart's bad. If the daughter dies I'll send a wreath. . . ."

The daughter did die, but not till a week later, by which time I was back in England. On one of my remaining days Nancy walked me to Souillac. I had been there before, once, in another year, and had pretty thoroughly explored that agreeable country town; today I just sat in it. About fifteen kilometres separates Souillac from Lamothe —by the road perhaps twenty, but Nancy and I "cut" through the woods. We had taken a picnic lunch, eaten it under trees, seen nothing all the way that failed to charm our eyes, heard only pigeons' voices, had crossed by ferry that loop of the Dordogne where the banks are cliffs and the water, bottle-green, flows at a great rate, had forged uphill by clover fields under a burning sun, glimpsed the cupolas of the Romanesque cathedral, and attained the High Street.

"Not bad going," said Nancy. "Two-and-a-half hours including the lunch break, and we didn't push ourselves."

She left me at the Café de Paris. Thankful for a seat, for the brown awning over my head, for iced lemonade, I watched her go off with her springing step—to shop, draw money from the bank, fix a date for the hairdresser's, God knew what else. Minutes passed.

A tall, pale man, quiet of voice, lame, emerged from inside the café and spoke to me.

"You are Madame Irene, are you not, Nancy's friend from England. I saw you both arrive. I live here, I've a flat just above." He gave me his name and took a chair at my table.

I had not met Albert Betz on that other occasion at Souillac, but certain things I'd been told about him came now to mind. He published *Les Editions de Point,* a review of literature and the arts. During the German Occupation the difficulties of bringing it out at all, let alone regularly, had been formidable. He had persisted. The printing works were clandestine, the contributors—writers, painters, engravers, photographers—used pseudonyms. The review was not political, not obviously, yet in its way a defiance. Its aim was to keep alive French pride in different aspects of the French creative spirit. The Germans smelt subversion. Often an article promised to Betz never turned up: the author had been arrested. I did not know what Betz had personally suffered in the war years; it was plain they had impaired his vitality and probable that his lameness was due to a wound. Since I found him unwilling to talk about himself, or about the Resistance except in very general terms, I brought up the countryside as a subject, its beauty, variety, and spoke of the joy I took in my walks with Nancy.

At this he smiled. Then seemed to brood.

"Nancy . . . Quelle étrange fille. . . ."

He had known her long? Only, he said, since the end of the war, when she had come hunting in these parts for a domicile. Did I think that her appreciation of a rural existence was genuine? Surprised, I assured him that indeed it was. But she was so cultivated, so sophisticated, Betz commented, so well-suited, one would have thought, to the life of cities, people, parties, the hum of ideas. I suggested she might be through with all that, having had a great deal of it, and that the country-loving element in her complex makeup was now uppermost.

"But that house!" he exclaimed. "It's isolation! Not a neighbour within hail. At times I fear for her."

"She doesn't fear for herself."

"Naturally not. Would she suppose that the sundry dubious characters who trudge up the lane at the back of her house on their way to that distant farm, to beg a bowl of soup or a doss-down in the hayloft, would knock at *her* gate with a request for these things, or for more, for money? Would it occur to her that even if one of them did, and he turned offensive, she couldn't deal with him? She might be able to, by force of personality and inherited gift of command. She might . . . On the other hand . . ." A pause and headshake. "When she has friends staying I don't worry. But this is only for portions of the summer. For weeks she is alone." The slow, gentle voice, which had dropped, took up again. "And her walks! She covers leagues of the country, companionless. You may ask what harm she could come to in a French Department on the whole agricultural and civilised, but there are wild regions in the Lot, and once, as she later confessed to me, laughing, she found herself benighted and slept among scrub on a hillside."

"In Spain she underwent worse hardships. . . ."

"During the Civil War. Oh, I know. And if the German war had caught her here in France instead of overseas, it wouldn't have been a matter of just 'hardships' for her. Up to the eyes she'd have been in the Resistance. Intrepid and prudent at first, intrepid and reckless as time went on, then captured. Then . . . No, one can't contemplate it. Only be certain she wouldn't have 'talked' and wouldn't have survived."

Often had I, on my part, turned from contemplation of it: of that "it" which chance, chance alone, had spared her.

"And she's brave on more than one level," continued this admiring friend. "On the mental as well as the physical. She speaks her mind. She'll stand up for someone unpopular, perhaps a Spanish refugee she has found work for in the neighbourhood. Or she'll give vent to some idea, point of view, embarrassing to those present. This when she *cares* enough—she doesn't always. But on occasions of her being really roused, not expediency, not discretion, not regard for her own reputation will keep her silent." Betz himself fell silent a moment, then said softly, "Elle a tous les courages."

Nancy appeared. Totally unconscious that she had been the subject of our talk, elegant, sinuous, her eyes full of light, her arms full of parcels, she dipped under the café's awning from the glaring street, and before the man could move had leaned and kissed him. "Mon cher Betz!"

He ordered her a drink. He said, "At least you don't propose, laden as you are, to *return* on foot? Even with your English visitor sharing the burdens?"

The burdens had dropped to the ground. She sat there, glimmering. "How do you feel, Irene? Shall we hire a taxi?"

But although I declared—with truth—that I was refreshed now, and more than willing to walk back, the gentle Betz insisted we should drive. He told the waiter to telephone.

Till the car came up, we drank and talked. And drank. And so pleasant was this interlude, so enchanting had been the day's earlier hours, with the sun-dappled woods and the great sliding river, that at a point I found myself exclaiming,

"Oh, I *don't* want to go back to England!"

They were touched. Almost together they responded.

"Need you?"

"Why not just stay?"

I shook my head. "Alas!"

It was not every summer of the 1950's, or of the early 1960's, that I managed a visit to Lamothe, and in 1964 there seemed solid reasons why I shouldn't even be invited. During her winter sojourn on the South Coast, Nancy had been pretty badly ill; nor were the summer months at home bringing improvement. She had had to make domestic changes, village "help" no longer met her needs, she had advertised for and secured someone who lived in. This stout, competent creature from Toulouse not only cooked (her main asset), but laundered and mended, chopped wood, clipped grass, and cheerfully ran errands. Not a chore hitherto undertaken by Nancy but the good creature shouldered it. There were inconveniences, of course, as well as blessings, in having her. For instance, she occupied the spare room. Scarcely her fault, since she had been *put* there; just the same, it had become unavailable to visitors.

Aware of all this, I was puzzled when in a later letter Nancy asked me to stay. Could I, she said, face the attic? There were few to whom she would dare offer such cramped accommodation but hoped I was among the few, and she did assure me that the bed itself, though narrow, was not uncomfortable. Hadn't I mentioned a possible visit to French friends at Cahors? If this visit was settled, would I please to remember that Lamothe lay very close. . . .

Of course I remembered, and had resigned myself to a single glimpse of the dear place from the train window as I was borne towards Cahors and then past it again on my return journey to Paris. But now I would be breaking that journey.

"Nancy, what just *is* wrong with you?"

She shrugged. We were in the garden, I had barely arrived, and though she had greeted me with all her old warmth, and those amazing eyes had not lost brilliance, the whole long frame had lost flesh— and how little it had ever had to lose!

"Doctors," she muttered scornfully. "I tried several in Nice last winter. Useless. *And* the one here in Souillac is useless. 'Lungs,' they say, or 'emphysema,' or 'chronic bronchial condition,' or 'poor circulation.' All *I* know is that I feel exhausted—perpetually." She smiled at me with a droll sadness. "I can't come walks any more. What walks we went together, you and I! Even last summer, when you weren't able to be here, I'd practically given them up. You'll have to go on your own. . . ." Then, as I began some protest, she declared, "I'd be vexed if you felt you had to stay beside me at all hours. In the evenings I'll love your company, but till then you must wander around . . . *please*. . . ."

And so, each day, I did; but to no great distance. Now to hillside farms with their old, beautiful pigeon-cotes. Now along by the stream, le Tournefeuille, that winds through the valley. The silver-cool water has so much lime in it that twigs, leaves, iris roots, grass blades, all oddments that in the course of months have not been borne further, but become stationary, have also become coated with minute crystals and look frosted. At these I peered, as Nancy and I used to do. We even, at times of great heat, bathed in this water. Then on I strolled, passed on my left the deserted mill that nettles and saplings were invading, took a stride on to the opposite bank, and turned towards home. Late afternoon light hung green in the sky, but days were drawing in, little of summer was left, the varied crops of these small fields had long been harvested, and the air, though windless, mild, benign, oven warm, lacked staying-power. It was not the air of June.

Up at the house again, I found Nancy curled on the divan with pencil and notebook.

"Nice walk, darling? Sit down. Take this section of an immense poem I'm working at, read it to yourself and give me your opinion. Your true one. To me the thing seems a mess."

The table, candle-lit, was laid for supper; at this season no meal but the mid-day one could be had out-of-doors. From the kitchen came sounds. Somebody stumped about, moved saucepans, collected plates. In a moment Madame Simone, the living-in servant, the too garrulous companion, would enter with the first course of an admirably cooked meal—and would herself partake of it. I bent my mind to the poem. It had a curious beauty, a quality of dream. It meant what? Nancy herself couldn't tell me. There was a great deal more of it vaguely in her head, she thought she would call it, if ever it was finished, "The Vision." I read on. Certain lines that impressed me I read aloud.

"Ces dames sont servies."

We rose, we two, and went to the table. Madame Simone, at the head of it, filled our soup plates, chattered of this and that, filled our glasses, brought the next course, presided. I was used by now to her being *de facto* hostess, and certainly she took no advantage of the position; all she desired was to save Madame Cunard every effort, even the smallest. Later, when she had washed up and retired to her room, leaving "ces dames" to themselves, Nancy said,

"About my poem. You won't see it complete, not on this visit, but I shall write another before you leave, a short one, and for you specially. . . ." She broke off, lifted a finger, and looked towards the shut door between the sitting-room and the spare-bedroom. "D'you hear her wireless? She keeps it low at this hour. But often in the afternoons she brings the thing out and has it on the garden table while she sews, and there it blares away with sloppy music, or some so-called 'serious' programme, and wherever I may be, upstairs or downstairs, or even beside her, I have to endure it. Of course," added Nancy fair-mindedly, "there's much *she* has to endure in this place. Compared with her own apartment in Toulouse, which she describes as 'moderne' and 'très chic,' my poor peasant's house with all its inadequacies must constantly appal her. Yet she never complains." A sigh. "Oh dear, that wireless!"

Impossible not to laugh, or, remembering the former peacefulness, not to sympathise. At the same time, could one be too thankful for the *care* with which Nancy was now surrounded?

On my last morning, Madame Simone assured me in the kitchen that this care would continue. Yes, right to the end of the autumn when Madame Cunard went South.

"Comptez sur moi," she nodded, pushing my tip into her apron pocket. "Je vais bien la soigner. Elle est si distinguée, elle a si bon coeur."

I left the kitchen for the garden. To Nancy my goodbyes were already said; since she felt at her weakest in the mornings I had forbidden her to get up. She had handed me a folded sheet of paper, saying, "The poem I promised you. It isn't long, read it sometime, in the train perhaps. . . . How I shall miss you!" But I sat down, the station taxi not having arrived, sat in the sun at the weather-worn table, and began to read at once. The poem had two verses. Its title was "Lambent." I give part of it here.

LAMBENT
(for Irène)

I

See how the sun sits fast on the calm land!
Into the small birds' songs runs a new piping rhythm,
Fresh moss and tiny plants grow in the wooden table,
Yet it will come, the cold, after this lambent spread,
This odd profusion of sun-hot on placid earth.
Ay, they will come, wrecker autumn and raw November,
The ever-perennial need of rough log fires.
Each day stays single yet, apart, to be serried
Into a future consanguinity
Of day-cum-day, called "that time" by memory,
But as yet each day's alone in the slow "not yet."

II

The lambent light's still laid over the land,
Bringing mild respite from anxieties . . .

I blinked back tears. How had she managed so perfectly to catch the mood—the season's mood, our mood? There *was* moss in the cracks of the rough table, the cold *would* come after this spread of sun, and these unmoving days that still were here be called "that time" by memory.

Out from the house bustled Madame Simone. She, not I, had heard the car come up. Into it, helped by the driver—whom she scolded for being late—she put my luggage, slammed the door on it and me, and waved us off.

No instinct, or none I attended to, warned me I was leaving for ever; I was sad simply at leaving. As Nancy, in spite of her poem's elegaic flavour, was sad simply at being left. Of course I had anxieties on her account—of course. Her cough was cruel, her thinness pitiful. But she had sworn to me, up there in the bedroom, to put herself in the hands of *one* good doctor (not vacillate between a number), trust and obey him, and get cured.

News of her during the winter varied; she seemed better, then less well. On a spring day she wrote that the weather was icy and 'flu as rampant on this coast as it appeared to be in London! She advised me *not* to come out as I had suggested doing, the mimosa and everything else looked hideous, prices were exorbitant, I should be wasting my money. There were further captious remarks. The only cordial one referred to the old, kind, rich friend, known to her since girlhood, in whose villa she was staying.

Then, as though her bronchial bouts were not enough, she had a fall. The hip bone was broken, she was rushed to hospital and operated on. Followed that period at the villa of lying flat, of two nurses in alternate attendance, of the doctor's daily visits. Later she sat up, for "they" feared pneumonia, but there was no question of putting foot to ground till weeks had passed, perhaps not till summer. In these grim conditions did her morale collapse? On the contrary. The post-cards I at intervals received—and that other friends of hers received—were spirited to the point of being humorous. She didn't pretend there was no pain; pain in fact was bad and constant, but only at times unbearable. She cursed it, she mocked at it, she *worked*. I learnt that she had again taken up that long, curious poem, parts of which I had read on my last visit to Lamothe. She had let it lie, she said, for months —through lack of belief in it or lack of will. Now it was absorbing her. Being thus "tied by the leg" was obviously a stimulus to one's writing powers!

I thought about her. Her pain, her bravery. Oh, I sighed, 'elle a tous les courages.' The words were not mine. They had been uttered by

Albert Betz, years ago at Souillac, when he and I sat together on a radiant day, talking of Nancy.

And still, although fifteen months have passed since she died, they recur to me: recur in the present tense as they were spoken. Even when I myself make comments on her, I'm liable to say, She "has" such generosity, or such daring, or such charm of manner, or such an interesting poetic gift. Then, mournfully, I remember, and correct "has" to "had." But that comment of the Frenchman's, whether I quote it inwardly or voice it to some friend, remains unaltered. How can "Elle avait" ever replace "Elle a"? How can a person like Nancy be no longer alive? She lives—here, there, with us, without us. She lives and "Elle a tous les courages."

nancy cunard

Poems from Poèmes à La France *and* Nous Gens D'Espagne

[Miss Cunard's mastery of the French language is well illustrated in the following poems. *Poèmes à La France,* an anthology of poems about France by British authors, was compiled by Miss Cunard during the war and published in Paris by *La France Libre* in September, 1946. The poems in *Nous Gens D'Espagne* were written between 1945 and 1949, mostly in southern France near the Franco-Spanish border. The volume was printed in December, 1949, in Perpignan.]

QUI DIT HAINE DIT RÉSISTANCE

Pour Aragon.

Qui parle de vérités dit: parmi elles
Sont celles qui vibrent, explosent, d'autres comme le bleu
                                             profond
De fiords qu'ignore le temps, ou un feu dans une barre de glace,
Patientent. Qui parle de vérités dit Haine, dit France.
Debout dans le blé, dans la mine, debout sur le château de
                                             Saverne,
Debout la Haine, l'Incorruptible,
Idéal, fait d'un peuple, unique nécessité.

France, épouse de la douleur, mère de ses fils, froide veuve,
Ta paix se nomme mort. Ta paix venue
Après la rupture des sangs, le délire du coeur, la torture rouge
Dans les nerfs et viscères; rictus, fin, *rigor mortis.*
Quelque part dans le tout subsistait l'heure vide, l'heure zéro—
La Haine y entra. Bien. A nouveau cette matrice concevra.

Son amant? Le nommé Haine. Elle en fait son amant unique,
Fort comme un talisman, lumineux, multiple comme poussière
d'étoiles.

La Haine comme une petite bête se glisse dans tous les sites,
Flâne sur les routes, s'ouvre la porte de toutes les villes,
Loge dans le miette de pain, et un grincement de rails,
Dans le vin du bistro et la gnole du matelot ivre,
Danse dans un talon de pute, entre les feuilles d'un bréviaire,
Dans la courroie huileuse qui tourne et le poinçon brisé du gniaf.
En avant, en arrière, la Haine! Dans les révolutions des essieux,
Dans le muguet du 1er mai et les fleurs oxydées de novembre,
Dans les feuilles tombées et les bourgeons rouges à venir,
Dans la mare et la brise et le gel, dans tout ce qui meurt pour
revenir—
Ah! Haine, comme tu gravis la courbe du cercle . . . ferme-le,
complète-le . . .
Voyez, voyez, cette matrice qui gonfle comme une lune
qui approche son plein.

LA RÉPUBLIQUE DANS LES PRÉS

A Picasso

Ah! ce train d'idées accompagnant les trains
Qui foncent vers les Pyrénées de la frontière:
"Si le vert est tendre, hésitant comme une promesse,
Jamais n'ai-je vu le coquelicot si rouge,
Mâle, mâle comme un cri de lutte . . ."
Les fleurs le disent pour qui les sait cueillir,
Les pois sauvages, l'un pourpre et l'autre jaune
Et du royal pavot le frère fluet:
        *Rojo, morado, oro**;
Point n'est besoin de drapeaux ni bannières,
Juin et Juillet s'accordent—
Les fleurs le chantent à qui les sait choisir.

(Carcassonne, Remparts, 28 Juin 1946)

* Rouge, pourpre et or—le drapeau de la République Espagnole.

LA BOTA

Sa panse généreuse arrondie au soleil
Prometteuse des demains qui couvent dans son flanc—
Demain est-ce espoir, poursuite ou mirage,
Demain, homme ou heure, message, papier blanc?
Elle va sur les monts chevauchant sur la hanche,
Complice des secrets, compagne des déboires
Du costaud ou du triste, du farouche, du furieux,
Epaulant la revanche, camarade en victoires—
                    La Bota*

                                        (Cahors, Octobre 1946)

  * La petite outre espagnole en peau de chèvre, compagne fidèle du paysan
et du contrebandier. Son vin âpre est le meilleur qui soit au monde, à condition
de le boire avec des camarades,—ou bien, seul.

A HIDALGO

Un camarade en face dans l'âtre,
Un toit, une table, dix doigts de vin
Combien j'attends la nef en rade,
Le moissonneur des lendemains.

Quel est ce messager subit
Qui vient renforcer mon désir?
Musique d'Espagne sur ondes d'Andorre
Ce 19 Août . . . Toi, vaincre, mourir—

Point ne mourus. Toulouse le sait,
Toi, dague d'Espagne et petite pierre
Qui roule et coupe et sait attendre,
*Guijarro** fine de la rivière

Qui libéra cette capitale—
Ah! mon ami, mon camarade,
L'absence est aussi terre d'exil . . .
Main si le bateau entre en rade

Finie alors une part des peines,
Quand on est deux ou trois: action.

  * La petite pierre au fond du ruiss eau.

Il faut que bateau entre en rade,
Que peines soient bues, mon camarade,
Et qu'on occupe la morte saison,
La morte, très morte saison d'attente,
Des Tables Rondes et Tapis Verts,
Des politiques, chantages, enchères,
*Cantamañanas** dans le dos
Et fausses promesses cent francs le verre.

Demain sera peut-être le tout pour tout,
La lutte finale, qui sait, de bout en bout . . .

Main entre-temps, mon camarade,
La table attend—arrive, arrive,
Espagne-Tolède—intégrité
Grave et intense et forte et gaie,
Viens, Segador†, ici en rade,
Cargo chargé des dix années.

Nous l'occuperons, la morte saison,
Tout comme avant—tout comme demain—
A condición de no llorar‡ . . .
Reçois le coeur, le pain, le vin.

(Bourg-Madame, 20 Août 1946)

* Chanterai demain—jamais aujourdhui.
† Le moissonneur.
‡ A condition qu'il n'y ait jamais de larmes.

jean lambert

Nancy Cunard

A Paris, en Mars dernier, j'accompagnais à l'Hôpital Cochin un ami dont la femme y était soignée. En cours de route, il me raconta que, huit jours plus tôt, Police-Secours avait amené dans la salle commune une vieille femme très maigre et très distinguée, au visage tuméfié; elle portait une valise en beau cuir remplie de livres et de photos. Elle avait commencé par demander du vin, qu'on lui refusa. Puis elle avait écrit longuement, fébrilement et signé un certain nombre de chèques. Un peu plus tard, on l'avait placée sous un masque à oxygène. En passant par hasard auprès d'elle, la femme de mon ami, s'étant aperçue que l'appareil faisait un bruit étrange, avait appelé une infirmière. La malade venait de mourir. Comme c'était arrivé quelques instants avant l'heure des visites, on avait rapidement transporté le corps dans un autre endroit. Quelqu'un vint, du Consulat britannique, pour se charger des formalités. Le lendemain, par un article de journal, les malades et les infirmières avaient appris le nom de cette femme, venue mourir si manifestement hors de son "monde", et seule: Nancy Cunard. "Hors de son monde"—mais, à vrai dire, il n'y avait là rien de nouveau pour elle, qui avait passé sa vie à fuir celui de sa naissance et à s'en créer un qui lui fût propre.

Tandis que mon ami parlait et que nous approchions de l'hôpital, se réveillaient en moi les regrets qu'avaient fait naître, quelques jours plus tôt, la lecture de ce même article. Car j'aurais dû aller à l'hôpital ce jour-là, où Nancy Cunard était morte; elle aurait eu, du moins, un visage connu auprès d'elle. Puis je me dis que je serais arrivé quelques instants après sa mort, et que je n'aurais d'ailleurs pas su qu'elle était là, dans cette salle commune, à quelques pas de la chambre où j'allais voir mon amie. . . . Celle-ci me redit ce que son mari venait de me raconter et m'offrit de faire appeler l'infirmière, qui pourrait ajouter quelques détails. Par une absurde crainte, je refusai—peut-être pour n'entendre pas parler avec indifférence de quelqu'un qui ne m'avait jamais paru indifférent. Aujourd'hui, me voici réduit, pour l'évoquer, à relire ses lettres, à appeler des souvenirs. Et l'amie qui, la dernière, m'a parlé d'elle, vient de disparaître à son tour.

Puisqu'on m'a demandé non de prononcer son éloge, mais de dire l'impression qu'elle m'a faite, j'ose me joindre à ceux qui l'ont beaucoup connue, si rares qu'aient été nos rencontres et si peu extraordinaires que soient les lettres—une vingtaine, dont de simples billets—reçus d'elle, que je viens de relire avant de les ranger avec celles dont le nombre n'augmentera plus.

C'est Norman Douglas que avait provoqué notre rencontre; ou plutôt, notre commune sympathie pour lui: la mienne, née simplement de la lecture de ses oeuvres; celle de Nancy Cunard, renforcée par sa familiarité avec le personnage même, auquel elle devait consacrer, sous le titre non réticent de *Grand Man,* un livre de souvenirs émus et émouvants, amusés et amusants. Ayant entrepris la traduction de *Siren Land,* et désirant écrire, pour les lecteurs français, une présentation de ce Norman Douglas encore (et toujours) très inconnu d'eux, j'étais curieux de rencontrer cette femme qu'il avait acceptée ou choisie comme compagne de route en Tunisie, ce qui supposait chez elle des vertus peu ordinaires, la gaieté, l'endurance, à la fatigue et au bon vin, la curiosité et la chaleur humaines, une parfaite désinvolture à l'égard des idées recues. . . . D'elle même, j'avais un peu entendu parler par des amis anglais, les uns avec une admiration amusée, les autres sans indulgence particulière. L'ami qui organisa notre rencontre choisit le parfait décor du Café Royal, au bas de Regent Street, dont le nom reparaît si souvent dans les lettres anglaises. Dans mon souvenir, je le vois rouge et or comme une salle d'opéra, mais c'est peut-être un effet de l'imagination.

Arrivé en avance, et assis dans un coin du café, j'eus tout loisir de regarder de loin la personne très maigre et très couverte de bijoux divers qui s'était assise à une autre table, attendant elle aussi. J'avais été certain qu'il s'agissait d'elle, avant même que je l'eusse entendue dire à quelqu'un qui venait de la rejoindre: "Il veut me faire connaître un Français que Norman intéresse. . . ." Notre ami commun, arrivé plus tard, fit le rapprochement.

Je mentirais en disant que je me souviens de notre première conversation; et je ne mentirais pas moins en disant que je revois parfaitement le visage de Nancy Cunard. Je revois le personnage, ou plutôt, un ensemble de sensations le recompose pour moi: souvenir, pour les yeux, d'un corps si maigre qu'il en était presque décharné; pour l'oreille, souvenir d'un cliquetis de colliers et de bracelets. J'étais fasciné par ceux-ci. Je vis par la suite qu'elle en possédait une collection considérable, car, à chaque rencontre, l'ensemble était toujours différent, abondant, surabondant même, mais toujours homogène. Je revois en particulier ce qui était beaucoup plus qu'une parure de corail, tant il y en avait partout. Certes, le personnage était peu ordinaire. Comme chez beaucoup de femmes, l'ensemble de sa silhouette s'était fixé dans les années qui, je suppose, furent celles de ses plus grands succès et de sa beauté, si bien qu'elle avait devancé sans le savoir ce retour vers les années 20 auquel nous venons d'assister.

Nous nous revîmes à Paris, à plusieurs de ses passages. Les circonstances de ma vie d'alors faisaient que j'habitais l'appartement de Gide, rue Vaneâu; je lui fis visiter un jour la bibliothèque. J'ai retrouvé l'écho de cette visite dans une lettre qu'elle m'envoyait, un peu plus tard, quand j'étais aux Etats-Unis après un assez grand changement dans mon existence, changement qu'avait suivi la disparition de cet appartement que nous appelions simplement "le Vaneau": "Rue Vaneau! Ainsi, pas même çà, avec tout son caractère, tous ses kilomètres de livres, n'était "stable et à perpété"! Jamais je n'oublierai notre excellent moment rue Vaneau: une si belle conversation (toujours son enthousiasme!) votre article sur Norman—et l'extraordinaire alcool d'oranges, "a cordial", je crois, en anglais . . ." (Je lui avais offert un modeste vin d'orange, mais l'avais corsé, à son usage, avec du gin). Et, un peu plus tard: "Je garde ce souvenir tellement personnel émouvant de la dernière fois que je vous ai vu, dans L'appartement de Gide."

Toutes ses premières lettres concernent nos efforts, d'ailleurs jamais récompensés, pour faire sortir sa traduction de *Fountains in the Sand,* ce récit du voyage où elle accompagnait Douglas en Tunisie, et ma traduction de *Siren Land.* Lettres d'affaires plutôt, mais qui s'humanisent assez vite, surtout après mon arrivée en Amérique, précédée d'un naufrage spectaculaire—d'où ceci: "Qu'eût dit Douglas? Il vous aurait posé des questions sur le déportement (?) de tous ces malheureux humains—qui sait, appuyant surtout sur le comportement de l'équipage" (et en effet, connaissant les Italiens comme il faisait, cela l'aurait intéressé). Un peu plus tard: "Je suis contente de vous savoir "à l'aise" aux Etats-Unis (moi qui, per forza, ne l'ai jamais pu être, *pas un instant:* 'les Noirs et les Blancs', et mon Anthologie *Negro,* et la Yellow Press et les faux frères, etc. . . .)"

Elle y avait pourtant acquis des amitiés, dont elle eût la générosité de vouloir que je profite. C'est par elle que je connus Langston Hughes, en ce temps où un blanc pouvait encore se promener dans Harlem. Je me rappelle revenant, de cette première visite, couvert de livres, dont *The Big Sea* et toute une série d'ouvrages pour enfants L'année suivante, comme je me trouvais dans cette retraite un peu sévère qu'est Yaddo à l'automne, elle me mit en contact avec Miriam Benkovitz, qui préparait alors sa biographie de Ronald Firbank, mais qu'elle-même n'avait pas encore rencontrée. J'enviai beaucoup Miriam de posséder, entre autres trésors plus littéraires, un carnet de blanchissage de Norman Douglas. Nancy Cunard avait toujours prétendu que je me serais très bien entendu avec celui-ci, mais je n'en étais pas aussi certain, car il y avait chez lui une truculence qui m'aurait sans doute ennuyé à la longue.

Nous ne nous sommes pas revus. Toutes les fois que je suis revenu dans le vieux monde, elle était dans quelqu'une de ses grandes villes, en Allemagne, en Hollande, en Espagne, à la recherche de documents pour ce qui aura sans doute été son dernier travail: une étude sur les anciens ivoires de l'Afrique. Elle revenait ainsi à son principal centre d'intérêt, ce monde noir qu'elle avait aimé dans toutes ses manifestations.

Cela est mince, j'en conviens, pour un hommage—à peine quelques traits de crayon dans le portrait que ses amis ont voulu dessiner d'elle. L'ayant si peu connue, rarement rencontrée, quand il était déjà tard dans sa vie et qu'elle survivait plutôt à l'image brillante fixée dans les années de la première après-guerre, j'ai pu seulement apporter le témoignage de quelqu'un que sa très naturelle originalité avait étonné et séduit, et qui conserve le regret de n'avoir pas offert à son dernier regard le réconfort, si c'en est un, d'un visage un peu connu d'elle.

herman schrijver
About Nancy

One day in Paris in 1946 Nancy and I were sitting outside a little bistro in the rue St. Honoré having lots and lots of drinks which she and Norman Douglas used to call "littlers." It was in August and appallingly hot and airless and the sky was silver-grey and cloudless and looked like the belly of a large dead fish. There was no one about except stray dogs and old women, for in that part of the rue St. Honoré—near St. Roche—after business hours and in August—there is no one about.

So there we sat—silent—on the pavement outside the bistro, waiting for more "littlers" to be brought to us before going on to dine somewhere much later on, and also waiting for the terrific electric storm which was bound to break.

Suddenly squeezing my arm hard and long which was one of Nancy's signs of great affection, she said slowly and deliberately: "Darling, I have never been so unhappy in the whole of my life as I am now." Her confession neither surprised nor shocked me, for during the many years that I knew Nancy, her mode of life was my idea of hell and we often discussed it together. After the last war Nancy was not only unhappy, she was also restless; she could not and would not settle down and even when she had bought and altered and furnished Lamothe Fénelon, in the Dordogne, and reassembled the broken fragments from the ruins of her lovely house at Réanville, it made not the slightest difference to her desire always to be where she was *not*. This passion—always to be in some very strange and distant land where one is not—is indeed wishing for the moon, or what the French call "lunatique."

I first met Nancy in London in 1931 when she was "a vision of beauty." She was tall—beautifully dressed in her own manner—and elegance was in all her movements and in all her attributes. She already wore the famous ivory bangles in various sizes and colours and my favorites were three Gold Coast bangles inlaid not with gold but with silver—and these she always wore—but in those days she very often wore thirty. Cecil Beaton did a wonderful portrait of her exactly as I remember her now, in a foulard dress with polka dots of heroic size; indeed much of Nancy was of heroic size.

The last time I saw Nancy was in the early autumn of 1963. She was a total wreck, bent double with emphysema, nevertheless smoking and coughing and drinking *sans cesse* and brighter than bright. With her wrinkled skin she looked much older than I remembered her mother at the end of her life. Only the eyes, the beautiful "star sapphire" eyes were the same, although dimmed, and her voice, to me always totally delicious—a tinkling voice—very high and girlish. I have never met anyone whose voice even remotely reminded me of Nancy's. I can hear it now.

It was during the last war that Nancy and I became great friends. We saw each other daily when for a time we both worked in the same Hush-Hush-House. Nancy had returned to London to do "war work," for above all she loved "causes." The Negro problem was of course her Cause No. 1, and the Spanish Civil War Cause No. 2. Nothing bores me more than "causes" and I often made Nancy laugh when I would interrupt her and say, "Darling, please, today no causes." One day when I asked Nancy what she hated most in life, she snapped without giving it a moment's thought—"injustice." On another occasion I asked Nancy if she regretted never having had a child? "Of course not," she said, "if I had wished to have a child I would have had one." And she would. It was stupid of me to have asked.

Nancy was a great hater and a great lover. A complete list of her hates and loves would be long and always incomplete, but apart from injustice she certainly hated her mother most, "Her Ladyship," as she always called her. She also hated England—"pestilential, darling"— but so was Paris *and* the French, and yet at the very end of her unhappy life she was thinking of coming to England to live in Brighton. She loved friendship more than anyone I know and colour and beauty as she saw it and where she saw it. She hated food passionately. "Fucking food, darling," she would say; "if only one didn't have to eat." And Norman Douglas once said to me that "Nancy has the appetite of a dyspeptic butterfly." It was true. The only food she liked was smoked salmon, one *very* thin slice and that was all. But drink and smoke, *ça c'est une autre histoire!* Norman Douglas, who was also in London during the last years of the war, was perhaps Nancy's greatest friend. She adored him and looked after him almost like a Nannie looks after a small naughty boy. What happy meals we had in Geoffrey Hobson's Chelsea house where I lived during the war and where Nancy and Norman often came to dinner and where good wine and good conversation always flowed extravagantly.

When the war was over and our daily meetings came to an end, Nancy went back to France to inspect the ruins of her once lovely and famous house at Réanville. It was where she had started her Hours Press, and where I saw the actual press in a ruined barn. Nancy's house had not been bombed. It was very carefully and very systematically broken up and looted by the Nazis, aided and abetted, I am afraid, by the villagers, for Nancy's name was high up on a list of intellectuals to be destroyed at all cost.

Victor Cunard, Nancy's cousin, used to say that Nancy hated comfort and loved to live like a peasant—a "15th century peasant *bien entendu.*" Of course, this was true. Nancy liked to sit on the floor, liked uncomfortable chairs and beds, and I have endless memories of cheap hotel bedrooms in London and Paris with Nancy sitting on the floor—I sitting on the only chair, or lying on the bed, admiring Nancy's latest treasures—ivory bangles, African *objets d'art* or fragments of Mexican potteries and beads. I am surrounded now with lovely objects Nancy so generously gave me.

As soon as Nancy left London after the war to return to France, our correspondence began and continued until the very end of her life. Her last letter is dated March 5th; she died on March 17th 1965.

When I look through these hundreds of letters and postcards, I see Nancy more vividly than ever and also her life, which to me was indeed *"une triste existence sur une terre étrangère."*

I am afraid that her soul will never rest in peace. It is the very last thing she would wish and I can hear her delicious little laugh. I always will.

w. j. strachan
Nancy Cunard

"The ball I threw when playing in the park
Has not yet reached the ground . . ."

As one gets older, one realizes the extent to which later life is a recap
of early days. From what Nancy Cunard talked and wrote to me
about in many scores of letters extending over two decades, I recognized her many childhood enthusiasms. Among these, fostered particularly by her kind of Alice-in-Wonderland friendship with George
Moore, a frequent guest at Nevill Holt and an adorer of her mother,
was her obsession with words and her love of wild flowers which she
would inspect and identify during long walks with the Irish novelist.
She would also pick up and collect pretty or unusual stones. We all
know how these interests developed. Her passion for reading and
writing verse, for translating poems from and into French and Spanish
with skill and bravura. Her collecting of "objets trouvés" foreshadowed
her more specialized feeling for African ivories, pre-Columbian carvings and enthusiasm for the sculpture of her contemporary in age,
Henry Moore. In one of her last letters, dated 2nd February 1965, she
wrote to me: "I write at once on account of what you say about
stones. You will love mine. So it was for YOU I was picking up
every one of those darlings I could see, often with difficulty, in the
general gravel of the place! This was at Pertenhall, Beds. (where
you have often written to me . . .). Well if Victor (Victor Cunard,
her cousin) liked tea and cake in and on silver, I adored those wonderful fossilized proofs of . . . yes, of who?" And on a similar theme,
concerning a stone she had collected, of which more will be said later:
"I have given Irene Rathbone the *ring* for Henry Moore—a devious
way of getting it to Henry via Geoffrey, via YOU. Irene also felt, as
I did, that it should not be sent through the post! (Though why not?)
Please look at it when it reaches you—an Avebury-shaped stone—
from the muddled coast between St. Jean Cap-Ferrat and Beaulieu. . . ."

As for her walking, during my stay at her house at Lamothe-

Fénelon in 1952, though considerably her junior, I found her pace exhausting but compensated for by all the fascinating local information she retailed as we strode across the fields and meadows. I have particularly happy memories of a walk to the Château Fénelon of which I made a sketch and the welcome pauses to identify wild flowers.

Physical appearance more than usually in Nancy expressed the personality. She might decry her mother's racialism (the "White Lady-ship" of her vitriolic pamphlet) which caused the rift between them, but—fortunately—she could not help inheriting Lady Cunard's beauty. When, after an exchange of letters over translations I was making of contemporary French Poets at the time of the Liberation, she sent me a card: "Café Royal at 6.15 pm . . . my *signalement,* old beige large coat with high fur collar . . ." But even this telegraphic description was hardly necessary, familiar as I was, with the Wyndham Lewis drawing of her, done in the twenties when she had been such a dynamic figure in post-war avant-gardism in Paris. She always wore clothes that emphasized her height and elegance, huge ivory bangles on her fine-boned wrists; heavy beads or coral ropes hung round her graceful neck and exotic-looking rings drew one's gaze to the exquisite, tapering fingers. But it was above all the eyes, clear, friendly which seemed to change colour—blue or greenish-grey with the light. These and her smile, unforgettable, made one feel an eternal youthfulness about her even when years of hectic activity and much physical pain were beginning to take their toll. Her conversation and letters, however, never ceased to be as lively and fascinating as ever. It was evident to me from our first meetings and exchanges of correspondence that she was a person who lived at a high not to say fever-pitch, prodigal of her nervous energy and—as I gathered later—of her money, in other people's causes. Little wonder that with her immense output in articles, translations, books, not to mention letter writing, she overstrained what must have once been an iron constitution and became too dependent on her "Romolo" as she called her rum and water which, alas, replaced more and more the good vin de Cahors which we used to drink at Lamothe. In a kind of way it seemed in character and inevitable. In a letter Sylvia Townsend Warner wrote to me from Frome Vauchurch she refers to Nancy: "I thought Nancy looked pretty well. She was very industrious while she was here. We shut her up with a fire and she ate through a great many overhanging jobs. It seemed to me that every time I went in with a little glass she was translating out of or into a different language. . . ." (March 27, 1947.) And I recall an early letter of Nancy's to me (January 9th, 1945) about Virginia Woolf on whom I had written a poem: "Having known Virginia . . . no, what I wanted to say was how she laughed when I said, in answer to 'the awful difficulty of understanding James Joyce' that one should read him with a good deal of strong drink, perhaps even a little tight (what Stulik used to qualify as 'hearing the anchels sing'), then, I said, many things become clear . . . I do mean this seriously. Consider Anna Livia Plurabella. It all invested itself with great meaning accompanied by the flow of wine. And Joyce appreciated drink very much, you know. . . ."

She was a strange mixture of many qualities one normally considers incompatibles; she supported causes with an almost Puritan-like fanaticism, yet unlike the majority of those who espouse causes, she was taken up most of all with human personalities; almost to a fault insofar as she must have been disillusioned on frequent occasions by some of the "lame dogs and hurt birds" that surrounded her. (I think for example of her sympathy with help for the poet and critic Joë Bousquet, bed-ridden since World War I injuries yet "pivot of the Resistance in the South West," with whom she put me in touch.) Never did this result in cynicism; she moved ahead to the next problem or task in hand. And this applied to some unsuccessful attempts to place her work with publishers who, after initial encouragement, turned her projects down. Fortunately her persistence with the two important studies of George Moore and Norman Douglas was rewarded. (*G.M.* and *Grand Man*) Alongside her deep appreciation of the high-browism of these twin heroes and her aristocratic taste in the arts was her sympathy with and understanding of ordinary people —from the family chauffeur from whom she learned her Russian to the woman who did the cleaning in her Lamothe home. No hint of patronage. In the same letter in which she writes apropos a bank staff strike in Andorra, very inconvenient for *her*—"Sept. 26. 19— 'How right they are—people are always right to strike. The mere fact means that all other ways have been exhausted. Strike, strike, strike, et vous aurez peut-être grain de cause. Gain de cause, I mean! Grain de cause!! Bravo typewriter! . . ."—she deals with another social problem: "I am preparing a report on prisons in Spain and shall send it to you for your edification." Note the tone of her description of the cleaning woman, referred to higher up. (Lamothe-Fénelon. November 16th 1950) "My little-old-woman-of-the-Lot totters about, stone-deaf, competent, undeterrable and a wonderful mender of old curtains ruined beyond service. . . ." She moved easily in any group, was as at home in a Mexican hovel as in Harold Acton's palazzo, La Pietra, at Fiesole. She was as outgiving to young people—as I had a particular opportunity of observing—as to her "grand old men." I recall how appreciative she was of a young pupil of mine who drew Lobengula's ring for her in Rhodes House (of all places!) at Bishop's Stortford. Among other contradictions, minor but intriguing, was the indifference she showed to "presentation" in her manuscripts and especially in her letters, frequently written or typed on the backs of old circulars, scraps of old bills, etc., which normally go straight into the wastepaper basket. Probably the habit dated back to war economy in the latter case, and in the former stemmed from her individual style of emphasis which in handwriting involved frequent resort to underlining and block-capitals, and, in typing, staccato dartings to and from the shift keys, so that some of her letters almost qualify in the Apollinaire sense as "calligrammes." Few would therefore have ever suspected her of running her own press (The Hours Press in Paris) and typesetting and composing herself and producing ten texts with bindings that have stood well up to time (with designs by Man Ray, Yves Tanguy and Frank Dobson, etc.) though her flair for discovering original authors, who include Roy Campbell, Samuel Beckett (*Whoroscope*), Laura Riding and Robert Graves, to publish is less surprising. These publications belong to the period before I knew her, which was when she was busy in London editing *Poems for France* and deeply absorbed in all that concerned resurgent France during the Resistance and after. Like scores of others (has anyone ever had more books dedicated to them?), I owed a great deal to her encouragement. She urged me to submit my first verse translation (a sonnet by Péguy) to the *New Statesman* and was delighted when it was published. She put me in touch with many of the poets whose work I was translating, including Aragon. When, after considerable struggles with publishers in France about authorizations, my collection of translations finally came out in England (1948). Nancy was ill in France, suffering from blood poisoning in her arm but managed to write (in pencil): "I am so ill still, can't write more. Forgive. I am touched, pleased, all, by your mention of me in *A. to A* and dedication. . . ." Whatever the scrap of paper or the local circumstances, her calligraphy was attractive and elegant. I praised it in a letter during her last illness and she wrote back: "And *now* what can you say of my handwriting? You praised it! Surely *no one* could possibly imitate this superlatively *tremblé* effect? 'Pulso nervioso' was the Chilean expression—I suppose in nice, strong, demotic English this can be translated as "the shakes." Due to bad blood circulation. . . ."

Her own translations at their best are very fine; sometimes I think certain of the translations of her own poems into French are oddly superior to the original English. She had a great gift for original, almost surrealist imagery—take the first stanza of her Noel, Amour, Guerre 1944

Décembre à la gueule de fer—
Voici la marée d'enfer
Où le brick Hélas prend la mer.

or

Triomphe des temps où Vie
Ne rime qu'avec Ennemi
Et le Non règne sur le Si

(what if she broke the rules—"to hell with the rules" one could hear
her say).

As all her friends know, she worked feverishly for France (first at
P.W.D.-SHAEF in London) during its darkest days, then after the
Liberation when things there seemed more hopeful she rallied once
more to her beloved Spain with whose Republican cause she had herself actively identified during the civil war. In a letter dated Aug. 24,
1946, she wrote: "Yes, Andorra. Five weeks there and much of it quite
wonderful. . . . As you know, I am ENTIRELY occupied with 'the
things of Spain' and shall not be back in Paris. . . . Literary matters
are simply a dead letter to me these times. Not for ever though. . . ."
Emerging from this Spanish period were her poems *Nous Gens
D'Espagne 1945-49,* remarkable poems in French (for an English
woman) written with the heart as well as the head. All contain
quotable passages but to me the most moving are lines in *Fou comme
l'Amour.*

La vérité comme une cravache,
La vérité au masque de fièvre,
La vérité—ce caméléon—
La vérité à bec de lièvre
                    (Quand il le faut)
La vérité—ce coup de dé
Immense et drue et volcanique,
Roublarde, gitane et ambulante,
Moitié hasard, moitié destin,
Ma vérité incandescente, Je t'aime—
Et tout réside dans l'âpre et fin.

Back in Normandy in 1948 after the time in Andorra, followed by
a prolonged stay in Mexico, she could write: "One way and another
here are my values for all the material difficulties and expense, *my*
values, as never could anything be in Mexico or in the Antilles. Rooks

and crooks and villainy beyond—here. And there? Many deserts. And here, pure wine. To your health in it, dear Walter."

Pyschologically (as well as *literally* most of her time) she was, like the two subjects of her affection, George Moore and Norman Douglas, an ex-patriot; partly as the result of being disinherited by her mother (tied up with the cause of it, her championing of the Negro in America), partly that she was by nature both pioneer and a rebel, a *révoltée avant la lettre*. Her authors and artists of the Hours Press, particularly Ezra Pound, Man Ray and Yves Tanguy could hardly be described as conformist; in her appreciation of Negro jazz she was well in the avant-garde. Many years after the publication of her *Negro,* she wrote to me: "How very interesting and nice that you should have a prize pupil who has got into the Negro world. I'd love to meet him one day. . . . In the April number of 'Europe' is my radio talk on 'Musique Noire des Etats-Unis' which finally got on the air here." Her interest in what has since become almost a craze is mentioned in the same letter (c. 1949) "It (the talk) is a very slight, condensed and horribly incomplete thing; no mention for instance of 'Negro songs of Protest,' 'Chaingang songs' which are superb." Seven years ago apropos *Negro,* first published in 1934 by Wishart, her magnum opus about which doubtless other contributors to this symposium who knew her at that date will have much to say, she wrote: (May 15, 1961) "I am so glad that at last Afro-America is taking more interest in its antecedents than it did when I was there in 1932. . . . How I wish I could give *you* a copy of my *Negro*—it is unfindable; when so, even in England, one sold last year for £18. In the U.S. it is worth over $60."

Nancy Cunard had little formal education. (She wrote to me, January 7, 1965: "All I could *learn* of poetry—or rather of its academic complexities was when Miss Woolf, the head of those horrible classes I was sent to in London, by Her Ladyship from the age of 9 to a little over 14 was this . . . 'ti-tum, ti-tum, ti-tum, ti-tum.' ") It is important to realize that she was virtually self-taught and that her vast fund of miscellaneous knowledge was simply the result of tremendous curiosity and that her experience of art and literature was largely from her direct contact with writers and artists of genius or talent and continual visits to the great museums of the world. If this lack of disciplined training can be discerned in her writing and more in her verse than in her prose, it is compensated by her individual originality of expression and above all her complete freedom from ready-made ideas. No letter writer could be less inhibited—her letters are spoken utterances and always bear the mark of their speaker. I would like to quote two examples. The first apropos Kokoschka (about whom I had been writing a review): "Kokoschka; Hotel Rousse Vernon, Eure June 21. Yes, he came to my flat on the Île St. Louis a great deal in 1924 and painted a portrait. I have never seen it, and my impression is that it was never finished, or at least it was not finished there! I had a squint at it one day and loathed it, simply loathed it—all cat-scratched in dirty purple. But some of his things I DO like. As I did him, fairly well. . . ." The second, simple, moving, concerning the memorial to Norman Douglas. (Hotel Pagano, Capri. March 11) "I wonder if you would like to meet Norman's biographer, Cecil Woolf, nephew of Leonard? . . . Norman's tomb here is very beautiful—green-grey-dark marble, completely simple with only the indications of his name and his dates and the Latin words "Omnes Eodem Cogimur"—which are completely mysterious to me. I went there yesterday in a cutting gale, and remembered there it was my birthday. . . ."

To re-read her letters is to recapture her physical presence; I remember vividly her first visit to us (January 7th 1945) when she sat on the floor by an open fire and talked and talked, striking off felicitous phrases the kind that had already fascinated me in her letters and ranging over a host of subjects, particularly poetry and translation. She communicated her enthusiasm for what one was doing and gave one's ego a tremendous fillip. I found her criticisms of my work most helpful. She suggested reviews that might be interested in publishing my poems and I recall her remark—with an allusion to her physique—about a poem I wrote on a painting by Derain and one entitled *Three Poplar Trees*. "Yes. I *do* like these two poems and surely a good quality review will appreciate them. Derain by the way not Dérain. The poplar is Chile's national tree—el àlamo—and they called me the alamo there—being long and thin." I realized then— as I do now—that her praise sometimes a little indiscriminate erred on the side of encouragement, a good fault.

When my interest in typography, after the coup de foudre of the Burlington House exhibition of French *livres d'artiste* in 1944, extended to the latest French illustrated books in this *genre* and finally took me to see Jean Lurçat at S. Céré in the Dordogne, Nancy invited me to stay at Lamothe-Fénelon in her new place, the slow transformation of which (it was a converted barn) into a suitable dwelling was to cost her money and much exasperation. Some time before she had written: "I have now a HOUSE, a nutshell building complete for every dis-comfort and in-convenience, and a veritable network of fissures, but I adore it—Provisional—The days go like small beads of the same colour and I am alone since weeks; though 'Géraldine' (Madame Géraldine Balayé) of Radio Toulouse-Pyrénées coming for three days, tomorrow. By her bed are 'A. to A.' and your own poems. She wants and plans to do a lot about English authors who love France. . . . Oh, I am being smoked, insidiously today, yesterday it was exuberantly, from below, through the floor. . . . Here is a draft of the translation I have just made of Kay Boyle's very fine Scottsboro poem in 1937 and copy of the poem itself. How inexpressibly glad I am to have the possibility of laying hands on some of my things again any way—at last. I wish I had known you in the Scottsboro years (32-35-36), you would have helped terrifically. Two at least of the boys are still in gaol, having got 'life'—the monstrosity of that country. . . ."

Thanks to her guidance and hospitality I found my way to most of the famous châteaux and caves in the Lot and Dordogne. The publisher Pierre Vorms (whom I had got to know through the painter and illustrator of Poe's *The Raven,* Prassinos) took me to spend a day with Lurçat, whom, after an exhilarating day of seeing and discussion, we left about midnight. Vorms put me down somewhere near Nancy's house; I got completely lost, but the early hours were warm and the nightingales were singing and I was lyrically happy in the anticipation of telling Nancy about the tapestries and illustrated books I had been shown by Lurçat, his ceramics, his dogs and above all his talk.

Lamothe-Fénelon was an anchorage where she was adored by the "locals," but gradually she had the feeling of being cut off from her friends especially in the winter months. But it was here that she did most of her writing, despite distant battles with publishers and nearer struggles against inanimate things—perennial, it would seem in Nancy's life. And so in the letter describing how busy she was with her translation of Norman's "Fountains in the Sand" so that there "has seemed to be not a moment for anything else, EXCEPT the usual chores and an APPALLING new one: lack of water in the cistern, cracked, as was the electric pump, by frosts—which means sundry grindings of teeth and impotent rages" she returns first to a request to find an exchange for a local-taxi-driver's daughter, then makes a reference to Hume Thorne and my Italian translations and finally to her book—" 'Grand Man' comes out (at last) this week," and a mild complaint about three "annoying typographical errors in it. Although I think, if such must be, the one about 'bristly wine' may have the approbation of every reader, including darling Norman."

The reference to Hume Thorne brings me to the gratitude so many of us owe to her gift for arranging contacts between people sharing common interests. Through Nancy I gained the friendship of many gifted and warm personalities, particularly Cecily Mackworth, Sylvia

Townsend Warner and Irene Rathbone. When in Italy I had intro-
ductions from her to Harold Acton, and during a stay at Venice to
Peggy Guggenheim in Asolo, Freya Stark and an old friend of Dia-
ghilev's whose name, if I remember rightly, was Signora Alix Cava-
lieri. For my part I was glad to have the chance of introducing Nancy
to the Italian writer (and directress of the Keats-Shelley Memorial
House in Rome) Vera Cacciatore whom she found "utterly charming" and of whose book *The Swing* she wrote: "I have just finished
Vera Cacciatore's very strange book in your admirable smooth translation. How eerie, how unlike anything else I know and rather terrifying. Particularly do I like 'The Bridge.' . . ." Also to Geoffrey Cot-
terell, a former pupil and author of *Tiara Tahiti,* and particularly to
Henry and Irina Moore as between her and them a very real bond of
friendship developed on which I shall enlarge later.

I would like to say something about her interest in the arts, since
she did a great deal to disseminate knowledge and enthusiasm just
after the last War both as journalist and as a translator. "Just finished
a long article on the Musée de l'Homme for the Burlington; lovely
photos with it . . . Am in rags. Damn the lot! . . . You should really
come and meet some of the poets." she wrote in a letter dated October
24, 1945, and a year or so later, "At this moment I am struggling with
a beautifully lucid but slightly technical 'Treatise on Aquarellisme'
by the painter Signac. It's a preface, I should think, to one of those
excellent art-books done by the Editions Braun. . . ." One hopes that
the manuscript of her book on African Ivories—on which she must
have been one of the greatest authorities to combine aesthetic judge-
ment with a real knowledge of the African people—will find a publisher.

Before turning to the phase in which her fight against illness—
illuminated, always by continued literary work and preoccupation with
her friends—predominated in her mind and saddened ours, I would
like to quote *in extenso* from an earlier letter (July 27, 1948) which
seems to reveal her wonderful gift for vivid reportage combined with
that inimitable personal touch which makes the born letter writer.
It was sent from the Hotel de l'Arche de Noe, Givery, Eure. "It's
divine here. Hot now. Days in fields, nights with absolutely fantastic
assortment of 'summerites'; an ex-Show Girl Ziegfield Follies style,
Diaghilew's nephew and a broken-nosed British ex-Russian priest, a
small brown irreducible french governess and my own strange beautiful poetic Irish-Red Indian-American 'boy-friend'—that was last
night's lot . . . and the girls like boys and the boys like girls in the
offing, and tonight Margaret Anderson and Dorothy Caruso . . .
Margaret, as you know, founded that admirable 'Little Review' in the

USA years ago with James [Jane] Heap (?)—the first to print Joyce. Dorothy is Caruso's widow. France, as you see, is getting to be France again. . . ." (Then the old battle with inanimate things.) "I am plagued, however, by my poor broken typewriter—what agony when teeth etc. break on that. I need it so, all day. Half-way through the Mexican book. O dear Walter, the awfulness of London. After 34 days in that unspeakable Empire ship, the 4 days in London were like the disgusting sham sweet at the end of a revolting meal. I loathed it. Once again! No more colonies, no more Mexico, no more travel for a long time. Just *France* and HERE. God, for a house. . . ."

Of course she did come over to England but at longer intervals. Meantime, I had direct news of her through continual correspondence, as usual, a mixture of reportage and opinions. Although she thought so highly of George Moore, she realized his blind spots. Apropos Zola (I had included a passage from *Germinal* in an anthology *Ici les Provinces,* Oxford University Press, I had edited), "What nonsense G.M. talked about him, practically saying he was a bit of a vulgarian, because of his style." In the same letter, an agreeable personal message, "The pleasure of seeing Geoffrey and friend (two gentle striding giants) was great. They seemed so able in encompassing all the diverse kilometres. Really, I loved seeing them, and wished it could have been much longer." The former, my son, was himself to form a link with Nancy, so sympathetic to young people and later— when Nancy was almost always suffering from illness—called on Nancy with his wife while on a tour of the Lot-Dordogne district.

The first reference to the Moore meeting was in a letter addressed from 9 Beaufort Gardens (undated).

"Would of course love to meet Henry Moore with you one day, but I can't say about coming to B.S. at this moment, as I am in a spate of troubles, worries and confusion mainly due to the Will and all its delays—So till we meet at the P.E.N. dinner. . . ." It must have been before spring 1952 since in the same letter giving me trains to Souillac she wrote (March 3, 1952), "In tearing haste. HOW much I enjoyed the day with you and meeting Henry Moore. . . . Would you please forward him this?" A year or so later, Nancy spent a few weeks at Much Hadham (staying at the Red Lion) and we had most enjoyable meetings here and at the Moores. But Hertfordshire cold was too much for her poor circulation. In practically every one of scores of letters to me there was always an affectionate message for "the dear Henry Moores." For example, Oct. 26, 1954: "I am just off to the Grand Hotel, Toulouse for a while—et région. Translation of 'Fountains in the Sand' (Norman Douglas' book which she translated into French) now finished . . . I believe I shall be meeting Manet's nephew next week in Toulouse. How very much one would like to hear any detail about Manet. Best thoughts to you all and to the Henry Moores." Or, May 15, 1961: "Once again what seems to become my usual request for aid and information. This time it is about a young Spanish student. Father-Angel Goded is the friend to whom went Henry Moore, de ma part, when in Mexico, and Angel (said H.M.) gave him a banquet with several of the intellectuals invited to meet him. So dear H.M. can tell you what he is like. . . . Angel Goded is one of the most honourable people I have ever known in my life. . . ."

The years between 1961 and 1963 I had fewer letters but many characteristic post cards and sometimes she would post off a packet of cuttings or photographs from exhibitions she had reviewed in the past. They consoled me for what seemed the dateless limit of her dear exile, and if I dwell on her last years it is because of my admiration for the tremendous fight she will put up against illness, not exactly stoically—that would be the wrong word, for she had to voice her protest, not against fate or death, just a desperate feeling of being prevented by pain and weakness from the tasks she had set herself to do. She was particularly anxious to complete her work on the Hours Press and find a publisher for it. In a letter of 23 June 1963 I find her first reference to the editor of the present symposium, "All my excuses, I shall read it now—and no doubt the young Prof. Hugh Ford arriving, I think, here tomorrow, to work the only collaborative way I can think of, on expanding my book on 'The Hours Press.' He is a dear. I am *so ill, all* the time and wonder how these things fit together (since well over 2 years). Sclerosis of the lungs, Asthma, Chronic bronchitis, Emphysema, Dizziness. Plus loathing of all food and utter weakness . . . Forgive not a longer letter. I am so ill! So much love to *all* of you and to the Moores."

In July marked (?) by her, 1963, from Lamothe, I received a letter from her which mentions so many of the things that bound us together—friendships, family, writing, that I would like to quote from it extensively.

"Dearest Walter, Thank you so much for your lovely letter, ending with those charming words of Henry Moore's and Irina—to who, much love please, when you next see each other. To think of you as a 'gran-da' may mean something to you all, but it means NOTHING to me, because since I've ever known you, I recognized an 'Immortal' whom no ageing would affect much ever. I LOVED Geoffrey and his wife here, for that so brief moment last summer, but was already ill as could be. MUCH worse now. And as you see, this has got into the typewriter. . . . Return here, after months in a Toulouse hotel-room

(LOVELY servants, all of them, and interesting), has been, and is HELL. As usual NO WATER . . . Who is 'WE'? you may ask. 'WE' are the delicious and so sympathetic young (New Jersey) Prof, (The reference is of course to Professor Hugh Ford, the present editor.) his wife and I; and the Prof and I work, daily, rather intensively, on that short book of mine on The Hours Press—'expanding.' He is lovely to work with. As for me, I see now that I ache all over. . . . Am perfectly ready to (at last) into hospital or cliniques. I thought they could do anything—which I feel they can't. Your beautifully produced piece (an off print from a *Connoisseur* article) on 'Le Beau livre' came. Thank you so much, as ever, dearest Walter—not only for many most interesting letters through the years, but for the admiration your continuous work gives me. And OH 'The Little World of the Past' (The translation I had sent her of *Piccolo Mondo Antico* by Fogazzaro.) How exquisite it is. . . . Forgive this terrible typing. If you knew how ill I feel, ALL the time—and that, dammit, must, I suppose, come out in notes and letters. So much love to you all (I can hardly walk to the village NOW!) Nancy"

The stone mentioned earlier I was able to take over to Henry Moore in the winter of 1964, and from Villa Pomone at St. Jean Cap Ferrat, Nancy wrote: "Bless you yet once again, dearest Walter. This moment came a delicious letter from Henry Moore saying how much he likes the stone and that it has many meanings, and that maybe, he may use one of them one day. I knew he would see it that way. . . . I adored your exquisite montage of autumn leaves and it went straight into my 'art-box' at Lamothe. . . ." By June, 1964, she had embarked on a poem despite a leg injury in addition to other ills. "The leg wound has finally closed up, but the lungs are like hell and that is why I did not write to dear Geoff to thank him for his exquisitely made card. . . . All I can do—DO is write. The long poem (in English) is already long. It will make a book. Don't ask me 'Who'll publish . . .'" In July she was back at Lamothe and wrote: "Dearest Walter . . . I wish to God YOU would send over one of your SENIOR pupils—art-knowledged, literary-minded, with a large empty suitcase, HERE, some time later . . . to remove a stack of worth-while books . . . Is it possible? Alas, I fear he could hardly sleep here, as I have en permanence a lovely French woman in that stone room you remember, and yet perhaps he could—if he did not mind the narrow attic which—praise be, has AT LAST re-become my own typing den, after years of disorder." Then another reference to the ring. "A little heavy to send. HE (Henry Moore) won't get his lovely creative finger into it. I can, just. Out of the sea. In stone, of course. Stonehenge period." Then back to the poem; "My POEM is, and I suspect will be in great abeyance while I am here, because of the 'House' etcs. . . . I think YOU and GEOFF will like it. Shakespearian (and archaic, as it starts) the break and what comes after will be very different. . . ." In a letter dated October 9, 1964, after writing about our early days—showing a remarkably accurate memory for years and even months connected with my first published poems and my time in Italy, she switches to, "HERE? I am near hating it. *Not* the land, nor yet the house itself (inconvenient as it is), but the fact of being MYSELF *in it at this time and ill*. Do you guess, or do you understand? The three leaves you sent me are so beautiful. I put them with paste on pale red paper under press—To keep! So much love." She battled on with her writing: "all my instinct begs of me is to lie in bed, sleep colossally, have a sup brought up on a tray, maunder about, grumbling, have a very strong drink of ROMOLO, and THEN put something on, and get to the typewriter (in proper temperature) to see 'what I have wrote the night before' copy it out roughly, correct like mad, re-type, like mad etc. etc. perhaps arrive at final minus-one version. . . . I admire scholars. I do not envy them. I do not ENVY anyone, for that matter, I envy and WANT the *time* I want for myself. Et c'est tout."

On January 30th from the Clinique Belvédère, Nice, a year ago to the day on which I am writing this—came a letter from her: "Dearest Walter, Thigh badly broken night of Jan 21 by inexplicable heavy fall in bedroom at Pomone . . . Agony just beginning to pass. Re-X-rayed yesterday. Good progress. May be able to return to Pomone in a few days. . . . It has been ghastly. At last I got into a room by myself and can sit up, but bedpan régime and not enough to drink. When there is drink (Rum and water: 'Un Romolo,' and sufficient wine) I compose like mad. . . . Thus I put the sequence (I refer to 'The Visions') in the poetry section in order and will see if I can use the typewriter in about three hours, when day shall have at last come. . . . Adenda:

1   2   3   4   5   6   7   8   9   10   11   12

'Dancing girls bore me bore me to distraction'
"This is the remembered example given by Sir Thomas Beecham illustrating some metre or other—a particularly hideous one, I think. What is it called. Not that *I* shall ever use it. What are 'Sapphics'? Meanwhile, what can I write about? I will try and think out what I am trying and failing to say to you as soon as I dare have the light full on. Oh. Walter! 'La Coca' would enchant you. She is from Perugia Province. . . . She is in four-square English 'the daily char,' une perle pour Pomone. Fat and fifty with *great* power in all she does. Those

dictones she serves me, most of them, I imagine, are pretty old. I have noted down quite a few. . . . There is also Adam (Monsieur Blu) and I think you have him at the end of the Fish Sequence. (Part of *The Visions* on which she was working so feverishly.) I put him into French (while in agony) . . . Will it ever come to seven today? For once I'd be glad of everyone being up early. I've had 2 hours' sleep, quite enough, and want to correct the lengthy and quite different sequence that immediately follows what we'll call the 'Seskypedaelian' page. What a beautiful word it is! P.S. Is your lovely Pavese 'Il compagno' doing well? . . ."

So, in the midst of all her suffering the same human sympathy in others, the quip, the burning curiosity.

During this period I wrote as often as I could, replying to her queries about rhythms and metres, and commenting on sections of her poem *The Visions* as they arrived. Out of one query about the Haycock Inn at Wanstead on the old Great North Road (now by-passed), she was surprised that I knew the legend. "Most glad you like my 'Barnabee.' So you knew him! How erudite. Or is he very well known? Lovely prints in my early edition. And The Haycock! How often I went there between 1914 and 1925 when my father lived there, dying before my eyes in Nov. 1925. The Nene! I've been on it, alone, for the first time in a canoe, before Sir Bache's astonished yet not displeased eyes. The current was often so strong that, alone, I could not bring the boat back, I had to tether it, and then a man fetch it." Here an interruption and the letter completed the next day (February 3, 1965) carried a cri du coeur "back at Pomone" (from the Clinique) "*Agony* Thigh" but also the triumphant "Heard my 'THESE WERE THE HOURS' *IS* accepted—by Southern Illinois Univ. Press." This was terrific news for her and one is glad that at least she could have this comfort in her last weeks. In January she had written to me: "Now that cursed HOURS PRESS book of mine. Written, and finished in 1959–60, it sought a London publisher, in vain. Hart-Davis, Senhouse of Secker and Warburg and I forget which others . . . Nix! 'Too special a subject!' . . . here, now Jan 14 . . . How everything I try to do gets interrupted."

"Well, The TSS, top-copy, has been with my dear young Prof. Ford, Hugh Ford, Trenton State College, Trenton, New Jersey, U.S.A., since August 1963. He spent a whole month at Lamothe, with his adorable French-Canadian wife, just before, and we went into everything together, every single day, and he seems to be thinking 'very highly of it.' BUT, *magari*, he is not a publisher. He tried Knopf, and Knopf NEARLY took it. Ya, 'NEARLY' . . . now one of the big University Presses has it in hand, and ONE (but not as yet, as far as I know, the necessary TWO advisors has sent in a favourable report. So there it is. . . ." More queries on the poem with a long letter dated February and February 26; February 12 another little note enclosing the end of the *Pub-Row* but with a charming sentence showing her affection for friends which no pain could quench, "Lovely letter from Geoffrey yesterday with pretty photo of Alison (his 18 month old daughter, my granddaughter), saying how she went round your house saying 'Book, book.' Delicious." Other notes about this time are filled with references to friends and acquaintances "darling Jean Guerin," the mother-in-law of the chemist from nearby Beaulieu "with flowers," "La Coca," the Italian "char," Monsieur Blu, "the itinerant gardener" —all inimitably described. Despite continual pain and weakness she battled on with her poem. In a letter dated February 9 she wrote, "Infinite thanks for all—of the greatest use in that very long sequence. . . . This is what I wrote all the time in the clinique to the first-of-all smirks of the innumerable nurses, then to their astonishment —the surgeon took the fact of my writing more seriously. . . . I came back here (Villa Pomone), delighted to be on a stretcher. Two days after (Feb. 5), what happened? Medical poisoning. . . ." Then follow details too painful to recount but which I think it helped her to describe. She continues, "I wish I had some pain-killer. But no. Forbidden (why?) *'Sufra na' mas'*—very current Chilean Spanish: 'Just suffer, that's all!' " She could still muster the energy, born of a lifetime's habit —of concerning herself with other people's problems. She wrote on a card dated February 14, 1965, "I see I missed answering a query of yours re. Yves Tanguy." Three days later a crowded postcard which seemed to sum up so much of her and her situation and struck an unusual, nostalgic note, foreshadowed by certain parts of her poem. The picture on the card—one of a series of five of Ship-Burial at Sutton Hoo, Suffolk, which she sent in rapid succession but only two of which carried messages—ran: "Feb. 17 Just this beauty . . . Might as well know the true, lovely things of one's own country. To say what? A. That I think of you with grateful dactylish love. B. That I am uplifted by the thought *of living in England again,* come late summer. C. That you will soon receive your véritable POULET from me: HUNGARY, this time—historical data on the great, historic battle, national disaster . . . wanted for brief mention in 'The Visions.' D. I shall want a small painting made (by YOU?) when arrived of the Osteosynthèse done on my broken HIP. Took tracings from medical books of 6 cols du fémur. You and Henry Moore will be enthusiastic. Expense continues appalling . . . (Later) 'Atalanta' letter just come. Such thanks." Ten days later (February 27), card No. 2 (her last communication to me), "Walter Dear, Please get in touch with a *very* great (French) friend of mine (we lived and worked together in France during three-quarters of the making of my NEGRO: before then he worked at the Hours Press (only at the end of it). So you see that makes more years than one:) Raymond Michelet 'Parallèles,' 172 rue Pelleport 172 Paris 20e.—I mean in connection with all your 'Beaux livres' activities. Hungarian questions to follow." The amazing intellectual curiosity and human sympathy of this undaunted spirit never let up in circumstances that would have defeated all but the bravest and most exceptional. Whatever the final judgements on the merits of this last poem, not even Marcel Proust could have shown greater heroism and persistence in the accomplishment of a piece of work. I am sure she had no great illusions about *The Visions;* these verses were partly a nostalgic return to past, half-remembered history and to her own past, partly a defiant protest against the body's racks, partly her unending devotion to the craft of words. "I should much like to know to perfection the modes of English poetry. How much would that serve one, I wonder . . . That will never make a poet out of anyone. What will. NOTHING—save by birth—and then work. Ah dear, I sigh. And so stop . . ." Less than a month later I had the shock of seeing her death reported in *The Times* and later, from Irene Rathbone, I received further news of the distressing circumstances surrounding it. I could not help—from the evidence of Nancy's last messages to me—interpreting her last journey as a desperate attempt to get back to England via Paris. Neither I nor her staunch and loyal friend Irene Rathbone with whom I had the mournful consolation of talking about Nancy at this time, could believe that that bright star had been extinguished; she who had raged against the dying of the light with such indomitable spirit had somehow seemed less mortal than ordinary people.

This is not the moment nor is it for me to attempt to assess her contribution to literature, but I am convinced that her personal memories of George Moore and Norman Douglas will last as long as interest in those great writers endures. Her *Negro* is and will remain a classic of aesthetic and sociological importance. What matters to us who knew her was her wonderful, radiant and generous personality, her devotion to her friends, regardless of race, country or class—the memories of our meetings with her, the pleasure she gave us with that vivid gift of spoken or written phrase, and above all, the deep affection that flowed from her like a tide.

henry moore

Postscript to the Preceding Account

Outwardly Nancy Cunard did not correspond with the mental picture I had formed of her from my previous knowledge of her activities connected with many worthwhile and often unpopular causes, her support for the Negro in America, for the Republicans in the Spanish civil war, for example. I expected a more militant physical presence. Instead, there was this elegant, sensitive woman whose very bone-structure seemed finer and more delicate than any one else's. She conveyed an immediate impression of gentle intensity. She had an abundance of nervous energy, and no matter how long you were with her, you were conscious of a burning enthusiasm, a perpetual giving-out whatever subject (and her range was enormous) came under discussion.

She had an innate feeling for sculpture, developed through her long familiarity with examples from early and primitive civilizations and her expert knowledge of African ivories. She had indeed a rare appreciation of form-meaning whether in man-made sculpture or in the kind of unusual *objet trouvé* she discovered and describes with such lyrical aptness in the letter quoted here, written when she was so desperately ill.

She was a dear, sweet, generous person one was always delighted to see and one feels enriched to have known.

LETTERS FROM NANCY CUNARD TO HENRY MOORE

Letter 1.

Lamothe-Fénelon
Lot France
Sept. 26, 1964

Dear Henry, Thank you so much for your very nice letter and it was most kind of you to write. Yes, I feel frightfully ill the whole time and nothing in the way of medecine is of help. It is sclerosis of the lungs and a very bad circulatory condition, I am told, with attendant chronic bronchitis. I am utterly despondent, incurable!

Your 'ring'! It should soon be with you, if by a devious route. What will you think when you see no ordinary 'ring' at all, but something made by *you* (I think)! A friend now here (Irene Rathbone, the novelist. A very staunch friend indeed when Nancy was ill.) also exclaimed on seeing it: 'A Henry Moore!' She is taking it to London and I will ask dear Geoffrey Strachan to call on her when she will give it him for Walter to give you. It is like Avebury as well as like you, and comes from the sea-shore near St. Jean-Cap Ferrat.

With much love to you and Irina, Nancy

P.S. Alas that you could not come here when at Les Eyzies.

Letter 2.

Villa Pomone,
Avenue Sauvan, St. Jean-Cap Ferrat, A.M.
France. Dec. 2, 1964

Dear Henry, Your lovely letter has just come to bring me joy. Of course the Stone has many meanings, as you say! First of all came to me 'something to do with Denmark'—a *hood* in stone, if such can be (and of course it can), and then 'some of the stones of Avebury, still urging themselves *out* of the ground, not at all sinking into it.' There must be yet others. Also, pretty well on first sight, returned the vision of *your* 'Warrior's Head',* which is almost as ancient, and certainly as immortal. I do not know what to call this exquisite thing of yours. I mean the beautiful, very complex, *and so pure* 'small' metal, redolent of feudal times, with whorls of iron(?) coming protectively, but also aggressively, curving over the 'face'. Do you see which I mean? I think you do. Other meanings too. Shakespeare seems one (I have been re-reading), and, indeed, the sea—most mysterious of all. Perhaps not only the sea, but the Mountain with it? In all, how much this stone sang to me of YOU. I

* [The "Warrior's Head" would seem to refer to one of the bronze "Openwork Head and Shoulders" of the 1950 period which Nancy would have seen in Henry Moore's studio. The "Helmet Head and Shoulders" of 1952 (which Sir Kenneth Clark showed and described in the television Henry Moore film in April, 1966) might also have been in her mind, though it has no "whorls" over the face. The title "Warrior's Head" might have occurerd to her through association with the "Warrior with Shield" and the "Fallen Warrior" of 1953/4.]
W. J. Strachan

called it 'Henry Moore's Ring' because I could fit its hole around my little finger.

Well no, I'm not better—but maybe not worse.

Much love to you and Irina, Nancy

cecily mackworth
Nancy Cunard

Nancy had the gift of ubiquity. She would appear suddenly, almost magically, when one least expected to meet her: in the Place de l'Opéra, wearing a tall leopard-skin hat; in a Venetian palace, metamorphosed into a society hostess, swathed in a piece of Chinese silk two centuries old; on a Channel steamer, perched at the bar, cool and slightly rakish, gulping brandy, sole survivor among the seasick. And always there was a little jolt of excitement, life's tempo quickened, people and things shifted into a new perspective and one found oneself transported into a world of violent and generally unreasoning loves and hates, of tremendous partisanship and at the same time of a fantasy that transformed landscapes, underdogs or whatever was preoccupying her at the moment, into something poetic, illogical and debonair. She created her own world and shared it, like everything else she had, with reckless generosity.

Perhaps it was something in the rhythm of her conversation. . . . It had a special kind of incoherence. Sentences, rarely finished, remained hanging in the air. One completed them in one's own imagination and this created a novel and stimulating kind of dialogue. When she came to Paris, we used to dine together at the "Petit Saint-Benoit," sometimes in company with Tristan Tzara, or some other friend from the Surrealist days before I had known her. I find a scrap of conversation recorded in my diary after one of these dinners. She had just returned from Bou Saada. "Through the windows there was yellow, then yellow, some pines and nothing at all. . . ." One was with her in the little desert train. There was no need to say more.

She would disappear as suddenly as she had appeared. Letters would arrive from Lamothe-Fénelon, where she had acquired a house and found herself faced for the first time in her life with the harsh realities of housekeeping ("I am so tired of making meals for self; to hell with eating"), or from Toulouse, where she would descend for months at a time in order to pursue some complicated political plot with a community of exiled Spanish Republicans. She wrote as she talked. A letter from Lamothe-Fénelon (still in the honeymoon stage) shows her at her most Nancyish. It is undated, but seems to have been written in 1949:

"Cecily dear, How sweet of you to have written; I'm glad to be in touch with you again. I had not your address. Is it 'permanent', do you like it?

"Ah but NOW I have a house: Incredibly small and elementary and I adore it and adore this region and know it and shall know it far better in time. I have no desire for Paris, and thank God this is 9 hours distant, which keeps away the bores and may not impede the few one really does want to see, who knows? But the house has taken all too much time already, on account of the state it was (and is) in. No sheets, etc. No lavatory, no water. Superb electric light and divine neighbours who load me with gifts, eatable gifts. I wish I had NEVER seen bloody Normandy. Had I lived down here from the start the whole of my life would have been different and I should not have lost everything.

"I wonder who told you where I was? Not many people have my address. Tzara maybe? The arm—it got all right finally, quite cured, having cost over 20,000 francs in the clinic, damn it. Here I can live as cheaply as a workman, and that's all too costly. Appalling is the situation, is it not? How do you manage in Paris?

" 'The Mouth of the Sword' is a very fine title, I think. Of what is the book? I shall read it with great interest I know. What speed you have put it in Palestine? My darling American friend, M, wrote just now that Palestine is the touchstone (of war-not-war) in the US. I hate the Americans more than ever, and with what cause; there are so hideously many of the rotten sort. Does hating get one anywhere, you may ask? Not-hating doesn't either, and hatred of filth seems just part of one, not?

"Cecily dear, can you do something for me? I hope it's not going to be a damn-bore, time-taking thing. It's this: someone has told me Carrefour published some kind of article about me in the course of September. I would VERY much like to have a *copy* of that. Would it be possible for you to see it and send it to me. I would bless you if you had the time or would ask someone to do this instead. 'La Bataille' published a part in August. I can't imagine why this sudden interest. They are going to be forced to publish some sort of denial of their invented filth. Do you remember how in London de Quilici (editor of *La Bataille*) was forced to suspend publication of his—then —*La Marseillaise* because of its attacks on Churchill or was it his attack on de Gaulle, or both?

"I will not fail to ring you when I come to Paris, who knows when. Do send a line soon and please try for Carrefour. Much love, Nancy."

No one could know Nancy at all well without realizing that she possessed some sort of genius. Only, like Oscar Wilde, she put it all in her life and kept only her talent for her writings. If she had ever written the Memoirs her publisher urged her for years to write, perhaps the genius would have appeared there in print. We spoke of the project the last time I saw her, but already it was evident that it was too late.

anthony thorne

A Share of Nancy

Affection not needed: it is here and implicit. Truth needed, yes, with good and bad, sometimes indistinguishable. Truth will never hurt the personality of Nancy, who passionately loved sincerity and plain-speaking—"the facts, please," she would say, "without any hooly-gooly."

But "truth" and "the facts" are always open to question, and I can offer only sincerity in my account of her, which must be a purely personal one. *My* share of Nancy, and entirely that.

Life arranged our meeting very oddly and took a lot of time and trouble over it—many intimations of her spread thinly over the years. As an undergraduate I heard of her notorious pamphlet *Black Man and White Ladyship* (of which I was to receive an inscribed copy many years later), knew of her association with Negroes and that it was founded on a deep sympathy with their problems and a love of their ancient cultures. And of their modern cultures too: a sure-footed understanding.

Then the path was laid cunningly, step by step. I met someone who had worked with her at the Hours Press at Réanville and in Paris, who told me much, perhaps too much, about her—her way of life there, without a word about her integrity. Then the pleasant shock of a photograph of her (Man Ray) in a magazine, like a dark negative, showing the back of her shapely head and a necklace of giant ivory beads. Then *Authors Take Sides,* an anthology of opinions edited by her during the Spanish War. Then an encounter with the White Lady-ship, her mother, at a Chelsea party where she was holding court. Then, in America, an unexpected remark from the late Claude Mac-Kay, poet-novelist of Harlem: "Your Nancy Cunard seems to think that only Negroes are never queer. But she should not be so sure of that, Anthony."

Then at last, after the inanely grinning gap of war, Nancy and I met in 1949—and ironically, after so many years of vague signs and signals, we saw a great deal of each other for an entire week, some-times twice a day, sometimes all day.

It was in Venice, late at night, when we were introduced: the three of us—Nancy, a mutual acquaintance and myself all teetering on the edge of an inky lagoon. I remember the conversation but took little part in it. After all these years I was staring at Nancy.

Her appearance? A girl once said to me: "I come into a room and at the end of it there's the most beautiful woman I've ever seen. Then as I get near her I realize that it's Nancy Cunard." Yes, she was raddled and distressingly thin, but the fine bone was there and the fire-blue eyes of a warrior and a smile ready for a quip. She made up her eyes very well, her mouth badly. A *bandeau* across her forehead, and escaping from it two "kiss-curls" (as I believe they were called) of the 1920s. Two commas, inverted, becoming to a typographer such as Nancy.

There was really no reason why she should have noticed my existence, but the very next night, after an opera in the Teatro Olimpico of Vicenza, we found ourselves embracing in laughter. We were in a kind of palatial public lavatory, the backquarters of a lush hotel, where people understood neither UOMINI nor DOWNE and doors banged indiscriminately and Germans spluttered noisily as they washed their faces.

"Oh, what a free-for-all!"

"Come to my party tomorrow," she said. "Palazzo Foscarini—don't try to find it, you can't. *Sometimes* the post arrives, *sometimes* friends, but never both. No, I'll come and meet you all at the Accademia landing stage from six onwards."

That next evening there was a violent storm and the rain came smacking down. Nancy in plastic was there to welcome every arrival from boat-bus, hung us all up to dry, gave us drinks, went back to the pontoon for more guests.

This time I deliberately baited her, when a turn of conversation allowed, by saying that I had lived for a short while in the Negro republic of Haiti.

"Did you, by God?"

We sat down together, established mutual friends and memories, and at the end of the evening found ourselves left with two Frenchmen who *would not go*. Nancy (her French was superb, though her Italian nine-tenths Spanish) asked us all to stay and eat. Eat? A saucer of mournful olives among all of us: my first knowledge of Nancy's appetite, which Norman Douglas described as that of a dyspeptic butterfly.

But the next night I persuaded her to dine with me at a *trattoria*, and it was there that we had our table-banging row. (Remembered by her years later and described in a letter to our *"zuffa-ciuffa* in Venice.") I don't know why I've never asked Nancy's other friends if they too had to go through this experience, but even at the time I realized that it was a kind of test. What was it all about, anyway? Yes, she had accused me of being "too bloody English," which made me lose my temper for a moment—but only for a moment. The shouting done and my hands already on the table, I began a drum rhythm remembered from Haiti, then saw her shoulders begin to lift in response and her head too. The row was over.

And the following night a very different Nancy, dressed in conventional "Government House" black satin though still with barbaric jewellery and the inevitable *bandeau* across her forehead. It was at a ball given in the Palazzo Rezzonico, to which we paid not the slightest attention, spending the entire night in talking on a balcony. She was thoughtful and sober, pained by memories of an earlier Venice, and suddenly, with the gesture of a priestess, poured a libation of champagne into the Grand Canal.

"For Henry," she said.

Henry Crowder, Negro-Indian, composer and singer, whom she had first met in this water-city, and who had influenced the rest of her life. It was he who had inspired her to compile her enormous anthology *Negro* (now very rare and costly). Let Nancy herself describe this man, as she did in a copy of *Henry-Music* which she later sent me:

"Dearest Anthony, this book* (how long after) of a man you would have loved *then as now,* of a man who introduced an entire world to me in 1928, and two continents: Afro-America and Africa—plus Music, the music of the Negroes of the U.S.A. (in Blues and Whole-Tone Scale). A most wary and prudent man, among many other beauties and qualities, who often said: 'Opinion reserved!' Whereas to me, nothing—nor opinion nor emotion nor love nor hate—could be 'reserved' for one instant on the score of the things this Man-Continent-People gradually revealed to me about his race and the life of his race. And now, with love—from 1930 to 1952. Nancy. Lot. France."

The libation which she poured that night over a balcony into the Grand Canal was for a lover who had died.

We left the *palazzo* in the early morning, both of us slightly drunk, and took a waiting gondola. I shall not forget that night—and to my perpetual amazement that same gondolier whom I ran into *eleven years later* still remembered Nancy. When I reminded him of our journey

* Crowder, Henry. *Henry-Music,* Hours Press, 15 Rue Guénégaud, Paris, 1930. Covers by Man Ray, Paris, photographs of African masks and ivories owned by Nancy Cunard. Poems by Samuel Beckett, Harold Acton, Richard Aldington, Walter Loewenfels and Nancy Cunard. At the top of his poem Beckett has the inscription: For Henry Crowder to sing. My own copy of the book is No. 85 in an edition of only 100 signed copies.

from the Rezzonico ball he said at once: *'Sì, e c'era una Signora francese, un po' ubriaca, che voleva sempre parlare spagnolo.'*

How was it possible that a gondolier, who must have had thousands of clients a year, could still, after that long lapse of time, recall Nancy unmistakably in a phrase?

The next day I left for England. Nancy stayed on in Venice for a while, then went to Rome and on to Capri, to be with Norman Douglas, before going back to France. (She had lived there since 1920, and bitterly resented being described by English journalists as "one of the Bright Young Things of the twenties." She wasn't ever here.) She sent me very many letters, and to bridge the gap before we met again I must quote her in brief, choosing only the flash of a revealing sentence or some paragraph that seems typical of her.

To give an exact date to these long letters would be an impossibility. I can only place them by their context. She would sometimes write the day of the month, rarely the year, but often adding the temperature. (She always traveled with a thermometer.) On one occasion she achieved an absolute triumph by heading a letter: "Souillac (your Hungerford), May 20, 1952, Temp. now (3.p.m.) about 72." You can hardly be more specific. But on another occasion there was merely a temperature!

These letters were sometimes typed (when she would have a running quarrel with her shoulder-slung portable, always going wrong) or else in pencil, alas, now fading. . . . They very often suggest the circumstances in which they were written, the typed ones on her stomach, lying in bed, and the pencilled ones—which seem to me the best of all—sitting at a café table in France or Italy with a glass by her side and a straw hat tipped over her forehead.

"NEVER ENGLAND FOR ME (please God). Do I have one more glass of *grappa*? . . . ? . . . ? to the same toast?"

"Venice 'in furs', nearly. I suppose, I think, I will leave in about 6 days. I would like to learn Italian. It has been a pestilential cat's cradle and I have stamped (and *bestemmiate*-ed) against these cobwebs of obfuscation—no man's mind being quick enough to clasp the word as it flies from Spain to Italy—from Catalonia to Venice......I HAVE NEVER, SO FAR AS I KNOW, MET D. H. Lawrence. Why does ****** like to think I do/did? Closest contact (if it can be called that) was in 1931 or so, when someone (Joyce? Aldington?) asked if the Hours Press would like to produce something of his. Answer: *theoretically*—highly honoured, but to me, personally, *not interesting*. This being said, a certain admiration (not more) for D.H.L.'s books. Less and less of it—*why*? Because to me a more and more disagreeable type of chap/character—hence 'I cannot dis-sociate the author from the work done.' Should one? Why not an 'anonymous pool' of writings? Exams are done that way. . . . I cannot have anything to do with SNOBBERY (with certain kinds of CROOKERY, certain gangsters, *and how*, YES). To push the point somewhat ridiculously further: Lawrence, what-he-stood-for, might be a *small fraction* of reason why I have left England *forever*. (1920.) Disgusting Lawrence."

"One is too patient, dear Anthony, too polite, too 'well brought up.' All this would seem scatter-brained to others (to hell with them) but not to you . . ."

"10.45 p.m. Where? Just off Piazza (for once). Shall I *now* dare to have a *grappa?* I have fore-fended it a-purpose during the writing of this. I will dare have a *grappa*. Here it is, a good dab on the page, drunk to your health forever. . . ."

". . . And God bless all good sailors with the freedom not only of the seas to them, but of the glory of the world around their lovely shoulders—they whose shoulders are the grandchildren of Atlas. . . ."

"*Continuity* will bring us together again. NOT IN ENGLAND, I trust. N."

". . . De B. was the little man who, to my stupefaction, came up to me in my 'all-scarlet' get-up that night in the Venice Theatre, to say '*Ça, c'est la plus belle couleur du monde—pour toutes les raisons.* . . .'" *

"Indeed I shall write you how I fare."

How I hate Rome. With such violence and vehement scorn right away that it suggests I might 'get to' like it and even love it—BUT NOT THIS WEEK—which is an old gag of the twenties or even before. A postcard when in the mood—I mean, when in the sun, with an olive and a drink at noon would be delicious to receive in the same way (*Norman Douglas's address in Capri follows*).

"Footballing priests and their foundlings are on the mount—why just this strikes me as being more obscene than lots of other things in life I can't imagine: either a priest OR a footballer, but, surely, not BOTH together in skirts. . . ."

"I keep on feeling that I ought to be doing something for Spain (literary) in connection with England. But what? It is the most dif-

* So many people assumed that Nancy was a communist. She was not. The impression was probably due to her having been twice to Moscow (where the bureaucracy appalled her) and to her having published pro-communist articles in her anthology *Negro*. But she once said to me: "I was never a communist— though I've sometimes wondered why I wasn't."

ficult matter to deal in, because people (in sufficient numbers) in England shy away from the subject 'like mad', possibly from a bad conscience still—as has often been said. . . ."

". . . talk, walk, read, write, translate—MAY IT CONTINUE."

"When you go on a long trip you should go ALONE, or with ONE proper person, not with all that huffle-scuffle-middle-muddle. I wish I had TWO GIANT NEGROES TO TRANSPORT ME AND CARRY MY LUGGAGE, AND CARRY ME TOO. Why two? So that one should not get lonely by himself: one ahead and one behind, majestically. Maybe this will come about one day. Next winter, if all goes well, I shall have ONE—not a giant, though, and not even 'pure bush', as obviously this dream-pair ought to be. I think you must meet him in England so that we can get all sorts of 'ducks in a row' (that's Harlem for plans)."

". . . and then to France, but not to England, my dear sir. NEVER."

But of course she came back to England. Not once but many times, and staying for periods as long as her income-tax problem—for she was "resident in France"—allowed. In a later year she was to be held prisoner in England—and then fined for being here. But that is another story.

At that time, in 1950, I lived with my family in Berkshire, in downs-country with a large garden overlooking farmlands, and after a brief stay with a cousin ("my luggage included a case of claret") she came to us there.

My wife, naturally a trifle shy of the formidable Nancy Cunard legend, was at once charmed by her wit, sense and manners and the two of them—both addicts of that habit, uncomfortable to males, of sitting on the floor—were shortly to be seen side by side on the hearth-rug in front of a log fire.

Far more surprisingly, Nancy scored an instantaneous hit with my son, who was then only five. One did not imagine Nancy having any point of contact with so small a boy, but he sat close to her gaping with wonder as she talked about the discovery of the caves of Lascaux and of the bull drawings of at least eighteen thousand years ago.

(This unlikely friendship between the two never ceased. She constantly sent him stamps that reached her from all over the world, remembered always his bonfires and fireworks in November, and when at University age Simon decided to be a botanist she sent him a long letter of praise and encouragement.)

It was clear from the start that Nancy was an easy guest. Never any question of her appearing in the morning. No, it was tacitly understood that a light breakfast reached her at about 8:30 and a carafe of red wine at eleven. Then, having typed on her lap in bed she would appear, bracelets clacking on her thin wrists, forehead *bandeau* over cheekside kisscurls and made up in the mode of the Twenties, for lunch at one o'clock.

She startled us once, that dyspeptic butterfly, by demanding a second helping. Of what? Nothing interesting, but a nursery-cum-Sunday lunch of a plain "joint and two veg." This inconsistency I noticed on other occasions: accustomed to a handful of olives a day, not for economy but from a dislike of more solid food, she would gobble up conventional London-pub dishes suitable for stout businessmen, saying that she had never eaten so well—which was probably true. Yet I have known her, in a good restaurant, demand that the food be served *at once* only to push it around on her plate. Often, when she appeared to be tipsy, it was not merely that she liked her wine too much—as people were only too ready to say—but that she liked her food too little. Thin, thin, she had no resistance to alcohol, and frequently fell down, sometimes in embarrassing circumstances: when, of course, she would be furious at any concern shown for her.

In Berkshire we went for long walks, and for the first time I noticed that curious gait of hers, light and springy, the knees flexing easily, rhythmically; and I, being suddenly reminded of the women of Haiti, thought that in her chequered cotton dresses Nancy was sometimes a Negress in all but colour.

Lovely to walk with, but infuriating to drive. Never having driven a car herself, she would try to distract one's attention. While dealing as coolly as I could with modern traffic in the medieval streets of Oxford I would hear: "Quick, Anthony, what was that building we've just passed—do look back—and the one on the right—no, I don't believe you saw it." I hadn't, couldn't, and barked at her.

After staying with us each time for about ten days—working first on her Norman Douglas book and much later on her memoir of George Moore—she would then leave us, but in a sense slowly and gently; for she would take a hotel room in the nearby town of Hungerford, where she had once lived, and frequently asked us to come to her.

It would be a gas-fire, this time, and she and my wife sitting on the floor beside it. Somewhere in the background her typewriter and that familiar altar of portable Lares and Penates that she had also established in the blue room of our house: a stretch of flame-coloured African cloth with carved Benin ivory bracelets on it and a bronze or two, conjured somehow from her meagre baggage. A few fine things that brought her the flavour of past years ("continuity, my dear Anthony . . .").

To be asked to dine with her there was usually disastrous, for after pouring gin into borrowed toothglasses for a couple of hours, she would say: "I think we'd better be going to the restaurant." It was of course black by then and the staff gone home. This put her in a towering rage, from which she would recover only when she realized that somewhere in her room—"where did I put it?"—there was a bag of olives.

What did she do in Hungerford? Prowled like a cat. She even investigated the local refuse dump from which she salved—they must have been under a heap of slow-cooling ashes—some extraordinary looking bottles. They were probably chemists' bottles, discarded a decade or two ago and made hysterical by constant firing. Not only, wildly distorted, had they an appearance of limpness which would have delighted Salvador Dali in his molten watches period, but the colours themselves had acquired an eerie kind of opalescence. They delighted Nancy who, giggling, insisted on presenting me with half a dozen of them.

After Hungerford—so long as "income-tax-time" allowed—she would go to stay with one friend and another,* and then leave for France, where she had bought a barn in the province of Lot, with the unlikely idea of settling down at last. Never, in all the letters that followed, could I find one word of praise for it. There was every known disadvantage plus some peculiarly French—petty little cheatings, tax fiddles to be sorted out while hostile village schoolboys hurled stones through windows just installed. Spring water only from a temperamental pump; occasional help from a stone-faced Madame Achille with whom she had a running feud: woodworm in the beams, and the place littered with "charming little *réserves de poussière.*" However, she did manage to work, translating Douglas's *Fountains in the Sand* into French: "like washing every sentence and hanging it up to dry." And then, as books could be sorted on to shelves and as summer lit the countryside, she was so happy ("though never about beastly Lamothe Fénelon") that she again dismissed curtly the idea of ever returning to England.

She was with us again that autumn with her shoulder-slung typewriter and the treasures without which she found it difficult to travel.†

* She had a reputation for keeping her very many friends in "separate compartments," but I have no personal experience of it. Where proximity and occasion allowed, one was gladly introduced to friends and relatives.

† ". . . as some, on arrival anywhere, open this or that, with me it seems to be the typewriter and its consorts and adjuncts that make any place 'home'. . . ."

November now, another Guy Fawkes night, and the gardener stoking a great bonfire and lighting rockets to please my son. To please Nancy also, for she was childishly fascinated—she who despised "prettiness"—with the small sparklers which you hold in your hand. Years afterwards I was to receive November letters from various parts of Europe saying "Now it is sparklers time. . . ."

When she was back in France I went to stay with her. The old barn, sturdily stone-built, seemed, with each room on a different level, to be climbing the terraced hillside in withdrawal from the tiny hostile village of Lamothe. Far below the broad Dordogne flowed between silver poplars, their tall trunks hidden by morning mists. In the fields there were long grasses and wildflowers, and in cultivated patches the tobacco plants severely restricted by the French government, jealous of its monopoly. Each short row bore clearly its owner's name, and not another plant must be added. Nancy shared my disgust with this tyranny.

Completely undomesticated, and with only vague promises of modern amenities, Nancy had nevertheless made a home, and every corner of it witnessed her past history and her personality. Personalities, I should have written.

In the kitchen, with its old French cupboards and its maddeningly impractical old French stove, she had pinned up on the wall a handwritten poster, which said, in French: "Today I had to pay for only five leeks the ridiculous sum of ****** francs." This was to remind her to be angry about it, and also to declare to the world that she had been cheated. I wonder that she had not nailed it to her front door.

In the living room, with its corner fireplace above which hung Manet's delicate *Etude pour Le Linge** (and beside it a jam jar filled with grasses and wildflowers which complemented the soft green-gold-pink tones of the painting) there was a table carpentered by her father, Sir Bache Cunard, and incongruously, yet right because this was Nancy's home, a primitive wall-hanging from the South Pacific. Green velvet curtains and shelves of books which would be a treasury to any historian of the literature of the 1920s, many with Nancy's curt marginal notes: "No, Harold has got his facts completely wrong!" "Never even met this man!" "Wouldn't have said such a thing in my life!"

---

* The picture was later brought to England for sale—heavy insurance, endless formalities. At Sotheby's it did not reach the reserve of £21,000 which they had put on it, and was withdrawn. Neither the Tate Gallery nor her bank would store it, and it found temporary refuge with an art dealer. It must have been inherited, after Nancy's death, by the female cousins who never even knew her.

There was also a good portrait of George Moore by C. S. Harrison which, lamplit by night, one could see from the kitchen.

The spare room had many more books and one other incongruity: an 18th century Venetian coffee table—"black boy"—a richly-clad Negro supporting a square piece of ebony. That Nancy could have endured even a pretty symbol of slavery astonished me. (This had once had a brother, kicked to pieces by the Germans at her Brittany home of Réanville during the war.) In furniture and books she had salved what she could.

Long walks in the daytime, and long walks they were, for Lot is a place of great distances: public transport is uncertain and determinedly inconvenient, and taxis cost a fortune. In these walks Nancy, barely touching the ground, would deride my red-faced attempts to catch up with her, but in one way and other, under burning sun, we managed to reach the obvious places like Lascaux and La Cave and Rocamadour and Sarlat and Souillac.

She was always as tactful a hostess as she was a guest—it was understood that one wanted to be left alone. While I went to explore, Nancy would sit at a café table and I would bring her a drink ("Anthony, your manners make me JUMP!") and she would wait for my return with paper and pencil in front of her and her head bent under a tilted straw hat. (At Lamothe there was a great pile of asexual straw hats which anyone could wear.)

Many comedies I remember: her astonishment when, after her complaining that mice ran up the legs of her kitchen cupboards, I suggested cutting the legs off and hanging the cupboards on the wall: my attempts to prepare meals for her, for she hated the stove and no wonder; since it was heated by twigs only, one was always trying to cook on a rapidly dying fire: her discovery on a shelf—"Oh, look dear Anthony, there's some *lovely old food*": her indignation when I attempted to wash up after a meal—"no, no! When Madame Achille arrives tomorrow she'll only say *'Rien à faire, je m'en vais!'*"

I must add that I was *not* fed on "lovely old food" but on the best meat that Nancy could buy—pre-ordered and collected from the post office—and on freshly-cut asparagus.

She herself seemed to eat well at this time and to drink moderately. One cannot guess what happened when she was alone. It was a house that needed a guest always: and over those vast distances of middle France many of her friends did manage to arrive, but there were long gaps.

So many images of Nancy and her home, so many memories. We talked through the nights, and from our talks so much emerged.

Of Henry again, and of Aragon, and of a Chilean poet. And of so many others who—including some of her relatives—seemed to be homosexual. Her references to their tastes struck an irrelevant and jarring note. I had already heard:

"I'm just off to stay with that old Auntie of Capri . . ." about whom she later wrote an affectionate and delicate book. But then also:

"She was out to produce three heirs—but all she could manage was three buggers. . . ."

". . . yes, he puts many people off, he is far too *chichiteux*. . . ."

". . . oh, that one, he's what Norman would call the *wrong* kind of sod. . . ."

". . . imprisoned, of course. In the manner of '*il courait les filles*' that one *galoppait les hommes*. . . ."

Yet many of these people she really loved. A disloyalty, a betrayal? I do not think so. It was part of Nancy's idea of honesty. People were what they were, so why not say so, even with a touch of comic malice? The fact that one might not have wanted to know, or that scandal travels even faster than bad news, simply did not occur to her. She never spoke about Lesbian acquaintances with the same freedom, however—in a tradition which seemed curiously British.

In those hot summer insect-haunted evenings she talked also of places and politics and of our common sympathies, and if we lingered at the kitchen table the face of George Moore was always shining at us from the living room.

On one occasion she spoke of Louis Aragon with startling bitterness and in phrases which I do not want to repeat. I had to ask her to stop, and she left the table as near to tears as Nancy could ever get.

There was no doubt that she had had many lovers: and yet it had already dawned on me that some of her accounts of recent conquests, or "unprovoked" assaults, were less than convincing, and on more than one occasion I could tell that they were imaginary. "It was an Arab boy who stole the ring you mentioned—yes, it was on a hill above Algiers—and he kept saying to me '*L'amour est toujours bon . . .*,' though really, it was like being raped by a *flower*." A situation which, in a different context and without the robbery, occurs in her account of travels in North Africa with Norman Douglas. There were many other love tales that were told with more wit than conviction. It became clear that Nancy, much loved and much loving, was beginning to have sexual fantasies.

The face of George Moore, brooding over us, reproached me, and he had reason to do so. For while Nancy was last with us in Berkshire I had persuaded her to omit one chapter from her book on him. Since then my conscience has suffered, and at this distance of time I feel I should add the missing chapter to my memoir of Nancy. There is no reason—*now*—why I should decree that it should be lost. But when she first wrote it I saw, perhaps mistakenly, all sorts of dangers. She was being pestered from every direction by journalists, publishers, *et al.,* for an autobiography. Had she written it frankly and in detail it could have made her fortune—but she was far too fastidious a woman, mentally, to commercialise her life, which had been a campaign waged with her whole heart and body. Somebody said to me: "Can't *you* persuade Nancy Cunard to write her life story?" I replied: "Well, I think she's doing so—as she prefers it—in writing the biographies of others." It was an answer of which Nancy highly approved.

The George Moore chapter is without sensationalism—*except in its context*. That context is that he was her putative father—this told me by Nancy herself, without comment—but the rumour was then current, and any one of many thwarted critics would have been only too glad to blow this delicately written incident up to giant size. She was too easy a target and could have been badly hurt.

I may have been influenced by suggestion, but it did seem to me that George Moore's eyes and Nancy's had the same blue intensity and the same droop of lid.

And then the scene changed as abruptly as the climate.

When my wife and I bought the lease of a house in London's Little Venice, overlooking the Regent's Canal, Nancy wrote quickly to say that she must take the furnished flat above us. Useless to tell her that the place needed re-decorating and that one was longing to get rid of the appalling furniture—no, she must have the flat *at once,* and all I had time to do was to reorganize the heating arrangements, to make sure that those bird bones would be warmed in winter.

People jeered at me. "Imagine taking Nancy on as a tenant. You'll regret that, won't you?"

Nancy arrived* and made her usual "altar" of reminiscent objects, and fell ill almost at once. If I have little to record of this period—except the insistent memory of her face out of a window, and she talking down to me in the garden below—it is because she suffered from so many disabilities, and some of them concurrent, from heavy bronchitis to a poisoned toe; and although I saw her every day, or else telephoned her, the phrase that remains most in my mind is: "Anthony, I feel dreadful."

We did as much as we could for her but had to guard against too much solicitude, of which she would have been highly intolerant . . . one had to tread carefully. My doctor remarked that she must have

* Early in 1959.

been undernourished for years. Dishes brought to her remained un-touched.

There were intervals in which she could struggle down to eat with us, and I remember with pleasure that she came to one Guy Fawkes party in the garden—no bonfires here but Victorian "fairy lights," rockets, and her beloved "sparklers." It was the last of them that she ever saw—and the last that we have ever had.

When she left here the climate again changed—and this time dis-astrously.

All Nancy's friends had hoped that, restless and fond of travel as she was, she would never go back to Spain. Her feelings about the Spanish Civil War were only too well known and she was obviously *persona non grata*. But to Spain she went determinedly, knowing that there are almost two policemen or soldiers to every civilian and that a word of protest from her, after a couple of glasses of wine, would land her in jail.

She came out of it with a cracked hip and a damaged mind.

Her letters of that period reflect what had happened to her—many of them as affectionate as ever but some, not surprisingly, full of irra-tional anger: "You simply have not understood my question!" And then the question, already answered, repeated again and again. Endless queries about the rights of a taxi driver in London compared with the rights of one in Ibiza. . . . The proposition of adopting legally a Span-ish dwarf who, like several young men whom she picked up at this period, was interested only in what he could get out of her. (He finally left her, to live with two men in Paris.)

Not only trouble in Spain but also in Switzerland, where, I gathered from official correspondence which she later showed me, she had flung her British passport from table to table in a café and then out of a taxi window. Trouble in France, and prison again in England: she was arrested for being "drunk and disorderly" in Soho, and spent another night in a cell after "creating a nuisance" outside the exclusively male Bath Club where a cousin of hers was staying.

My wife—I was abroad at this time—had a disturbing experience. The bell rang after midnight and there was Nancy having a violent argument with a taximan. She had lost her money somewhere and her baggage too—suitcases full of valuable ivories scattered over the stations of London. It was a weekend, and my wife had just enough money to pay the fare, but no tip. "No tip anyway," shouted Nancy. "He tried to have an affair with me, he even pushed my head under the wheel."

She came in with a paper bag full of ham sandwiches which, refus-ing the offer of other food, she then ate, hurling the crusts into the empty fireplace. At one point she picked up a Fornasetti ashtray, demanding: "Is this supposed to be pretty?" and was about to hurl it after the crusts when my wife stopped her. She had to get Nancy to bed before they were both out of their minds.

"*No* sheets!" protested Nancy as clean ones were produced.

"If you sleep in this bed," my wife said firmly, "you will have sheets." Nancy gave way.

Restless in another bedroom my wife contemplated the possibility of the house being burnt down over her head. (It could have happened, for not long afterwards Nancy showed the familiar and expected signs of incendiarism, and on one occasion, in another flat, set fire to her clothes, declaring: "I shan't need *these* any more!")

In the morning Nancy telephoned to ask who else would give her a roof, intending to make a round of visits in London—and it is interesting to remember the distinguished friends who found reasons why they could not see her.

When I came back to England she was already in an asylum, "certified insane." It was a dismal place in the East End, doors firmly kept open (why do they have doors anyway?) and a shuffling procession of people who giggled momentarily, staring at one another. There was Nancy, lying on the coverlet of her bed, fully dressed and with the usual bandeau across her forehead. Instinctively you looked for the little altar of ivories and beads spread on a bright cloth, and then was thankful that it was missing: for this room, this cubicle in this place, she must never make her own.

There was a Negro with her,* a young man just arrived from Ghana. Hearing somehow that Nancy was in this hospital he had come to see her for the first time, bringing flowers and a photograph of himself. It was gradually beginning to dawn on him what kind of hospital this was, and I admired the coolness and good sense with which he came to accept the situation. But alas, when she demanded some matches he gave them to her and she tucked them one by one into the hem of her skirt, like a refugee hiding jewels, and with an expression of cunning that I had never seen on her face before. As for his photograph, she had put it on a high window sill with its *back* to her room, his face looking out on to the busy passage beyond. "There is no point in having a photograph," she said, "unless *everybody* can enjoy it."

---

* The name of Nancy Cunard, like that of George Padmore, seemed to have travelled round the world. Not only her anthology *Negro* but her impassioned appeals for the defence of the Scottsboro boys seemed to be as well-known in Africa as in Harlem. She was constantly receiving letters from coloured people whom she had never met and was never likely to meet, and if they *were* coming to Europe they somehow felt all the safer in knowing that she was here.

A young Indian girl was giggling mirthlessly in the doorway. "Sometimes at night they bang on the doors and walls," Nancy told me, "and then I bang too. I love doing that."

Letters to be posted, please. One to the Home Secretary to protest against this scandalous treatment of her, and then—one must be prepared for anything—another written in Russian (so she said) to Khrushchev, who would be sure to use his influence to get her out. And then—shown to me with great pride—and how unlike that evening in Lamothe when she had denounced him—a loyal article written by Louis Aragon in a French newspaper, demanding her immediate release and exposing the rigid unfairness of the British legal formalities.

Her solicitor and many of her good friends were trying hard to rescue her: her family would do nothing at all and pretended that she did not exist. The situation was appallingly complicated and at times seemed hopeless. Then of course, being forcibly held in Britain, she became liable for British Income Tax as well as French. That final blow confirmed her forever in her hatred of this country, and when about a year later she was able to leave it she never returned.

But during that year much had been achieved. She was transferred from the unforgettable East End Asylum to happier surroundings at Virginia Water, and she was able to struggle back to life as we conventionally live it when an old friend of hers, a journalist, the late Louise Morgan, guaranteed to the authorities that she would take Nancy into her country home for "mental rehabilitation." Louise said at the time that it was one of the happiest tasks she had ever undertaken.

Nancy's letters to me during this period are oddly flat and colourless, like a schoolgirl's account of a rural holiday with pleasant bucolic tasks —picking fruit, vegetables, flowers. I suspect that she was still under sedation and allowed a minimum of wine.

Pause. And then a letter from France. She was back.

This was the last phase, and since Nancy never returned and my wife and I chose Italy rather than France, I can give no eye witness account of it. The rumours of mutual friends suggested that she had again involved herself with some shady figures but there was no major scandal: and her many letters to me, on which I prefer to rely, speak of much work.

A book on the Hours Press*—the private press begun by her at Réanville in the 1930s and then moved to Paris—this, so often dis-

---

* In early 1965, shortly before she died, Nancy sent me an inscribed off-print from *The Book Collector*. It is entitled "The Hours Press—Retrospect—Catalogue—Commentary."

cussed, was now her main concern. Yes, she would at last write about the authors she had published at that time: many of them, such as Samuel Beckett, were then unknown, but had been warmed and sustained by her enthusiasm. Though the Hours Press period had been short it had been one of great activity and importance, and I think that in writing of it she wrote half her epitaph—the other half being *Negro*.

This project was greatly encouraged by a visit to Lamothe by Professor Hugh Ford and his wife, whom she found most sympathetic, and it must have been largely due to their enthusiasm that the long delayed book was finished and its American publication arranged.

". . . a chapter on each of all the books produced, with as much as I could remember of their authors at that time. What a diverse company it was and thank God those days are over! I would gladly be a typesetter again, but not a publisher, no! UNLESS with the ideal partner, of course. . . ."

And then this work, which had sustained her more than food, was over. She fell ill again.

". . . Sometimes things reach such a point in ill-being of a general kind I have exclaimed: 'Which is best: to BE ill and NOT feel ill— or not to be really ill and feel like hell lengthily?' And have opted in favour of the former. . . ."

It was too much to hope that Nancy was back on her feet. And when she left Lamothe to stay with two old friends at a villa in the South of France, it seemed that she was attacked not only by a series of vague and concurrent illnesses but by real disasters. First of all she fell down "one of those flights of steps that decorate the French Riviera" and cut her leg badly. "The gash was 20 centimetres long (vertical) and to the bone was the incision, I think. Having suddenly found (a) little French tape-measure in typing bag yesterday, I did measure it. . . ." ". . . I am indeed ashamed of myself, as one generally is when ill. . . ." ". . . the hell of a doctor: remark his splendid name: Jézequel. . . ." ". . . coughing and asthma and loathing of food. . . ." ". . . Did I tell you it was Aragon who said that anyone who had had a very serious illness, or who had been severely operated, generally developed tacchycardia? Aragon has been the ONE man in all my life to talk intelligently to me about medicine, etc. He was 'aide-chirurgien' in the 1914 war; he was the same at the start of the 1939 one. He cured himself of consumption at the age of sixteen or so (not wishing to tell his mother*s*) by breathing regularly and deep on his way to college, and by drinking bullocks' blood. Those mothers never knew. . . ."

Nancy was in bed for some time, cursing, and as soon as she got up she fell again from weakness and not only broke her hip but cracked several ribs (she enumerates them in her letters). It is small wonder, knowing Nancy, that her answer to continual and severe pain was to compose a long poem on the subject of *Pain,* many stanzas of which she sent me. Some of them have a mediaeval setting, and I think that one can find in them a faint reflection of George Moore. . . . It would have been a remarkable poem if she had been able to finish it.

Even through her pain she wrote to me.

". . . Must a person believe in a 'God' of some kind so as to try to get through life—'Pie in the Sky' and all that? Why not *here* and *now?* Had I to choose a God, I would opt for inter-kindliness—and not more. And THAT covers the end of all wars. . . ."

Then—this horrible story is hearsay, but from several sources—she went to (a) Nice hospital and then to a train for Paris ("I'm held together by bolts and screws"); was arrested at the end of her journey for not having a ticket, found refuge in flats of friends, and then went into a hospital where she died. It was on 17th March 1965, exactly one week after her sixty-ninth birthday.

A depressingly thin little ceremony in the English church. But after all, her real relatives were all over Africa and America, and there must be many who think, and will go on thinking, perhaps for many years, that Nancy Cunard is still alive.

In her very last letter to me she returned to a former theme: Continuity. "Despite, despite," she wrote. "And that word *Despite* means Continuity. . . ."

ADDENDUM

THE BACK LIKE A WEASEL'S

Now where was the subject first mentioned, in Ebury Street or during one of his visits to Paris? It was in Ebury Street one afternoon in the middle twenties, I remember, that those words spoken in a matter-of-fact tone, a sudden aside in the conversation (even the preparatory gesture was confidential) left me dumbfounded.

"I wish you would let me see you na-aked."

He had me amazed and he went on and on with his urging. The sound of that sonorous "What is the ha-arm?" rang in my head long after I left him. It might be a passing whim.

"I am sure you have a lovely body. Now Why won't you let me see it?" he began as suddenly, several months later. I told him there was a long scar on one side of me, he would hate the sight of that.

Oh no, such a thing meant nothing: "I knew a woman who had two. Her body was beautiful all the same and she had many lovers. Think what pleasure it would give me to see yours."

Thus, on five or six occasions, always unconnected with anything that had been said, it would come: "I do wish you would let me see you naked."

At no time between us had there been any "passages"—the word he sometimes applied to amorous tentatives—unless that delaying kiss, now on the cheek, now on the lips, *un vrai baiser plantureux,* could be called such?

"Why won't you give me this pleasure? I am an old man. Come now, what possible harm can there be in that?"

How did he look in those long-gone times when "She was as black as the raven and I as golden as the sunflower"? His racy expression about being "a great dab at making love" aroused no disbelief in me. Thinking of G.M. as an impetuously temperamental lover in his own time, I felt, all the same, that my naked body fitted our relationship at no point.

Yet, at seventy-three one should know one's own mind, and the words which at first made me laugh were saddened when time, ever-passing time, began to accompany them: "I am an old man. . . ."

He may have been as impetuous a lover as he pleased in all those "yester-years," but in truth he was a little difficult to attune oneself to at the first moment of meeting. Some days there was a surface formality about him, or he might be "in a mood," or, in the noise of Paris, unable to hear immediately what was said. Whatever the reason, a slight hesitation might lie between us, before the give and take of conversation began to flow. A pause, a phrase, a silent—how different his rhythm was to every other rhythm in the Paris of the twenties.

He was staying at Foyot's in the spring or summer of 1925 and it was there, he said, we should dine. The formal moment past (was he ever aware of it himself?), we sat in long conversational harmony in the quiet restaurant with its old red plush seats, appreciating the burgundy still left in front of us at the end of the perfect meal, and as he talked I was thinking yet again how the Paris of the seventies, with himself in it, would have been a great time to have known.

After dinner we went up to his sitting-room, where, at ease in an armchair, G.M. continued talking of France and of painting, of Dujardin and of Mallarmé near Fontainebleau, and then suddenly broke off.

He would often do that with an exclamation that cut short whatever had been engaging his mind, and the subject of the body in the nude was certainly not approached by stealth. No little *entrée en matière,* such as "the flesh tones of Renoir," came to usher it in. The words were as sudden as ever, said, this time, with a good deal of wistfulness:

"I do wish you would let me see you naked. I am an old man. . . . Oh! Let me at least see your naked back!"

Now, equally suddenly, something within me said: "Do this!," and without more ado, facing away from him, I took off all my clothes, standing motionless a few feet from where he sat. How lightly, how easily it came about. My clothes left me, lying in a graceful summer pool on the floor, as if they had slipped away of themselves. The night was warm and the mood serene. Without hesitation, my long, naked back and legs were at last in front of him and the silence was complete. It would be full-on he was looking at them and I did not turn my head. Of what could he be thinking? At length came a slow, murmuring sigh:

"Oh, what a beautiful back you have, Nancy! It is as long as a weasel's. What a beautiful back!"

Then, never turning, I put on my clothes again with the same ease. What might he find to say now? He would often be thinking about my back, he said; perhaps he would use it.

And "use it" he has. It is the back of the Irish peasant woman, Brigit, married by the priest to old, nigh-moribund Tadgh, as the last months of the venerable harper's life go by on the island in the lake at the end of *Ulick and Soracha.* A good sight of her naked!—begs Tadgh, that he may give shape, in his talk with the pilgrims who come to him for the great story of the lovers, to the body of the Princess Soracha. Thus, looking at Brigit, dies Tadgh.

So when you read of the back that is like a weasel's with a dip in the middle, that back is mine as he saw it, with never a word or a gesture, but only a long, slow sigh to end the silence in the room.

Nancy Cunard
July 28, 1955.

(Alas, not for inclusion in her book on George Moore, yet written for it all the same. The first version has now been somewhat corrected, and this is the final one. Sept. 17, 1956. Lamothe Fénelon, Lot, France.)
(*Signed in her handwriting*) For Anthony Thorne

louise morgan (theis)
My Nancy

[Miss Cunard's confinement at Holloway in 1960 ended when she was permitted to join her old friends Louise and Otto Theis, whose house near Battle became her home until the end of the year. Her friendship with the Theises began in 1925 when Louise reviewed *Parallax* favorably in *Everyman*. Meetings, usually in London, and a long and intimate correspondence followed.

The following passages were taken from unposted letters and notes found among Mrs. Theis's papers, all of them written while Nancy was either at Holloway or staying at Battle. Regrettably, the Theises died (Louise in 1964, Otto in 1966) before completing their memoirs on which they had begun working in the early sixties.]

9 July 1960

Dear Sir or Madam:

One of your residents (that is, patients at Holloway), Miss Nancy Cunard, is a family friend and has been for nearly forty years. My husband and I are devoted to her and would do anything for her. She has never shown signs of insanity with us, and when I visited her on Friday, yesterday, she was her usual self, except, as is natural with age, more individualistic and contemptuous of authority than ever. But NOT insane! She feels the world has been against her, as indeed it was throughout all her childhood and youth. She got the habit of rebellion in her cradle and nursery, and had an army of nannies and governesses, one after the other, to "control" (not educate) her by a mother who knew nothing and cared nothing about children and was jealous of her as she grew up. She made a good job of ruining her only child. But she did not kill an innate gentleness, loyalty, and utter sweetness of nature which overflows like a suddenly unfrozen fountain in the presence of understanding friends. She is an artiste manquée, a "sensitive plant" which has been trodden under foot, and sends out tiny feelers from a hardened root. The sweetness in her never fails to respond to sweetness. I had a perfectly normal visit with her. I can tell you that it was one of the most hideous shocks of my life when I learned she had become a certified lunatic.

[On October 19, 1960, Mrs. Theis recorded the following impression of Nancy's arrival at her home in Battle.]

Nancy's handkerchiefs were made "out of red and white check gingham sewn with black thread." She arrived wearing an "olive green patterned chemise, cheap, thick stockings, pale cream moccasins." She had taken in the sides of her red suit by herself, but the "slit was too far up the back, and the olive green chemise showed below the narrow skirt." She had no nightgown. She wore no hat, but carried a number of scarfs for head and neck, one a brilliant orange red made of veil-like material from Woolworths. As always she carried a typewriter (new), "lots of books, letters and other papers in a cheap, light-colored suitcase."

Nancy has "no sense of values in my fashion. She thinks 3/6 for a good tin of fruit fantastic, but three gns. for a bottle of whisky doesn't mean a thing to her.

She is firm. Once she says she will or she won't, nothing will move her. She is honest without reservations of any sort, or calculating the consequences. She is brave. How brave? Practically fearless. She has the profoundest sense of loyalty. She has the capacity for endless friendship with any number of people.

Yesterday the doctor came and suddenly said to her something about Holloway. Then as smoothly as silk it happened that he signed a card to say he had treated her for five or six weeks and found her perfectly competent to manage her own affairs.

My dear John (John Banting),
Nancy and I go to Hastings tomorrow on our last refurbishing bus ride. She will come back wearing her grand new coat. . . . Nancy has had new teeth from Mr. Edworthy (they really fit, but she won't admit it!), and elegant lined boots from a little shop in old Hastings, and underwear made by a dear little woman round the corner who charged only 5/ for an exquisitely made chemise, and a suit and overcoat from Margaret, who is an expert tailoress like her mother and grandmother before her. In fact she's nearly completely fitted out, including a good suitcase. . . .
How I have worked to open her eyes to certain things about which she harbors the deadliest illusions! Otto has begged me not to go on trying but I can't help myself. I thought, inspired, when she was

coming here, that I would reform her! I've worked daily with every ounce of brain I still possess to rid her of some of her "spoiled girl" attitudes, her intolerance, her hate—which springs up like a viper in the innocent grass. I think I have made some impression. But I fear it all will go, because her memory is so bad, and she lives so much in the instant. She is one of the few I love with my whole heart and soul, and I feel bitterly disappointed that I have not been able to do more for her.

She has slept well, been warm and free and beloved here, and there has never been the shadow of a shadow between us or between her and Otto. "Otto, Merlin"! she will say, or "Merlin, Otto"! and throw him a kiss. Yes, we have been very happy together, and what evenings of talk! Endlessly springing up, hour after hour after hour. Plains, forest, mountains of it, always fresh, always new. We turn on the radio only for news. We read several papers a day, and the weeklies, and stuff sent from USA and from Spain and Mexico to Nancy. Luckily, I have learned cooking and housekeeping in the past seven or eight years, or I should be dead by now. I came to it fresh, and it still interests me, and I cook and wash and clean as if I were a young-married in a new house. Me, at seventy-five. Nancy inspires me because though she has no really deep appreciation of food, she knows all about it. . . .

She is well, so far as she can ever be well. There is a good touch of the malade imaginaire about her. Sometimes I think she really has learned that she must keep out of Holloway. . . . I do believe, unless her memory lets her down, that she will be careful.

I need to get back to my writing and to a less complicated life. She is the best possible guest—a miracle of guestmanship—but I need peace and aloneness for a while. I don't think I could have done this for anybody but Nancy. And she has been an angel of tact and understanding. It's been a wonderful experience having her in these peculiar circumstances.

[Letter addressed to The Official Solicitor, Royal Courts of Justice, following Miss Cunard's departure for France in December 1960]

13 January 1961

Dear Sir:

I have been meaning to tell you how grateful Nancy Cunard has been to you. You were the first official to treat her with kindness, and she was touched by it. "He is so kind and understanding," she would say. Or, "What courtesy. What understanding. I like him so much."

It was a relief to me to see your letters. There was always a semi-collapse at sight of the buff envelopes until yours began to come. You may like to know that you helped her enormously in a very difficult effort. We are such old friends (since the middle twenties) that I would have done anything for her. But I no longer have a maid—and my husband, who is in his 80th year, is not robust. So you see how much I welcomed your letters and the cheering effect they had on her. She lost her "phobia" about officials.

I am getting cheerful letters from her in France, thank heaven. She found the house at Lamothe (shut for a year) not so damp or cold as she had feared, and nothing—none of her treasures—disturbed. Local people, all peasants, are being very helpful. Her handwriting is strong and vigorous, not spidery as it was when she came here. I think my husband and I anchored her, for the time being at least.

w. k. rose
Remembering Nancy

It was probably in Spain, the summer of 1957, that I first met Nancy Cunard. When trying to work this out with Charles Burkhart, who introduced us, I said, "Of course, she would have known precisely the day, the month, and the year." This remarkable memory for times and places was but one quality that seemed on first discovery paradoxical in Nancy. Later I would recognize that it was only my insufficient imagination that caused me to be surprised. Nancy was an authentic individual, and in 1957 I hadn't known enough such to be prepared for the way she battered my preconceptions about character types. Why not be a passionate romantic, pursuing high principles and low pleasures, and at the same time a fiend for accuracy, worse than a librarian? I remember her on that first occasion, late one night on the Gran Via, pointing out the hotel room where Hemingway had stayed—in 1937, I *think*—and telling us the day and hour she had visited him there.

From that summer till her death we were friends, seeing each other as often as we could when I was abroad, writing when the Atlantic separated us. "America giveth and it taketh away," she would say when it came time for me to return to the States. Quoted this way, the expression sounds melodramatic, or at least excessive. Coming from Nancy, with her talent for making the moment count, her lack of self-consciousness, and her beautiful responsiveness, it seemed simply right. I belonged to the generation that came to maturity in the disillusioning cynical years of World War II and its aftermath; so I was not prepared for her kind of authenticity. She taught me, long after we had learned to doubt it, that there could be such a thing as a *sincere* adult, that it was possible to be intelligent and sensitive and still wholly on the level. To me the discovery was doubly exciting for having as its subject someone notoriously immoral in the eyes of convention—a lewd woman, a drinker, and a fellow traveler.

Knowing Nancy in her last years was an education in history and literature as well as in life. She, along with a few of her coevals, gave me an insight into the truth of the 20's that its writers seemed always to be shadowing. Lady Brett, Catherine, Daisy, Nicole had all seemed to me, before Nancy, vivid, compelling heroines on their white chargers of independence; but I couldn't help suspecting a degree of sentiment in their creators. These women's ineffable *style* seemed just too fine. Fitzgerald at least fixed his eyes on the worm of selfishness and privilege that spoiled the golden apple. But he too was bemused by the glamor of his classy thoroughbreds, their integrity shining diamond-like through the mud of their social condition and of their own licentiousness. Then came Nancy, looking like a greyhound, telling the truth as if there were no choice, yet making a wreck of her personal life and always ready to fling obscenity and insult at offenders. She is said to have sat for Iris March and Lucy Tantamount, and to these I think can be added the heroine of Lewis's suppressed *The Roaring Quean*. But knowing her was to know better the meaning of those more significant Bretts and Daisies, the lovely martyrs to beauty and truth in a world hell-bent on pleasure. The kinship is, I think, substantiated by William Carlos Williams' *Autobiography* of the youthful Nancy and Iris Tree in Paris.

Nancy's attitude towards age struck me as particularly characteristic of her kind. When I knew her in her late fifties and early sixties, she showed none of the usual feminine concern for years—in herself or others. For her, people were OK or they were not; she gave her affection and approval to the OK ones with as little regard for age as for social distinction or professional eminence. Her seniors like Brigit Patmore and Otto Theis she treated just as she did her contemporaries like Iris Tree and Lady Diana Cooper and Peggy Guggenheim, or as she did a young American like me. Though I was her junior by about twenty-five years, I found in her no trace of the envy or age snobbery that usually colors such relationships.

Nancy's mother, referred to always as "Her Ladyship," was a San Franciscan, and Nancy took great pleasure from the fact that I was from there, too. We also had in common Wyndham Lewis. She had had a brief and checkered affair with him in the early 20's, and while she came to loathe his politics of the 30's, she stayed an admirer of his drawing and writing. I was working on Lewis's letters in London in 1958–59, and Nancy was spending that winter there. She was always coming up with a buried fact from that splendid, unsentimental memory or with an obscure friend from the early days who might be helpful. Recalling Lewis's vagaries as a lover, she told me of their departure from Venice, where he had been her guest. Two gondolas were needed to get the luggage, Nancy, Lewis, another friend (male), and a maid to the train. Nancy took the other friend with her, putting Lewis in the boat with the maid. Lewis, easily offended, was in such a rage by the time they reached the station that he didn't speak, she said, till they were half-way to Paris.

Her talk was full of precise, evocative recollections. When I visited her in her beautiful little barn in Lamothe-Fénelon, she took me for a long ride in a hired car. She knew the area like the back of her hand, having first discovered it in the 20's, she told me, when she had gone on a walking tour with directions provided by Pound, who wanted her to know his troubadour country. Now there were more monuments to the fallen *maquis* than reminders of Bertrans de Born, and we stopped at every stone marker to read the names of these heroes of hers, and incidentally *"pour prendre un verre"* if there was one in sight. In Sarlât she walked me to the oldest and best buildings, making each locked church the occasion for another *"tout petit verre."* Later, she insisted that the driver stop on a bridge over the Lot so that I could admire the river. No sooner was I out of the car than a *gendarme* appeared to tell us to move on, we were holding up traffic. All of Nancy's instinct and training for rebellion welled up instantly, and there she stood in that dreamy landscape going for the poor fellow, her stream of invective bringing an edge of foam to her tight, cracked, badly rouged lips. He was a polite and attractive young man, and in the end I think she asked him to come have a drink with her some time.

This scorn for authority and some hectic behavior in London landed her at one point in a public mental institution in Surrey. Going to visit this elegant and sympathetic creature in that great Victorian brick madhouse, her room a pale green cubicle, I felt too poignantly the absurdity of her fate. Kafka or Brecht could not have designed a more grimly ironic situation. She was ill and miserable; she could not get at her money to hire a lawyer; she wanted to write and they would not permit her to have her typewriter. But she was her gallant self: "Look, darling, the door has no latch."

I prefer to think of her sitting during long afternoons in the kitchen of Otto and Louise Theis's tiny Sussex cottage. She would be staying with them, or the two of us would drive down from London for the day. Louise would go to the cooler for a bottle of her elderflower wine, not yet ready for drinking. No matter, we would sit there sipping the delicious golden stuff from large rummers, the talk usually literary, quick and allusive, the little room so full of cheer and good feeling we soon forgot its ancient chill and did not notice when the faint sun disappeared entirely.

On one occasion I was giving a party and had asked Nancy to come and meet a woman friend of mine who was working on Pound. "Why should I talk to the bloody woman about Ezra? I've already told *him* all I have to say about him." But she came, and I can see her sitting there in one of her outfits that looked so very "period" and yet neither eccentric nor pathetic. A heavy wool suit, I think it was this time, purplish or black and white, beautifully cut, but with the skirt too long, or too short. Around her neck a marvelous necklace of African ivory, as yellowed and elegant as the old Parisian shoes on her long, narrow feet. Her reddish hair was graying, rather frizzy and pinned up with no great care. And her eyes, like those of Elizabeth Bishop's fish—

the irises back and packed
with tarnished tinfoil
seen through the lenses
of old scratched isinglass.

They flickered, taking in every one in the room, curious and alive, wary too.

Her gestures were inimitable. One involved holding her elbow against her side, the arm going straight out in front, and at the end, the hand raised, palm outward, fingers slightly curved—like some Massenet heroine holding off the worst. Or standing, she would move her knee out at some unlikely angle, her foot slightly raised and turned to complete the line from thin hip to long toe. At the same time, an elbow would be crooked, so that the forearm made a right angle with her side. I know Nancy was aware of her "look," for she always arranged herself in one of these stances when I started to take a snapshot of her. But there was nothing of the poseur in this. Rather, it partook of the gay intelligence and unique style that enchanted so many of us.

miriam j. benkovitz

A Memoir: Nancy Cunard

Nancy Cunard died alone in Paris on 17 March 1965. Two days earlier the police had brought her, ill and confused and unaccountably bruised on the face to the Hôpital Cochin. She could not recall her name. She immediately asked for wine, but she could not be allowed it without a doctor's order. She then asked for pencil and paper, and on that first day she spent hours writing. As her condition worsened she was forced to put aside her papers. And just before the commencement of visiting hours on March 17 Nancy Cunard died, mercifully unconscious since she was still alone.

The irony of these circumstances is almost too pat for belief. Nancy had an urgent need to serve her fellow men and a conviction that their fulfillment depended on liberty and justice. Her involvement with her fellows was the core of her life. That is what makes Nancy Cunard memorable.

I came to know her through my work on the novelist Ronald Firbank. In 1954 I sent her a letter asking what she remembered about Firbank, and she replied with a long account of him. Soon she began to send me newspaper clippings, book catalogues listing Firbank's novels, and various anecdotes of Firbank—something her cousin Victor had told her, a memory she herself had just recovered, a suggestion from Nina Hamnett. I kept asking questions, and Nancy never failed to answer them.

We developed a steady exchange of letters, and with each one she seemed more and more a revenant from another time, the very spirit of recklessness and furious achievement which the world had had to an unusual degree, at least in my eyes, in the Twenties. I went back to her poetry, published in volumes long out of print, and of course I found there all the confirmation I expected. The last sonnet in the sequence called "Outlaws," a poem about two fabled lovers, was enough:

One thinks to hear them crying in the wind:
"Life was so bitter to us—but we chose

The living, stressful moments from this close
Denying, gray existence. If we sinned
We bear our joys and crimes with equal heart,
And punishment is nothing. We have known
All sweet and sharp adventures, and are grown
Heroic-hard with life. You cannot part
Our twin minds from each other, and we sail
Proud and forever on the clutching sea,
Grown element again; the heaven's breath
Makes clear our souls with space; life does not fail
As we have used it." . . . They shall ever be;
Summer has set upon them but not death.

But I found the real magic in Nancy's letters, for they are full of the names and places, the intimacies, of the twenties. In one, Nancy Cunard and Iris Tree are together in the Café Royal writing verse; in another there is Nancy in a gold suit and a gold mask and top hat at the "Bal du Comte de Beaumont" having her picture taken with Tristan Tzara. There is the bistro in Montparnasse, the Jockey, with its "wild swoops of tenebrous colours all over walls and ceiling" and its bottles of colored water "apothecary-style" and its owner Hilaire Hiler at the piano each evening, "vamping till ready, on and on and on." There is "La Puits Carré," the old Norman farmhouse where Nancy set up her Hours Press with the help of William Bird and the machines he had used for his own Three Mountains Press. There is the Wyndham Lewis room in London's Eiffel Tower Restaurant. There are Louis Aragon, Diana Manners, Norman Douglas, Man Ray, Langston Hughes, Paul Eluard, Virginia Woolf, and how many more. The flavor of the whole decade was in the note Nancy sent me from Palma: "Lord how this land does need, would love, and could use some of the real-and-true Am. music—such as 'Beat it up. Beat it up' (Drums)."

Someone had told me that Nancy Cunard even dressed as she had in the twenties; but when I questioned Jean Lambert, whom Nancy had introduced to me by letter after he came to the artists' colony Yaddo to finish his book about his father-in-law, *Gide Familier,* he was no help at all. He replied (correctly or not), "Women always dress in the fashion of the time when they were most loved. But with Nancy—where does it end?" I looked long at Wyndham Lewis' sketch of her, done in 1923, and the photograph, made by Cecil Beaton in 1930, in which she wore her legendary African bracelets. Obviously these could convey nothing about her appearance in the 1950s, and I was plainly curious. I wanted to see for myself.

At last, on Easter Monday in 1959, when we both happened to be in London, we met for the first time. We had arranged to dine at one of the few restaurants open on that holiday evening, the Majorca, which Nancy had described as on Brewer Street just off Regent Street near the Café Royal. My anticipation was great enough to make me early, and I sat watching the door for her arrival. Promptly at eight she came—or to be more precise, glided—in, a tall, thin woman in a leopard coat and hat. The hat was a cloche and, while it was not exactly of the late fifties, it did not belong to the twenties either. Neither did the rest of her clothes. For a moment I felt disappointment; but in the flurry of acknowledging each other and getting seated and ordering the first drink, I forgot it and I never thought of it again. Since then her appearance has hardly mattered; I have to make an effort to recall that her eyes were the blue of a northern sky at mid-day and her hands, competent but without grace. Although Nancy looked slightly ill, as she was, her thinness had a beautiful strength and angularity. I remember little else of that evening except that I understood, even then, that Nancy Cunard had a distinction in no way dependent on styles. And I know that we sat late, finally emerging into the cold spring night, quieter at the end of the long bank holiday than most London nights.

At subsequent meetings, usually in restaurants, we both had much to say; and because I prompted her to do so, Nancy spoke again and again the names of the twenties and of her girlhood. She talked of her parents, Sir Bache and California-born Lady Maud Cunard, and of the novelist George Moore. Because Moore is in it, we went once to see the copy of Orpen's painting of the Café Royal hanging in its brasserie. She talked of André Gide's "terrible intelligence" and the crisp bureaucratic manner which Louis Aragon had developed. She referred with wonderful irreverence to Buckingham Palace as "Old Buck House," and when she spoke of the jazz musician Henry Crowder, she added happily, "Honey, what love we did have."

Only in retrospect did I understand that while I may indeed have been in the ambiance of another time with Nancy Cunard, she was not memorable because she had known James Joyce or sat with Norman Douglas and the Sitwells in a Florentine trattoria. Nor did the gallantry of her life make her so. Nancy Cunard was notable for her faith in the emancipated human spirit. In the winter of 1924, from her flat in the Rue le Regrattier, where the old clothes men passed "all morning and each morning" and the river Seine rushed by full to the brim, Nancy had complained to Ronald Firbank that "at least half life is defending oneself from the intrusion of people." Nevertheless she was passionately involved in helping them to liberalize themselves.

She began The Hours Press so as to publish avant-garde writers, and possibly the publication in which she took most pride was Samuel Beckett's *Whoroscope,* because it was Beckett's first book and his first opportunity. Nancy Cunard's zeal in the cause of equality for the Negro was unflagging. "As little as I believe in class distinction," she told me, "I can much more easily understand it than colour distinction." With George Padmore she wrote *The White Man's Duty* in defense of all colored peoples under colonial rule, and she objected vigorously to the sentence given the Negroes accused in the Scottsboro (Alabama) Case, a sentence finally reversed by the United States Supreme Court. Nancy affirmed her ardor for racial equality, intellectually, by making that monumental anthology *Negro.* Her dispatches to the *Manchester Guardian* and the Associated Negro Press from Spain during the Civil War were vehemently pro-Loyalist. Indeed Fascism was so hateful to her that in 1943 she worked endlessly to help organize the massive protest against the release of the British Fascist Party's leader Sir Oswald Mosley from prison. Ezra Pound's war activities bewildered her. "He was so generous," Nancy said about Pound, "and then he got this thing with anti-Semitism." Nancy spent the years of the second World War in London after a harrowing journey from France by way of Portugal, Curaçao, and Cuba. Once in London, she devoted her energies to the Free French in their struggle against Nazism. But she also feared Communism as another kind of tyranny; she wrote in 1962 to say how concerned she was for Cuba.

Nancy Cunard knew that she lived with an impossible ideal. A letter sent me from her home at Lamothe-Fénelon, France, on 19 July 1959 reads, "Today's date has such a meaning for me: the beginning of the war in Spain, 23 years ago! And I could never, somehow, get to finish the long epic poem on all that—which is bad. Too many of my writings have been thus, and I feel ashamed, for it should not be final: the inner sense that arises within me that 'Neither war ended as it should and that was what stopped me, by cutting off the inspiration and the impetus.' So saying, I am thinking of other poems of mine during W W 2, in London, which were to have been a little book—unfinished."

But she could hardly relinquish the hopes and convictions of a lifetime. Within a month of her death Nancy was still at work on a poem called "Visions Experienced by the Bards of the Middle Ages." It was meant to discredit war. Nancy Cunard, as another of her pieces of verse said, scanned "the crossroads of a violent world," and in spite of what she saw there—impotence, folly, evil—she kept her faith in the redemptive possibilities of justice and freedom for all men.

charles burkhart
Letters from Nancy

How lucky to have saved her letters! Otherwise, what memories of Nancy hadn't washed away, hadn't slipped down the stream, would be all I had of her, and what I had most vividly would be the last memory of her, a memory of too much pain.

This was in Gourdon, in the late summer of 1963. Nancy had just come out of the hospital where she was being treated for emphysema and was staying at the ugliest hotel in the Dordogne or perhaps in the world: raw, white, and new; downstairs a salon/cafe of pinball machines, local youth, and nervous young proprietor; upstairs, tiny rooms furnished and paneled in raw orange pine, so new it oozed under thick varnish. Creaky wooden stairs and narrow hallways, wardrobes which screamed when touched, plumbing, though new, French and implacable. For a village hotel it was extraordinarily noisy; the wood upstairs served, I suppose, as acoustical chamber for the noise of the pinball salon, and there was the noise of the rain (was the roof made of tin?)—it rained incessantly during those two or three days, though August and September there are usually sun-baked, a time of lizards and blackberries and nightingales, when the rivers—the Lot, the Vézère, and the gray Dordogne—begin to run thinner between red banks.

When Nancy was able to leave her raw orange cubicle (where she had an old suitcase or two, as she always did, full of manuscripts or correspondence or ivory, and a bottle of rum, her favorite drink, on the bedside table), she descended and sat in a corner of the pinball salon, writing her letters, drinking rough red, which she would occasionally ask one of the boys to share a glass of, catching her breath between Gauloises. Still writing, but desperate; dazed and bemused with pain and with the drugs they gave her at the hospital. I had just arrived in Paris for the winter and met Herman Schrijver there and we had decided we must at once visit Nancy; Janet Flanner said it would be "an errand of mercy." And we arrived in Gourdon to find the rain and the raw hotel and Nancy, able to walk five steps before she must stop to catch a little breath into her incredibly thin body, able to talk only a minute or two before rage overwhelmed her. She was always like a cat, and her rage was like that of a puma encaged, an ocelot or a cheetah; green eyes blazing like a cat's, she pounded the table weakly and gasped in her fury, "If I could breathe!" Anger at everything, at the food she would not eat—she crumbled up bread and made little balls of it in her plate; at the doctors who were expensive and wrong; at Franco, all Fascism, and the world.

She was a good hater, and of course at the same time she loved things and people very deeply, things more than people, I sometimes think, and she had at one time loved her stone house at Lamothe-Fénelon. The second morning we hired a car and a woman to drive it and went out to see Lamothe, some few miles from Gourdon. We drove too fast on those wet roads, and Nancy at one point said, with an access of breath, with sudden firmness and resonance, "On ne fait pas la tour de France, madame!" Lamothe itself one could hardly enter, grass so thick by the gate; the house which I remembered as steeped in the sun and splendidly open and full of air seemed crouched and defenceless in the rain. It was crumbling; the books, precious books some of them, were mildewing; on the mantelpiece where the Manet had sat, there were a few old wine bottles, spider webs, odd rocks, metal or wooden scraps, objets trouvés from the days when she could walk; musty sad debris of all that famous and brilliant and energetic life. I helped her to make a list of some bibliographical details on her Hours Press books for an article that was to appear in *The Book Collector,* and Nancy and Herman and I sat on the floor of the upstairs study and went through the trunk that contained her ivories, what remained of them. A nightmare: the cold and the rain and the mildew and the pointlessness; but at one moment, when she held a favorite ancient bracelet to her cheek, she crooned something I could not hear and gave me a look of dim, remote ecstasy, as if I would understand.

I did not understand any of it, nor do I yet, such suffering and such rage. One can call it rage against the coming of the night; this scarcely clarifies. The next day Herman and I left for Bordeaux, assured that Jean Guerin was coming to fetch Nancy the following day, to take her further south for the winter, and Bordeaux seemed more severe and dix-huitième than ever after Gourdon and what had happened or had not happened there. I think that must be the way she died, over a year later, in Paris; in such suffering and such rage. Not mad, but maddened.

If it were not for her letters, then, the memory of Gourdon would be final. But there they are; testimony. Out of them spill photographs and telegrams, her urgent requests, her lavish affection, her great and various interest in life. Other visits to the Dordogne, and many an expedition together. Instead of the pained white uncomprehending face, to which a translucent hand held yellow ivory, I can see Nancy in my letters, bedecked with chunks of amber, walking lightly and rapidly at my side, hear that cool, voluble voice, hear her laughter.

A memoir of someone else is always a memoir of one's self, unless one could, school of Sitwell, construct a persona, inflexible, grand, inevitably patronizing; one's memoir would begin, "Nancy Cunard!" It would be the kind of thing Nancy, who never was anyone but herself, would find comic. She was much more humorous than witty. She was without snobbery, though always, in some miraculous way, a lady, even when she was assaulting a policeman with intent to kill or, with other intent, an African exchange student in the back seat of a big black London taxi. Drunk as the devil she could throw herself fully clothed into a bathtub full of water; she could, with incomparable elegance, grace a reception for Tzara at the French Embassy. Indecencies about the dead? There are none.

The use of any voice except one's own to describe her would be an insult in the face of her irremediable honesty, so that the bare facts are in order, and they are that I first met Nancy in 1950, when I was an American student at Oxford, and, having found out a Paris address for her from Samuel Beckett, wrote her about George Moore's letters, which I was collecting. Hers from GM had been destroyed by the Germans in the sack of her house at Réanville, but later I found copies made by Joseph Hone, who wrote Moore's life, in the National Library in Dublin—copies which I gave to Nancy for her book *GM; Memories of George Moore*. Our interest in Moore started us. Could it be true, I once asked her, towards the end of one of those long drunken Soho luncheons where the waiters wanted us to leave and we wouldn't, could it possibly be true that she was GM's daughter? She had a way of pressing her hands together in front of her lips and looking judicious and merry and wicked: "Oh, darling, I don't think so, I'd *like* to!" GM, fond of her for many reasons, because of his devotion to her mother, because of Nancy's beauty, because she was the beginning artist and he the grand old man of letters, asked her to undress for him, he must see her "bum," to use his word (and the word he uses in *Aphrodite in Aulis*), which she did, giving him, I think, the scene between the aged Tadhg and his young wife Brigit in GM's late novel *Ulick and Soracha*. I lived in Ebury Street for two years, GM's own "long, lacklustre street of Ebury," and Nancy and I walked from my place at 63 Ebury to 121 Ebury, where GM spent his last years, 1911–1933, to see the ground floor converted into, as I remember, first a hairdresser's and then a Finnish travel agency. A little farther down the street was the lovely house where the infant prodigy Mozart had dwelt.

But there was something more basic than GM between us, and this was the fact that I was American. After seven years in England I returned to America—"What America giveth, America taketh away," she said several times in letters of that period; and when I returned to Europe each summer and talked with her about America I found that she had developed almost a mystique about it. She could be gay about "jolly old Ellis," where she had been interned, but, unpredictably, there erupted a furious diatribe against "cellophane," symbol of American falsity. Her ambivalence was greater because she herself was part American; when I moved to Germantown, a suburb of Philadelphia, she wrote, "Germantown: my forebears helped to found it—proved!"

She sometimes called me "the second American." Here was the heart of the matter. The first American for her (between whom and my own second rank a great gulf was fixed) was Henry Crowder, the Negro jazz musician she knew in the late Twenties and Thirties. After Henry, nothing was the same ever again—Negroes, America, herself. As the following letter will show. It is dated April 24, 1955. That winter in Washington, D.C., Henry's home, I had tried at Nancy's request to find out what had become of him. And I had found out:

> And so Henry is dead—
> How extraordinary it is to me to think of the way this news comes to me. It will be so to you—as if a branch were to fly off a tree across one's walking way, to tell one something from another planet. That it should come to me in this manner . . . Do you know that, otherwise, I should *never* have known? . . . Is *this* what happens when one asks a friend to look for the long-past? I could say "yes". Pretty obviously, I should never have seen him again. He might have been dead from 1935 to 1947, for all I knew. Henry made me—and so be it . . . I don't know WHO could think of words, or even thoughts, with which to thank you for writing about this. I am at a loss. But I know that doesn't matter at all, because our instinctive selves have much akin. All I feel is a kind of stupour, an amazement, that YOU should be in this, dear Charles. It seems, perhaps, connected with the amazement it was for me to know Henry at all—in Venice in 1928—"Introducing America." That covers it. And then, all the rest. . . . I am finishing the litre of 'rough-red' to your health, amazed, amazed for ever that you, darling Charles, should be the messenger of Henry. Others have loved me more (?), and I, perhaps others. NO, probably not, for me, has this been true. In any case: Henry made me. I thank him. And that is the steèle.

If he was her creator, she re-created him over and over in her letters; she told time by him:

> And you now 32. What was I at, at that age—OH! It was the year I met Henry in Venice, in October. I was printing; the Hours Press began then.

And, out of Henry, the visit to Harlem in 1932, the enormous anthology of *Negro* in 1934, and her life as champion of the Negro cause. My thanks for a copy of *Black and Unknown Bards* she had sent me in Philadelphia led her to these reminiscences:

> Glad you like "Black and Unknown Bards". Yes, Stirling Brown is the best, and what an enchanting man (met in 1932 in Boston). And you see many Negroes. (I had my hair done at a coloured hairdresser in Philadelphia and could *not* think why all the attendants seemed so odd in behavior, as if rather flustered. At the end they confided with many smiles that I was the first white woman ever to enter that shop. And my being English did not appear to explain it all away! *Oh really,* said I to myself!) How I wish *WE* had been able to know each other during that long visit of mine to Harlem in 1932. So much was there *we* would have laughed about together—which I could never do properly with the Negro friends. It was a very bitter-sweet time, all of it, and I longed for an American white friend with feelings such as mine— but alas, nary a one. The only friend not of "the race" got scared at the newspaper rumpus and was too serious about everything to have a sense of humour *as well.* Lord, how we could have got about, you and I. (This was while I was collecting the Afro-American part of "Negro".) Those threatening letters from rabid colour-haters would make a splendid exhibit of "moronism". There must have been fifty or so (there were many letters of commendation as well). In all, there was everything from threats of being "taken for a ride" and deserving death for "the betrayal of your race", through pornographic outpourings, up to 3 proposals of marriage (from whites). How mad it all was. I kept all this, of course, but, alas, the War caused *nearly* all to disappear from Reanville.

"Nearly all"—but some of them she showed me later, certain priapic splendors.

Nancy's championing of the Negro, of the anti-Franco Spaniard, of any oppressed man anywhere, was, I am sure, largely sexual in origin, as—again I am sure—such championings generally are. To say so is not to lessen their beauty or goodness. But, because Nancy would not have liked such pontificating, I will not explore the connection I felt between her high, even aristocratic breeding and her sexual/

political drives. Her breeding was most obvious to an American like myself when I saw how the other English reacted to it; not so much the tendency to servile flunkeyism among the older generation of waiters, charwomen, etc., but among people of her class the instinctive and unconscious recognition of Nancy as "one of us"—to use Conrad's term. Nancy's strong anti-authoritarian impulses—she was more anarchic than Communistic, I would say—led her into such difficulties as anyone who knew her knew about, problems with visas and with the police. Others will know better than I how many times she was in prison. She had absolute personal courage. It was not a case of the brave man being that man who can overcome his fear. Nancy simply had no sense of fear, and this made remarkable the political/racial/sexual experiments of Harlem, Spain, and elsewhere.

"Damn all our enemies!" one of her postcards ends. She was of course a born fighter, and once again, a good hater—particularly of places. Culled from various letters: "Life here /Lamothe/ is HELL" . . . *"Who wdn't* hate England!" . . . *"horrible* London!" . . . "I *hate* France" . . . "Belgium was really beastly" . . . "That country /Spain/ seems always to be like a rock on which one's hopes are broken. . . ." I can still hear the hiss of her breath when she said, *"Pestilential* Paris!" Early letters, those of 1951 and 1952, describe the difficulties of building the house at Lamothe (she told me that "old goofy Ezra" had first introduced her to the Dordogne), and it never was really quite right, whether it was local children breaking her windows, or her servant, Mme Achille, who went insane, or simply the staggering heat. This is why so many of her letters are marked "de passage"—no one traveled more, but whether it was to visit a place, Altamira or Algeria, or to get away from a place, Lamothe or London, one had the sense not so much that she traveled as that she was driven. She carried her own Furies with her in an ancient valise, along with amber and rum and ivory. They drove her on that last impossible journey northward to pestilential Paris, and there they finally left her.

I seem to be too much remembering rage. Here is something from a letter of December 4, 1953, to offset:

I see that Tuesday is the Immaculate Conception. How *can* it be? Unless, of course, Jesus was as oddly gestated as conceived: 17 days, or 1 year and 17 days? (This is the kind of thing that puzzles me no end, always.)

There was great gaiety with her, often. She was quite convivial, and always liked everyone, without exception, on meeting. She liked parties, and gave them; there was one in Jimmie's back bar at the Cafe Royal on Boxing Day, 1953, where she introduced me to Herman Schrijver. Having met my good friend the actor Hugh Paddick she was determined to see the play he was in at that moment, *The Boy Friend,* then running at a theatre in Swiss Cottage before its transfer to the West End. The night we went we'd had a long day of antiquing, in Peckham and elsewhere, and arrived chaotically late and disheveled, to find that the seats Hugh had arranged for us were directly behind Princess Margaret. Nancy paid no attention to royalty, but some little pained attention to *The Boy Friend:* "Oh, no, darling, the Twenties weren't like that!" Afterwards, meeting the cast and the director and Sandy Wilson, she was several times addressed as "Lady Cunard," which, in view of her feelings about her mother (whom Nancy never called her mother, always "Her Ladyship"), was at least ironic.

Other expeditions: the best of all was to Bath and Bristol—that part of England, her favorite part, she said. We saw the improper giant of Cerne Abbas, and gorgeous robes made of feathers in an ethnological museum, and two friends she was immensely fond of, Sylvia Townsend Warner and Valentine Ackland, at their house in Dorset. We bought vigorously and as cheaply as possible; in Bristol I found two oil paintings of baby chickens under a ragged sofa in a junk shop, my kind of Victoriana, which Nancy rather deplored, and Nancy bought two small alabaster urns. There was always a grand vernissage in our rooms at night after our shopping; the first thing was to clean, with warm water and soap, and then to display, as in a museum, except that we used the floor or the bed and Nancy's silk squares, a cup made of horn, a papier-mâché snuff box, a model of a pyramid, a ruler made of various marbles, wooden beads from the South Seas. We drank more whisky and the room grew muggier with smoke and the objects grew lovelier, and we congratulated ourselves on them at length and made plans for the morrow.

Her taste in art was for the prehistorical, the non-European. Avebury or Les Eyzies concerned her deeply; she loathed rococo. In the summer of 1957, when we were in Madrid with Bill Rose, Nancy and I hired an old taxi and went to Toledo. En route through hot dry fields she showed me where she had fought in the Civil War, "behind *that* hill," and by the time we arrived in Toledo the heat had gathered itself into a fist. We were two minutes at the cathedral, which she hated, and I too, because of, within, its sickly decorations and tinselly pieties, and without, the saprophytic cluster of souvenir shops, full of junky Toledo-steel letter openers and paperweights. We looked at the El Greco paintings in his house nearby and then for coolness' sake went to sit in the old synagogue. But even with the heat, and Nancy was ill, already beginning to be ill most of the time, I remember the Toledo expedition as exhilarating.

I do not remember, even, that the final effect of visiting her, three or four years later, at the asylum of Virginia Water, where for some months she was committed, was unhappy. I never for a moment thought she was insane, though she did insane things; maddened, but not mad. And the gardens were lovely there, and Nancy was full of projects for when she was released—she usually had so much underway that it was rather funny, the busyness of it; she was grace itself in offering us tea, and beautifully grateful for the fruit and chocolate and cigarettes we had brought her. It was London that seemed insane to return to, vague, huge, meaningless.

She could mean so much because she was more herself than other people are themselves. She was more characteristic of herself than they, as one says that some Goyas are more characteristic than others. But she was various and surprising, never monotonous; her energy saw to that. Losses live on, there will be no more letters, and I can state my own loss best by yet another line from a letter: "Sure I'm *you*, because you're *me*." What I lost, with Nancy, was one of my identities, which had come to life with her, and which, when she left, left too.

clyde robinson
Nancy Cunard in Mallorca

It was the little café El Brindis on Plaza Santa Eulalia in Palma de Mallorca where I first met Nancy Cunard, an early evening in August, 1958. I came out of the café and recognized her at once from Cecil Beaton's photograph (with the African ivory bracelets) which she had included of herself in her book on Norman Douglas. The heat was frightful and the city had recently cut down all the old plane trees in the square.

She was seated at a table on the terrace busily writing in a sort of school copybook, and sipping a glass of "vino blanco." I paused in front of her and said: "I'm terribly sorry—but aren't you Miss Cunard?" I shall never forget those extraordinary pale blue eyes which looked up at me from under a high turban of veils! Nor her *voice:* "Yes, I am Nancy Cunard. Who are you?" I told her my name, that I had been living in Mallorca and how much I had liked her books on Norman Douglas and George Moore—all I knew of her work at the time. She asked me to sit down and have a drink, a "trago." We talked half an hour or so, mostly questions from her. Apropos of what I don't remember, but she mentioned having met and liking Helena Rubenstein. I had to leave for an engagement, to which I arrived late. She said she *might* have to leave Mallorca in the morning but would drop a note at my hotel. And she did. Unfortunately when I got it she had already sailed for Marseilles.

Weeks passed. She had left me a bank address in London, to which I wrote. We began a correspondence—eventually a hundred letters or more from her before the tragic end in Paris. And what immediate, graphic, Spain-nostalgia or of Harlem, wonderful, sad, at times very funny and always thoughtful-of-one letters she wrote! Later, after she returned to Mallorca, she would send me a midnight or dawn note when we were in the same hotel: "Written this very moment *en todas las Españas*" . . . For she did come back to Palma, from her stone house at Lamothe, in time for dinner together at the Hotel Cannes New Year's Eve, 1959. Afterward we went to a party Geraldine

Spencer and Russ Sully were giving in their flat a few blocks away, and Nancy loved the "procession" en route. I was to provide the food, which Mediterranean fashion was simply arranged on open trays and carried by us with the help of "botones" from the hotel. When midnight struck we were all trying to consume "the twelve grapes" in Spanish tradition and dancing at the same time to a recording of "Scheherezade." . . .

What to say of that month of January with Nancy in Mallorca! Milder that year than usual and the almond trees blossomed early. I never knew what to expect. The year before she had investigated the "talyots"—prehistoric Cyclopean constructions or round stone mounds found in remote spots on the island, the original purpose of which still a mystery. One of Nancy's friends in Palma was the "taxista," Juan, and shortly after her arrival she engaged him to take us to Llubí—a more primitive Spanish village one can't imagine, outside of which lost in some fields was a "talyot." So off we went, Nancy chattering away in Mallorquin dialect with Juan. There is a snapshot of us together near the site, Nancy leaning against a typical Mallorquin stone wall with a garland about her she had quickly put together and holding a stick she had picked up. For all that, looking very British with a "riding crop." . . .

Nancy never forgot she was a Cunard. Rarely was there an extended conversation in which she didn't mention her mother, Lady Emerald Cunard—"Her Ladyship," as she always referred to her. Who can know at what point or the why in her childhood or in those London years of the early Twenties ("three balls a night") she revolted against her mother and her class. In any case, it was a violent interior revolution and she never looked back, on principle. And "on principle" (to use an old-fashioned term—and yet in many ways Nancy, too, was oddly "old-fashioned": in little personal ways, not ever in thought or perception) she was rigid, implacable. Like her mother? She was never a Marxist—one afternoon we were lunching on the terrace of a "fonda" overlooking the harbor of Palma. Suddenly she remarked: "There's a Cunard ship—the orange smoke stacks, you know . . . Here on one of those tripper cruises. . . ." Later she spoke of buying a car in pale blue, with the Cunard arms to be emblazoned on the doors. . . .

We spent much of our time together in hole-in-the-wall cafés. . . . Nancy had a genius for ferreting out "joints" and Gypsies! She saw again old friends—George and Helen Seldes, a crippled veteran from the Civil War on Menorca, a waiter in the Bar Bellver; she met Louis and Eveline de Sonnenberg and Juan Mariá Thomás—a Spanish priest with whom I had collaborated on a music-drama festival in Bellver Castle. We talked and talked. From time to time she would disappear in a taxi with Juan on something very "secret."

It was at this time she was experimenting with a sonnet form in several languages simultaneously, each line to scan and rhyme according to the scheme: French, Spanish, English, Italian, German, etc. She made it work. Later in 1960 I wrote her from Germany and of the fantastic new Munich. She answered with recollections of her visit to Dachau right after the war and of "swallows flying at dawn out of the black ruins of a church." When the Nazis compiled their "black list" of the British, under "C" Nancy Cunard was next after Winston Churchill.

And until I met Nancy I thought I was observant. She and I would walk down the Calle de los Olmos, lined with little sub-pavement shops, which I had passed month after month. She would spot a straw napkin ring, a red painted flute, a simple lemon wood salad fork and spoon, none of which I had noticed before. *"EYES AND NO EYES"* she often repeated. . . . She was intensely aware of each moment and immediately projected herself and her intelligence on each new discovery, sensation, happening or person. Each experience was drained of all its elements. At the same time she had an almost perverse disregard for the simplest amenities in life, a paradoxically sybaritic asceticism.

Then she went to Valencia, returning in two weeks. She was most concerned with the condition of political prisoners in Franco's jails and devoted much of her time in raising funds to help them. I see her sitting in the lobby of the Cannes, writing at a low table, and when I would come in she silently held out her right hand—a gesture for humanity, actually. . . .

I left for France. We had a last drink together at the "Formentor"—a café she liked, and oddly the meeting-place of all the Spanish bourgeoisie she hated most. She said: "No good-bys." But it was just that. I never saw Nancy again. In 1961 I returned to America. The letters and poems, the first fragments of her "Troubadours" epic, a few last notes came across the Atlantic from London, Toulouse, Cap Ferrat. Somehow we both felt we *would* meet again.

géraldine balayé
Nancy Cunard

Nancy Cunard? En 1944, je ne connaissais ni son nom, ni son oeuvre, quand je croisai dans un restaurant de journalistes—récemment sortis de toutes les presses clandestines de France, d'Espagne, d'Italie et d'Angleterre—une grande femme d'allure . . . stratosphèrique, mais en réalitè très Irlandaise.

Il était impossible de ne pas remarquer l'intelligence de son regard, la noblesse naturelle de son attitude. Et beaucoup de mes confrères écrivains combattants—sortant de maquis comme moi—l'avaient apprèciée: Aragon, Cassou, Francis Crémieux, René Laporte, Louise Mamiac, Wurmser, Rémy Bouchoux. Deux de nos journaux avaient accueilli nos articles.

Dans une de ces feuilles N. Cunard venait de publier des notes sur la résistance espagnole. Particulièrement sur ses séjours en Andorre et Catalogne qui inspirèrent les beaux poèmes "Nous gens d'Espagne."

Ces articles furent l'entrée en matière des premiers mots que j'adressai à Nancy la suite de notre conversation au sujet de la résistance qu'elle avait en dernier lieu, si vaillamment vécue à la B.B.C. de Londres, fut le prélude d'une amitié qui devait durer jusqu'à sa mort . . . et que j'essaye de prolonger jusqu'à la mienne.

Ni les lointains voyages de l'une au Yucatan, en Afrique de Nord, en Europe Occidentale, en Russie, ni les enchainements de l'autre aux Londres de l'O.R.T.F., ne devaient rompre l'union de deux pensées à la cause de l'humanisme et de la liberté.

Si certains critiques ont voulu enfermer la pensée de Nancy Cunard dans le moule étroit des politiques partisanes c'est par erreur. Toute l'existence de cet être vibrant fut vouée au combat universel pour la paix.

En évoquant ce visage pâli par l'effort du travail intellectuel, et par la révolte ressentie devant l'injustice humaine, on ne peut qu'y relire la pitié, la générosité et l'amour de l'Amour.

En 1944–45 Nancy décida de s'établir dans le midi de la France, à Lamothe-Fénelon. Avant la guerre de 1939–1945 elle y avait fait plusieurs séjours avec Henry Crowder et du jeune Raymond Michelet, à l'Abbaye de Carennac. C'est là qu'elle travailla (ainsi qu'à Paris en l'Île St. Louis avant guerre), à terminer son livre remarquable sur l'art nègre: *Negro*. Celui-ci fut avec son travail inédit sur les ivoires afro-américains, le point culminant de sa grande érudition.

Je suivis Nancy dans son aventureux projet d'installation dans le Lot.

Pourquoi aventureux? Parce qu'avant 1948 date de la mort de sa mère Maud Cunard, mon amie était presque sans ressources financières. Une modeste maison (genre refuge de berger) dans le hameaude Lamothe (à l'emplacement même où naquit Fénelon de Salignac) fut nôtre abri.

C'est là qu'aboutirent d'abord, les livres, manuscrits, photos de l'Hours Press. Nous allâmes les retirer en 1946 d'un hangar, parmi caisses et malles, éventrées lors de la bataille de Normandie et du débarquement anglais (1944).

Ce voyage à Vernon, près de Clos Normand, et de la demeure de Claude Monet, aurait été un calvaire si nous n'avions pas extrait des "Débris de la Guerre," tant de lettres célèbres d'Aragon, d'Eluard, Ezra Pound, et les manuscrits de *Negro*—tant de photos précieuses aussi des "ivoires," accompagnés de leur historique. Le tout déposé d'abord dans notre ABRI de Lamothe Basse, fut ensuite transféré à Peyrouro, (et confié au notaire français de la succession à Souillac, pour être remis aux héritiers de N. Cunard.)

Ceci fut fait au moment de la vente de Peyrouro (pierre des heures) en octobre 1965.

En 1948 j'avais suivi Nancy Cunard dans son déménagement de l'Abri, à Peyrouro. Il s'agissait de reconstruire une ferme abandonnée et d'en faire un ravissant manoir, où plutôt un sanctuaire de souvenirs littéraires. Là prirent place en plus des lettres ou manuscrits de Stirling, de René Crevel, de James Joyce, de George Moore, quelques tableaux de Picabia, de Manet, quelques meubles venus de Londres (après le décès de Maud Cunard). Nancy perdit sa mère peu après un voyage au Mexique et Yucatan.

A son retour elle commença à écrire ses souvenirs sur G.M. Nous traduisions aussi plusieurs textes d'Aparicio et de Valle Inclan. J'ai fait plusieurs émissions a l'O.R.T.F. sur 'Poèmes pour la France,' cette belle anthologie sur les écrivains anglais, qui ont écrit au sujet de la Résistance 1940–1945.

Les deux maisons de Lamothe-Fénelon Lot virent éclore une quantité d'articles, de traductions, de livres dont Norman Douglas *Grand Man*. L'élaboration de ce livre nécessita plusieurs séjours de N. Cunard à Capri, en compagnie de l'écrivain célèbre, qui devait mourir 5 ans plus tard dans l'île où repose maintenant son corps, et son oeuvre rayonnante.

Le printemps et l'automne de chaque année voyaient revenir Nancy dans la demeure lotoise qu'elle adorait. Ensemble nous allions rendre visite à Pierre Betz, directeur du Point, à Breton (St Cirq la Popie), à Jean Lurçat aux Tours St. Laurent—Vers nous venaient parfois les cousins: Victor et Edward Cunard, Arthur Johnson, Irène Rathbone, Randall Swingler, Kay Boyle, Jean Lurçat, rénovateur en France des splendides tapisseries d'Aubusson.

Mais c'est surtout de George Moore que N. Cunard parlait sans cesse.

Un jour les manuscrits et livres de Nancy ainsi que les illustrations de Hours Press furent déposés contre le mur extérieur, inondé de soleil de la maison, Nancy s'assit sur le gazon au milieu de ses livres; son visage émacié éclairé par le rayonnement bleu de ses yeux paraissait surnaturel, jamais écrasé par aucun reflet de ce monde, fusse-t-il celui de son éternelle robe rouge, sa couleur préférée. "It's a good color," disait elle.

Je pris de cet ensemble quelques photos. Malheureusement celles-ci furent brûlées par elle même avec beaucoup de ses derniers manuscrits à St. Jean Cap Ferrat en 1964 et la veille de sa mort à l'hôtel Continental (Paris). Excès d'intensité d'une vie humaine, qui ne pouvait se continuer dans un AILLEURS roi de l'Absolu—du Parfait.

Cependant son oeuvre doit rester vivante dans le sillage infini du souvenir de ses innombrables amis. Elle doit même ressortir des murs et de la nature de Peyrouro de Lamothe, cette ruche construite sur le berceau de Fénelon. Une ruche vibrante à jamais de pensées. Le département entier du Lot se souvient de cette marche en avant (nous arrivions à boucler des "little touring" de 15 à 20 km par jour), et partout Nancy laissait sur les "livres d'Or" l'empreinte de ses pas et de son âme. Cabrerets (Castrum capri), là les collections de masques et sculptures afro-américaines rapprochaient N.C. d'une histoire et préhistoire qui la passionnaient et complétaient parfois ses souvenirs sur l'art NEGRE. C'est à Pech-Merle, aux Eyzies, à Altamira que N. prenait des notes et faisait preuve de la plus grande érudition.

La résistance physique et morale de notre amie-écrivain, était inouie, jusqu'aux années 1959–1960. On pouvait à peine suivre le rythme de ses 6 à 8 heures de composition journalière à la machine à écrire, ou de ses interminables randonnées dans les Causses du Lot. Pélerinages aux villages tristement célèbres de Gramat, d'Oradour sur Glane, de St Julien. Ossuaires des grands massacres nazis. Elle en écrivait et envoyait des photos à Valentine Ackland. Parfois aussi elle s'arrêtait longuement dans les grottes, témoignant des arts pacifiques humains, et opposition à l'idée de guerre qui l'obsédait. Equidés de Lascaux, Bisons du Mas d'Azil ou d'Altamira, "Cervus megaceros" ou "Venus Steagine." Les vieilles pierres des châteaux de Rocamadour, du "Montal" de Jeanne de Balzac, du Castel Novel de Jouvenel, du château de Fénelon près de Salignac, lui servaient de but de recherches historiques. Mais cela lui paraissait insuffisant tant que nous n'avions pas franchi toutes les frontières latines de France, d'Italie, et d'Espagne. D'Andorre nous allâmes en Espagne basque, à Bilbao, à Santander où elle visitait les amis espagnols éprouvés leur distribuant argent et vivres.

Si Nancy ne fut pas déçue par la classe de quelques écrivains espagnols comme Roma ou Aparicio, par contre elle se heurta presque toujours à l'incompréhension humaine, celle-ci lui coûta en plus de sa fortune, sa santé.

Vers 1954 je retrouvai Nancy à Frascati, sur une indication de son adresse qui me fut fournie aimablement par Jean Guérin et son ami Walter à St. Jean Cap Ferrat. A Rome nous eûmes plusieures conversations littéraires avec l'aimable Arthuro Johnson. Nous allâmes avec lui voir l'artiste que N.C. admirait le plus sur le plan social et artistique: Chaplin (*Limelight,* Rome, 1954).

A Orvieto elle s'arrêta ensuite longuement devant les Signorelli "toujours éternels," un de ces pléonasmes qu'elle aimait. Entre temps elle aimait converser dans les "bistro" de Frascati, de Ciampino, de Grotte Ferrata avec ouvriers, cheminots ou jockeys. Je la vis un soir, écrivant d'une main sur une table de café, mais soutenant de son épaule gauche la tête d'un marchand de journaux qui s'était endormi près d'elle, harassé par la tâche de la journée.

Un ou deux voyages à Capri suivirent le voyage à Rome. C'était pour y retrouver Macpherson et Norman Douglas, le Sagittaire, "Sagittarius Grand Man" afin de terminer son livre sur lui.

"Les congrès du Pen Club?"

Nancy aimait à y assister. Et nous y allâmes plusieurs fois à Nice. En coïncidence avec quelques visites à l'exquis Denis Saurat, alors hâbitant à l'hôtel Victoria de Cimiez.

Vers 1955 séjours à Londres, que de batailles avec les éditeurs, à part deux éditeurs amis qui surent l'aider, ils furent cause de la destruction de la moitié de ses oeuvres par elle-même. Que de projets cependant pour enrichir cette oeuvre, je l'entendis s'exclamer "Je veux voir le Kenya et la Gold Coast et revenir aux Antilles. J'ai appris une chose en faisant mon Norman Douglas, c'est la discipline d'écrire. J'aime écrire pendant plusieurs heures. Mais pas pour arriver au résultat auquel j'arrive en France et en Angleterre! Non! De l'autre côté du monde on ne se plaindrait pas de mes productions . . . mais ici . . . ! Quelles difficultés!"

Noël 1958. N.C. passe ses soirées à Londres chez Schrijver ou Banting; elle devait ensuite ramener John Banting pour un séjour à Lamothe-Fénelon. De Londres elle m'écrivit qu'elle avait beaucoup aimé le film

West Side Story, mais peu les Hemingway. Par exemple *The Old Man and the Sea.* Elle habita alors chez Anthony Thorne l'écrivain, visita Cecily Mackworth (qui faisait alors partie des services de l'information à Paris) et le professeur Strachan. Elle n'oubliait pas ses amis américains dont le poète de couleur Langston Hughes.

C'est en septembre 1964 que nous fîmes notre dernier séjour à Lamothe-Fénelon. Nancy sentait bien alors qu'elle vivait ses derniers jours, ses dernières heures dans ce sanctuaire de sa pensée qu'elle nommait "mon joli Peyrouro." Elle enveloppait le portrait de George Moore, sa bibliothéque, sa petite chambre mansardée, le paysage entier de la vallée bleue sous noyers touchés d'or par l'automne, d'un immense regard tendre. Elle voulut même le dernier dimanche de mon séjour près d'elle, se séparer de sa gouvernante, Madame Simone Logeay, pour essayer de descendre une dernière fois dans la vallée. En pantoufles, la marche ralentie par l'asthme, accrochée à mon bras pour ne pas tomber, elle accomplit héroiquement cette promenade; me parlant à peine mais ramassant parfois à nos pieds une pierre dorée ou une de ces branches de noyer incrustée de mousse artistement décorée par la nature. Et puis ce fut un au revoir où je pus à peine maitriser mes larmes. Huit jours plus tard je recus une carte rédigée comme une supplication: "Passerai deux jours à Toulouse me rendant ensuite à St. Jean Cap Ferrat. Rends-toi absolument libre."

J'avais compris que notre habituel au revoir allait se changer en adieu. Quarante-huit heures encore pour absorber dans mon âme l'aspect physique (déjà fantomatique) et spirituel toujours prodigieux de cette créature qui résumait à elle seule l'histoire d'un demi siècle de philanthropie raciale, en même temps que les pionniers de nos Arts et Lettres universels.

Un dernier dîner fut fait à la "Frégate" de Wilson tout près de la chambre du Capoul où aboutissaient régulièrement ses lettres à ses chers amis Thérèse et Hugh Ford. Ils étaient devenus ses plus chers correspondants, surtout après leur séjour à Lamothe-Fénelon.

Nancy partit en octobre 1964 pour son avant dernier voyage. Elle alla, accompagnée de Simone Legeay retrouver Jean Guérin au Cap Ferrat. Sa correspondance d'abord enthousiaste se changea bientôt en déchant. Il y eut plusieurs chutes sur le pavé de Pomone. Déterminées autant par un état de cachexie que par la "consolation" à base de rhum. L'une de ces chutes détermina une fracture du col du fémur, suivie d'une douloureuse opération.

Et cependant jusqu'à son départ pour Paris (12 ou 13 jours avant sa mort) Nancy écrivit ses poèmes aux troubadours (nous tous), ses séquences à Marco Polo, ses poèmes au sujet des chiens "Shih-Tzus" dont 4 ou 5 naquirent entre ses mains, toujours largement ouvertes—

jusqu'au bout—à l'accueil de la vie. Elle aima "toute" la vie, mais particulièrement celle des plus pauvres, des plus humbles "vivants."

En février 1965, Nancy Cunard décida de partir pour Londres, accompagnée de Paris à Londres par la journaliste Janet Flanner. Ce voyage fut le pire de ses calvaires humains.

Il devait aboutir d'abord à Orgeval, chez une excellente amie l'écrivain américain Solita Solano. Celle-ci secourut non plus Nancy Cunard, mais son fantôme halluciné; avec un grand courage elle réussit à la mettre entre les mains de ses docteurs à l'hôtel Continental. Mais là son destin mortel devait s'accomplir. Relevée agonisante sur le trottoir devant l'hôtel, Nancy devait être transportée à l'hôpital Cochin. Elle y mourut quarante huit heures plus tard.

J. G. Barney, conseil britannique de Sa Majesté la Reine d'Angleterre m'apprit que ses cendres reposaient dans l'urne N. 9016 dans la crypte du Columbarium de Père Lachaise à Paris.

Ceci écrit en toute vérité passera comme toute parole humaine.

Mais tant que tournera la terre, l'oeuvre humaine et poétique de Nancy Cunard ne passera point.

allanah harper

A Few Memories of Nancy Cunard

Nancy Cunard was a fiery and furious angel, like the angel in Mathias
Grunewald's triptique or the angel in Rainer Maria Rilke's *Elegies*—a
terrible messenger descending with fiery sword upon bourgeois hypocrisy and those ignorant persons who discriminated between race or
colour of skins. If as Dante wrote, "Heaven and Hell reject the luke-
warm," Nancy will certainly come into her own.

Nancy personified the rebel. She revolted against the luxury of her
mother's house, the arrogance of the rich, the vulgarity of the fashionable, with "their brain of feather and a heart of lead." She rebelled
against their snobbery and false values, their complacency towards the
suffering of minorities, their false morality which did not come from
within but was imposed from without and not acted upon. Nancy
will be remembered as a valiant fighter for the equality and rights of
coloured people and for her admirable anthology, *Negro*. Her violence
sometimes did more harm than good, because she lived her beliefs
and exemplified them in her own life. She was not a theorist. But
extreme behavior, though not always agreeable, does call attention to
abuses and exploitation. She reacted to her conscience with passion.
She did not just sit back and wait; or sit back and watch, as most
people do. She was fearless and reckless, consuming herself with burning intensity. She would not have understood our contemporary use
of dialogue in order to better understand beliefs other than our own.
Nor would she have understood Krishna's, "Action is in inaction, inaction in action." No "middle way" for her; she was "entières," as
the French would say. Whatever she did, however violent she was,
Nancy always looked more distinguished than other people. She had
great beauty and elegance. Her enormous eyes resembled a tiger's. She
seemed to walk on air, she was so lightfooted; she moved with the
rhythmical swaying movement of a graceful bird.

Nancy had in some ways an innocent, an almost naive belief in the
causes she so strongly upheld. She seemed incapable of abstract reflection; or of separating political reality from her own emotional concep-
tions. I ventured once to point out that Stalinism was very different

from what her idealism imagined it to be. She gave me a withering look, as if to say poor creature—she has been listening to reactionary propaganda.

My first contact with Nancy Cunard was most unfortunate. I was at the time editing *Echanges,* a quarterly review of English and French writing. The first number appeared in 1930 when Norman Douglas was unknown in France. I wrote to him in Capri, asking for permission to translate something of his. He answered, saying that he had nothing new to give me at the moment but that I could use whatever I chose from his published works. I chose *One Day,* which Nancy had published in her admirable Hours Press, mainly because the edition has been limited to 150 copies and therefore was known only to a very small circle. I informed Nancy of my intention and asked her permission to publish a translation.

A few days later on returning to my hotel, I was told by the barman that a lady had asked to see me and had left a letter. He said that she had threatened to kill me and that she was in a most strange state. I opened the letter the contents of which were so upsetting that I felt shaken for the rest of the day. I have long lost the letter, but it was roughly this:

> If you dare to publish *One Day* by Norman Douglas, I shall have you summoned by the Authors' Society. If you say I know you or your publication, YOU ARE A LIAR! I have never heard of you or your magazine.

Three pages of invective followed. I told Norman Douglas of Nancy Cunard's refusal. He wrote back saying, "Go ahead." With this encouragement, I did. One Day appeared in *Echanges.* I never heard another word from Nancy, who had apparently got over her anger or had other things to think about.

Not long afterwards I recognised her in a restaurant, dining with her friend Louis Aragon, both superbly good-looking and completely engrossed in each other. I had seen her at parties in London when I was very young, but she did not know me. I thought that it was better under the circumstances not to reveal my identity; I did not want to have something hurled at me.

It was not until 1947 that I really met her. I was living in Normandy at the time; Nancy lived a few miles away near Vernon. A mutual friend brought her to my house. She was charming, gentle and had not the least recollection of the aggressive letter of nearly twenty years before. Nancy asked me to dinner the following week and we subsequently visited each other regularly. She was her best in her own house, entertaining young men who aspired to be poets, or anti-Fascist Spanish refugees, to whom she gave shelter. I remember one evening two Spaniards playing Flamenco music, for which I had a passion; I could not resist attempting to dance. Nancy did the same, but her lightness and temperament turned her into a Spaniard, while I remained horribly Anglo-Saxon. The sight of her gracefulness put an end to my floor stamping and I retired in shame. It was then that I realised what human warmth and delightful manners she had, and when she liked one she was overflattering and kind. One evening I gave her a copy of *Horizon,* in which I had written an article on the poet Léon Paul Fargue. Nancy called to the other people in the room. "Look," she said, "Allanah has written a lovely thing on Fargue. I am going to read it aloud." She read: (I quote only the first verse.)

Gare de la douleur, j'ai fait toutes tes routes.
Je ne peux plus aller, je ne peux plus partir.
J'ai traîné sous tes ciels, j'ai crié sous tes voûtes.

One can understand why Nancy loved this poem.

The last time I saw Nancy was in 1962. She blew into my house in the south of France, like an autumn leaf in a gust of wind, so light she seemed and fragile. She had become so emaciated that her skin was stretched over her bones. She asked me to lunch with her on the port in Cannes. She was very gentle, asking with rather sad humility, "Do you believe in God?" I said that I had always been attracted to religion, especially Vedanta, but that nevertheless I had a few years before been received into the Roman Catholic Church, in which I found the fulfillment of all religions. "You are a good woman," she said, looking at me with tenderness. "I wish I could believe in something."

That was the first time I had been called a good woman, and I hope the last, being so far from that estate. Her overestimation filled me with confusion and mortification. I quickly changed the conversation to contemporary poetry. Nevertheless, I had observed how resigned and lenient Nancy had become. In the past the very word Catholicism would have called forth vehemence. I do not wish to infer that she was no longer true to her vision, or had lost faith in her ideals, for that would be untrue, but age and suffering and disillusion over the results of her lifelong fight for equality and liberty had wearied her.

"Do you remember," she asked me, "dining with me at a hotel I was staying at near Vernon?" I recalled how she had transformed the small hotel bedroom into a "Nancy room," mainly by the display of her magnificent collection of huge ivory African bracelets. A painting or two she loved and African designs on skins hung on the walls; coloured scarves and a few books of poetry lay about. She needed nothing more, apart from the usual young man, usually a potential poet, occupying the only comfortable chair.

"Is that all you remember?" she asked.

I then recalled two men who sat at a table in the corner of an otherwise empty dining room. There was something odd about them. They kept straining to hear what we were saying.

"Well," she said, "the hotel proprietor told me later that they were detectives who followed me everywhere I went. They believed I was a Communist agent. They could not differentiate between a left-wing anti-Fascist, which most decent people are, and an active Communist agent. Thugs!"

Soon after, Nancy left for her house in the Dordogne. I never saw her again. To the last she was true to her vision. When I think of the manner of her death, I am reminded of Dylan Thomas' great poem,

> Do not go gently into that good night,
> Old age should rave and burn at close of day;
> Rage, rage against the dying of light.

As we know, although gravely ill, she escaped from the confining walls of the hospital, free to live or die as she wished. She fulfilled to a strange degree the meaning of Rainer Maria Rilke's poem,

> O Lord, give everyone his own death, the dying which comes out of that living in which he had love, sense and need.

These lines by Réne Char could serve as her epitaph:

> Ce qui vient au monde pour ne rien troubler ne mérite ni égards ni patience.

kenneth macpherson

Ne Mai

Nancy Cunard appeared for the first time in my life in 1928. After that, because we both tended to rush about in pursuit of interests and causes, she turned up or, rather, flashed from time to time in my rather stormy skies like summer lightning which omits the bellow of thunder. I met her that time by appointment at the old Café Royal in London one winter evening and, of course, since I love dragonflies, I loved her at sight.

She looked exactly as I had seen her look in photographs, with her mother's eyes, shaped like arrowheads, but more searching, more elated, perhaps more tragic, but no less humorous, and her kiss-curls under her toque were as ever pinned round carefully. I always used to wonder why she used hairpins in these adornments instead of setting them and spraying them, since that was the way she wanted them to look and the hairpins were a bit of a clutter.

First and instant impression: exciting, dotty tigress-dragonfly. No: cheetah. And, of course, woman of passionate opinions. Then, seated, one *heard* her.

They talked of Sarah Bernhardt's voice, and as an infant I heard it, cracked to be sure, and she had one leg, and was, to my innocent mind at least—instructed by mum—a miracle. I could believe this because I quaked with excitement. Nancy's voice was then and remained, a miracle. And so was the way she walked. Often she looked terrible in thrift shop finery of a decade gone, but the inbred chic, even when most clownish, was an accomplishment, and she flowed swiftly forward, as I have said like a cheetah, and also rather like a slim splendid fish.

I must get her to Venice now for a moment, when, at a luncheon party which I will describe, she sat beside me and told me that she had been walking over the Rialto Bridge, and that some boys had called out: "Bella Americana, ciao!" "Non é un'Americana." "Come *no* un'Americana? Nient'altra." Enraged, not by the insolence and loutish usual ridicule, she had shouted, passing swiftly: "Ne mai!" She then asked me: "Can you say ne mai?" I remember saying it was more usual to say *giammai,* but she said they cottoned-on anyway and shut up.

As she told me the story, repeating *giammai!,* she flourished her hand in the air (clutching her handbag) and caused our hostess, Miss Peggy Guggenheim, to twitch nervously and shake her earrings which looked like metal garden gates. I think Alexander Calder had designed them, or perhaps it was that a big mobile by him was fussing and fidgeting in the draft over our heads.

I then asked her why she had shouted ne mai, and she said, repeating (again waving the arm) *giammai!* that it was because Italians thought Americans more awful than wonderful, though their admiration was clotted, hot and randy; coveting first the mighty dollar and then perhaps a less cramped way of life. Had I not noticed, in Rome especially, how the young imitated them and had switched from Campari bitters to Whisky-a-Gogo? I suggested that she herself, being part American, had been perhaps a bit edgy. Nothing of the sort, she said. What she minded—anywhere and always—was applauded imbecility. One fool would jeer, and the other louts find in him the mouthpiece of their own idiocy and love him. Such parades of doltishness were the easy way out.

She said: "Sometimes I think they have determined not to learn: the *fatal* revolution! Perhaps they were demoralised by the horrors of the resistance?"

I said I thought that that should have made men of them, and at once she said:

"It made men of the Spanish."

Did she not think much of Italian men?

She did, emphatically and often, and had to concede that among them was a shabby sleaziness hard to duplicate elsewhere. They could be as heroic as they could be abysmal cowards; but cowardice mattered little if at all, except that the coward was the show off, the caffone. I think the Rialto Bridge rudeness had shaken her.

At this luncheon party, besides Miss Guggenheim who gave it, were Mary Reynolds now dead, herself a distinguished woman whose great friend was Marcel Duchamp, and I suppose, as well, all the great painters of the day: Picasso, Braque, Ernst, Tanguy, Cocteau (not *quite* looked up to), cher-maître Breton, and so on. And there was Miss Guggenheim's ill-fated daughter, Pegeen, with long primrose-pale hair like Alice in Wonderland. And there were two other gentlemen who need not be mentioned, except the one of them who proudly displayed a tortoiseshell cigarette case he had bought that morning.

"Is it real?" asked Mary Reynolds, who knew her Venice.

"Of course," he said with dignity. "Imitation tortoiseshell breaks. Real tortoiseshell doesn't. Besides, I paid the earth for it!"

"Doesn't break?" said Mary Reynolds. "You're sure?"

"Absolutely."

"Interesting. May I see it?"

She handled it.

"It looks very real," she agreed, and flung it across the marble floor on which it exploded in a thousand fragments.

"O, it wasn't," she said as the proud look of a man who has just been able to explain Linear B slowly was replaced by incredulity.

Nancy, whose eyes could fire with as wicked a mirth as you are likely to come across, now took fire but she said: "You must have it swept up bit by bit and take it back and show it to them and make them give you a real one."

"I'm sorry it wasn't real," said Mary Reynolds and Miss Guggenheim was laughing her head off. Pegeen was looking pensive and far away.

At that time the gondolieri were on strike in protest against the competition and harm of motor craft.

It was at this awkward moment that Nancy's expression of contained mirth changed to one of concentration, and she was no longer paying attention to my patter which I had turned on to help redeem the moment.

Leaning forward, so that I could see her only in profile, she barked: "Ma *bisogno* darli qual'cosa! *Bisogno!*"

I looked up and saw that a man had approached from the garden behind and was addressing himself in a muffled voice to Miss Guggenheim.

"Certainly not," said Miss Guggenheim, being firm. "How dare he enter a private property without permission?"

Nancy reminded me later: "We were the only two who gave anything."

The man was collecting for the cause of the gondolieri; a worthy one.

I hope we did not offend our hostess.

Another generous impulse I remember hearing of from a friend, while Nancy was in Rome where I was then living. She was being driven by this friend, a lady, on a hot day up to the restaurant on top of Monte Cavo, south of Rome, where you paid a toll to use the private road. At the toll gate there were half-stripped labourers sweating under the solleone, the August sun. To their slightly startled pleasure, Nancy leaned across her hostess, offering cigarettes, thrusting across the wheel a packet of Gauloises, saying in Spanish: "Amigos! Cigarillos!"

It was at the house of this same friend whose husband, a scholarly British Francophile who nevertheless lived in Rome (his wife was Italian) was beginning to have lapses not so much of memory (he would go on and on quoting Apollonaire) as of reason and sat mumbling crossly at luncheon; Nancy was on his right. When he came out with a disastrous rudeness directed at his wife, it was Nancy who, with immeasurable elegance and instinct, thrust the ghastly moment, as it were, out of the room. And it was dismissed, light as a feather. The story is not for telling. Nancy's staggering tact is what mattered. Never have I seen social catastrophe demolished by so light a touch, and in that hauntingly beautiful voice; the triangular eyes, compassionate and smiling, restored order to a shattered equilibrium.

She was far less tactful when she brought out her foolish book called *Black Man and White Ladyship,* a diatribe against her mother which did no good to the black man, much harm to Nancy, at least financially, for she was more or less cut off, and failed less to insult her mother than expose in herself a vindictiveness which, if it had to rise to the surface, should have been shouted in a boudoir and not set up in print.

As I have written, both she and I were championing various causes. One of hers, as we know, was the Negro. She would have enjoyed the present resurgence of independent determination. I, myself, lived for an exciting year with coloured friends in Harlem and all of them loved Nancy and all deplored her. "Nancy's back. We're in trouble!" They said, in effect, that brandishing fists at possible unoffenders tended more to startle or annoy than make converts. When she was refused a visa to the United States, I got furious telegrams from the West Indies which I answered with sympathy, but, unlike de Gaulle who was an important guest, an unimportant Scot with a visitor's visa couldn't very well storm the White House or bang shoes on a table in the United Nations Assembly.

At one of the public dances she organised in London to raise funds for some Negro welfare committee, she stood up to address the floor. "I take it," she said, "that we are all friends of the Negro." And a churlish bass voice with more resonance than Nancy's microphone was heard to say: "Negroes don't need no friends." I think it was more an instinct of self-protection than of aggression, like my American Negro friends who said: "Hold onto your hats, kids, Nancy's back!"

After the war she came to Capri.

As her friends know, she loved Norman Douglas, my great friend, perhaps almost as much as she had loved George Moore. Up at our villa we saw a lot of her.

These times, and later in Rome, were the last of our times together. I have always wished that she or I had been more accessible to each other's company, but dragonflies and cheetahs don't stay still. When we did meet it was always exciting, often exhilarating, but these times were crumbs instead of the whole loaf.

I cannot give dates. Although I keep a diary, up to a point, I keep it in idleness and months are blank except to name places visited. It hardly matters.

In her kind book about Douglas, she has written generously of her good times at the Villa Tuoro. What she omitted to say was that she herself was responsible for so much of the laughter and joy we all then shared.

I must wind up this brief note, not with anecdotes which could go on and on, but with an appraisal—my own—of an extraordinary and marvellous friend, not in relation to myself, except insofar as any perception has to be one's own, but in relation, as a passionate humanist, to her life and times and the terrible historical panorama across which she and her friends and foes had to move; she more than many of us because she cared more than most of us. It is wonderful, and rare, to be able to say of someone, that no ignobility, no shirking, no evasion, ever entered their thought or action. Nancy was the prow which takes the storm and cuts through its boil and impact and will not heave-to but, if necessary, break.

She was a hothead, she was detraquée, she was utterly pure, and drove that energetic, skinny body and lean impassioned mind and infinite kindness and compassion to the limit of her strength.

At last, of course, the prow had to come to grief. But we, whom she had to leave, are the ones to grieve, and to remember with gratitude a splendid, dotty genius who hated compromise. Ne mai!

Appendix

nancy cunard

A Few Notes on Roy Campbell

I believe I met Roy Campbell when he first came to London in 1918, or it may have been early in 1917. It was with T. W. Earp, the poet who had talked so much of "the Zulu," a strange, young, new figure who had recently appeared: about him Earp managed to set a certain amount of mystery, possibly because he was so very much impressed by him. To Earp he was clearly a prodigy. I puzzled over the term, "zulu": a swarthy South African perhaps? Why I did not ask Earp to which race he belonged I cannot imagine and rather expected to see a South African Negro.

We met in the Brasserie of the Café Royal (alas, gone now). A tall, adolescent, strong, loose limbed youth with dark hair and red cheeks sat next to Earp; now and again his eyes would flash, he was vivacious yet seemed a little shy, or reserved, and contrasted much in appearance with the fair haired, precise, high voiced English poet. Earp radiated admiration for Roy's poetry; we should see, oh indeed yes, we should see that this was going to turn into someone to be reasoned with. His predictions were frequently voiced, Roy had, obviously, been a rich "find." I never knew Campbell at all well and it must have been generally in company with several others that I saw him, perhaps most often in what was loosely known as "The Room" at one of Montague Shearman's intimate little parties of six or seven where various intellectuals sat enjoying his generous drinks, gazing at a beautiful Matisse, the first that the barrister had brought back from Paris and which, to some people, was controversial. That dates it: 1919–1920. By then Roy Campbell knew many people in London and if he had been looked upon at first as rather a *rare avis* or something of a rough diamond, he was by now quite at home in England. Our main contact was years later, in 1930, when I published some excellently written verses of his in a volume merely called "Poems" at my Hours Press in Paris. The slim, tall volume in the same format as that chosen for the poems of Robert Graves, Harold Acton, Walter Lowenfels and others was hand set and the edition of 200 signed copies printed on very good Vidalon paper, bound in vermillion paper boards with red leather, gold lettered spine, with the two drawings by the author on its covers. It was over-subscribed before publication and had some fine reviews—which unfortunately have disappeared during World War II. I forgot the exact figure but it was between £70 and £80 that I was able to send the poet as royalties. How agreeable to think that, for once, poems had paid their author, and very well, indeed, for not more than 24 pages.

But of course we had some kind of contact beforehand so as to talk of publication. Yes, it was the summer of the previous year that we met in the South of France, while he was living in Matigues, and it seems to me it was there. Travelling with me at that moment was Henry Crowder, an Afro-American pianist whose six songs were then written for me to publish. Knowing more then than in 1918 about the general reaction of many South Africans towards people of colour, I certainly wondered how the meeting would go. It was excellent, and a beautiful, friendly welcome was that of Campbell to both of us. I do believe that snapshot of him (so indistinct) water-jousting must have been given me then. Or perhaps we met in Site—I know I have seen this fantastic tourney only once and it was the waters of that port. But I simply dare not affirm that Roy Campbell participated on that occasion. To do so would be one more example of the wishful thinking that connects and identifies what *may* have been two separate things! I *think* I saw him joust: more I cannot and will not say. It is a very skilful yet rough and at moments violent spectacle, the aim of the jouster standing upright with his pole at the end of the narrow boat being to push the jouster on the other boat into the water. The pole is used as would be a lance, while these long boats that have to be very precisely rowed by some six men or so approach each other, come abreast, pass (the tilting being achieved or missed), veer round and return to the attack. How unfortunate that I cannot recall if he was one of the jousters that day. He certainly talked of it interestingly. Everything went very smoothly during the printing of his poems, which was not always the case with all my authors, and he was easy and agreeable to deal with. I had several letters from him, I know, in that small, sloping, rather pinpoint writing of his; alas, they too, as all letters written to me by literary friends, save a very few, disappeared during the war, in my house in Normandy. I imagine Roy's mss. also have gone to light some pilfering French peasant's fire. I did not see him for years after that, nor, for a long time, know where he was living.

My surprise was very great indeed, when as a journalist in Madrid at the start of the Spanish War, in October, 1936, Spanish and Latin American friends one day indignantly exclaimed to me, that Campbell was actually with the Franco armies then approaching Toledo. They were intensely shocked that a poet should feel like taking side of the Fascists. While assuring them that some writers, indeed, had, such as Ezra Pound—my own astonishment and disappointment at him continued. The next meeting was a chance one, in London, in September or October 1941, as Robert Nichols and I, who had been dining, prepared to plunge into the blackout of Charlotte Street. Suddenly in the doorway stood Roy Campbell and it was so long since we had met that I did not at first recognise him, while Nichols hissed into my ear that it was he, "the horrid pro-Fascist." As we talked away without stopping, a roar arose in the dark, from Campbell, "I'm not, I'm not a Fascist, Nancy! I am a Requite." What is the difference! The Requites, the Foreign Legion, the Moors, the Germans, and the Italians were all with the Fascists, to the same degree, during the Spanish War. And yet, after this, Campbell and I did meet again, and that was the last time of all I saw him, we had a long talk. It was in Oxford, about the time that Paris was being liberated, in August 1944. Neither of us mentioned anything to do with Spain. It would have led too far and might have ended in great anger after much very bitter argument. That afternoon it was of the Negroes he talked, and very sympathetically. I had not realised that he felt such friendliness towards them and seem to remember that he had some kind of military job with them earlier during the war.

Early in 1950 a long article by me on Spanish writers in exile came out in London and I was soon, and frequently, being told "Roy Campbell is very angry with you on account of it!" I will say this gave me more than anything else an idea of what he had become (or of what he had ever been?). It seemed so ludicrous, so infantile, to take unto himself, i.e., to resent my statements of fact, along with appreciations of the literary merits of these poets and writers. He could have answered them on writing, I thought. But hardly been able to make a polemic, for the fact remained clear that practically all the best brains of Spain had left rather than submit to the various forms of suffocation and censorship and animosity that came in along with Franco's rule. About this time too, he was going to make what sounded like a hard physical attack on Stephen Spender, who had been an eminent pro-Republican during the war in Spain. "Swashbuckling rambunctiousness" some called it; and others "a great lack of dignity." I am unable to say if anything actually happened between the two.

"Masculinity" is certainly one attribute that Roy Campbell could have claimed. It is, in fact, the first adjective that comes to my mind to apply to him. This "he man" stuff grew upon him, I thought. Although I do not remember seeing him actually aggressive, he had the reputation of being at times quarrelsome and overbearing and full of threats. The row with Spender has been called "the permanent row." Another went on with Hugh MacDiarmid. John Gawsworth took his defence, and no doubt his real friends found him warmhearted as well as sometimes hasty. I do remember with enthusiasm the way he talked of the African Negroes that day in Oxford while the tact of both of us, in such utterly opposite camps, was equal in not referring at all to our partisanry in what had been a very serious thing in Spain. I liked and admired his drive, his vitality and energy and, indeed, many of the beautiful lines and images in his early poetry. All more the detestable therefore seemed his allegiance to Franco. He really was one of the very few poets and writers of Great Britain to take such a line; and (I think he can be said to belong to England as well as to South Africa). Having issued a questionnaire to poets and authors in England in 1937 on the score of the Spanish War and Fascism in general, I could assess the general feeling. Pro-Republicans were greatly preponderant among the 147 replies that were printed. The score of "neutrals" and the five or six pro-Franco answers were also published in "Authors Take Sides." I wish I could have sent this question to Campbell, but, as he was in Spain with the Nationalist forces, it would not have reached him, nor did I know where to send it. The phrasing of his answer might have been interesting and I should have published it with the rest, of course. Or maybe he would not have replied.

How can it have come about that he was on the side of Franco? The reason lightly tossed at me, as it were, by Nina Hamnett, the painter, who knew him, I think, very well, was "Catholicism!" That's where it has led him! which left me rather surprised. Others in England who had no particular feeling about the Spanish War supposed that what attracted him was "all the action and excitement." But why on that side, I wondered. Had he radically changed, or had he always been ready for this? He had been living in Spain for some years, had he not, by 1936? He knew Spanish very well; he must have imbibed and absorbed many things of the country and ways of feeling and thinking of those he had lived most among—and they would hardly be Spanish grandees, business-men or officers, supporters of Franco. I always thought of Roy Campbell as a democratic person: he was not surely a "class snob," but at ease with working people, a good mixer too.

Change or no in himself there was a great change in his poetry. I say this thinking of his "Flowering Rifle"—how different to, say, "Flaming Terrapin." It contains a very high percentage of tirades and diatribes against jews and marxists and there is precious little about Spain itself or the events of the war. The poet Lorca is seen, or purported to be seen, as a sort of poor, deluded creature who should not have been on the side he was on and got shot for it. This is really horrible, and is a falsification of Lorca. I will say that "Flowering Rifle" seems to me a tub-thumping lengthy piece of boredom. No matter how unsympathetic, it might perhaps have been revealing and interesting had it contained merely a few facts.

All of us who were very deeply affected by the Spanish War and its issue were further amazed, a little later, that it should be Campbell who translated so much of Lorca's poetry, the ally of those who shot the Spanish poet. It is to me incomprehensible that he could manage to accord these two directly opposite things. Speaking from the purely literary point of view, as far as I can judge from being able to compare only a few of his translations with the Castilian originals, they are quite true to the text, keep to the meaning, read very smoothly and—no mean thing—are English poems in their own right. But that does not alter the fact that Lorca was the victim of Fascism, on account of his friendship (perhaps most) with so many of the poets and other intellectuals active on the Republican side. He was shot, without accusation, trial or condemnation, by those, as he showed, that Campbell himself held in admiration. As you perceive, to me Roy Campbell is a queer figure and you note that because of his attitude during the Spanish War I cannot do else than feel against him and deeply so. I do, however, retain my admiration for his vigorous nature and for the beautiful lines and images in much of his early poetry.

(Miss Cunard's remarks on Roy Campbell were written in 1958 in reply to an inquiry from a South African professor.)

nancy cunard

Letter to Ezra Pound

Gourdon, France
June 11, 1946

Ezra Pound
St. Elizabeth's Hospital
Washington, D.C.

Ezra,

I have been wanting to write you this for some time—for some years—but I could not do so because you were with the enemy in Rome. You were the enemy. I will write it today from Gourdon, a place you know. You will have received the note I sent you from Rimont, near St. Girons: this letter is the one it announced.

Your address was sent me by a person in England who had a letter from Bill Williams in which he said you wanted to communicate with me. Williams has called you "misguided." I do not agree. The correct word for a Fascist is "scoundrel." I am aware of the symposium of six American writers who have tried to white wash you, in which the word "misguided" was applied. I cannot see what possible defense, excuse or mitigation exists for you—in the name of "old friendship." As with W. C. Williams—though it be. Nor do I believe anything concerning the "advanced stage of schyzophrenia "madness" etc. that was used as means to secure your non-execution. I do not believe you are insane or half-crazy. I think you are in perfect possession of your full facilities, as before. I may be wrong. The symposium was mentioned in a French review, with comment, and evoked due contempt for the writers.

Having heard you on the air speaking from Rome, there might be some excuse for calling your talk that of a man insane. It was idiotic, the more so in view of facts that you already belonged to history. But then, by that count, Goering, Goebbels, Hitler, Streicher, the whole gang of criminals, were just "merely" insane. Fascism uses the same hatreds and the same lies the world over. Fascism is not insanity, unless evil itself, all evil, be insanity (a point that can certainly be argued psychologically and philosophically, *in the abstract*. War is not abstract.

I will quote some of your words: "What I mean to say is . . . the greater the ignorance of a people the easier it is to lead them to the slaughter—like the Russians." This was said by you in April 1943, when it was damn-clear to the nazis even that the Russians were neither "ignorant" nor being led to any slaughter at a time when Stalingrad had ended some two or three months previously, as a very great victory for the Russians, a very great defeat for the Germans. Stalingrad, one of the great decisive moments of the war. I also monitored a talk of yours when I worked with the Free French and it was evident you were hard-pressed to say anything at all. You praised the opportunities people had in Fascist Italy as opposed to the snobbery of England. An expert on Italian life under Fascism will be qualified to say how true or not this is. What I personally know is that one million or more Italian workers, some good number of intellectuals included, got out of Italy so as to live without repression in France. And now I have come to the word "intellectual." It is inconceivable to me that an "intellectual" should collaborate with Fascism. Every single thing you reviled and blasted in your first Cantos was happening in Italy in a modern form around you—corruption, oppression, murder, plus the added vulgarity of Fascism—the tub-thumping, empty, ostentacious, vainglorious, fifth rate demagogy that I should have thought you, as an artist, would have loathed more than anything.

Now on a personal plane this:

The last communication from you was your answer I duly printed in my *Authors Take Sides* to the question addressed by me in 1937 to writers on the issue of Spain, France and Fascism. Your words were something to the effect that Spain was "an escape mechanism." With a stab at the Bank of England. The fact that Hitler and Mussolini were making their start of World War II in Spain and that all the best things of Spain were being massacred, meant nothing to you. I have participated myself in these events and shall again participate, in whatever form the liberation of Spain has to come. It is no "escape mechanism" for me.

The last communication before that was a note from you which came on Christmas Day, 1935, during the Abyssinian war, telling me that you hoped I realised that the Ethiopians were "black Jews." To begin with, ethnographically, I think this is false. And secondly I do not see the point, even if they were "black Jews." Incidentally, for several years, I thought you were Jewish yourself, Ezra. What could it have mattered, one way or the other?

You are not the only intellectual who has chosen Fascism, who has lied about clear, straight and self-evident issues. But you *are* one of the rare few poets of any merit to have done so. I maintain, and have maintained in argument with those who never appreciated your poetry, or with those who want to "cheat" now because of your Fascism, that you were a very fine poet indeed, unique, I think, in contemporary English. *I mean, up to the time* of the XXX Cantos. Collaboration with Fascism will not efface *that fact accompli.* Nor will that *fact accompli* excuse your collaborating. I cannot understand how the integrity that was so much you in your writing can have chosen the enemy of all integrity.

And now I want to record the things I personally place on the good side, the good things I have to remember of you: In 1915, when I first knew you rather vaguely at that time, you were an intellectual—revolutionary. With your then fine critical sense and "feel," with your generosity and kindliness, you took up the defense of the young, the unrecognized. In 1921 you helped me greatly with your criticism of poetry (of my poetry then too); you threw light for me on thinking straight, on composition, on eschewing the tautological, etc. Your Gaudier Brzeska book, which contains much constructive criticism of art and writing, as I remember it, is very fine. (And that the really good work of art should be "as hard as the side of an engine"—what better definition could there be?)

It is you I have to thank for a very great deal, of my early love of France. For it was you who told me (with that love, yourself, and knowledge) of the Quercy and Languedocian regions, and who told me where to go—to Gourdon included, where I am today, and where the friends of your friends shot 23 people two years ago because the invasion had occurred and because of the French patriots. As an American maybe you did have a little prejudice against Negroes (despite the sophistication that should attend all good contemporary American intellectuals on that score). If so, all the nicer your charming and appreciative ways with Henry. My Henry of colour. Do you remember how often we were together? Henry loved you—so did I, always, then, and before then up to the last time I saw you in 1928. I know, I knew only years later, by chance, that you remonstrated pretty sharply after I had been disinherited because of Henry. That was fine of you, Ezra.

And now I will tell you this of my life today. Réanville, my house, is in ruins, thanks to the Germans who lived in it and to their friends, the French Fascists. Among all the smashed windows there was one that held the wind still, for the reason that in lieu of glass someone had torn the pages out of Rodker's vellum edition of your

Cantos and had crucified the cover against the window-frame. That is what I found of you in my house on return. The allies of your friends threw many books down the well, burned, destroyed all of the African things you used to admire. Nothing is left but some fragments to prove there was once something. Perhaps you will be glad to hear that the Fascist mayor of that village (Fascist already before 1936) who is the direct cause of the ruin because it was he who sent the Germans to my house, is still mayor, despite every proof against him.

If you are glad, you will be gladder yet to learn that, up till now, not all Fascists have been punished in France and that they continue to do their best to prevent this country from recovering its normal life. They will not succeed to the limit of their hopes, because there are people determined enough to prevent that.

I think that is the gist of all I have to say to you, Ezra. I should merely repeat myself if I expanded it. Besides, you probably know all this already. The concept of "misguidedness" does not exist for me on your score.

Nancy

Reply from E.P. 1 Aug. 1946
Motto at top of stationery: "J'ayme Donc Je Suis"

My dear N.

What the blue beggaring hell are you talking about. I had freedom of microphone to say what I liked—namely the truth that your shitten friends were afraid to hear. Your "friend" who busted the Tempio @ Rimini, etc. etc.

Sur me on both side, but truth suppressed for 40 and for 200 years.

Bill W. an ass who won't face historic fact. Wish I had Henry's address.

notes on contributors

Acton, Harold (b. 1904), born in Florence (where he now lives) and educated at Eton and Oxford, lived in Peking from 1932–1939, studying Chinese drama and occasionally lecturing at the National University of Peking. The author of several volumes on modern Chinese poetry and plays, he has turned in recent years to Florentine and Neapolitan history and Italian art history. In 1956, he published *The Bourbons of Naples* and five years later *The Last Bourbons of Naples.* His lively autobiographical book, *Memoirs of an Aesthete,* appeared in 1948, and he is now at work on a second volume of memoirs.

Aragon, Louis (b. 1897), poet, journalist and novelist, after a brief period of service in World War I and an association with the Dadaists, became one of the founders of Surrealism. Breaking with other Surrealists in the early thirties, he became a leader in the Socialistic Realism Movement and began his journalistic career, serving on the staff of *L'Humanité* and *Ce Soir.* In 1936, he won the Prix Renaudot. Shortly before World War II he began a series of novels about Europe before and after 1914 under the general title, *The Real World.* He joined the Resistance Movement during the war, edited a clandestine paper, *Les Etoiles,* and composed poems for the Maquis. Six volumes of his poetry appeared during the war years. In the 1950s he was editor of *Les Lettres Françaises.* According to Janet Flanner, Aragon is recognized as "French Communism's undisputed intellectual, literary, and artistic leader."

Arlen, Michael (1895–1956) became a naturalized British subject in 1922, eight years after the publication of his first novel. It was *The Green Hat* (1924) that made him a celebrity and a wealthy man. Though he produced a book nearly every year following his success, his popularity gradually waned. During World War II he spent two idle years in Hollywood.

Balayé, Géraldine was formerly a professor of art history at the National Conservatory in Toulouse, her home, and for many years she conducted a literary forum on a Toulouse radio station. A frequent companion of Miss Cunard in the 1940s and 1950s, she assisted in making translations for *Poems for France* and other volumes. A poet herself, Mme. Balayé has completed a book dedicated to her friend called *Poèmes à Nancy.*

Banting, John (b. 1902) was born into the "center" middle class in Chelsea. One of the first London Surrealists, he began to paint in the early 'teens but had to work as a bank clerk, a "naked" life-class model, and a porter in town hall. Having failed medically for service in World War II, he made official films and worked as an air raid warden. A member of the British Communist Party for one year (1940), he is now non-political. Whenever possible he prefers to live in southern France.

Benkovitz, Miriam (b. 1911), professor of English at Skidmore College, was born in Chattanooga, Tennessee, and educated at Vanderbilt and Yale. In 1963, her *Bibliography of Ronald Firbank* appeared as one of the Soho Bibliographies. A regular contributor to professional journals, she is now at work (simultaneously) on a biography of Ronald Firbank and an edition of a group of letters from Richard Aldington.

Boyle, Kay (b. 1903) left America in 1921 to live abroad, mainly in France, and before returning to the United States twenty years later she had gained a wide reputation as a novelist and short story writer. In 1946, she went back to Europe as a *New Yorker* correspondent. Now on the faculty of San Francisco State College, she continues to write, her last novel being *Generation Without Farewell*. Miss Boyle has also begun editing letters and books by writers she knew while living in Europe, one of which is Robert McAlmon's *Being Geniuses Together*.

Burkhart, Charles is professor of English at Temple University, Philadelphia. He is the author of books on Ivy Compton-Burnett and Ada Leverson and has written extensively on modern British literature.

Carril, Delia del, affectionately called Tia Hormiga by her many friends in Santiago, Chile, her home, was married for many years to Pablo Neruda. Recently her paintings have attracted wide attention in Europe and South America.

Délano, Luis Enrique, the Chilean journalist, historian and novelist, has written on the social and political life of his country and Latin America. His novels include *La Base, El Viento del Rencor,* and *El Rumor de la Batalla.*

Duff, Charles (1894–1967), Irish journalist, translator, essayist, created a sensation with his satire on capital punishment, *A Handbook on Hanging.* During the Spanish Civil War he edited two pro-Loyalist newspapers and following the conflict undertook the publication of *Spanish News Letter,* which lasted until 1948. Translating *The Gypsies* by Jean Clébert in 1963 inspired him to write his own book on the subject called *A Mysterious People.* His last work, *Six Days to Shake an Empire,* an account of the Irish Rebellion of 1916, reflects his long and deep interest in Ireland and its people. "They are a lot, those Irish," he once commented, "including myself."

Flanner, Janet (b. 1892) has lived in Europe (except during World War II) since 1921, mostly in Paris. Her first "Letter from Paris" appeared in *The New Yorker* on October 10, 1925, the year the magazine started. Miss Flanner published a novel, *The Cubical City,* in 1926; a collection of articles called *American in Paris; Petain: The Old Man of France;* and *Men and Monuments.* She has translated two books by Colette. An indefatigable traveler and writer, she has been decorated with the Legion of Honor, and is a member of the National Institute of Arts and Letters. In 1966, she won the National Book Award for non-fiction writing. *Paris Journal* is her latest publication.

Garnett, David (b. 1892), a member of the well-known literary family, opened a book shop (with Francis Birrell) in Soho after World War I. At the same time his first two novels, *Lady into Fox* and *A Man in the Zoo,* became popular successes. In 1923, he joined Francis Meynell's Nonesuch Press as literary advisor, and for years he was book critic for *The New Statesman.* His novels, urbane and imaginative, number over a dozen. Recently he has been writing a series of autobiographical books.

Gellert, Lawrence, a Rockefeller grant recipient, has helped widen the field for better study of the "grass roots" of American literature. He has published three volumes based on original research, numerous critical articles and is represented in major native folklore anthologies. Perhaps his best known book is *Negro Songs of Protest,* which he collected in the late twenties. He lives in New York.

Gilbert, Morris has been a member of the working press all his life, starting modestly in Yonkers and moving on to the *New York Tribune, Herald Tribune, New York World Telegram* and *New York Times* in various hitches. George Jean Nathan and H. L. Mencken made him their successor as editor of *The Smart Set* until they sold it ten months later. He also worked as a correspondent in Paris, London and Rome at various times and produced a novel and some short fiction and verse. As one of Gilbert's city editor's would say, as deadline approached, "Just one little word after another." That is a summary of Gilbert's life.

Gordon, Eugene was a member of the writing staff of the *Boston Post* from 1919 to 1935. His articles have appeared in the *Mercury, New Masses* and *Nation.* In the late thirties he worked on the *Moscow Daily News.*

Green, Nan joined a British medical unit during the Spanish Civil War. Her husband, a member of the International Brigades, was killed during the fighting. Except for the years 1952–1960, when she taught Spanish in China, she has been connected with some sort of work for Spain, and has since 1943 served as secretary of the International Brigades Association. She lives in London and works in a publishing house.

Harper, Allanah was editor of *Echanges,* a quarterly review of English and French literature, from 1930 to 1935. She is the author of *All Fond Trivial Records,* an autobiography, and numerous articles, including a recently finished essay on the poetry of Edith Sitwell. She lives on the French Riviera and is now writing a second volume of autobiography.

Hart-Davis, Sir Rupert (b. 1907), since 1946 director of the publishing house that bears his name, attended Eton and Oxford, became a student at the Old Vic in 1927–28 and an actor at the Lyric Theatre, Hammersmith, in 1928–29. He was director of Jonathan Cape from 1933 to 1940, and during World War II he served in the Coldstream Guards. His biography of Hugh Walpole appeared in 1952. He has also edited three volumes of letters: *George Moore, Letters to Lady Cunard* (1957), *The Letters of Oscar Wilde* (1962) and *Letters to Reggie Turner* (1964). An avid book collector and reader, he was recently knighted.

Henderson, Wyn, a typographer and director of private presses, was assistant to John Rodker at the Ovid Press and Sir Francis Meynell at the Nonesuch, a founder of the Aquila Press in 1929, and manager of Nancy Cunard's Hours Press in 1931. She later became Miss Peggy Guggenheim's secretary and organized art exhibits at her art gallery, Guggenheim Jeune. In her book of memoirs, *Confessions of an Art Addict,* Miss Guggenheim admires her former secretary's "common sense, tact and social grace." She now resides near Chichester.

Hiler, Hilaire (1897–1966), American artist, musician, Paris night club owner (Le Jockey), poet and raconteur, was one of the most familiar figures in Montparnasse during the twenties and thirties. His theories on color techniques, which he called "color-forms," appeared in *Some Directions and Dimensions of Color, Light Shades* and *White and Scarlet Permutations.*

Hobson, Anthony has been a director of Sotheby's, the London auctioneers of books and works of art, since 1949.

Hughes, Langston (1902–1967), the vibrant and prolific chronicler of Negro life in America, wrote many books of poetry, plays, short stories, novels, anthologies, TV scripts and opera librettos. His friendship with Miss Cunard is briefly mentioned in an autobiographical volume, *I Wonder as I Wander* (1956). In 1961, he was elected a member of the department of literature of the National Institute of Arts and Letters.

Hutchinson, Mary is the wife of St. John Hutchinson, K.C., both of whom were friends of Nancy Cunard since her early grown-up days—and particularly then.

Kokoschka, Oskar (b. 1886), born in Vienna, is now a British citizen and lives in Switzerland. Before World War I he published several plays and worked as a teacher in Austria, Germany and Switzerland. An emigré during the twenties and thirties, he painted landscapes, portraits and compositions. His paintings now hang in the principal European galleries, and recently he has had several large retrospective exhibits in Europe and America.

Lambert, Jean (b. 1914) is professor of French at Smith College. Though the recipient of a "licence de lettres" in German literature, he also has a vast knowledge of English and has translated books by several English writers. In 1936, he became acquainted with André Gide and eventually married his daughter. He has written about Gide (*Gide Familiar*), Jean Schlumberger and Henri Bosco, has published two novels and two collections of short stories, and is now at work on a third volume of short stories.

Lowenfels, Walter (b. 1897) shared with e e cummings the Richard Aldington Award for American poets in 1930. Before returning to the United States in the mid-thirties, he published *Apollinaire, Elegy for D. H. Lawrence* and *The Suicide*. Politically active until around 1955, he has since published a large amount of work, including *Walt Whitman's Civil War*, several volumes of poetry, *To An Imaginary Daughter*, and very recently, his first best-seller, *Where Is Vietnam? American Poets Respond*. Along with other projects, he is currently writing an autobiography. He lives in Peekskill, New York.

Lye, Len, Australian film maker, artist and writer, designed covers for books published by the Hours Press and the Seizin Press of Robert Graves and Laura Riding. His own Seizin Press book, *No Trouble* (1931), contains letters written to friends while working on his film, *Tusalava*. At present he lives and works in New York and is connected with the group called "Contemporary Voices in the Arts."

Mackworth, Cecily, though born in Wales, has always maintained close connections with France, where she now lives with her husband, the Marquis de Chabannes la Palice. In her book *I Came Out of France*, she recorded her experiences of the German invasion of France. *A Mirror of French Verse*, containing translations from various English poets, reflects her enthusiasm for French poetry. She has also written *The Mouth of the Sword*, concerned with the Middle East, a novel, *Springs Green Shadow*, and a study of François Villon.

Macpherson, Kenneth operated the Pool Press in the late twenties and early thirties with his wife, Bryher, and together they published the film review, *Close-up*, and the book *Film Problems of Soviet Russia*. Pool Press issued Mr. Macpherson's novels, *Pool-reflection* and *Gaunt Island*. For many years a resident of Italy and a close friend of Norman Douglas, he was appointed Douglas's literary executor following the author's death in 1952. He now lives in Cetona.

Michelet, Raymond (b. 1912) rejected his middle-class training, including a traditional university education, in favor of the revolutionary movements of Rimbaud, Marx and Freud. He joined the French Surrealists and participated in their explorations during the 1930s, and for awhile he assisted Nancy Cunard at the Hours Press. "J'ai appris d'elle," he wrote of Miss Cunard, "ce que je savais d'André Breton: que la liberté et l'amour sont deux choses sans prix, et qu'il ne faut jamais composer avec ce qui prétend vous en barrer le chemin." His home is Paris.

Milne, Ewart (b. 1903), a Dubliner, has been a sailor, a student teacher, an ambulance driver and courier in the Spanish Civil War, a land worker and estate manager during and after World War II. His volumes of poetry, notably *Letter from Ireland, Listen Mangan, Jubilo,* and *Boding Day,* as well as his contributions to journals and newspapers, have brought him considerable recognition. He now lives in England, where he has just published *Time Stopped,* a poem-sequence with prose intermissions.

Moore, Henry (b. 1898) was born in Castleford, not far from Leeds, where, following service in World War I, he attended art school. He continued his training in London at the Royal College of Art. His drawings of Londoners huddled in underground stations during the air raids of 1940 brought him considerable attention. Following the war his sculpture was constantly in demand. He lives with his family in a 15th Century farmhouse, in Perry Green, Hertfordshire.

Mortimer, Raymond (b. 1895) was for many years reviewer for *The New Statesman*. A devotee of the visual arts, he has written appreciations of Duncan Grant and Edouard Manet. Another selection of his work was issued in 1942 under the title *Channel Packet*. A Francophile since the age of six and an irrepressible traveler, he now divides his time between London and Dorset. He is at present a reviewer for the London *Sunday Times*.

Nichols, Robert (1893–1944), poet and dramatist, attended Oxford and served briefly in the Royal Field Artillery in the First World War before assuming the chair of English literature at the Imperial University, Tokyo, from 1921 to 1924. He married Norah Denny in 1922 and before returning to England worked for two years in Hollywood. His volumes of poetry include *Aurelia* (dedicated to Miss Cunard), *Fisbo,* and *Such Was My Singing, Poems 1915–1940*.

Plomer, William (b. 1903), born in the Northern Transvaal, Africa, and educated at Rugby, traveled widely in Africa, Greece and Japan before settling in England. A novelist, poet and short story writer, he was commissioned to write the libretto for Benjamin Britten's opera *Gloriana,* which was performed at the coronation of Queen Elizabeth in 1953. His *Collected Poems* appeared in 1960.

Putnam, Samuel (1892–1950), journalist, editor, translator of Rabelais and Cervantes, served as Paris literary correspondent for the *New York Sun* from 1929 to 1933, and in 1931 founded *The New Review,* one of the important little magazines of the era. His book of memoirs, *Paris Was Our Mistress,* contains amusing recollections of Montparnasse in the twenties as well as several fine portraits of significant European and American writers.

Rathbone, Irene is the cousin of the late Eleanor Rathbone, M.P., and of the late Basil Rathbone, the actor. During World War II, she was much in contact with exiled European writers, the French particularly. She has contributed articles to the daily paper *France* and to the monthly *La France Libre.* Her works include *We That Were Young* (war novel); *They Call It Peace; When Days Were Years; The Seeds of Time; Was There a Summer?* (a long love poem set in Provence).

Robinson, Clyde is a poet and decorator. For several years during the fifties he organized and managed an artistic and historical festival on Majorca. He lives near Philadelphia.

Rose, William edited *The Letters of Wyndham Lewis* in 1963. He is professor of English at Vassar College and the author of numerous articles on modern literature.

Sadoul, Georges (1904–1967) was born in Nancy, where his father directed the review *Le pays Lorrain.* Among the first to rally to the Surrealist Movement, he worked for awhile on the *Nouvelle revue Française* and at the Hours Press. In 1930, with Louis Aragon, he represented the Surrealists at the Kharkov Congress of Revolutionary Writers. From the 1930s on, M. Sadoul specialized in the cinema. His outstanding work is a five volume "histoire genérale du cinéma."

Schrijver, Herman, who lives in London, is an interior decorator of international fame, art collector and essayist.

Seldes, George (b. 1890), American journalist, joined the press section of the American army in France during World War I. After a stint with the *Chicago Tribune* and a few years off for painting, he began writing journalistic books, beginning with *You Can't Print That!,* which cover the history of the United States and Europe over the first third of the century. After World War II he edited the newsletter, *In Fact. Tell the Truth and Run*, the author's record of his forty years in American journalism, was published in 1953.

Solano, Solita substituted for college three years in the Philippines, surveying and building coral roads (MacArthur used them in Leyte). Before leaving for France in the early twenties, she spent five years as dramatic critic and editor on the *Boston Herald-Traveler* and one year as dramatic editor on the "old" *New York Tribune*. She has published three novels, short stories, and a volume of poetry. During the past thirty years she has edited many books, and for five years she worked as secretary to the Russian mystic Gurdjieff. Etymology is her special interest. Her home is near Paris.

Strachan, Walter, who is Second Master and Head of the Modern Language Department, Bishop's Stortford College, England, has translated a book of French poetry, *Apollinaire to Aragon;* French, German and Italian novels by Jean Cocteau, Hermann Hesse and Enrico Emanuelli; and books on French and German art. He has published two volumes of poems, numerous articles on French *livre d'artiste,* and has just completed a full length study entitled *The Artist and the French Book, 1900–1967.*

Theis, Louise (Morgan) (1885–1964) first knew England (she and her husband Otto became British subjects in 1941) in 1909 while gathering material for her doctor's thesis on academic drama. After World War I she settled in London and contributed to *The Outlook,* of which Otto was associate and literary editor. They married in 1926. In 1932–33 she edited *Everyman* and wrote a series of articles on writers at work. She began her long association with the *News Chronicle* in 1934 as a special correspondent, becoming just before World War II the highest paid woman on Fleet Street. Her book on the Sun Prayers of the Rajah of Aundh called *The Ten Point Way to Health* (1938) has been universally translated. Following her retirement (she was nearly seventy), she began exploring the hitherto unknown world of the kitchen and produced in a brief time two books, *Inside Your Kitchen* (1956) and *Home Made Wines* (1958).

Thorne, Anthony (b. 1904), a graduate of St. Paul's and Oxford, has published many novels, two of which, *So Long at the Fair* and *The Baby and the Battleship,* have been made into films. He was a British delegate to the P.E.N. Club Congresses in 1952 and 1953. His criticism has appeared in *New Writing, Vogue* and *Argosy.* He lives in London.

Tree, Iris, the British actress and writer, daughter of Sir Herbert Beerbohm Tree, had her first theatrical success, with Lady Diana Manners, in *The Miracle* in 1925. Recently she has appeared in two films, *La Dolce Vita* and John Huston's *Moby Dick*. A long poem called *The Marsh Picnic* appeared in 1966, and she is now working on a book of memoirs tentatively entitled *In Praise of* . . .

Viers, Henri, historian and painter, retired to La Mothe-Fénelon (the village in the Lot where Nancy Cunard lived the last fifteen years of her life) after having spent over fifty years in Paris. Now, besides enjoying the company of the people of the Lot, he has undertaken a historical study of La Mothe-Fénelon and its environs. In 1966 an exhibit of his paintings was held in the ancient village church. M. Viers is also a book collector and a specialist in the work of Louis XIV and Louis XV.

Waley, Arthur (1890–1966), the scholar and translator of Chinese and Japanese literature, helped popularize Oriental writing with his translations of *The Tale of Genji* and *Monkey*. His historical views were expressed in *The Opium War Through Chinese Eyes* and *The Secret History of the Mongols*. He was at one time a curator of the British Museum. He was a Fellow of the British Academy, and in 1953 he received the Queen's Medal for Poetry.

Warner, Sylvia Townsend (b. 1893), English poet, novelist and short story writer, had her first novel, *Lolly Willowes,* chosen as the first Book of the Month Club selection. She joined other British writers in 1936 and journeyed to Spain, where she participated in the Congress of Writers and served as secretary of Medical Aid to Spain. She has written several volumes of poetry and over twenty novels and collections of stories, the most recent being *Swans on an Autumn River*. She lives in Dorset.

Williams, William Carlos (1883–1963), the poet, novelist and physician from Rutherford, New Jersey, wrote a delightful account of his experiences among the expatriates in the twenties in his *Autobiography*.

Woolf, Leonard (b. 1880) worked for several years as a civil servant in Ceylon before he returned to England and married Virginia Stephen. One of the "Old Bloomsbury Group," he founded, with the assistance of his wife and Barbara Hiles, the Hogarth Press, which published several of his stories. Long recognized as historian, political essayist, reviewer and critic, he now devotes his time to his autobiography, a fourth volume of which, *Downhill All the Way,* has recently appeared.

bibliography of nancy cunard's writings

I. BOOKS AND PAMPHLETS:

Outlaws. London: Elkin Mathews, 1921.
Sublunary. London: Hodder and Stoughton Ltd., 1923.
Parallax. London: Hogarth Press, 1925.
Poems (Two) 1925. London: Aquila Press, 1930.
Black Man and White Ladyship, An Anniversary. London: The Utopia Press, 1931.
Negro. London: Published by Nancy Cunard at Wishart and Company. Miss Cunard's contributions were: "The American Moron and the American of Sense—Letters on the Negro," "Scottsboro—and Other Scottsboros," "Southern Sheriff" (a poem), and "Colour Bar." 1934.
Ethiopia Betrayed—Imperialism, How Long? (Unpublished) 1936.
Authors Take Sides on the Spanish War (ed.). London: Left Review, 1937.
Psalm of the Palms and Sonnets. La Habana (Unpublished) 1941.
The White Man's Duty, with George Padmore. London: Hurricane Books, 1942.
Man-Ship-Tank-Gun-Plane. London: New Books, 1944.
Poems for France (ed.). London: La France Libre, 1944.
Ballad of Réanville (Unpublished).
Poèmes à la France (ed.). Paris: Pierre Seghers, 1947.
Nous Gens D'Espagne. Perpignan: Imprimerie Labau, 1949.
Grand Man, Memories of Norman Douglas. London: Secker and Warburg, 1954.
GM, Memories of George Moore. London: Rupert Hart-Davis, 1956.
Sonnets on Spain (Unpublished) 1958.
Visions Experienced by the Bards of the Middle Ages (Unpublished) 1963–1965.
These Were the Hours (Forthcoming).

II. CONTRIBUTIONS TO PERIODICALS, NEWSPAPERS AND BOOKS:

1916
The following poems by Nancy Cunard appeared in *Wheels: An Anthology of Verse* (New York: Longmans, Green and Company): "Wheels," "The Carnivals of Peace," "Sonnet," "Destruction," "Remorse," "Uneasiness," "From the Train."

1921
"At les Baux," *The Observer*

1922

"The Solitary," *The New Statesman,* XX (Oct. 28, 1922)

"I Am Not One for Expression," *The New Statesman,* XX (Dec. 16, 1922)

1923

"Sonnet," *English Review,* XXXVI (Jan. 1923)

"Trasimene," *Saturday Review,* 135 (June 2, 1923)

1926

"In Provins," *The New Coterie,* 2 (Spring 1926)

1927

"Simultaneous," *The New Coterie,* 6 (Summer & Autumn 1927)

1930

"Equatorial Way," in *Henry-Music* by Henry Crowder. Hours Press, Paris, 1930.

1932

"Black Man and White Ladyship," *The New Review,* II (April 1932)

"Collect to the Virgin," *Contact,* I (May 1932)

1936

"F.A.S.C.I.S.M.E.," in *Les Poétes du Monde Défendent le Peuple Espagnol,* No. 1. Miss Cunard edited and published six numbers of *Les Poétes* during the Spanish war.

1937

"To the Mothers of the Dead Militia" by Pablo Neruda. Translated by Nancy Cunard. *Left Review,* III (April 1937)

"Almeria" by Pablo Neruda. Translated by Nancy Cunard. *Left Review,* III (Aug. 1937)

"Three Negro Poets," *Left Review,* III (Oct. 1937)

"Madrid" by Jacques Roumain. Translated by Nancy Cunard. *Left Review,* III (April 1938)

1938

"Yes, It Is Spain," *Life and Letters Today,* XIX (Sept. 1938)

"To Eat Today," *New Statesman and Nation,* XVI (Oct. 1, 1938)

"In Spain It Is Here," *Voice of Spain*

1939

"The Exodus from Spain," *Manchester Guardian* (Feb. 8, 1938)

"The Refugees from Perpignan," *Manchester Guardian* (Feb. 8, 1938)

"The Soldiers Leave Their Battlefield Behind," *Manchester Guardian* (Feb. 9, 1938)

"At a Refugee Camp," *Manchester Guardian* (Feb. 10, 1938)

During the Spanish Civil War Miss Cunard despatched many articles to the Associated Negro Press (Chicago), *The News Chronicle* (London), the French publication *Regards* (Paris), Sylvia Pankhurst's weekly, *New Times* (London) and to the General News Service, which provided service for the British colonies, India and the Far East. She also contributed to Charles Duff's publications, *Spanish Newsletter, Spain at War* and *Voice of Spain.*

1942

"October Saturday Night in the White Lion," *New Times* (Dec. 26, 1942)

1944
"Pensées en Tunisie" by John Gawsworth. Translated by Nancy Cunard.

1945
"Letter from Paris," *Horizon*, XI (June 1945)
"A Message from South-west France," *Our Time*, 5 (August 1945)
"Foreword" in *African Empires and Civilisation*, by Raymond Michelet.

1949
"News from South America," *Horizon*, XX (July 1949)

1950
"Decade of Exile," *Arena* (Feb. 1950)
"Impressions of Italy," *Life and Letters*, 65 (June 1950)
"The Watergate Theatre," *Life and Letters*, 65 (June 1950)

1962
"A Poem for Spain" by Hubert Juin. Translated by Nancy Cunard. *Political Affairs*, XLI (Sept. 1962)

1964
"The Hours Press," *The Book Collector*, XIII (Winter 1964)

index

Nancy Cunard

References to Miss Cunard's Books and Writings

about the editor

Hugh Douglas Ford was born in Washington, New Jersey, in 1925, and was educated at Dickinson College, from which he received a Bachelor of Arts degree in 1950, and at Stanford University, where he earned his Master of Arts degree in 1952. He received his Ph.D. from the University of Pennsylvania in 1962.

He has taught English since 1952, first at the College of Wooster, Wooster, Ohio, then at the University of Pennsylvania; he is now professor of English at Trenton State College, Trenton, New Jersey. In 1965, Mr. Ford was Fulbright Lecturer in American literature at the University of Chile.

An interest in Spain led to the writing of *A Poets' War,* an analysis of the powerful impact of the Spanish Civil War upon British poetry. While gathering material for this book, Mr. Ford became acquainted with Nancy Cunard, whose knowledge of the conflict was not only deeply felt but encyclopedic. In 1963, they collaborated on a history of Miss Cunard's private press, the Hours Press (1928–1931), called *These Were the Hours.*

Mr. Ford is now completing a study of the Anglo-American private press movement, and he is co-editor of an anthology of American literature being prepared for use in South American universities.

He is an enthusiastic traveler, art collector and bibliophile.